Spanish American Literature in the Age of Machines and Other Essays

Spanish American Literature in the Age of Machines and Other Essays

ÁNGEL RAMA

Translated and Edited by

José Eduardo González and
Timothy R. Robbins

Published by State University of New York Press, Albany

© 2023 State University of New York

All rights reserved

Printed in the United States of America

No part of this book may be used or reproduced in any manner whatsoever without written permission. No part of this book may be stored in a retrieval system or transmitted in any form or by any means including electronic, electrostatic, magnetic tape, mechanical, photocopying, recording, or otherwise without the prior permission in writing of the publisher.

For information, contact State University of New York Press, Albany, NY
www.sunypress.edu

Library of Congress Cataloging-in-Publication Data

Names: Rama, Ángel, author. | González, José Eduardo, translator. | Robbins, Timothy R., 1980– translator.
Title: Spanish American literature in the age of machines and other essays / Ángel Rama ; translated by José Eduardo González and Timothy R. Robbins.
Description: Albany, NY : State University of New York Press, [2023] | Includes bibliographical references.
Identifiers: LCCN 2022055890 | ISBN 9781438494494 (hardcover : alk. paper) | ISBN 9781438494500 (ebook) | ISBN 9781438494487 (pbk. : alk. paper)
Subjects: LCSH: Rama, Angel—Translations into English | Latin American literature—History and criticism. | Literature—History and criticism. | LCGFT: Literary criticism. | Essays.
Classification: LCC PN849.L29 R36 2023 | DDC 860.9/98—dc23/eng/20230302
LC record available at https://lccn.loc.gov/2022055890

10 9 8 7 6 5 4 3 2 1

Contents

Acknowledgments	vii
Introduction: The Density of Literary History *José Eduardo González*	1
1. Mariano Azuela: Ambition and Frustration of the Middle Class (1966)	13
2. Criticism and Literature (1971)	47
3. Spanish American Literature in the Age of Machines (1972)	55
4. No More Demons (1972)	65
5. The Two Latin American Avant-Gardes (1973)	77
6. Literary System and Social System in Spanish America (1975)	93
7. Literature and Social Class (1976)	109
8. The Literary System of Gauchesque Poetry (1977)	129
9. The Boom in Perspective (1979)	171
10. A Research into Ideology in Poetry (The Diptych Series of *Simple Verses*) (1980)	219
11. Narrative Technification (1981)	263
12. Literature within an Anthropological Framework (1984)	315

Appendix: Publishing History of the Essays in This Volume   325

Notes   329

Bibliography   365

Index   377

Acknowledgments

We would like to thank Amparo and Claudio Rama for kindly granting us permission to translate this collection of essays. Needless to say, *without their support* this book would not have been completed. We would also like to thank the academic journals *Revista Iberoamericana* and *Hispamérica*, where "Indagación de la ideología en la poesía" and "Tecnificación narrative" were originally published for allowing us to reproduce and translate these articles. We are indebted to our editor at SUNY Press, Rebecca Colesworthy. Thank you for your assistance and for believing in this project. We also appreciate the kind and helpful feedback we received from our anonymous reviewers.

Introduction

The Density of Literary History

José Eduardo González

Born in 1926 in Montevideo, Uruguay, Ángel Rama, like most public intellectuals in the developing world, wore several hats in his youth: author, editor, critic, translator, publisher, actor. During the 1950s Rama turned his attention toward creative work, producing fiction and writing plays. In 1958, he was put in charge of the literary section of *Marcha*, a political weekly newspaper, and he began his transition into one of the most important Latin American intellectuals of the twentieth century. It was in the pages of this newspaper that Rama began to introduce to the South American public of that region the work of little-known contemporary authors such as Gabriel García Márquez, Mario Vargas Llosa, Alejo Carpentier, and other writers who would go on to achieve a commercial and critical success unprecedented in the history of Latin American letters. As a literary critic, Rama began to develop a sociological approach during the 1960s, influenced by the Frankfurt School and Walter Benjamin. During this period, Rama was inspired by the Cuban Revolution and the idea of creating a different socialist society, independent of the interference from both the Soviet Union and the United States, but by the early 1970s, when the Soviet influence on the Caribbean Island increased, he cut ties with the Revolution. His unique interpretations of Latin American literary history, in particular his readings of important literary movements or periods—for example, modernismo, gauchesque poetry, the literature of the Mexican Revolution—increased his visibility. In 1973, a military coup d'état in Uruguay forced him into exile in Venezuela where he worked for several years and started Biblioteca Ayacucho, an ambitious editorial project to publish scholarly editions of classical Latin American texts. In 1980, he moved to the US, but his petition for a resident visa was denied because he had been classified as "communist subversive" early in his career.

The initial reception of Ángel Rama's work in American academia occurred in the late 1980s and early 1990s, in departments of Hispanic literature that were beginning to mirror the transformation of literary criticism caused by the wave of postmodernist ideas and approaches, and the rise of theory that had been impacting the English literature departments. It was unavoidable that literary critics in the US read Rama looking for "concepts," "tools," or "theories" that could be not only applied to other "texts" or cultural objects but also reinterpreted as a contribution to, for lack of a better term, the postmodern discourse and its critique of social constructs. Those reasons perhaps allow us to understand the immense influence Rama's "theories" of narrative transculturation and of the Latin American *letrado* held for Latin American criticism and other fields associated with Latin American studies at the turn of the century. I use the term theories with quotation marks because the idea that conceptions of culture developed under specific social conditions could be transported to another region and applied to a different situation was very problematic for Rama, as is evident in a few of the essays in this collection. The historical circumstances of his reception explain that most of Rama's critical work, which cannot be easily operationalized and reused as free-floating "theory" remains understudied and inaccessible in other languages. Logically, the first of his books to be translated into English was *The Lettered City* (in 1996) as it was already having an important impact in the field of Latin American studies in general.[1] The next year "Processes of Transculturation in Latin American Narrative" was published in the *Journal of Latin American Cultural Studies*.[2] In this article from 1974, Rama presented for the first time his theory of narrative and it became the basis for his book *Transculturación narrativa en América Latina* (1982). The latter has been translated with the title *Writing Across Cultures*.[3]

We get an incomplete picture of Rama's interpretation of the Latin American literary field if we depend only on those two books—not only because he studied a wide variety of topics that are not covered with the theories of transculturation and the letrados (as an incredibly prolific writer, Rama's bibliography surpasses fourteen hundred items[4]) but also because he was purposely studying those topics from a very limited perspective. For example, in his theory of the letrado, Rama simplifies the history of the intellectual in Latin America to focus only on the relationship of this social group to political power. Likewise, the theory of transculturation studies only a small number of cases of authors from mid-twentieth-century Latin American literature who have successfully, organically, negotiated the modernization process. As I introduce some of the themes related to the essays included in this collection, I am taking the opportunity to show how they add complexity to the view of Rama's work that we get from the materials that were previously available in English, namely *The Lettered City* and *Writing Across Cultures*.

Rama believed that real literary criticism always took place in newspapers and magazines, where it could reach a large audience, and not within the sterile setting of university campuses.[5] "Criticism and Literature" (1971) is a short essay that Rama wrote for *Sin Nombre*, a literary review in Puerto Rico, one of the places where he worked as a literature professor. While reflecting on the unique situation of the Puerto Rican literary field in which, he says, a double circuit has emerged, one composed of authors who utilized their influence and social capital to receive undeserved recognition for works that are unoriginal or of questionable quality, Rama comments on what he understands is the purpose of literary criticism. His reflections on the many functions of criticism with regard to literature and to a society's decision about which cultural paths it must follow in the future go beyond a simple view of criticism as historical research or as arbiter of taste. While there is a T. S. Elliot-esque feeling when he assigns criticism the task of connecting the present with the past, creating a literary corpus, Rama is also seeking to emphasize that the system created by literary criticism cannot be reduced to aesthetics but depends on evaluating many social options (moral, economic, or religious) affecting the creation of a literary work in a specific historical moment. That would also include "many options that emerge from the cultural demands relevant to present day society." Criticism, then, is not just a passive cultural act—it plays an active role in helping society to "discover itself," which explains Rama's preoccupation with the quality of literary criticism in Latin America. Hence his rejection of structuralism, as he understands that such an approach requires the assumption that one can detach a literary system from a cultural system.

One can also observe in "Criticism and Literature" Rama's belief in the power of literary criticism to organize hierarchically, that is, to create a coherent, organic whole out of disparate elements. This does not mean, however, that he is arguing for a flattening/simplification of literary history. On the contrary, most of his critique of the literary criticism of his time actually focuses on urging critics to avoid simplistic periodization and recognize the rich complexity of the literature produced in Latin American nations, to take into account the diversity of social groups represented in them.

Ironically, simplistic periodization was one of the problems plaguing the posthumously published *The Lettered City*. As mentioned above, this book analyzes the origin of the Latin American intellectual, or letrado, as resulting from a situation of colonization in which the power of the written word—whether through the creation of laws, rules, or maps—seeks to control a non-European reality that must be molded and controlled. However, as the study moves from colonial times to the different stages that come after independence, it becomes evident that the preoccupation of intellectuals is focused on surviving as a group, that is, maintaining the privileges that they obtained from the simple fact that they have access to the written word in a region where the masses have remained illiterate and do not have access to the main means of communication. Unfortunately, this vision of the letrado as self-interested, as mainly involved in protecting their connection to a political power that validates their position when faced with new challenges—modernization, increased public literacy, the emergence of new professionals that challenge their supremacy—fails to show Rama's awareness of the field of forces that Latin American intellectuals had to navigate at each historical juncture.

Early critiques of Rama's *The Lettered City*, like the one found in Julio Ramos's *Divergent Modernities*, understandably centered on the problem of periodization created when trying to encompass such a large span of time. Arguing that Rama puts in the same letrado group two completely different authors (Sarmiento and Rodó) from the mid- and late nineteenth century "because both were public servants," Ramos shows that Rama's periodization "does not take into account the different discursive fields that grounded their respective interventions. In fact, these fields were traversed by different subjects, different modes of authorization."[6] No doubt Ramos is correct with respect to the need to establish differences between the literary system (local and regional) in which these writers worked but wrong in suggesting that Rama's work was not attentive to the overlapping between letrado ideologies. In fact, attention to this type of discursive disparity is a trademark of Rama's criticism. Nothing is more central to his critical practice than his call for Latin American scholars to pay attention to what he used to call the "density" of literary history. For example, looking at nineteenth-century literature, in "Literature and Social Class" (1976), he argues for the existence of two main layers where works coexist simultaneously but independent from each other. One of them is always supported by important social institutions, the other one is not. In Latin America, he explains, the division into two productions is associated with a series of ideas, among them the tendency to place urban and learned writing on one side and rural life and oral or folkloric art on the other. Each layer is characterized by addressing a specific public through the literary forms they employ. But this simple opposition is complicated when the concept of class is introduced. He gives the example of two mid-nineteenth-century Brazilian writers, born around the same time, writing for the same newspaper, and working with similar themes, who develop two different styles of writing (one cultured, imitating a Romantic style, the other more realistic, cynical, using awkward language) that reflect two different worldviews. "It is not necessary to resort to the biography of both authors to find the causes of these differences," writes Rama, because their literary choices betray their class affiliation. The same presence of social classes with different worldviews applies to works produced on the other side of the spectrum, directed at rural groups, such as gauchesque literature. Given the centrality of "class struggle" for the historical development of the region, for Rama it seems incomprehensible to believe that literary history is not able to show the importance of that separation for classifying Latin American artistic production.

There is no doubt, then, that in *The Lettered City* Rama has chosen to present to us a condensed and flattened version of the history of intellectuals in Latin America, and one need look no further than his reading of Azuela as just another member of the letrado group: "Mariano Azuela specialized in critiques of intellectuals, members of a social group which he despised despite belonging to it himself . . . Azuela's paradigm of intellectuals in the revolution has a long tradition in Latin America and draws on a commonplace of the popular imagination regarding the representatives of the lettered city: an undisguised awe of the intellectual's capacity to manipulate language, whether in oratory or writing."[7] In contrast, the analysis we find in one of the earliest essays included in this collection, "Mariano Azuela: Ambition and Frustration of the Middle Class" (1966), is a masterful study of ideology and political commitment. Rama studies the political situation that leads Azuela to make the decision to openly use his writing to advance a political position, not without first covering the author's process in deciding to which social group he should adhere. In the process, Rama paints a picture of the multiple interests at play during the revolutionary period and the positions that intellectuals took, which were far from being homogeneous. As opposed to the simple description that "Azuela despised intellectuals while being one of them," Rama shows how Azuela's rejection of the traditional intellectuals affects his approach to literary form. When in *The Underdogs* Azuela creates a literature with testimonial intentions, in which "the things narrated in them are happening and the author is constantly referring to contemporary facts or situations," he is distancing himself from the dominant forms employed by the literatos at the time. Pointing out Azuela's portrayals of modernista poets detached from reality, Rama explains how he makes fun of their art for art's sake credo, criticizes their "escapism," and ridicules the titles of their works ("Agonies of the Marble," "I Search Now for the Heights of Serenity"), which appear senseless when contrasted to the reality of the ongoing revolution. Azuela "[not] only caricatures the typical modernist poet who after 1910 becomes a survivor," explains Rama, "but also the 'colonialists' who, right in the middle of the revolutionary period, continue to fantasize about reconstructing long-gone societies."

It is ironic that the same Ángel Rama who wrote extensively asking Latin American critics to pay more attention to the nuances and discontinuities of literary history, warning others about oversimplifying the field of forces in a literary system, is now often judged by a book that does not display these qualities. In spite of the originality of its thesis, the absence of the type of density and complexity in *The Lettered City* that one expects from Rama's writings at times makes the best known and most used of his texts in American academia look like an outline, a mere blueprint of a building that was never completed.[8] In contrast, his earlier work is characterized by the author's constant, almost obsessive return to topics already studied, rethinking and improving his analysis with each new look. Two of the essays included in this collection are examples of a topic to which he kept trying to find the correct approach. In "Literary System and Social System in Spanish America" (1975), his preoccupation with avoiding "a lineal, progressive literary history lacking in density" that happens when Latin American critics try to impose a prioritization based on Europe's artistic development leads him to propose the idea of literary sequences or series. Some of these sequences are based only on artistic manifestations whereas the other series will be "non-discursive in nature, but rather technical, economic, social, political, and so on, and they will be found forcefully linked with literary sequences by reason of the structural interdependence of an ensemble." But the topic behind this research is the problem of mediation, the complex processes through which social reality manifests itself in the literary text. With the idea of series, Rama seeks to avoid presenting literature as responding directly to economic or social forces. All series are autonomous, but the literary text possesses the capacity to combine other discourses and "return[s] them to society as an indivisible totality."

He keeps coming back to the idea that language plays an important role in the process that links the literary text to the worldview of a social group represented in an artistic text. In the last essay that Rama wrote, "Literature within an Anthropological Framework" (1984), he was still attempting to discover in the relationship between language and community a solution to the problem of arguing that the text always shows traces of the social context in which it was created. Rama begins by summarizing the importance of the field of anthropology for Latin American literature. He mentions that this discipline's contributions—for example, the introduction of cultural relativism—have impacted artists in the region, allowing them to evaluate positively regional cultures. But for Rama the most interesting aspect is anthropology's notion of a "collective production of culture." Anthropologists, he says, look for this collective expression in arts and languages. This does not mean that individual artists disappeared but that artists worked with collective patterns that carried the values of their community. It allows us to see literary works as "cultural organic expressions, immersed in the complex web of relations." As a "truncated model of the culture that informs it," we can read society in the text. Thus, when anthropology analyzes primitive languages trying "to find in language the objectification of a worldview that undergirds the community that uses it," it is unwittingly advancing the idea that those values and beliefs as well as communal aspirations are part of the literary text, whose raw material is language.

A close relationship between language and worldview is one of the main components of *Writing Across Cultures*, the other one of Rama's books available in English. The theory developed in it, well-known among Latin Americanists, argues that faced with the influence of modern literature produced in Anglo-European countries, some Latin American authors, concerned with the preservation of regional traditions, respond by looking for local equivalents to modern techniques and structures. The local culture does not die when replaced by the modern, but rather it is updated thanks to the work of the transculturator. Transculturators do not passively accept exterior influences and adapt them. More exactly, their work is the result of a double process of selection. At the same time as they decide which foreign influences they will accept, they are analyzing their own culture for the purpose of rescuing traditional elements that are compatible with the modernizing forces. They are by no means the first Latin American authors to respond this way, but they appear to be the most successful at the time Rama wrote his book (1982). Rama sees this tendency to find local equivalents at many other moments (with varied levels of success) during the history of twentieth-century Latin American literature, and in each of those moments he discovers that there are also authors who have the opposite reaction, wishing to leave behind the local context and join the "universal" culture. His essay from 1973, "The Latin American Two Avant-Gardes," is the first place where he suggests organizing literary history around the two major poles of attraction, the foreign or the Latin American literary systems: "For some, the avant-garde [literary work] . . . required readers to apprehend the European literary system from which it took its models as they were consuming it. Two operations of appropriation had to be performed at the same time. . . . I do not think it was clear to [Latin American avant-garde authors] that adopting a European literary system imported with it other cultural elements. . . . [However, there is another group] whose works were created within a Latin American literary system. They drew from its structures and contributions, modifying and adapting them to new realities." The historical shapes these two positions take logically change according to the forces or issues at play (as well as the players), and understanding which authors Rama includes on one side of the pole or the other, it seems to me, is an important corrective to how his work has been received in the US.[9] While in American academia his book on narrative transculturation is often mistakenly seen as the summa of his critical work, is actually a study of a particular reaction to the developments within the mid-twentieth-century literary system. The fact that Rama focused on the contemporary period and included popular writers like Gabriel García Márquez and Juan Rulfo has made the book more attractive and controversial, but in a way, this study is no different than the books he dedicated to modernismo or to the gauchesque genre. In each case, Rama focused on a group of writers or a "movement" whose art inclined toward either the European or the Latin American literary system. In the case of transculturators, however, understanding how contemporary developments in technology and in artistic technique have transformed the literary field is important to the origin of Rama's theory and why he saw it as the "correct" path at that moment.

On the one hand, the question of technology in Rama's work originates in his readings of critical theory—his writings included here are clearly at times a response to both Benjamin and Adorno, for example, and in that sense one can understand that they become intertwined with his concerns with literary technique. On the other hand, this is a topic that in a Latin American context cannot be extricated from the peripheral position of these regions in terms of use, consumption, and especially invention of technological machinery, or, in the case of culture, innovations in artistic technique. Rama read Walter Benjamin in Italian and possibly French translations in the mid- to late 1960s, before the German critic's writings were available in Spanish. "Spanish American Literature in the Age of Machines" (1972) is a short essay, written as a reaction to these early readings of Benjamin, specifically the well-known essay on technological reproduction to which Rama's title alludes. Noticing how rapidly technology has changed since the end of WWII, Rama is not interested in questions of how technological reproduction undermines authenticity, as the German critic was, but in what the process of making technologies economically viable for a greater number of people means for literature. For Rama the increased use of reproduction technologies such as film and sound recording has transformed the content of literary works, but not because writers have to compete with machines in replicating reality. Technology, he says, has transformed how authors conduct their research, offering them the means to document the world outside more objectively and to study it. His reflections on art are, however, wrapped in a more general concern about the invasion into the Latin American market of all kinds of "machines." When he wrote this essay in 1972, Rama felt that Latin America, a marginalized region in the world economy, was becoming filled with mechanical objects produced abroad, with a forest of foreign products that block access to reality, and this would result in heterogeneous literary works. About ten years later, when he writes "Narrative Technification" (1981), these concerns have moved to the forefront. During that period, the world economic crisis that took place after the 1973 oil crisis made evident that Latin American efforts to replace imported goods with the import substitution industrialization (ISI) model of development had failed, and this prompted a deeper reflection on the relationship between technology and artistic technique. Rama's essay investigates the idea that techniques are created as a response to social changes in a specific cultural context; they become, like the "machines" in the earlier essay, imported products that invade the Latin American cultural space. A simple application of techniques created for other social formations, imported and applied locally, is likely to result in a failure, in a disharmonious artistic object that reveal a schism between form and content.

Rama traces the different stages of this conflict between local content and a foreign form, from the turn-of-the-century modernistas and their strive for professionalization to a contemporary "internationalization of literary techniques" as they have come to form part of a "common heritage." But the problem with this perception, Rama will argue time and again, is that techniques, if left unchanged, will bring with them the context in which they originated: "One can also suspect that universal techniques that are adapted to narrative and applied to a Latin American content subtly drive a transformation of this content within equally universal patterns." At the end of "Narrative Technification," Rama retakes his ideas about the two avant-gardes and presents transculturation as the appropriate response to the globalization of culture and as the latest step in the history of Latin America's relationship with literary modernization, but not the only way. Both cosmopolitan writers' and transcuturators' approaches "are equally valid to sustain artistic production at the highest level" and even those authors who accept the urban world can reconnect "to the origins, to the defenseless zones, to the marginal characters."

The last characteristic that I want to call attention to in this selection of essays is Rama's attraction for studying what one could call group behavior in literary history, an idea directly connected to the notion of literary systems mentioned above. Rama began to think about "literary systems" in the 1960s, influenced by the work of Brazilian critic Antônio Candido who in 1957 published *Formação da Literatura Brasileira*. Candido defined a literary system as a group of literary works interconnected through three common elements: a group of authors (more or less conscious of their role), a reading public, and a form of communication among them. The main purpose when thinking of these connections in terms of a "system" is to emphasize not competition (which is not to say that this element was not present) but continuity. In "The Literary System of Gauchesque Poetry" (1977), for example, Rama studies the early national literatures of the River Plate region. On one side, he sees the members of the Literary Salon, whose work, even after independence, continued to consider the Romantic literature produced in Spain as the model of high literature. On the other side, there are those writers looking for a public among the lower classes, writing for gauchos and the rural population. Rama's essay focuses on gauchesque authors' awareness of their position in the literary field, the range of topics available to them, and, above all, the public they are seeking to reach and the ideology connected to that audience. Their literary choices, artistic formulas they try, and the different ways to make their works available are aimed at creating a tradition: "They see themselves as members of a literary movement, declaring themselves followers, refiners, simple disciples, and rarely disagree with past works or authors. In few occasions one can corroborate how literature comes out of literature and in turn engenders literature, in a succession that goes from fathers to sons, from teachers to disciples, and from texts to texts." While Rama believed that at the end of the nineteenth century writers began to see themselves as individual players within the literary marketplace, he continues to find traces of group behavior in his work on modernismo and later movements. One can even detect a similar approach in his essay about the commercial context in which the Boom writers achieved success. One of his best-known texts, "The Boom in Perspective" (1979) explores the role played by new media and publishing houses in the creation of this literary phenomenon. When read alongside the study of the gauchesque style, it is easy to see that Rama is focusing on the same elements (a group of authors, a reading public, searching for the correct form to deliver a content), but the Boom authors seem to have less control, as if, now that they have become professional writers, the old literary system has been invaded by new actors. Rama devotes a few paragraphs to explain how the attention received from popular magazines and TV transformed our perception of the Latin American author, but the most important part of his essay is without a doubt his study of the marketing strategies employed by the European and regional publishing houses to increase their sales.[10] After the Boom—after Latin American authors have "conquered professionalization"—Rama seems to be suggesting with his analysis that functions he used to assign to criticism (organizing the past, helping reflect on future cultural options) and to the literary system (creating a public, testing and finding the appropriate forms) are now in the hands of the world book market.

The last few years have seen an increased interest in Rama with studies in both English and Spanish focused on different aspects of his work.[11] While the theory of transculturation and the letrado theory still receive attention, there is also research into previously neglected areas of Rama's work that is being used to produce innovative readings of contemporary (and world) literature.[12] The present volume seeks to contribute to rekindling interest in the rich and diverse work that Ángel Rama produced.

Translators' Note

We have updated Rama's endnotes using the Chicago Manual of Style, adding or changing information to make his references easier to find for contemporary readers and replacing his quotations with translations available in English. Editor's notes have been added between brackets to distinguish them from Rama's original notes. Rama occasionally writes "America" or "Our America" to refer to Latin America and always uses "North America" or "North Americans" to designate the US and its inhabitants. Sometimes he makes a distinction between Spanish America, referring only to the Spanish speaking countries and literature from the region, and Latin America, when he wishes to include Brazil and Brazilian literature, but sometimes he uses them interchangeably. When a Latin American literary text has been translated into English, we refer to it using the title of the translation. When no translation exists, we have kept the title in Spanish.

1

Mariano Azuela

Ambition and Frustration of the Middle Class

I. Azuela's Ideological Perspectivism

Some of the works that Mariano Azuela wrote between 1911 (*Andrés Pérez, maderista*) and 1918 (*The Trials of a Decent Family*), including, of course, his famous text *The Underdogs* (1915), form part of the first period or proto-period of the novel of the Mexican Revolution. Among the problems that one finds in the literature from these years is that of the relationship between narrative images and real images. This a literature where there is evidently a documentary and testimonial intention; texts created as the things narrated in them are happening and the author is constantly referring to contemporary facts or situations. Critics, for that reason, focused on the author's veracity. Beyond the merely historical interest on the topic, there is the problem of reflecting real life in a literary text, and the capacity of a writer to express his time, especially when he is actively taking part in the events. At the least, it allows for an analysis of the elements that determine his worldview, and the way these elements are transformed into specifically narrative materials. Even the bloodiest "tranche de vie" can become an index to calculate an author's worldview and his strictly artistic creations.

Manuel Pedro González offered an early critique of the revolutionary narrative as he was listing its basic features:

> Another detail or characteristic of the revolutionary novel which separates it from previous narratives is its limited and 'historical'

realism. It is excessively faithful to the historical fact. In contrast to novelists from the previous generation, these authors are not inventing anything, their creative fantasy hardly intervenes in the text and their imagination limits itself to capture social facts in narrative prose and dialogues. Not only is this defining characteristic of the revolutionary model that separates it from previous novelistic models, but it is also a limitation (a defect) that clips the wings of this creation and puts them under the weight of historical reality.

By restraining their inventiveness and faithfully copying facts and characters of the revolution, these novelists do not let their imagination roam free in their writings and, instead, turn the literary text into a document, a more or less faithful portrait of a moment in the history of Mexico, thus diminishing its aesthetic value in the process.[1]

On the one hand, it is true that the documentary character of these texts, as González notices, forces them to focus on facts, and the revolutionary novels have a higher dependence on historical events than in other imaginative products. These types of testimonio novels are without doubt related to historical novels. But, on the other hand, the critic describes the relationship between narrative and life in a simplistic way, as a mere appropriation of the real. Applying a highly problematic theory of reflection, González assumes that it is unproblematic to transpose them: "[These novels are] a faithful copy of the events and characters of the revolution." If it were like that, we would be dealing with historical data needing no interpretation and of immense value for history scholars.

We suspect that the relationship is not that direct. In Mariano Azuela's late literary confessions, for example, he explains:

> The novelist—has said [Vigny]—is a poet, a moralist, a philosopher. A historical topic for him is nothing more to him than the canvas on which he must weave his work as a novelist. Because above the positive reality there is a higher reality, higher in quality, ideal. A writer must be above all an artist. Mummies should stay in their niches and not come out of their tombs, lest they become dust. Readers prefer Stephan Zweig's *Marie Antoinette*, Strachey's *Queen Victoria* or Maurois' *History of England* to all

the César Cantús in the world, just as we prefer Vasconcelos to all others who have described the life of our latest revolution.[2]

Besides protecting the idea of a creative space and not letting authors be transformed into history's amanuensis, if that is even possible, the most important part of this text is that it postulates the existence of two planes that have to be managed simultaneously, in different and complex operations, so that the writer can create his work. One of the planes is what Azuela calls "positive reality," which seems to be referring to historical events, tacitly accepting that it is possible to obtain a global view of them. The second plane is the "ideal reality," which he considers superior in value and for that reason rules the positive one. Here one can perceive echoes of Rubén Darío's famous verse, "Ideal forest that complicates the real," which expresses the same theory about ideal concepts acting upon and modifying the concrete reality of our historical lives. Likewise, the example Azuela gives is significant for the text, "We prefer Vasconcelos to all others who have described life during our latest revolution." With the statement he is showing that he personally follows Vasconcelos's "ideal reality," he is recognizing that he was employing revolutionary history as a canvas on which to paint a "higher" reality. In fact, one can find evidence of Azuela's ideas in his novels and notes as well as in Vasconcelos's long autobiography.

When a man of Azuela's philosophical convictions speaks of an ideal, he is not referring to the Platonic realm of pure ideas but to a system of moral and socio-political beliefs with which he judges the reality of his time. On a first level, and from a purely personal perspective, these are Azuela's own ideas. They would arguably be influencing his view of reality. However, it is impossible for him to have access to a totalizing knowledge of the universe and he can only come into contact with a fragment of it. He can eventually postulate this fragment as paradigm of the whole, but it will never be anything but a small part of a dynamic world and as a consequence it is evident that the writer should have a reduced use of the "positive reality." Antonio Castro Leal took into account these two methodological precautions when he said:

> A direct view of a new and impressive reality (whether it came from simple witnesses or those responsible for shaping it) is one of the characteristics that facilitated the birth of the Mexican Revolution. That this direct vision affects the narration in the

form of autobiographical aspects is obviously not only natural but also unavoidable. One can easily understand, on the other hand, that visions and aspects change according to circumstances and the mood of the witness, and also the type of reality he has the chance to contemplate. All the novels of the Mexican Revolution during this first period demonstrate to different degrees an autobiographical character.[3]

—not only biographical but also partial. José Luis Martínez emphasizes even more these autobiographical deformations of history when he points out that novelists write their works as memories or as true pieces of personal justification, to the point that they lose all objectivity and think of themselves as the center of the events happening during that period. Although this does not strictly apply to Azuela's revolutionary period works, the observations of this critic allow us to situate them as works with firm polemic intention: "These works are characterized by their status as memoirs more than novels. They are almost always personal pleas in which the author, similarly to what happened with the authors of our Chronicles of Conquests, explain his fundamental intervention in the Revolution, for which all of them will claim they were central pieces."[4]

Although very frequently critics lump together under the label "novels of the revolution" materials that have little or nothing to do with the narrative genre and that would perfectly fit the definition of memoirs or autobiographies, the author is prominently present even in those texts that are presented strictly as novels, as in the case of Azuela's works—not as character, not even as the axis of the action, but as an eye that looks at things and compares them to an ideal. Indeed, it is not only his personal interests (desire of power, monetary gain, fame) that move his pen, because the austerity and disinterest with which he always behaved is well known, but his intellectual interests. His works are pleas that correspond to a biased view of the events, but this biased view, far from being controlled by minor personal worries, responds to his socio-political ideas. That is why his literature is essentially political, more than historical, and political in the militant sense, as it corresponds to a party man.

Of course, he is not a party man in the strict sense of the term, as a member of a political organization (even though he was a fierce member of Francisco I. Madero's anti-reelection party, whom he worshiped almost like a lay saint), but in the general sense of a man of very well-defined ideological positions who believes firmly in them, around which he has created his life and for which he fights against what he sees as error and evil. To be a party man is to be, as in Drummond's verse, a divided man, a being limiting himself to a sector of reality, knowing what he is missing but confident he will be compensated.[5] Mariano Azuela himself admitted this in his memoirs, with his reaction to the failure of the hopes placed on those replacing Porfirio Díaz, when the idealists saw that the same corrupt elements remained in power and slowly began their work of corroding Madero's movement. If the assassination of Madero throws Azuela into direct, personal action, joining the revolutionary groups, the fraud that follows Porfirio Díaz's resignation turns him into a belligerent narrator. It was a moral reaction in both instances: the writer couldn't withstand the national indignity.

> Since then I stopped being (consciously or unconsciously aware of what I was doing) the serene and impartial observer that I tried to be in my first four novels. Whether as witness or actor in the events that will later serve me as basis for my writings, I had to be (and in fact, I was) a biased and passionate narrator. By my own free will I had chosen a mental position during the great renovating movement and I wanted and was able to keep that position until the end.[6]

This passionate view, I insist, was not influenced by personal gain, as happens in Vasconcelos's autobiography, and was the result of the "ideal reality" of Azuela's political convictions. That was the origin of the political novels that begin with *Andrés Perez, maderista* and culminate with *The Underdogs*. Because of this characteristic, one cannot say that we have here the mere expression of a man, of an educated citizen of Mexico. Political ideas belong, by definition, to a group of men, to a sector of society, to a class, whose members recognize themselves as having a common will and a similar interest that might or might not be an idealization. The fact that after the re-edition of *The Underdogs* Mexican society of the 1920s was able to recognize in it their recent revolutionary history was due not only to the artistic virtue of the images but to the political and philosophical worldview expressed in those images, which embody that moment of the Mexican institutional process. In the same way, when Azuela constructs his novels in haste, as the events are happening, he is expressing not only his indignation, his fury, his criticism, but also the feelings of a social group that agrees with his judgment.

This political aspect, inseparable from the narrative of the revolution, is linked to certain points of view that have resulted in great debates, especially during Lázaro Cárdenas's administration. Literary critic José Luis Martínez summarizes the problem thus: "It is worth noticing that most of these works, while revolutionary in spirit as well as because of their topic, are the opposite of that. It is not strange to find in them disillusion, accusations and tacitly, an ideological detachment from the Revolution. It would be wrong to call them revolutionary literature and the name they have, in spite of its imprecision, is preferable."[7] They are not anti-revolutionary novels, rather they contain a curious interpretative duality about the events and they are especially critical of the of the civil war that after 1913 became part of Mexican reality. Depending on the political views dominating during different periods of Mexican life, these novels were either considered a legitimate expression of the revolutionary process or were attacked as the manifestation of a reactionary spirit. The dual interpretation they have received corresponds to their dual nature, and several hypotheses have been formulated about the topic.

We have to mention the hypothesis, among the most recent, by Enrique Anderson Imbert, who explains that

> the Revolution of 1910 in Mexico (one of the few Spanish American revolutions that actually changed a social and economic structure) sparked an entire novelist cycle. Now, it is the novel's prerogative to describe real anecdotes, not judge ideal objectives. The objectives of the Revolution were noble; its anecdotes, horrifying. And thus, the novelistic cycle of the Revolution, because of its courageous realism, seemed anti-revolutionary. An easy paradox to solve: the desire for justice is also a desire for the truth, and because they were revolutionaries, those writers denounced without hypocrisy the brutalities of the people who took up arms.[8]

I don't think the paradox can be solved that easily. To begin with, the novel of the Mexican Revolution, as Azuela understood it, always combined real anecdotes with evaluations of ideal objectives, which is generated out of this clash. Of the two elements that enter in conflict, it was not the second, the ideological system, that was affected and needed to be fixed or discarded, but the first one, the realism that became the target when it did not conform to the ideal canon previously known. This operation does not simply refer us to the "desire for truth" because it is not an abstract and universal entity, as the endless historical conflicts teach us, but a concept shaped by an epoch and, within that epoch, by the diverse social and political groups. The operation Azuela employs refers us to the theory of ideologies, not as a way to rationalize group or personal interests but as coherent systems established during different time periods and societies, which are used to understand reality and measure phenomena. The parsimonious analysis of Azuela's novels between 1911 and 1918 allows us to follow the various inflections of an ideology, at moments implicit, at other times openly expressed, that not only determines the materials of the intellectual debate—discussions among characters, meditations on the events, editorializing about the encounters—but also, in a more general and subtle way, reaches down to all the levels of the novelistic creation. This includes not only the choosing of events or the creation of characters but also the stylistic forms to be applied and the composition of the scenes. It never stops being the "ideal forest that complicates reality," and perhaps one should remember that in 1911 Mariano Azuela is already thirty-eight years old. He is no longer a young man who is touched and transformed by the intense events of the revolution. He is a man carrying spiritual and literary baggage, which he brings from his origins, his family background, the educational environment in which he studied, with ethic and social concepts already formed in his mind. The fact that he is writing contemporaneously to the events he is watching saves us from the typical deformations of the memoir of authors who recover the past from completely different (personal and social) situations and with a richer and more complex interpretative perspective. The spontaneity of his writing, the immediacy of the historical events in which his work is situated, leaves very little room for a dense and meditated intellectual elaboration. In his literary composition, the author describes his sensations and communicates the quickness of his choices and the problem of having to judge constantly. For that reason, he does not get any help from the accumulation of past time, the ratification or rectification of the value of his choices according to social consequences, or the strategies of a political action. The writer's decisions are controlled by what in Lukacsian terms is known as a perspectivism resulting from his ideology. "It is the perspective, the *terminus ad quem*, that determines the significance of each element in a work of art."[9]

Mariano Azuela belongs to a small, rural middle class family. Within that environment, making their ideals his, he lived and received his formation until the revolutionary storm. His frank realism, his wonderful sense of nationality, his petite bourgeois sensibility, his rigid moral views, and his respect of order, work, and precision have their origin in the environment from where he comes. He also gets his critical spirit, which is needed to establish distances and measure errors from his background. It is significant, and he himself acknowledged it, that his novels about middle class life are the weakest and that he judged very harshly his involvement in the revolutionary period. Within his class, because of his specific intellectual role, he occupied an intermediary place, with an inclination toward the popular sector, which explains both his revolutionary novels and his participation in the military whirlwind: "The humble classes have attracted me in inverse proportion to the middle class to which I have always belonged. Perhaps because I am closer to this vision, its endless, turbulent shades have confused me. Out of my observations I must report a passionate, but perhaps unfair account. I have been less sympathetic to the novels about the middle class."[10]

In his partisan storytelling there is an implicit set of values, including especially a mode of evaluation that comes from his origin in a socially ascending middle sector. To mark their boundaries one needs to first consider the sociological significance of the middle class toward the end of the Porfiriato. Even though Azuela, as we mentioned above, maintains a relationship with his environment not of dependence but of criticism, he also internalizes the ideological worldview in which he was born and surreptitiously employs it in his creative work.

II. The Middle Class before the Revolution

In 1908 *Pearson's Magazine* published an interview that Porfirio Díaz gave to a North American journalist, James Creelman. It was later translated in the Mexican newspaper *El imparcial* and has been considered the moment that triggered, or at least motivated, the anti-reelection campaign that led to the destruction of the Porfiriato. Upon reading it, Madero and his followers, which was a good sector of the country, found an opening for the possibility of a peaceful change in the national situation by means of the political tool of an election. The violent frustration of that path would lead to the turbulent times of the Mexican Revolution.

The rhetoric in that interview is controlled by the journalist, while the realism corresponds to the old general, who is cautious about the reporter's anti-reelection insinuations; he was after all North American. Explaining his presidency, Díaz discloses that he thought the moment of democratic maturity had arrived, which would make possible the application of the expression "effective suffrage, no re-election" (which became Madero's slogan). Díaz responds to a statement by Creelman about the composition of Mexican society thus:

> "It is commonly held that true democratic institutions are impossible in a country which has no middle class," I suggested.
>
> President Díaz turned, with a keen look, and nodded his head.
>
> "It is true," he said. "Mexico has a middle class now; but she had none before. The middle class is the active element of society, here as elsewhere.
>
> "The rich are too much preoccupied in their riches and in their dignities to be of much use in advancing the general welfare. Their children do not try very hard to improve their education or their character.
>
> "On the other hand, the poor are usually too ignorant to have power.
>
> "It is upon the middle class, drawn largely from the poor, but somewhat from the rich, the active, hard-working, self-improving middle class, that a democracy must depend for its development. It is the middle class that concerns itself with politics and with general progress.
>
> "In the old days we had no middle class in Mexico because the minds of the people and their energies were wholly absorbed in politics and war. Spanish tyranny and misgovernment had disorganized society. The productive activities of the nation were abandoned in successive struggles. There was general confusion. Neither life nor property was safe. A middle class could not appear under such conditions."[11]

Leaving aside all the elusive elements that Díaz employs in his interview and some improvised sociological explanations about the absence, for many years, of a middle class, it is worth pointing out the clear description of an entirely new event (the visible emergence of a middle class) which, in general terms, Porfirio Díaz situates perfectly and whose benefits he appears to understand, at least in word.

This social transformation has been taking shape under the stern Pax Porfiriana. A number of groups, with barely coordinated actions, have been creating an intermediate layer between the families of wealthy landowning (and even partly industrial) caciques, on one side, and, on the other, an immense mass of agrarian population. They have been opening their own path with great difficulty, especially in the capital and in the provincial urban centers, and by 1908 they possess a certain amount of power, even if full of contradictions. They are still weak economically in comparison to the bourgeoisie associated with the Porfirian regime, and their momentum is about to be stopped during those years by governmental concessions to foreign powers, but they have in compensation found in their education or in vocational training a good instrument to advance socially and to become an emerging public opinion that is beginning to pressure the military state.

Porfirio Díaz's famous slogan, "little politics and lots of administration," in practice was a political response to the economic conceptions of Limantour, the secretary of finance, who believed that for the country to progress they needed the inversion of foreign capital and the capacity of a tenacious bourgeoisie, which could enrich themselves without problems, employing all means available, even illegal ones. The same slogan helped the discrete growth of the middle class, which during a long, obscure period at the end of the nineteenth century took advantage of the possibilities for development available during the Pax Porfiriana.

Even though the Maderista movement presented a black-and-white picture of the Porfirian period and this partisan view only grew stronger later on, an analysis of the economy of that long period of Mexican life shows a process of development and progress that resulted in an important national growth. Out of this process an incipient proletarian sector was emerging, united through anarchist ideas that arrived in the country in the late nineteenth century. Feeding from this proletarian sector and from the peasants who were kept with an iron grip in low living conditions, this process allowed the upper classes to enrich themselves greatly but it also tolerated the development of the middle class. Saving little money at a time, taking advantage of their small businesses, educating themselves, they slowly acquired a status as a secondary ally to the dominant class and provided the country with a team of administrators and a network of commercial distribution, as Porfirio Díaz acknowledged in the previously quoted interview.

The growth in exterior commerce (between 1872 and 1910 it goes from fifty million to almost five hundred million), the intense development of the railroad (by 1915 Mexico had laid down twenty-five thousand kilometers of railroad tracks), and the early oil extraction companies, which allowed Mexico to export twenty-five million barrels a year, meant that more specialists were needed. Given the disdain of the upper classes for poorly remunerated careers and given the incapacity of the lower class to provide the staff, the middle class was able to appropriate those tasks.

Out of the middle class came public and private administrators (though there was a ceiling to how high they could go), university staff and professors, and groups of school teachers. These became their ambitions because they thought these positions allowed them to socially advance toward the centers of power. José Vasconcelos's autobiography contains plenty of references to his youthful years and the belief among the middle class that it was only possible to improve one's social status through education. Thus, speaking about his rich classmates who, because of the democratic environment in Campeche, were studying alongside the poor ones, he notes: "We got even with them in class by being the best. Lino Gómez, from a humble Tabascan family, was my rival for first place; all the best students were from the middle class. They were rich, Why would they care about learning? They had lands, young Indian girls, and old slaves!"[12] We will see later in more detail that this way of optimistically clinging to education the young José Vasconcelos shows corresponds to the spirit of the middle class from which he comes. His mother has patiently taught him that knowledge is the only possible way of achieving his ambitious dreams of getting ahead—a young middle class man cannot aspire to any type of knowledge, but only to that which will propel him to a socially advantageous position. Vasconcelos himself explains: "I was not fond of studying law, it had the advantage of assuring me a well-paid and easy profession. In reality, it was my poverty that drove me to become a lawyer. If I had been born rich, I would have stayed as an assistant in the physics lab and I would have gladly taken again the entire science program."[13]

To facilitate its members' access to such cultural spheres, the middle class had to acquire a good enough economic base, something they usually did as small business owners (many sons of grocery store owners obtained university degrees in the first decades of the twentieth century), as small rural properties owners, or, usually, by carefully managing the income coming from a bureaucratic job. The last one was Vasconcelos's case, while the first one was that of Mariano Azuela's father. In his *Autobiografía del otro* [*Autobiography of the Other*], Azuela remembers his father's first savings:

> When my father balanced the books after his first year as a merchant, feeling miserable he went to "The Gold Mine" and said to his rich brother.
>
> "Here you have the three hundred pesos you loaned me to start 'El Tíguere.' I couldn't save a dime."
>
> My uncle very bluntly said to him. "Stop pretending. You have lived with your wife and son for a year without having to borrow from anyone; you are the sole owner of your store and don't owe anyone anything." My father's store was very busy. They sold bread and shoe repair nails, lard and medicinal herbs, natural honey and copper sulfate, cheese, tequesquite and all sort of miscellaneous products.[14]

The position of the middle class with respect to the wealthy landowners as well as with respect to the bourgeoisie of the regime was dual. On the one hand, they intensely criticized their rapacity, their despotic use of power, their never-ending greed for everything; on the other, they wanted to create alliances with the purpose of getting advantages, increase their economic base, benefit as a result of their collaboration from the speculations only allowed to the upper classes. What pushed the middle classes toward a confrontational attitude and led them to dispute the upper classes and their businesses was the latter's resistance to middle class upward mobility and their exclusory conception of the nation, which the upper class understood as their property.

In order to achieve that within the peculiar structure of the Porfirian state, where the gate to obtaining land, concessions, businesses, and governmental support was in the hands of the political power, the middle class aspired to put in practice sections of the 1857 constitution, no longer in use and violated, that would allow them to gain administrative control of municipalities and of the central power. The middle class's battles were mainly political in nature as they were interested above all in displacing the upper class rather than in abolishing privileges. Only reluctantly, they will later accept the large peasant masses' claims for equal rights, admitting later that if the masses were cautiously managed they could strengthen the middle class's position. But originally the middle class's claims were exclusively political. Hence they would find their perfect expression in Madero's ideology. He opened the possibility of a pact between a sector of the upper class bourgeoisie and the middle class, obtaining from the latter a support that was important at a moment when it had become necessary to replace general Díaz.

Maderismo became the ideology of the middle sectors, and that is why the continuous support of their cause began with enlightened citizens. As the confrontation grows, this group will produce the Revolution's leaders as well as its doctors. That is how Silva Herzog sees it. "Among the members of the middle class one could find the best educated, most intelligent men and the persons with the highest moral characters in Mexican society. From the middle class came several leaders, perhaps the best of the 1910 Revolution."[15] In the idealized version of Madero's last days that Azuela painted, the trusted collaborator, who in narrative terms is the leader, is an engineer who possesses all the qualities the middle class praise: honesty, responsibility, industriousness. And in his mouth Azuela puts a phrase that exemplifies the notion of constant loyalty: "Mr. Madero is not an intellectual, but he is worth more than one: he is a hero and a saint."[16]

The presence of the middle class as actors and leaders of revolutionary events had not been noticed until recently because once the Maderista revolution started and awareness grew of their incapacity to singlehandedly overthrow the military might of the old Porfirian regime, they had to appeal to the help of the popular sectors, especially the peasants, and the latter invaded the scene, progressively imposing their demands and obscuring the middle class's initial involvement as well as their subtle activities throughout the second, third, and fourth decades of the twentieth century.

From the perspective of the years that have passed since Madero's book appeared, the actions that led to the definite triumph of the middle class have become visible. "In reality the Mexican Revolution was not only able to allow the transition from colonial development to a semi-capitalist national development. From a dependence system that limited the benefits of its development to a small group of foreigners, bureaucrats, military and rich landowners, the Revolution has moved to create a system that increases the benefits of development, that allows the expansion of the middle class, the rural bourgeoisie, the qualified workers."[17] Pablo González Casanova's observation is from 1962, when there was already an ample historic perspective to evaluate the results of the revolutionary movement and recognize those who directly benefited from it. An approximation to the issue is found in sociologist Nathan L. Whetten's interpretative synthesis of his research (1950), in which he was precisely studying the trajectory of these classes: "In opinion of the writer, the revolutionary programs have had the following effects upon the class structure: (1) improved somewhat a lot of the members of the lower class—this has probably been the most important result of the Revolution; (2) stimulated an increase in the middle class; and (3) shifted the composition of the upper class."[18] If we understand fully Whetten's reference to improvement of the middle class as the transition of a rural sector to the middle class, this corroborates Pablo González Casanova's observations about how this class benefited the most after the revolutionary period was over.

In the meticulous works of Iturriaga one finds a similar conclusion. Using the years 1895 and 1940 as boundaries and taking into account the increase in population in the different classes, Iturriaga arrives at the following conclusions about the dynamic growth of each one of the social classes: "Taking as basis for comparison the rate of population growth in the upper class, that is, as 1, the middle urban class developed at a rate of 17.49; the middle rural class increased at a rate of 19.93; the popular urban class increased at a rate of 11.76 and the agrarian popular class at a rate of 1.84."[19]

One must recognize the operational capacity of the middle-class groups, a characteristic of their down-to-earth views, as John Johnson has explicitly explained. "The middle sectors' conduct between 1917, when the Mexican Constitution now in force was promulgated, and 1940, when the election of Manuel Ávila Camacho paved the way for the urban middle groups' emergence as the primary influence in formulating and administering national policies, offers unusual examples of their ability to survive in a wide variety of political climates."[20]

Although he recognizes the importance of the middle class for the beginning of the revolution, Johnson tends to undervalue their intervention during the second revolutionary period, asserting that "between 1920 and 1940 the middle sectors' influence over political life was highly indirect and negative" and that "the middle sectors were the last to lay claim to the nation. In the meanwhile they fought to protect the foundations upon which they proposed to build when they could again decisively affect policy-making on the national level."[21] It is true that there appears to be a withdrawal of the middle class after 1920 as they feel submerged in forces they do not control and let these forces assume political control. They even feel unfairly bypassed by a lower class that lacks preparation. This withdrawal is only in appearance and it is compensated with the effort they put during this period into broadening their financial base and getting stronger while they wait for their moment.

Their presence, in one direction or the other, in one trench or the other, is constant throughout the entire revolutionary process. To think otherwise would be to not recognize the complexity and disparity of the middle sectors. They are composed of a wide range of groups that include an upper level, educated and rich, linked to urban commerce, and a lower level of rural workers and small landowners. Their diversity explains their capacity to remain operational throughout the revolutionary storm. It also explains the flexibility that allows them to move from one spectrum of society to the other, taking advantage of the variety of relationships they have access to for being centrally located in the social body. In Iturriaga's statistical tables one can follow their ascending movement, from decade to decade, especially in the urban centers where they never stop growing between 1910 and 1950.[22]

This has been a long and sometimes difficult development resulting from the dynamics of upward mobility characteristic of this group. At the beginning of the twentieth century, the middle class has acquired the clearest consciousness of the need to obtain political power and the economic and cultural possibilities that come with that. At a moment when the rural masses have not even thought about the problem, when the urban proletariat is just beginning to organize and educate themselves as a class, the middle class has already achieved a level of development that leads them to covet political power.

Who were the members of the middle class? How did they earn a living? What were their views? Silva Herzog characterizes them in the following terms. "The middle class was composed of engineers, lawyers and doctors with very few clients, elementary school teachers, office staff, store clerks, small business owners, qualified railroad workers, successful craftsmen, and so on. One can place in this class or social category those who at the turn of the century were making approximately between fifty and one hundred pesos a month. Those who earned a bit more, lived with some comfort; those who made less, thirty or forty pesos a month, lived in shame and poverty."[23] If we classify them, we have an intellectual or educated sector composed of autonomous workers (professionals) or dependent ones (teachers), which was probably not a very large percentage, but this intellectual sector was important and it possessed a luster and social recognition that other sectors of the middle class lacked; a public or private bureaucratic sector that always belonged to those in lower levels; a sector composed of small, independent business owners; and finally, a small sector of skilled workers.

A quick image of the middle class situation within the social formation is given by Vasconcelos in the previously quoted autobiography, when he describes life in the Mexican Altiplano, in Toluca, contrasting it with the life he was experiencing in the border town of Piedras Negras:

> A great number of Indians dressed in blue and white, with dark skins, trotting as they walked while carrying a load on their shoulders, passed early in the morning toward the market. The creoles also went out to church, but afterwards they would go back to isolate themselves behind their glass windows. Only on Sundays, around noon, they came out well-dressed to stroll around the "Portales" downtown as they listen to the sounds of a military band. A few rich landowners stood out socially because of their frequent visits to the capital and to Europe, but they do not know nor greet their neighbors. Employees and their families stroll around the same places, but not even the most basic conversation between the groups is ever started. The same distance, another abyss, separates the middle class, "poor but decent," from the Indians who walk along the stream and listen to the music, but located far from those who use European clothes. Foreign to that world of well-defined social groups, we stayed away. . . . Strolling around Toluca one could see Indians stupefied under the weight of their loads, who were too shy to greet anyone, and the landowners in coaches, who were too arrogant to greet anyone. Between them, there was a reserved, untrusting, silent and impoverished middle class.[24]

This image, which is from the late nineteenth century, was going to change around the first decade of the twentieth century. The reservation, confusion, and silence of this class gave way to a more belligerent attitude, and the opinions of its members began to have some weight in the cities. They noticed the landowners and the companies getting rich within the demarcations approved by the government, and they observed the simultaneous impoverishment that the agrarian groups suffered because of that. They noticed the foreigners and those locals granted government permits, enriching themselves with mining and oil industries. They noticed the first attempts by the workers to unionize and protest. They realized that wealth was closely linked to power, concentrated in the authority of General Díaz and his group of "scientists." They knew that their opportunities to infiltrate that golden wheel were scarce as the upper classes fought to keep themselves abysmally separated from the rest of Mexican society. At the same time, they had developed a keen nationalist sentiment and hierarchy of intellectual values that made them feel as the true representatives of their country and the ones capable of helping it move forward.

But, as Johnson observed for the rise of the middle class in all of Latin America, they lacked any political experience, and because they had no homogeneity and no history of fighting for their group, they were not ready for violent action. They felt more at home in a library, behind a desk, or behind a store counter than in the middle of the street. That is why they tried, as long as possible, for a peaceful change and that is why they strongly supported Madero's movement. Later on, the middle and the lower classes learned to recourse to action, failing and reaffirming themselves time and again. Even as the masses of peasants occupy the revolutionary field, the middle class continues with their activities, which must be analyzed closely to understand how different their personalities are in behavior and ideals during the revolutionary storm. The fact that they became by definition the intellectual class during this period, and that because of their rationalist drive they felt the need to explain and define themselves in relation to contemporary events, gives us plenty of material for studying their ideas.

III. Education, the Instrument of Power

As we have already pointed out, one of the preferred means for the middle class to achieve upward mobility was education. It was not and could not have been a free choice but the result of adjusting their ambitions to the reality of the time. Located in-between two sectors that were growing more apart every day (a vast majority of peasants and workers who were becoming poorer and a small minority of Porfirian upper class members that were becoming richer) and because of the many reasons that prevented them from joining the upper class, the middle class took advantage of the path available to them: education.

The middle class was the group that benefited the most from Barreda's reform and positivistic education. In fact, it was meant for this group, hoping to provide it with the intellectual preparation needed to achieve the liberal plans of reform. The development of the nation needed to create an administrative apparatus to achieve its goals, as can be observed in the increased number of public servants under Porfirio Díaz, paralleling a similar increase in private activities spurred by the expansion of agricultural, commercial, and industrial businesses.

The upper class was in no position to fill those administrative positions as they had already assigned themselves political and economic leadership roles; they were disinterested in other activities. When the rich landowners thought about preparing their sons to become political figures in the regime, they sent them to get an education outside the country (that was the case of Francisco Madero himself, educated in the United States) or employed the private education of Mascarones in the capital city. This was the result of the habitual upper class belief in the foreign superiority and distrust of the national values, but it was also prompted by their desire to keep a distance from the middle class and from a type of education (the famous "preparatoria" designed by Barredas), which, while it was useful for the creation of skilled people needed in the country, did not conform to their philosophical worldview. The dictator himself had recognized it in his interview with Creelman: "The rich are too much preoccupied in their riches and in their dignities to be of much use in advancing the general welfare. Their children do not try very hard to improve their education or their character."[25]

With ever more exclusivity the middle class consecrated themselves to the possibilities that education opened for the preparation of both administrative roles and independent professionals, thus creating the education staff necessary for those positions. They helped to strengthen and prolong an ideology that, in practice, tended to slowly undermine the absolute power of the upper class. This is one of the reasons for the attacks that, beginning in the 1880s, were hurled against the positivistic education model (Montes's plan[26]) with the intention of dismantling that fortress of the middle class that was the escuela preparatoria (elementary school), even though it was not fulfilling their idea of upper mobility. The other reason for attacking positivistic education was the perennial need to prepare technical workers who were simply servants of the regime, lacking their own ideology. The actions show how little understanding the authorities at the time possessed about the link between socioeconomic groups and intellectual problems.

From their intellectual preparation the middle sectors extracted a pride that allowed them to justify their ambition to stand out in the rigid social conglomerate of the period. The knowledge they acquired gave them—in their eyes—the desired social status, imagining that it was compensating for the real socioeconomic base on which the social hierarchy was based and that it was then inaccessible to them. Vasconcelos's autobiography is full of sharp observations about this situation, as he experienced intensely and dramatically the lack that came from his social situation. One can even reinterpret his political and philosophical opposition to the Porfiriato based on this lack. As so many others, he perceived that the social ladder was constructed in accordance with wealth, and he understood it as a reflection of the influence of politics over the economic plane. He even tried to find a philosophical explanation for it:

> The vile political situation did not allow ambition any other path than achieving financial success. Turning money into an all-powerful entity and replacing the image of God with that of Caesar. And worshiping Man leads to the sin of the golden calf. Because if all we have is Man, then all we need is gold to have power. Under the Porfiriato, as it is today, gold is the measure of all values. . . . Money and pleasure, privileges of those worthy; pain and work, the inheritance of the inferior ones, who perhaps should disappear. Thus was the sociology of the time.[27]

This crude view of reality, with its dark overtones, offered by someone outside the circle of usufructuaries, is an approximation to the concept of culture that Vasconcelos expresses when remembering his youth:

> We were concerned about being, not about "Culture." This new religion of Science, which we overcame, did not touch us or inspire us. For my part, I never valued knowledge for the sake of knowledge. On the contrary: knowledge was a means to increase power and to finally save oneself. Knowledge as a means of achieving the supreme essence. Morality as a way to measure glory, not empty stoicism. Such were my rules, whose objective was the conquest of happiness. I was not interested in anything that was in the middle or in-between; I had a strong desire to conquer the essential and the absolute.[28]

This conception of learning and culture as efficient instruments to achieve power (both within the real and limited society as well as projecting it to the universal and superior field of knowledge) responds to the middle sector's desire for conquest in the process of developing. It is a reenactment of some of the main ideas of the bourgeoisie when they began to dominate the modern world. It is important to underscore that it was the only viable way the regime left them as a result of its ambiguous position toward the middle class. The government had given them the means to prepare themselves intellectually and gave them a way of earning a living within the bureaucratic apparatus, showing respect for some of their most treasured characteristics: hard work, honesty, decency. But the government was careful not to give them access to greater power and tended to make them dependent on the central power, turning them into passive regime collaborators. The regime had achieved the support of a sector of the middle class, neutralizing their ambitions, and during the years of revolutionary unrest required extreme servilism. But it was unable to get support from the most advanced part of the group as they were requesting the economic transformation of the country, their incorporation into the country, and the displacement of the rich landowners.

Until his fall Porfirio Díaz counted on the support of a sector of the middle class, ready to strengthen and expand the base of his power. Both "Reyismo" and Maderismo, which were the two big political groups of the middle class, tenaciously sought to reach a compromise with Porfirio Díaz, and it is difficult to determine to what extent that was his big mistake because the middle class possessed very little real power and they were deluding themselves by thinking that their intellectual preparation compensated for the weak bases supporting them. They would not have been able to defeat Porfirio Díaz—when he refused to negotiate with them—and remove the upper class from power if they had not appealed to the popular masses, having no other choice but to join them. The smartest ones, distrusting the masses, understood the situation and used all of their resources to achieve a peaceful and slow transition of power—even though they knew it meant establishing an ambiguous pact with the dominant classes through the military power in charge of the country.

Vera Estañol, who was one of the last ministers of Porfirio Díaz's government and later, when Madero fell, became a member of Huerta's cabinet, gives us a great illustration of the middle class and their zeal for education. Because he is a representative of conservative thought, this gives us the chance to study clearly the upper class's opposition to the middle class's use of culture to advance. It also shows the upper class's desire to see the members of the middle class take up manual tasks that would situate them at the level of skilled proletariat. It is the dream of having citizens achieve intellectual development exclusively through a technical route and thus obtain a better working economic machine. That dream was contaminated at the time with the desire to imitate what they had heard about the United States and the lack of prejudice of the North American workforce for manual labor. They did not consider that the peculiar industrial organization in the United States allowed its citizens to achieve a higher income, whereas in Mexico, as in the rest of Latin America, the highest it led to was the position of foreman. Remember, for example, the struggle of railroad workers to be recognized as professionals.

Vera Estañol says:

> Our middle class have felt such aversion to the factory or the worker. Careers in the scientific and literary field have exerted such a fascination over them because of the respectable fortunes or enviable fame acquired one professional or another. Or perhaps because of the social recognition that traditionally those who obtain a diploma have enjoyed, or because for the spoiled rich boys, student life is just a dissimulated pretext for laziness and licentiousness. There is no father or mother who, when thinking about their son's future, is not thinking about turning him into another Pardo or Lavista. No matter how many have failed trying, the alluring image created by the few who have triumphed has not diminished. . . . The irresistible inclination to become lawyers, doctors and engineers resulted in the creation of the special class of professional proletariat—those who after years of study and great sacrifices acquired the coveted title and when they started practicing realized that a piece of paper is not a guarantee of wealth.[29]

The reference to the failure of professionals with which Vera Estañol explains the overabundance of public servants is not entirely false, but it is in contradiction with the argument used at the time to bring in foreign professionals (not only engineers and chemists came from other countries, especially the US, but also lawyers who opened their law firms in the capital). "A government post was for these men the dream job. Few working hours, a desk job, job security, possibility of promotion depending on having good connections and a recommendation from their bosses and the ministry. In short, bureaucracy in all its splendor, empleomania in full-swing. And when there were no government jobs, then the dream was working behind a desk or a counter in banks and commercial companies. This was the sphere of action of the bourgeoisie and the middle class in Mexico and it determined their economic situation."[30]

The disdain toward the middle class and the distrust of their educational zeal is visible in the text. We cannot accept, without making some observations, Vera Estañol's explanation about the creation of a bureaucratic system. It was not born out of the paternalism of the Porfiriato but because the development of state activities grew as the country began to develop economically. On the other hand, it is true that the job ceiling put on the intellectuals of the middle class, limiting their ambitions, is a valid explanation for their resentment against the government. Even though they were the best educated citizens, they were not allowed to occupy key posts. This is a better explanation for the generalized resentment and not Vera Estañol's analysis, which portrays it as an upshot of the educational system for which Justo Sierra advocated: "The professional proletariat was the second unavoidable consequence: minds developed half-way, damaged by an excess of offer and the lack of demand. Resentful spirits, unfulfilled ambitions, unrealized professional dreams. This was the ferment of social disintegration."[31]

The educated sectors of the middle class were either public servants or professionals; that means one was dependent, and the other, autonomous. The most generalized ambition was to move from the former to the latter. Vasconcelos recalls the hatred his father had for the dependent worker (and in his case, without any official protection). The attitude exemplified the idea that there was nothing better than becoming a professional and being able to work without a master. "My father infected me with his hatred for bureaucratic life: 'One cannot make a career out of that, he used to say, one needs to become independent.'"[32] Similarly, there was also a constant ambition to go from private administration to public. On the one hand, it provided greater security, as Vasconcelos observed in relation to the decline of the city of Campeche: "The poor central governance, in destroying Campache with its levies and chaotic laws such as giving Yankee companies the rights to coastal trade, forced half of the population to emigrate. As a consequence, hundreds of families became part of the bureaucratic proletariat."[33] "Trapped in a silent, deliberate disaster, the middle class sought refuge in the charity of the ministry managing the few jobs available in the capital."[34] On the other hand, official employment carried more social prestige and, as a consequence of the political stability during the Porfiriato, a greater possibility of having independence and leading a moral life. Even though Vasconcelos is speaking from an anti-Carranza point of view, one can see the truth of his observations about the Porfirian bureaucracy. "Contrary to today's public servants, during the Porfiriato people could preserve certain decorum when doing their jobs. They knew that a majority of judges were honourable and administrators were honest."[35]

Perhaps one can notice this not in the corrupt government workers depicted in Mariano Azuela's *The Flies* or in his *The Trials of a Respectable Family*, but in the minority of bureaucrats that were the first to militate (and thus sacrificed the most) in the Maderista group. These were men who preserved a sense of incorruptible dignity. The violations of rights they witnessed, even if it made them a bit skeptical, did not destroy the moral hierarchy to which they held on in times of corruption. The social structure assigned them the role of mediators, which kept them protected from direct contact with the most brutal and unfair events. Instead, they found themselves working on the written documents justifying all the injustices. The double nature of their middle position allowed them to be both forced collaborators with the regime and, at the same time, its moral censors.

A text by José Rubén Romero documents the guilt the members of this group feel when seeing, face to face, the social injustice with which they collaborated. The same text allows us to observe how much less mediated private jobs were at the time and, as a consequence, how problematic they were for one's moral conscience. In his novelized autobiography, Romero recalls what happened in one of his first occupations as a young man:

> A notary, an acquaintance of ours, noticing the bad situation we were experiencing, suggested to my father that I go work for him, copying documents. We accepted, anxious to earn some money, and I started working in his office. At first I liked the job. I used to copy the documents mechanically without paying attention to their meaning. To this I must add that the notary had a very attractive daughter who liked me. But as I got better at my job, I began to earn my boss' trust, who put me in charge of interacting with the clients. Then I saw so much misery, injustices, and plundering that I did not want to continue copying those disgusting papers. Poor unsuspecting Indians who would give up their inheritance for a few dollars to spend them in a religious celebration. Executors without conscience stealing from minors. Priests who tricked widows into trading their houses for funeral prayers. And I was benefiting when I copied

those felonies thus contributing to senselessness and injustice. Many times I was paid fifty cents for my signature to function as a witness of these indecent crimes certified by a notary. My father and I agree that I was not going to return to the firm.[36]

Both public servants and those we can already consider intellectuals (professionals, educators, writers) generated a notion of culture as a superior value and they were its main consumers and beneficiaries. That notion of value became the criteria to be employed in the re-categorization of the social body. They automatically became the head of the new order, distinguishing themselves from the upper class but also from the ignorant and illiterate masses in the country and wielded against them the same arguments the old paternalist state had once used. Intellectual and civil servants formed a subgroup within a social class and intensely developed their class consciousness, which allowed them to recognize each other as a coherent group.

IV. Intellectuals in the Revolution

To become a "biased and passionate narrator" implies that behind the author there is a citizen who is judging the surrounding reality in terms of a morality, a philosophy, a philosophical doctrine. Beginning with *Andrés Pérez, maderista* the critical character of Azuela's narrative grows, and his work becomes a partisan analysis of the society of his time.

The regional "caudillos" and the political elite during Huerta's presidency are targets of strong critiques, which, due to his sarcastic writing style, take on the appearance of caricatures and grotesque creations. Similarly, he heavily censures the excesses of the masses of peasants and their leaders. However, the sector that gets the bulk of the criticism is the one closer to the author and which he knows intimately as he comes from the same petite bourgeois background. We are talking about those representatives of the rural lower middle class (to whom he dedicates his novel *The Bosses*); the representatives of the small town upper middle class linked first to Huerta and later to Carranza (this group's troubles are depicted in *The Tribulations of a Respectable Family*); the state public servants whose social origin and worldview also place them in the middle class (they are the pretext for the chaos in *The Flies*, a novel that can be compared to pre-expressionist art forms); and, in particular, the intellectuals, for whom he reserves the strongest invectives. Intellectuals appear in all the novels from the period we are studying, from *Andrés Pérez, maderista* whose plot is mainly focused on them to *The Underdogs*, where one of the main characters is Cervantes, the intellectual who joins the rural uprising.

Of all these sectors, none gets a stronger reaction from Azuela than intellectuals. When he talks about them he moves into defamation and collects insults without measure, breaking away from the narrative strategies giving direction to his work. His passion overrides the literary rules he has adopted, giving way to a political pamphlet full of insults.

This virulence has to do with intellectuals in the country dividing into the three organized forces that were aspiring to power in 1910: Porfirian reelection supporters; "Reyismo," an alternative that was also a continuation; and the dissident stance of Maderismo.[37] Vasconcelos evaluates the distribution of intellectuals among the three politico-ideological currents as follows:

> Almost all the best known intellectuals and the youth who were entering politics for the first time, all of whom were more or less benefiting from the regime, joined the Reyistas. Jesús Urueta, Luis Cabrera, Zubaran, who will be future ministers under Carranza, were Reyistas and considered Madero's actions a crazy adventure. Those of us who followed Madero were as unknown as the masses that were joining him along the way. The upper class intellectuals, slow to make up their minds, stayed with the old regime, either wearing a Reyista mask or supporting Limantour and the scientists. Our schoolmates became divided. The most brilliant ones, José María Lozano, Nemesio García Naranjo, followed Pineda and the scientists. The Ateneo group stayed away from politics but most of them sympathized with Maderismo.[38]

This description resembles Jesús Silva Herzog's conclusion, which in turn confirms Federico González Garza's interpretation: "Indeed, one could argue that in 1910 and 1911 most of the intellectuals were in some way linked to the Porfirian regime. The few who were honest and joined the Revolution from the beginning, were less than a dozen."[39]

During the first decade of the twentieth century Mexico underwent an accelerated crisis because the dominant political structure was inadequate for the real socioeconomic organization of the country. It is normal that in those cases the destruction of old values creates, first of all, a general state of confusion. The apparent homogeneity is destroyed, and the fragmentation increases because of all the different tendencies. This situation necessarily forces a revitalization of intellectual life because the intense social polemics require analysis and interpretation. The demand for intellectual products increases as the confusion and insecurity of life creates a need to urgently understand the new situation and seek guidance.

It seems relevant to quote here Alfredo Maillefert's memories from this period: "The first thing that happened then was that newspapers acquired an importance they didn't have before. We didn't use to read newspapers (only the illustrated versions on Sundays), but then we started to read them daily. We (and this plural includes not only myself but also those around me) didn't use to talk about politics and began to get interested in it. The entire city was talking politics."[40]

We have to remember that it was Madero's book about presidential succession that started the polemic. It was a good example of the type of intellectual analysis that society was demanding. It made sense that the polemic grew through the only tool of intellectual exchange available at the time: the newspapers. Contributing to them were not only reporters (who had recently appeared, responding to the jobs created by the popularity of this mean of communication) but also modernista writers and poets who, following the pragmatic example set by Gutiérrez Nájera, had found in the newspaper a way to support themselves and the possibility of creating intellectual work for which they had no other outlets. But these newspapers, because of their peculiar economic structure that made them dependent on the central power and its interests, lined up with the Porfirian government. They forced their writers to start a virulent anti-Maderista campaign that did not shy away from using insults and lies. It became clear that intellectuals were subordinated to the interests of the regime and especially to the upper classes. That it was not as evident before was because up to this moment the peace created by the regime did not need intellectuals to openly defend it. As soon as the Porfirian Pax was broken it was revealed that the government was not representing the interests of the entire nation as it pretended. Intellectuals showed themselves as corrupt servants of the regime and had been given the typical ideologizing task of hiding the economic and political objectives of the government of Porfirio Díaz (and later on, of Huerta), employing theoretical justifications and singing the government's praises.

It was the small intellectual group of Maderistas who made evident this situation of dependence and forced the Porfirian intellectuals to abdicate their roles mentally and ethically. The sole existence of this Maderista group, their resistance, their militant criticism, unmasked the pretended national unanimity and the fake apolitical attitude of the intellectuals in the regime (or those who pretended to oppose power joining Reyismo). It was shown that they were at the service of a specific sector of society that was economically supporting them.

The characteristic position of modernista intellectuals enters into crisis. Having accepted the division of work resulting as a consequence of positivism, they had withdrawn to a sphere exclusively dedicated to literature. They had rejected the functions traditionally assigned to poets during Romanticism, which included moral, social, and patriotic tasks. Their rejection of society and their need to dedicate themselves seriously to their art, attitudes with which the modernista poet sought to placate his moral conscience, were now an object of vilification. In *The Flies*, Mariano Azuela employs a text by Díaz Mirón, who at that moment had become a supporter of Huerta, to sarcastically demonstrate the fake modernista disdain for society. "There are feathers that can cross a swamp and do not get dirty. . . . My feathers are of that kind," Mirón would say, defining not only the untouchable nature of the poet but also, hypocritically, the possibility of existing in the swamp of reality without being contaminated. Put in the mouth of one of the characters, Matilde, who is ready to accept any heinous act to survive during difficult times, the text acquires an obvious sarcastic tone.[41]

In the same novel, Azuela uses another character, Neftalí, to denounce modernista intellectuals' "escapism." To ridicule them, he places the young "nefelibata" in an anguishing dependence on reality that transforms his emphasis on the sublime into grotesque and vain gestures. "Neftalí was lying doubled up against the side of the hut, fagged out, disconsolately surveying the disaster of his shoes. He answered Don Rodolfo with a grimace which, interpreted, meant: 'You are quite aware that I live in my ivory tower, that my spirit floats serenely above the eternal snows, indifferent to the trifles you call revolution.'"[42] And in *The Tribulations of a Respectable Family* the same topic centers around the poet Francisco José, supposedly the author of books titled *Agonies of the Marble* or *In Praise of Serenity* that caricature not only the typical modernist poet, who after 1910 becomes a survivor, but also the "colonialists" who, right in the middle of the revolutionary period, continue to fantasize about reconstructing long-gone societies, thus keeping alive some of the traits of modernista escapism.

Azuela's technique is very simple and is based on using strong contrasts. In chapter 6, "On the day after our arrival," Francisco José has just finished reading "with a voice full of emotion and his eyes wet" his poem "I Search Now for the Heights of Serenity" when Archivaldo interrupts him, saying, "The Federal troops, disbanded, are returning to the city. They have suffered great defeats in Zacatecas and Guadalajara."[43] Here not only is Azuela making fun of the idea of art for art's sake but he also shows its secret alliance with a social order rigidly established, the one the defeated federal troops were defending. As an example of the exasperation that Azuela felt with this type of intellectual (the kind of human beings about whom Dante would have simply stated "let us not talk of them, but look and pass"[44]) we can find other outbursts like this one: "Francisco José, as usual, took refuge in the water-closet to shelter his esthetic sensibilities from the ensuing quarrel."[45]

Although Azuela belongs to a previous generation, he leads and moves ahead of the new artistic tendencies that characterized the writers of the 1910s. Vasconcelos was a better representative than Martín Luis Guzmán of a group that, beyond subtle political differences, had as a common denominator the Athenaeum of Youth. Those artistic tendencies were submersion in the social reality of their time, a strong will, and responsibility to educate the emerging social, middle class group.

For the same reason, Azuela realizes the first coherent effort to restore dignity to the twentieth-century professional writer in Mexico. But he can only do that, given the peculiar historic-cultural circumstance he is experiencing, if he is drastically militant. To achieve this, he unconsciously adapts one of the directions described by Karl Mannheim as the options available to intellectuals in that epoch of sociological interpretation of the world that begins in the mid-nineteenth century.[46] In other words, he tries to insert himself in a social group, tries to turn himself into one of them so he can express their view, give them a voice, and make sense of their interests as much in the plane of intellectual reasoning (ideologies) as in the plane of artistic sensibility (literary works). This is how he was able to obtain for himself a stable and justified situation within a generally unstable and unjustified period.

As said above, Azuela expresses the worldview of the small middle class embodied in Madero. Azuela translates Madero's worldview and therefore his interests, as Azuela is part of that class because of his origin and formation, but that would not have been enough to turn him into a spokesperson for the group. It was necessary for him to discover his connections to other men of his class through a lucid awareness of being like them. Having realized the difficult situation in which this sector of society found itself, he transforms himself into a combatant (a "partisan and passionate narrator"). It is when he belligerently takes action that he discovers his class and polemically assumes it. He makes this class his own as a community of interests fighting against a common enemy—the existence of this enemy led him to become part of a zone of society with other men who think like him.

Given the specific field of activity, his fight begins as an attack against the Porfiriato intellectuals, especially those who were notorious for publicly defending the regime in the press. When he opposes them, perhaps Azuela is not aware to what extent he is also an intellectual serving a cause. He will continue to do so until the defeat of 1915, which is psychologically prolonged a few years, even though his service will contain contradictions because of the special situation of the middle class during those years. Even if he had not expressed it programmatically, the militant use of literature and the substitution of words for bullets can be easily corroborated in some of his texts and novels focused on intellectuals: "I thought you were one of those Mexican pseudo-intellectuals, herd of pen-wielding slaves full of meanness, eunuchs whining about peace, incapable of shedding a drop of blood for their siblings, for their country, or for their own kind; cowards who spend their lives ceaselessly filling their bellies and are satisfied with having their names mention as another one of the miserable and corrupted servants, good only for singing to their masters' sluts."[47]

Beyond the concept of intellectual servitude, Azuela attacks positivistic notions by contrasting them with the generous idealism the middle class presents as new philosophy as the century begins. Such idealism responds to the reestablishment of a criteria based on collective social sacrifice, which the middle class use as a fighting weapon. That sacrifice, of the national and patriotic kind, is meant to be a rejection of the pure selfish subjectivism (both economically and philosophically speaking) on which the power of the upper bourgeois classes is based. Azuela associates the intellectuals-turned-journalists with literary authors as they both exhibit two traits of selfish subjectivism: venality and defection of the national cause. "Writer! There is no doubt: we, men of letters, are unbearably pleasant guys. I swear I have never come across a single member of this fauna in my life without feeling the most sincere desire to see him burst like a toad."[48]

For Azuela there is evidently a link that ties journalists and writers to the political powers and turns them into spokespersons for that social class. His attacks will be based on moral reasons, combating the idea of intellectual "servitude" itself. In a passage from *The Bosses*, intellectuals are associated with politicians and they are both defined as servants of the upper class: "You only have to read the opposition press to see intellectuals and politicians in all their nakedness—faithful copies of the cultured and wealthy classes. Disgusting! They stink of mud because they sprang from it, they breathe it, they eat it, and in it they are reproduced. When they show themselves in the newspapers or in the courts, they make me think of toads escaping from their puddles, raising their ugly heads to the sun that blinds them."[49]

Another passage in the same novel establishes a curious comparison between two social types, the intellectual and the proletarian, linked because of their position as servants. The passage allows us to measure the distance Azuela takes from the second one, whom he sees as belonging to a lower social level, but at the same time confusedly points to an opposition that, during this historic period, only Flores Magón was able to see. Azuela says: "The most ignominious depravity that the Revolution of 1915 has exposed is an abject intellectual class that drag their bellies through the mire and lick the boots of everyone in high places. We know that there are two kinds of slaves in Mexico: the proletarians and the intellectuals; but, while the proletarians spill their blood in torrents to win their freedom, the intellectuals fill the press with their nauseating slobber. The ignorant poor command our admiration; the intellectuals make us hold our noses!"[50] These words were put in the mouth of Rodríguez, who is representing Azuela's ideals with the exception that the character believes in utopian socialism (Azuela considers this unrealistic and a weakness). And one can see in them the distance that Azuela keeps from the proletarian servants. He would have never considered, like the petite bourgeois intellectuals suggested when a strong conscience among the proletarian class emerged, becoming a servant for this class. He belonged to a different sector, but he was also unwilling to become a servant of the middle class, and he even rejected ethically the concept, not because he stopped completely representing it but because its members notoriously failed to challenge the Huerta dictatorship and give meaning to their own revolutionary movement. This leads Azuela to become isolated and to self-criticism.

The failure of these new social sectors in the field of politics and the field of battle was too visible and Azuela could not ignore it, especially because he was a close witness of their indecisions and weaknesses. His literature during this period contains many critical references to the problem, especially in his novel *The Bosses*. Twenty years after the events, this is how he saw it: "The active participation the middle class had in the revolutionary movement started by Francisco Madero had many heroic and valuable episodes like the story of the Serdán family in Puebla, but most of them were humorous and grotesque because people were treading on shaky ground, they were absolutely ignorant of how to do politics. Those who were overthrown were masters at politics and that was a fundamental reason for the fall of Madero's government at the moment it had just begun to work."[51] Juan Viñas and his family in *The Bosses* represent the best virtues of this class, their emotions, their hard-working attitude, and even the quiet lyricism of their grocery stores. At the same time, Azuela shows Viñas's lack of heroism, his dependence on the upper classes, and above all the tragic inefficiency of the urgent action needed in view of the national circumstance. The seeds of the critical vision the novelist offers of his fellow members of the petite bourgeois can be found in those deficiencies and the successive failures that result from them. Even though they are presented in his books as part of a warm circle that Azuela knows well because he lived among them, this does not diminish the bitterness of his criticism. In his notes "The Novelist and his Environment," Azuela explains that "the humblest classes in society have always attracted me in reverse proportion to what happens with the middle class, to which I have always belonged. Perhaps because I am too close to them, I am overwhelmed with the endless variety of shades in them. Based on my observation I must necessarily report what I see with passion and perhaps I am unfair."[52]

The failure of the middle class is the vital experience, close and heartbreaking, that feeds Azuela's narrative cycle between 1911 and 1918. In the first work of this period, *Andrés Pérez, maderista*, the topic is clearly stated and perceptible in the resolution of the work: fraud achieves its maximum expression in Andrés Pérez, the coward and accommodating intellectual turned into a spokesperson for Madero; Antonio Reyes, the authentic Maderista representing the educated sectors, is killed; the popular uprising, with Vicente as leader, is defeated with the participation of his own fellow members, blind servants of the established political power. If this is how the narrative cycle starts, its conclusion appears in *The Tribulations of a Respectable Family*. Among drama, mistakes, and frustrated acts of rebellion, the narrative illustrates Procopio's growing skepticism and ends in resignation. A little bit like Voltaire, who makes his puppets go through a thousand adventures so that at the end they recognize that "il faut cultiver son jardin," Azuela forces his characters to recover in the end a philosophy of the defeated middle class. Procopio and his family will start working as employees; they will create a cozy environment, intimate and private, in their house; they will go back to carefully saving their money, with the criteria Juan Viñas expressed in *The Bosses* when he says that everything consists of "patience, honesty and stick to it"[53] but no longer with the ambition of one day competing with rich people. They only aspire to limit their ratio of ambition so that it coincides with their real possibilities, thus generating the illusion of happiness. That is how Procopio agonizingly explains his philosophy to his wife, whom he has won back for this enterprise. "Look, this is true happiness, the happiness of trivial joys, because the other, the Happiness which is written with a capital does not exist; it is a mirage, a mournful lie. We all have the same chance to achieve happiness. All depends on putting the inner and outer worlds in harmony."[54] The old, enterprising middle class that wanted to obtain power lost their hopes, now considering them "crazy," and begin anew to reconstruct their economic base starting from zero. They will still have great opportunities to participate in power but for the moment they have abandoned definitively their revolutionary zeal. They will look for other paths to move ahead, now from within the cities to which the social storm has forced them.

In the same way, the narrative cycle of 1911–1918 begins with images of confusion in the first pages on *Andrés Pérez, maderista*, symbolizing the chaotic state of the country, the subversion of values, violent agitations taking over society, and the expectation of great events: "Later, everything was confusion. People rushed, avid with curiosity, towards 'la Profesa' ";[55] they put up fences at the street's entrances and alongside sidewalks. They stopped slow and solemn vehicles, automobiles stopped making noise; a triple row was created, then came another and another one. At the end, everything was confusion and disorder and traffic was interrupted. Artisans mixed with elegant, perfumed people, humble seamstresses like bewildered varnished dolls. But in that group of dissimilar people there was one predominant expression in their eyes and gestures: anguish and indecision, sensing that something was going to happen."[56]

The images of the urban world that close the cycle in *The Tribulations of a Respectable Family* are also dark. But what we are now given is the diminishing figure of the main characters located within the early macrocephaly of the capital, being part of the modern urban space. Gone forever are the provincial idealization and the semi-aristocratic hierarchies of the landowners there. " 'Who, now,' I thought, 'are the Vásquez Prados of Zacatecas? Where is the well-gloved hand raised to salute us cordially as we pass? Where is there a single head bared respectfully and inclined humbly on seeing us? Cold countenances—disdain, apathetic, insolent. Nothingness! The hateful city! Yes, here we are nothing more than a tiny drop of water in the immensity of the ocean.' "[57]

This defeat, which Azuela bitterly recounts after eight years of hard work, shapes his view of things as he recognizes when explaining his work retrospectively. He says about his writings that he "put all his passion, bitterness and resentment of defeat"[58] or when he explains that beginning with *The Tribulations* "I felt totally cured of my personal resentments and the hyperesthesia that I got from that disaster."[59] To this failure he owes his isolation and his attitude of sharpshooter, from where he contemplates reality. He remained marginal to the social group to which, because of his origin and worldview, he was looking to be part of, and he does not find any other group to join. Perhaps, being nearly forty years old, he could no longer achieve a new integration.

The failure of the middle sector to topple the upper classes opens a path for the lower classes, peasants, and sometimes proletarians to act. It is them who beginning in 1913 occupy the historical stage. It is with them that Azuela will fight and it is about them that he will offer his pessimist account in his major work, *The Underdogs*. But it is in *The Tribulations of a Respectable Family* where one can find Azuela employing his critical and belligerent style to judge the lower sectors of society. He says: "Wild-haired people, pockets bursting with Carranza's paper money, half dead with hunger; humble clerks, dressmakers, small rentiers, orphans, the infirm: the middle class condemned to a double torture in their intimate contact with the vile, mean rabble, for whom nothing was ever any better or any worse and who now, all puffed up with pride, spat insolently in their faces."[60] The resentment Azuela was talking about, and that originated in the defeat of the middle class, will only grow in the face of the lower classes' sudden and disordered rise to power. The admiration that he feels for them as courageous warriors (chapter 3 in *The Underdogs* describes the first encounter, where brutality is mixed with a heroism turned impulsiveness; chapter 18 in *The Tribulations*, where the narrator cannot hide his inexplicable admiration for Zapata's and Villa's ragged armies as they enter Mexico City) will not obscure his repulsion of the advance of groups lacking preparation, almost barbarian sectors, who take power because of their strength.

Azuela's situation becomes, with some variations, like one of those "Types of Intelligentsia Formed of Displaced and Blocked Persons" Karl Mannheinn described, specifically "those intellectuals whose social expectations are thwarted." In the short period of time that goes from 1910 to 1915, Azuela witnesses the greatest possibility of rise for his group, their complete failure, and their replacement by an inferior social group that perceives the middle class as if it were the upper one, and he proceeds to attack it directly in the same way:

> A stratum which is abruptly thrown back upon its original position does not emulate the upper classes but assumes a defiant attitude and develops contravening models of thought and behaviour. The situation itself makes such attitudes probable; to what extent they become acute depends on secondary factors, as for example the capacity to articulate and to evolve a counter ideology. Where the conditions for the crystallization of an articulate opposition do not exist, resentment becomes covert and its expression confined to the individual or his immediate primary group.[61]

That is, unless the resented one is a writer. He is capable of expressing an articulated position and creating a clear and coherent ideological body and a corresponding artistic sensibility. But he is not capable of making his intellectual action embody a social movement because he is an isolated element disconnected from his original group, which he is able to see critically from his new situation without breaking the connections that tie him to it. After 1925 that group begins to consolidate itself in the cities, begins to develop under a new battle plan, and rediscovers Azuela's work. *The Underdogs* is successfully republished. The writer has found his adequate social medium. His work begins to feed the ideology of the middle class, giving them an interpretation of recent history. They thus close the cycle of idealization of the past, which presented a nostalgic look at not only the colonial past but also the Porfiriato, so many times remembered by Vasconcelos and Azuela as a period of peace and order. That is the beginning of the cycle of the novel of the revolution, a long chapter of testimonial accounts with the purpose of integrating that violent period into the worldview of a class that was again beginning to seek power.

2

Criticism and Literature

Some clichés seem ineradicable. They are so fiercely ingrained in the wisdom of common people that they always shine and accompany other ideas. They end up being prestigious forces of habits. That is the case with certain ideas about criticism; they force us to start a reflection about the topic with a series of negations. However, we should not forget that Maurice Blanchot has re-thought many of these common places from a critical point of view and perhaps we might surreptitiously be referring to them.

Criticism is not *something* added to the literary work. And even if it is a "metadiscourse," as Barthes points out, because it is elaborated from a previously existing literary discourse, that does not make it an appendix, nor a persistent and repetitive shadow. Criticism *is* a fully developed work afflicted by the same problems a poem or a novel possess. Not only does criticism have a guiding role, but its position within the vast, plural, and dynamic structure of literary periods is as central as the one creative works occupy.

If we had to summarize its function, we could say that criticism grants literature its existence because through its interpretative discourse an original composition becomes part of the field of culture. Criticism is in charge of determining the place of a work of art among other literary works and at the same time its place within the plurality of cultural meanings originating in other disciplines (philosophy, anthropology and sociobiology, etc.). Criticism transforms the literary work into an object inextricably integrated into the totality of culture. During that complex process, criticism oversees the exchange of values that gives culture its organicity. It selects, organizes hierarchically, and explains. It incorporates the materials upon which it is acting into a systematic and value-granting structure. To this synchronic action, we need to add a diachronic one. Only criticism is capable of integrating the past and the present through a homogenizing reading that finds a common denominator for all epochs, styles, and aesthetic projects. In that way it both modifies and completes the hierarchical system of each period. At the same time it shapes a literary corpus that is not tied to the social limitations of a specific historical time. In fact, such a group of works and meanings prefigure profound possibilities within society that connect the past to the future. They make the dominant tendencies within a specific idea of civilization visible, taking into account its remote origins as well as its contemporary manifestations.

We are not in the presence of "literature" if the only things we have are isolated and scattered literary works, no matter how good they are. Instead, they become integrated into a system—because that is what "literature" is—the moment criticism consolidates them as part of its explanatory discourse. The previous observation, a tautology on which structuralists built their work, must be complemented with two points frequently rejected by the structuralist thesis. The literary system exists within and depends on a cultural system and cannot be detached from it. In other words, literature as such cannot be removed from the meanings and options of the culture from where it emerges, whether these are moral or social options, economic or religious ones. And for these reasons, the options of the present determine the *literary system* in whose circumstances a society will discover itself. I am not talking only about the aesthetic options but also about the many options that emerge from the cultural demands relevant to present day society. In other words, the literary vision of the past is born out of the vision of the present and the latter, in turn, comes from society building options. In this way, performing critical evaluation does not require society to be bracketed. On the contrary, society reacquires its key position in this intellectual process, even if it did not have it in the literary works that were its pre-texts.

Thus, for criticism to establish the system, the first step is evaluating the literary present. Facing contemporary culture with the intention of evaluating it, criticism assumes, explicitly or implicitly, an aesthetic position. It is then when it acquires a reflexive consciousness and the guiding cultural principles emerge. As Hauser already observed, neither Wofflin nor, later, Spitzer would have been able to reinterpret the legacy of the Baroque if they had not taken as their starting point the aesthetic lessons gained in their era from the appearance of impressionism in painting and symbolism in literature.[1] This is why we can say that criticism is an adventure in the same way that, as it is widely recognized, literature is. Like new literary works, criticism has a vivid origin, expresses an original vision, and modifies the ideas received. They both emerge from the same group of writers, from similar experiences and similar struggles.

If the work of art is usually situated at the crossroads of national and international lines, criticism also needs to coordinate local traditions, topics, and tendencies with global aesthetics and philosophies. This is especially true in the marginal zones of culture that make up the third world.

In this region, criticism becomes more systematically coherent as a response to an increase in fragmentation and a diminishing sense of totality. A national literary history yields the pseudo spirit of a more rigorous system than a Spanish American, Latin American, or Hispanic literary history. And in these, the coherence will be greater than in a Western or universal history. As a system expands, its laws become stricter and more specifically aesthetic and ideological. When the system is reduced or localized, it allows for better, more concrete representations and more flexibility in its artistic demands. These expansions and reductions affect both the content of criticism and its methodological tools.

Thus, in many Latin American regions or countries (in Colombia as much as in Puerto Rico or Panama) criticism has not been able to develop in its fullest, distracting itself with marginal, sometimes damaging, solutions. In Puerto Rico, reflections on literature oscillate very visibly between two extreme positions, with a large empty section in the middle. Normally, that middle section is where literary criticism would bloom. The first of these two poles is not unique to this country. It is such a common practice in Latin America that it has become a secondary or secret circuit of intellectual life. It has its own associations, congresses, magazines, literary pages in newspapers, networking, and books existing at the margin of the main circuit, where real culture occurs. We are talking about the survival of a literary provincialism that is supported by a sort of lodge of mediocre people. They depend on a regime of cronyism to survive. Far from wanting to establish a tradition of literary criticism, they aspire to establish a society of mutual aid ("I praise you so that you praise me") whose paying members increase in direct relation to their literary incapacity. They are a legion, like demons, and they possess channels of communication and public activities and benefits, sometimes as important as those of real writers. Within this pseudo-intellectual circuit the role of the critic is performed by the writer himself, as a sort of second job, with the objective of "pane lucrando" [earning a living]. In fact, it is done to achieve literary survival.

The amount of incense the writer burns is equivalent to the amount of help they hope to receive. And their intellectual existence will depend on it. These creatures, like infernal demons, become a corporation created out of fire, sulfur, and smoke. Politically, they seek the protection of the state agencies, to which they pay the necessary homage. They will be for the most part ornaments of the establishment (this means any establishment) because they lack ideological positions or political knowledge as well as any real public usefulness. Thus they can barely aspire to be given the decorative function that sometimes the political power requires as complement to the pomp surrounding the throne. Their loyalty to the status quo derives from the absence of a real public that reads and pays attention to them and that forces them to depend on the charity of those in power. In that way they prolong anachronistically the regime of patronage characteristic of the aristocratic centuries.

This strange literary fauna of literature has not been analyzed so far. They have merely been the target of the intellectuals' silent disdain. However, it is a sociological phenomenon as important as serious literary culture and has a profound impact on Latin American societies, especially in those where the educational process is still very recent (such is the case of several Caribbean countries). Thus, for example, to that dark and conservative literary circuit we owe the imitative presence of certain literary forms that keep alive the modernista style at a popular level. Likewise, because of their combination of simplistic formulas with conventional morality and neutral socio-political positions, we owe to this regime of favoritism the literary models that are being taught to children in schools and to students pursuing secondary education. It has promoted an inefficient, vague, and anti-intellectual image that Latin American scientists attached to the humanities and it is why they look at them with disdain. The distance between science and humanities that dates back to colonial times has only grown.

This lodge of mediocre writers has a powerful position in Puerto Rico and possesses academies and newspapers, followers and mundane salons, but it is not a phenomenon unique to the island. One could deduce that if their practitioners have a more grotesque presence there than in other regions, it is because they have at their disposal a lot more financial resources. The "mediocre intellectual" has a similar presence in Venezuela and for the same reasons, and again in Mexico, for reasons related to the "royal court" culture created by the long-governing political party in power.

However, what is specific to Puerto Rico (and the situation is only comparable to Colombia's) is the other extreme of the literary reflection:

university research. The texts that the thesis-producing machine spews with unchanging regularity year after year should not be confused with literary criticism. In addition to the methodological deficiencies of a material that is still being ruled by the anachronistic model of the "Miguel de Cervantes-Life-and-Work" variety and where any stylistic study is realized as a reflection of author's life, it is not new to argue that there is a disconnect between "living" literature and academia. Vossler once argued that this was the origin of his critical renovation.[2] For a long time now, most writers have had no interest in university degrees. Their works are born outside the classroom. Since the time modernismo founded the Spanish American literary field, the gap between literature and academia has only increased, even though for obvious economic reasons many writers have become university professors. This, however, has not changed them: they live within these small and annoying jackets without having gotten used to them. Positions like "writers-in-residence" invented by North Americans have only resulted in writers losing prestige. The financial security offered by the university does not compensate for isolating oneself inside the university campus and losing touch with vital and creative horizons.

Literature, and within it literary criticism, rarely resigns itself to academia's domesticity. Obviously, university research and criticism, when done with a high level of academic seriousness, helps to increase knowledge about literature (e.g., Etiemble's thesis on Rimbaud). However, only rarely has academic analysis helped determine literary value in a specific cultural community. Reasons for this could be many and it is sufficient to mention a few. Tradition make these studies impermeable to methodological renovations (late nineteenth-century stylistics arrived at Latin America in the 1940s, via the Buenos Aires center of research; how long do we have to wait for everything else?). There is also a habitual lack of knowledge in the schools about the problematic of contemporary literature: specialization, which is required but reduces the intellectual panorama. One does not expect academic research to cast light on the present but on the past. But even accepting that, it is difficult to find a researcher that has spoken better about Darío than Octavio Paz or about Martí than Cintio Vitier, and both of them are only poets.

To sum up, one must admit that the university has had a formidable role in the education and democratization of Puerto Rican society and that it has been an important instrument in its social modernization. But it does not fulfill a similar role for the literary field or for contemporary cultural products. The same can be said about other universities, even some as prestigious as Mexico's famous Universidad Autónoma. In that country, at the margin of academic products, there is a hierarchical critical tradition that is the result of Alfonso Reyes's work and also of the admirable work of Octavio Paz (to the point that one could talk about an "Octavio Paz school of criticism"). Their work has allowed the integration of literary products into a great structure that has no equal in the continent. Instead of traditional critical texts, they employed free-form essays to study reality creatively. Thus, they have been able to implement models of behavior and great interpretations of literature as a system within a vast cultural system.

Finally, I see another two great stumbling blocks in the development of criticism in Puerto Rico. Beyond the lodges and flavorless fraternities, Puerto Ricans group themselves within another type of organization: political parties. In a country that is deeply and justifiably divided for political reasons, attacks against ideological adversaries can be masked as literary criticism of their poetry or narrative prose. And equally prejudicial is the uncritical defense of a comrade arguing for the supposed excellence of their literary work instead of accepting that it is because of a solidarity based on ideas held in common. The belligerent group of supporters of nationalism and independence, which is where one can find the best intellectuals in this country, have employed that type of uncritical judgment. It is true that this type of political cronyism is a superior version, not to be confused with the simple cronyism previously criticized, because it assumes shared ideological values. But it fails as it does not pay attention to the specificity of the artistic work.

The second stumbling block is the endless confusion of private and public life, of personal and social interest, of literary and economic fields, of artistic interest and financial investments, of ideological manifestos and bureaucratic preoccupations. All of these establish an always-present ambiguity in the behavior of the writer, which is even more problematic when we are talking about criticism. A critic needs independence of judgment as the first condition to work and that is only possible when there is real personal independence. The potential critic lacks the economic resources—the possibility of freely publishing—and even lacks the demand of an intellectual market, which still only pays attention to those looking to ingratiate themselves. In addition, the critic is constantly besieged by mundane, social, and economic interests, which, when they become unbearable, lead to acts of compassion and to cronyism.

For that reason, one can imagine that true criticism (so urgently needed for Puerto Rican letters) can only emerge from a zone where socially established values are decidedly questioned—only within such a zone can criticism have the necessary freedom to do its job, as long as the critic is not asked to be a mere soldier in a cause because at that very moment he would disappear. His independence and his work, simultaneously from within and from outside the cultural process, are the keys to his historical task.

3

Spanish American Literature in the Age of Machines

Spanish American literature is an art from a peripheral zone, frequently mirroring what happens in the world's cultural centers. In other words, following a logic of action and reaction, it reacts appropriately to foreign pressure. As an artistic product, it tries to solve the contradictions of the system that generated it. It tries to do so by incorporating foreign art forms into products that can both represent regional identity and suggest the possibility of an autonomous artistic future. Such behavior explains several features that apparently define contemporary Spanish American literature: the wide variety of its themes, a complement of its totalizing desire. It also explains the tension between the conflicting elements that form it; the ambivalence and sometimes semantic imprecision of the materials employed; the energy of a creativity transformed into voluntarism.[1]

The degree of autonomy this literature has already achieved—especially the poetry from the 1930s and narrative and poetry from the 1950s—should not make us forget that there is still a considerable degree of dependency that marks it but should not be confused with the study of legitimate literary influence. This situation results from simultaneous activity in both artistic zones. While Spanish America is trying to overcome disadvantages to reach stages of development already existing in the most industrially developed world, the latter is also looking to improve, using its current position to reach higher levels. To use a sports-related analogy, the other team also plays.

Proof of how far the South American field of letters has advanced is the quality of its literary products, which compare with (and for some surpass) those from some parts of Europe. Something similar happens with the economy and its impact on urban zones in the continent. However, celebrating this apparent victory might make us lose sight of newly created situations in which dependency and foreign influence are exposed in all their nakedness. The idea of a partial victory [over dependency] comes from some declarations by Mario Vargas Llosa, repeated by others afterward, about the superiority of the Spanish American novel in comparison to the European one, especially the French novel. The so-called decline of the French novel (even though one can understand Spanish American readers not being interested in it as their local reality strongly requires their attention) is unlikely. And attaching the "decadence" label to the entirety of European culture repeats the gesture of Marxist critics toward avant-garde literature in the 1930s, or, even before, that of the European bourgeoisie itself toward its dissidents in the nineteenth century. Beyond those problems, arguing that literature from a peripheral zone has acquired the same level as the one coming from a metropolis that used to rule the planet but now is reaching the autumn of its life does not prove that dependency is extinct and autonomy has triumphed. It simply hides a shift in the terms of the debate. The problem reappears in all its harshness once we focus on other centers of culture, such as New York or San Francisco, or, better yet, once we try to understand the nature of contemporary foreign influence and its impact on artistic creations. For that we need to stop looking for a specific imperialist metropolis as the origin of the problem and recognize its universal specificity.

We should not look for the foreign influence in a group of specific literary works, nor in artistic forms detached from those works, which have acquired meaning in themselves. We need to look at the conditions that in the world's cultural centers came together to support and to give life to works and forms in which a new cultural horizon solidified, created by the entire society. We could look for its point of origin in an element that helped prolong the splendorous life of capitalist societies at the moment when a debilitating world war appeared to have led societies to their twilight. We are talking about the technological revolution born out of that very conflict, which violently grows until the middle of the century, securing for these societies a new historical period of domination. Not only were the conditions of life modified and improved—in our opinion, to the detriment of their counterparts in third world regions—but also there was a profound transformation of the nature and composition of life, the basis of social taste, the forms of perception, and the instruments of exploration and domination of reality. The art that in the US and in some European countries—Germany and France, especially—is created during the period of the technological revolution is very different from the progressive and anti-fascist prewar art. But it was also different from the avant-garde art of the 1920s, which was contemporaneous with regionalism and neo-realism in other parts of those countries.

There is no more flagrant example than the big wave of objectivist narrative of the postwar period, which acquired different shades in each European region. Among Italian writers (Cesare Pavese) it included powerful emotional undercurrents, among the Spaniards (Juan Goytisolo) it functioned as social protest in a period of censorship, among the British (Allan Sillitoe) it was tinted with proletarian ideology (coinciding with the rise of the Labour Party) or with refined snobbism (Ian Fleming). But, as Cesare Pavese argued in his lectures on British literature, all of them were responding to the initial example set by North American literature, which gave us the great objectivist school, with Hemingway at the head, and a powerful legion of detective fiction writers led by masters such as Hammett. It was the first time that literature was adapting to the conditions of life imposed by technologies that had existed in the US for a long time before appearing in the Europe of the Marshall Plan. Thus was the story of North America experiencing modernity and the application of its laws before France repeated itself—as when in the nineteenth century Poe was a precursor of the French art for art's sake movement. The impact of the early technological systems appears in North America in the 1920s at the most basic levels of literary creation. Initially literature developed two different modes of confronting technology, one romantic (Lovecraft) and the other realist (Hammett). But the idea only achieved a balanced execution with the narrators that formed part of the lost generation. The latter term turned out to be a prophecy fulfilled during the war when a technological revolution took place that later, during the time of peace, began to distribute its products. It wasn't noticed immediately, which explains how early European existentialism became a legitimate interpreter of human beings during the anti-fascist resistance. But toward the middle of the century, younger writers reacted to this revolution in their art, which began to progressively adapt to it.

The representation of three previously mentioned elements (taste, perception, instruments) in particular works of art had an impact on the Latin American zone. However, because of its apparent neutrality, technological instruments have become the most attractive element, both within art and outside of it, in the real world, and also the one that has been most easily adopted. From kitchen tools to office desks, appliances became part of daily Latin American life, impacting especially the bureaucratic high middle class. Not only the apparent neutrality but also the ease of use of mechanical objects contributed to their incorporation into peripheral zones, far from where they were invented. The incorporation of machines is justified as there are utilitarian purposes for machines, and incorporation merely involves using and applying them. More difficult to explain is the emergence of the idea of a polished product characteristic of a good part of the pre-beatnik North American writing and which responds to the demands of refined industrial production. By the same token it is very unlikely that Latin Americans start adopting the same regime of work characteristic of elaborated industrial production, but they would accept the products from that system even if using them ends up looking unrefined and even surrealist.

Technological instruments were integrated into literary creations after the Second World War mainly as objects in a literary landscape, generating the dissonance typical of a surrealist montage (picture the image of an urban landscape increasingly becoming populated with machines). But instruments also functioned as a way of penetrating reality and, at the same time, becoming an impenetrable barrier mediating that reality. Thus, by becoming reality itself, they relegated art and literature to a product of second or third degree, created from secondhand and prefabricated materials. The result was a monumental bricolage created out of a universe of mechanical products and industrial waste, mixed with Lévi-Straussian pleasure.

The difference between this use of mechanical objects and the experience of technology during the first decades of the century with the futurist manifestos is well-known. The Italian futurists, the German expressionists, the North American abstractionists (like Eugene O'Neill or Elmer Rice) created works about the relationships between men and machines. But the writers from the second postwar period, fulfilling the prophecy of the pre-war objectivist authors,[2] wrote works with the help of machines, assuming as correct the perspective created by the machines, obeying their demands. The clearest notion, as mentioned above, was the recently acquired but unhappy belief in objectivity, an idea unveiled by the use of technological instruments. But the effects of technology in other intellectual disciplines was even more direct and this prepared the way for its impact on literature, as is obvious in some Spanish American examples.

In sociological field research, the use of mechanical tools seemed to validate their ambitions. The improvements in systems for capturing sound and images seduced researchers. It facilitated the task of penetrating reality and promised a faithful reproduction. The difference between two beautiful books, Pozas's *Juan Perez Jolote* and Lewis's *Los hijos de Sanchez*, is not only the amount of economic resources available to the authors but also the use of modern mechanical instruments. While the first one depended on a personal recreation for its construction, the second one resulted from the contributions of a mechanical register. Imitating this transformation of the social sciences, literature began to explore the new possibilities created by the presence of technology. Authors began to recreate, from a personal (even subjective) perspective, the materials that the machines were objectively recording. Two paths became popular. The first one, responding to the realist preoccupation with social protest, reacted by replacing the progressive realist novel practiced before the war with the testimonial novel of the sixties. The change from the literature of Jorge Izaca to that of David Viñas is substantial. Overall, it meant freeing narrative from the restrictive and propagandistic model used to present progressive revolutionary ideas. The adventure of impressionism and fauvism began when the development of photography freed painting from the demands of capturing a true reflection of reality. In the same way, the technological improvements in field research are now being used to capture the ideas of rebel movements in the form of documentaries, film-journalism, testimonial recordings, and autobiographical tales. They have created a new and valuable genre, which we call "testimonio," and its impact on literature has been immediate. Given that no novel can complete with a testimonio in terms of veracity or in authentically recording reality, the novel has been forced to use creativity differently. To explain it better, placed at this crossroads, literature has been pulled into two different directions. Let's look at one example, contemporary Cuban literature. We perceive different creative tendencies in two of its best young narrators. For Norberto Fuentes, literature is violently transformed by the use of direct testimonial reports. Its volatility is noticeable in the stories from *Condenados de condado* and the materials collected in *Cazabandidos*. For his part, Reinaldo Arenas transports literature into a world overflowing with imagination that, on the one hand, allows for subjective expression (*Celestino antes del alba* [trans. *Singing from the Well*]) and, on the other, can recreate a historical and global event and contaminate it with subjectivity and imagination (*El mundo alucinante* [trans. *Hallucinations*]). Out of these two solutions, the second one has been dominating the last fifteen years of Spanish American narrative. There has been a notable decrease of the so-called revolutionary novel in favor of the imaginative novel, whose role model, created in 1967, was *One Hundred Years of Solitude*.

The other tendency notoriously influenced by this age of machines corresponded to a new representation of the spoken language within literature, which also facilitated a major improvement over the old *costumbrista* (*criollista* or Creole) formula that depended upon phonetics, as many regionalists (from Mariano Latorre to Rómulo Gallegos) practiced it, allowing the approach of a new formula where the main key was the syntax and where the spoken language completely absorbed the literary discourse. That is what happens in Guillermo Cabrera Infante's *Three Trapped Tigers*. Once writers' perception of speech became sharper—because technology had objectified it—it was possible to develop an analysis of it; they were not concerned, when capturing speech, with occasional phonetic irregularities but rather with its general structure and other aspects that came with it: the social and individual views made transparent by speech, the greater proximity and truth of its realism, the objectivity it brought to literary discourse, which did not prevent writers from expressing their subjective views through variations and connections. In addition, narrative's focus on linguistic expression sanctioned a critical perspective of cultural materials. Simultaneously, the affirmative handling of some elements that we could call "ignoble" meant an emphasis on a realist style—applied preferentially to vulgar sectors of the middle to lower classes—and an artistic dignifying of its original forms. In the novels of Manuel Puig or Jorge Onetti one can see different ways of utilizing, in the River Plate area, this recently discovered field.

Narrative learned the application of new tools through applied sociology, but literary criticism got it from journalism. For journalists this meant greater rigor and precision when doing interviews free from the limitations of orality. However, it must be pointed out that two of the best Latin American reporters—Elena Poniatowska and María Esther Gilio—did not systematically use recorders. When the practice of journalism acquired a greater degree of objectivity, this affected the literary field. Current affairs magazines had been turning writers into celebrities, applying to them the same public scrutiny that was previously reserved for movie stars and football players, though the resulting interviews were clearly of a higher level. The star treatment became accepted by literary critics who, tape recorder in hand, interviewed writers. However, unlike magazine journalists, they were not interested in discovering curiosities about their personal lives but in knowing more about their ideas, methods of work, influences, sources, aesthetic theories, and critical opinions. In the case of very popular writers (Gabriel García Márquez) the result was almost dangerous. The author himself proposed valid interpretations of his work, explained its origins, and analyzed its creation, giving acceptable clues and rejecting those of others. The author actually became a critic of his own work and the critic was reduced to another attentive reader and someone in charge of registering the author's opinion. In Luis Harss's book (*Into the Mainstream*) the practice of recorded interviews still alternates with the use of other sources and with a critical editing of the materials. But in many of the books that came later, everything centers around capturing the interview and criticism is replaced with apparently objective information.

It is in the dramatic arts where the elements of technological revolution have an immediate impact and on occasion even acquire a protagonist role. In theater, as Roland Barthes has pointed out, there is an "informational polyphony" that juxtaposes many languages, including speech but also languages of lights and colors. The traditional setup became complicated because of the fast development of technologies and corresponding new languages. The traditional "three-act play in prose" was replaced by a show of disconnected scenes (a series of sketches or a collage of diverse materials) where the music, singing, and dancing acquired primacy. Here too, the North American theater scene of the postwar era became the most influential model. It was a desperate (and more technologically oriented) imitation of early twentieth-century German expressionist theater—one could contrast Bertolt Brecht and Abbie Hoffman to see the similarities in substance and the differences in ideological circumstances.

The Latin American adaptation of this theatrical tendency followed the original models less than the versions mass media promoted and made popular with the public, like *Hair*, which established the structure of the common play of the last fifteen years. In the case of theater, Latin America's response to foreign influence was an emphasis on social and political protest as representatives of regional identity and views of the future. There is a singularity and coherence in the dozens of works that were written in response to local circumstances with the desire to turn them into instruments of social action, expressly anti-imperialist. It is true that the socially critical character of this type of theater is already present in the original foreign model. However, the Latin American adaptation not only intensified that critical aspect but it transformed it into the central element of theatrical performance. At the same time, Latin American authors cleverly took advantage of their lack of resources using basic components and turning them into an artistic opportunity that allowed them to connect with the sectors of the low middle class in Latin America.

But for the most singular aspect of the response, we need to look at how the concept of objectivity was understood. The cultural centers of the most developed countries in Europe and in the US used objectivity as the basis of a literature from which they could build an art interested in acquiring true knowledge of the world, learn how to eliminate contradictions, and use technology to validate reality. We can see it in Nathalie Sarraute's analysis of "tropisms," Italo Calvino's reflections based on scientific theories, and Lawrence Ferlinghetti's manipulation of information in his poetry. All of these are examples of using speculative knowledge to look at the world as a form whose meaning is foreign to man and needs to be unveiled.

Latin American writers have behaved very differently. There are exceptions, like Octavio Paz and Julio Cortázar, in whose work one can find a similar type of approach to reality, and a few poets scattered over the continent who practice a very austere art. But in general the tendency has been completely the opposite. Writers have tended to impregnate objectivist literary products with a discourse populated with subjective interests on everything from sexual desire to social protest, expressed as an anxious willingness to confess. Hence there is a vivid interest in Spanish America for those foreign authors who have challenged the modern technology-influenced literary styles. This is the case of Dylan Thomas and Alan Ginsberg in English language poetry.

Such a subjective approach places the Latin American writer again as a social or scenic protagonist in contemporary history. But this takes place within a curious and at times contradictory manipulation of materials that appear to have been very carefully and scientifically fabricated, although they are fragmented, disconnected, and incapable of establishing a coherent field of meanings. Hence, we should not look for explanations in those materials but in how writers shape them, in the huge bricolage their work becomes. Its meaning and aesthetic value is the result of combining a convoluted group of foreign elements that can only be appropriated through their fragmentation. Evidently, all collages or techniques of composition of autonomous pieces reminds us of a byzantine mosaic, but the only resemblance that contemporary Latin American art has to that type of composition is its abnormal lavishness, its impressive contradictory, and its irregular elements; otherwise, it lacks the byzantine canonical organicity. It is an *ars combinatoria* whose laws of composition do not follow any specific school or social-cultural norms. It is simply a direct reflection of particular minds. The subjective approach to literature, because it is not being applied to traditional elements but to objects from global technology that are invading Latin American cities, generates discord and noise. This is what we hear in a poem by Cardenal, a story by Salvador Garmendia, a tale by Salvador Elizondo, a novel by Jorge Onetti, an artifact by Nicanor Parra. On the other hand, Latin American writers who have joined the universal process of culture (Carlos Fuentes or Mario Vargas Llosa) appear more capable of overcoming all of these problems and achieving a balance that corresponds to the lessons of the masters such as Paz and Cortázar. Those closer to or living in a particular Spanish American situation and among dissimilar elements that form part of it can today be faithful witnesses of a conflict that—beyond any type of social, political, or moral issues—will decide the fate of the continent.

4

No More Demons

[**Editor's Note:** This essay was part of a debate that took place in the pages of the Uruguayan weekly *Marcha* and republished in other newspapers in the region in 1972 between Ángel Rama and Peruvian novelist Mario Vargas Llosa. The debate started as a result of Rama's largely negative review of Vargas Llosa's book *García Márquez: Historia de un deicidio* (*García Márquez: History of a Deicide*, 1971). The book's main thesis was that novelists are plagued by "demons," that is, life experiences that have a lasting effect on writers' minds. The only way to exorcise those demons is to invent a fictional universe in which they play the role of God. Rama criticized the Peruvian author for employing an archaic view of literature and for not possessing a modern critical apparatus. Taking cues from Walter Benjamin's "The Author as Producer," Rama asks Vargas Llosa to abandon his outdated definition and start seeing writers as consciously creating intellectual objects in response to demands of a society or a social group. Visibly offended, Vargas Llosa responded in an article titled "The Return of Satan" that his view of the creative process was more comprehensive than Rama's as it allowed the inclusion of irrational, private aspects as opposed to seeing it as a "social product." Rama's "No More Demons" is the third text in this debate and he takes the opportunity to explain in detail why Vargas Llosa's view of authors as "isolated individuals" is useless for a literary critic and to describe his own idea of writers as mediators between social groups trying to transform Latin American societies and the reading public.[1]]

I.

My friend Mario Vargas Llosa is mistaken when he opens his reply ("The Return of Satan") asserting that my note "Vade Retro" was an exorcism against his book *History of a Deicide*. I indicated exactly the opposite. If I would have analyzed the book, I surely would have praised the joy of many literary interpretations, the vivacity of the biographic reconstruction. I would have corrected errors of information and lamented its ignorance of many scattered literary and journalistic works by Gabriel García Márquez, but above all I would have criticized the "form" employed for the essay; I would have fatally called it a nineteenth-century approach.

In doing this I would be applying the criteria that I have previously used to criticize this type of approach,[2] which follows the model of "Miguel de Cervantes, life and work" that Spanish universities wearily demand for doctoral theses and that, due to Federico de Onís's influence in the Instituto de las Españas,[3] has stifled the functioning of North American departments of Hispanic Studies, so inferior methodologically to the centers of English literature of the same universities. It uses a rigid structure, direct heir of Romantic historicism and biographism, inconceivable before Thierry and Sainte-Beuve,[4] which conquered nineteenth-century academies: knowledge is organized around a biographic recounting, which the historical frame encircles, chronologically analyzing production as the confrontation of the individual and the world, to crown it all with a chapter on style.

If such a "form" is understandable in a young doctoral candidate, it is unheard of in a writer distinguished for his experimentation with narrative forms. This would suggest that the archaic contamination of the thesis affects the essay's form, or that it allows us to see a contradiction that is becoming visible in Mario Vargas Llosa's production and that places novels, or some of his lucid essays about current issues, in opposition to the thesis that he has proposed (about the decadence of Western narrative with respect to that of Latin America, about the unhappiness of the writer as the source of the literary work, about the presumed creativity of the periods of revolutionary imminence) that are far from having been proven. In the same vein, his book is not presented as a "monograph," but as an "essay" that attempts the "description of the process of fiction writing from a concrete author." The author disdains the title traditionally used for 90 percent of this type of study (*Gabriel García Márquez: Life and Work*) and chooses a more pompous one, *Gabriel García Márquez: History of a Deicide*.

This thesis and not the book was the target of my note. I criticized it, not so much for its errors but for being outdated and for understanding that to use it now is detrimental to the effort of Latin American culture to employ more rational levels of thought in accordance with the transformational projects of its society. With this or other theses, Vargas Llosa will continue to write good novels, but I fear that the application of them will not bring admiring young writers good results.

As Mario Vargas Llosa begins by saying that this critic did not read well and as he considers that his analysis was correct, there remains no other way out than to elevate readers to judges of these notes and to copy for them some defining statements. Let me start by asserting that I am happy to check the modifications that Vargas Llosa's article introduces, tempering earlier cutting affirmations and advocating a conciliatory eclecticism. We can start with a selection of quotes from the second chapter of the book:

1. The vocation of novelist is not chosen rationally: a person does not submit to it as an absolute but enigmatic mandate, but more through instinctive and subconscious pressures than rational decision making.

2. *Why* a novelist writes is viscerally mixed into the *about what* they write: the personal demons of their life are the themes of their work.

3. A writer does not choose their themes, the themes choose them.

4. All novelists are rebels, but not all rebels are novelists. Why? In contrast to others, writers do not know why they chose this profession, they ignore the deep roots of their disagreement with reality: they are blind rebels.

5. If a novelist does not choose their themes, but rather is chosen by them, the conclusion is, in some form, depressing: the novelist is not free.

6. Not responsible with respect to the themes of their work, the novelist is completely free—that is, free to deal with their obsessions, with their lucidity—in the enterprise of evicting their demons, of objectifying them through words in fictions that, for them, are truly exorcisms.

7. A writer does not invent their themes: they plagiarize them from a true reality, in the form of crucial experiences, which deposits these themes in their spirit as obsessive forces of which they want to free themselves through writing.

8. The novelist is a dissident: they create an illusory life, create verbal worlds because they do not accept life and the world as they are (or as they believe they are). The root of their vocation is a feeling of dissatisfaction against life: each novel is a secret deicide, a symbolic assassination of reality.

One could add many more but I believe that these concepts are sufficient. I said that they constitute an example of archaism because they replace concepts that the Romantic aesthetic popularized. I added that they concede a fundamental role to irrationalism as was the case of this aesthetic: the vocation is irrational, the themes emerge irrationally and control the writer; the writer is blind in their rebellion against the world, they are not responsible for their themes, and as a consequence, they are not free and the literary work functions as an exorcism against the hostile world that helps the writer achieve their individual freedom. In their work, together with a vision of the real world, the writer will put their dissatisfaction to try to destroy the hostile world, even though they know that they will fail: this symbolizes the attempt to kill God, creator of that world where the unhappiness of the writer originates.

All of this has not been, obviously, invented by Mario Vargas Llosa: they are clearly dated concepts. There is no possibility at all of applying them to *Rameau's Nephew* or *Candide*,[5] examples of eighteenth-century narrative, but neither can they be applied to numerous earlier works that were made on commission, as was the norm for art for millennia. It troubles me to imagine how Vargas Llosa would study *The Aeneid* that Augustus commissioned of Virgil in light of very poor Romantic psychologism and one should note that a good part of the critical effort of the twentieth century sought to unload certain great classic works of the patina imposed by Romanticism, as is the case with Shakespeare (see Jan Kott's book[6]), with Cervantes, or with Dante. Neither is it possible to apply such a critical approach to contemporary art, despite the fact that it continues to be dominated by conditions (economic and social) that the bourgeoisie imposed on taking power after the cycle of revolutions, and I do not believe that Vargas Llosa's obvious admiration for Sartre's existential psychoanalysis—which one cannot recklessly connect to

Sainte-Beuve—can lead to a revision of *Proposed Roads to Freedom*.[7] I believe that neither can it be applied to the novels of Brecht, Calvino, Günter Grass, Fuentes, or Carpentier, and even the work of García Márquez. In fact, when Vargas Llosa includes the latter among the "marginalized," it seems to me, he is ignoring some of García Márquez's central trends that explain the public's multitudinous acceptance of his work.

It is normal that with the methodology of our time (which includes such disparate things as the reconstruction of rhetoric by structuralism, post-Jungian psychoanalysis, Western neo-Marxism, transformational grammar) we can carry out a coherent reading of all past literature that, as Barthes would say, would introduce it in the system of our language, but it is unthinkable to do so with a method that corresponds to the previous century and that, despite diachronic imbalances of Latin American culture, does not enter into its present projects of expansion nor into the trajectory of universal evolution.

II.

Mario Vargas Llosa's view of narrative creation is not only irrational. It is also restrictively individualist, lacking the social perception of the writer and their works, and is enriched by the individual exceptionality that marked the historical origins of the thesis. It sees human life as a rending conflict between world and person where the latter is the "recipient" and not the "agent" of history, the solitary "marginalized" and not the "part" of some sector, group, or movement; the "one" against "all people" because that "world" (of Dilthey's analysis) cannot be anything but "society." This conflict seems to be productive since the literary work departs from it as a resurgence of this fracture, what Echeverría would have called "the consolations."[8] In other words, it primarily serves a particular, psychologically compensatory function, and only in a second stage, which is not part of the deliberate objectives of the author, can it serve society if and when it is received.

The individualism of this position becomes exacerbated by irrationality given that the writer does not understand the causes of their marginalization, they simply suffer it, as a victim that cannot reach the plane of rational thought that, on understanding their situation and their causes, will allow suffering to dissolve so that they may act on the world.

Vargas Llosa extracts his position from the most traditional line of Romanticism and the subsequent era of *poète maudits*, but in the same period some great narrative works propose a different model. Setting aside Balzac, Stendhal, or Dickens, no one fails to note the belligerent ideological meaning of Sarmiento's *Facundo* or Mármol's *Amalia*, products of a Romantic thought that was more offender than victim and whose thematic, social, and even specifically political purpose is well known.[9]

Vargas Llosa forgets that the writer is not a cloistered individual sitting in opposition to a totality that is the world but that they form part of a social group, class, or movement, that there is not a single person struck by the coldness of the world, nor struck in such a unique form, who does not find similarly affected beings. Furthermore, as members of a community, they end up molded by the cultural conditions of their country, period, and social sector, participating from that national, historical, group, or class plane in the evolution of their society and as a result expressing values that are not strictly individualist but inherent in the coordinates that can only be defined as "social." It does not consist, then, of the fracture with the hostile universe that condemns Byronian heroes to destruction, but rather more realistic and legitimate confrontations of the social sectors, or the demands of these sectors that are already under the regime of patronage or under the regime of the market or under the regime of the party. The "excellent" Walter Benjamin's explanations[10] (inherited from Marx's "old" aesthetic ideas) made of nineteenth-century art and artists (without any shame I recognize that I used them, along with those of Fischer and other Western Marxists to write my book about Rubén Darío[11]) depart from the recognition that ideas translate real lived experiences of the authors since existence is what determines conscience. They are not far from the interpretations that German sociology of knowledge has made, taking Max Weber's work as point of departure, and which cannot simply be equated to Marxism.

All of these materials concur to a progressive social understanding of culture that obviously is not capricious nor a brusque political remark but is merely the consequence of the universal development of civilized societies, visible to any scientific analysis. In a lucid text, Karl Mannheim revised human history as a succession of definitions of man in relation to values that have been elevated to the category of absolutes: for a long time, God; for the long Romantic period, history; for the present times, society.[12] And this last one is the result of the overwhelming growth of contemporary social structure. I believe that Martí was the first to perceive this new condition of artistic creation in our America (or at least I argued that in my essay "Dialectics of Modernity in José Martí"[13]) when in 1881 he exclaimed, "To an indeterminate people, an indeterminate literature. But as soon as the elements begin to unify, the elements of their Literature condense into a great prophetic work."[14] Such a thought, which traverses the best Latin American essays of the century, and that so clearly appears in Mariátegui, has allowed the Brazilian anthropologist Darcy Ribeiro to recently situate the perspective of the future culture in terms that are diametrically opposed to those that Vargas Llosa employs. Ribeiro said, "In fact, a new civilization is being born. All we know about its culture is that it will be more uniform in the whole world and will be based increasingly in explicit knowledge and in rationality."[15]

In the sense that this secular line precisely interprets the historical process, one cannot say, in a Solomonic manner, that all ideas are obsolete, but those that correspond to a surpassed stage that is only conserved in cheap imitation, and even more so in archaic societies like ours, are particularly outdated. The ideas that are fully alive, from very diverse fields, recognize the basic need of a redefinition in terms of social matters, taking into account the person and their work as part of that perspective. This does not have reason to be eternal, it will be substituted by other findings of humanity of which, as Sartre said, our children not ourselves will take charge.

It is known that when one talks of these ideas, particularly in societies where structures predating modern urbanization survive (even within their monstrous cities as the cautious Medina Echavarría perceived[16]) people startle and think that the abstract and rationalized forms, intellectual discussions, economic and educational planning, and cultural programs all put in danger their "personal treasure," the inimitable marvel of their intimacy. It is not coincidence that when these conditions emerged in Europe, as a consequence of technological and industrial revolution, the literary reply of Romanticism included the concept of the unique and original themes that correspond to the inimitable treasure of individuality—exacerbated in that historical juncture—in opposition to the concept that for centuries dominated the educated elites: the incessant re-elaboration of themes that belonged to the common heritage or to the demands of society's powers.

Neither did those ancient ones lose their "personal treasure" nor will those who today incorporate the rational recognition of their social sectors with their unique requirements. For this, I believe that we should begin by situating the line of evolution and transformation of our America and accepting frankly the intellectual debate on an adult level. The objective decided, one can adjust the method with exactitude. I never thought that Georg Lukács's *The Destruction of Reason* could be defined as an "intimidating noise."

III.

In "The Return of Satan" Mario Vargas Llosa argues that the "demons" that he uses in his book *History of a Deicide* function as metaphors—as I expressly pointed out in my note—defending the right to employ them and exalting their explanatory capacity. I am completely in agreement with him. It is because of this cognizant function (that Whitehead attributed especially to poetic language) that we feel obligated to question ourselves as to why Vargas Llosa went searching for metaphors in the Romantic panoply. We arrive at the conclusion that he did it because he depended on the secret harmony that exists between these ideas and the ideology that gave birth to them in their time period.

Thus, the conflict "man-world," literature as exorcism and individual psychological reparation, irrationalism of the thematic choices, and blind rebellion agreed with these demonic metaphors that abounded in Romanticism, representing the idea of a competition between Man and God (in contrast to Balzac who had already recognized his competition with the civil registry) or the nihilistic bent of the destruction of reality that dominated the "cursed writers" represented in the destruction of God, as was seen in Uruguyan Ducasse's beautiful *Maldoror*.[17]

The metaphors that he selects are the ideas that he selects. In the same way we use others (producer instead of deicide) that correspond to a manufacturing world and to the construction of an object destined for social consumption.

Within Vargas Llosa's argument there is a reply that should be attended to because it is reasonable. He observes that one can hardly characterize his position as idealistic given that he attributes the schism of the writer with the world to real events, even though they may not be comprehensible to them. Certainly, the idealist element with which the remaining points configure the extreme Romantic thesis fail here. He talks of "a corrupted relationship with the world" that he explains thus: "9. Because their parents were too complacent or severe with them, because they discovered sex too early or too late or because they never discovered it, because reality treated them too well or too poorly, with an excess of weakness or force, of generosity or egotism." As can be observed, they are all relationships situated in the field of psychology, and, to a greater or lesser extent, they are all imbalances that emerged in the formative period with respect to a presumed norm, which places this genetic process close to Freudian formulations, as Vargas Llosa comes to corroborate in his article saying that he accepts Freud's ideas but "complements them" in his analysis.

It is useless to analyze such vague and journalistic texts like the one quoted above, trying to insert them, in order to understand them, into a half-century-old debate in the psychoanalytic field and the search for alternative theories after 1912. That debate has been characterized by the attempt to surpass Freud's biological and psychological assumptions to reconstruct a community of unconscious human knowledge, in Jung's theories, or a sociological historicism in the line of Freudian revisionism, or an improvement of the limitations of Freud's theories, whether it is Reich's somewhat extravagant Marxist version,[18] or the recent Fromm-Marcuse debate.[19] Vargas Llosa apparently understands vocation in terms of Freud's scheme (found in his analysis of Leonardo da Vinci), with which the literary work ends up being a narcissist compensation in the face of an oppressive reality that reinstalls the pleasure principle. It is useless to attempt a discussion of this thesis—or redo what has already been done—while not clarifying with greater rigor Vargas Llosa's position on the point.

But quote "9" allows some clarifications. I do not know if Mario Vargas Llosa, who reproached me for using very general formulations that he reads with amusement, perceives: (1) the vast generalization of his affirmation on the genesis of the writer, more adequate to psychopaths; (2) the intimate tie he decrees between the writer and social illness, with its foreseeable results in literary content; (3) the underlying conviction that the world, reality, society is one, monolithic, and homogeneous and not a variation of positions, groups, lines, and philosophies in constant dialectic process within which the writer is situated. Freud himself arrived at the latter idea when he analyzed the authoritarian coordinates of the society where he was formed, which influenced the parameters of his initial psychoanalytic theory; (4) the underlying idea that the writer is the person that is outside reality, that is the "dissident," which means that either they are not part of reality or one has to conceive of an extra-reality in which to place them; (5) the foreseeable consequence that the literary work is created, exclusively, as the sickly product of negation, which makes unintelligible the vast majority of works of art in the history of the universe, and only the ones produced during the last one-and-a-half centuries (out of the three thousand years of literature) are comprehensible.

When Vargas Llosa affirms that "at the irritation of some lazy people, a writer is completely responsible for their mediocrity or their genius," he supremely validates the effort of the writer at their workstation (and, in passing, devalues the difficulties that our Latin American reality frequently brings to the most determined will of the creator). However, he is not equally demanding with the creator's task of taking the impulses they receive and transferring them to the plane of conscience and rationality nor with their need to adjust their work to the demands of the sector, country, or cultural zone to which they belong.

Because of all of that, I considered that the proposed thesis is archaic, at its heart Romantic, applicable to writers that belong to this aesthetic trend but only in the sense that it simply collects approvingly their arguments. It does not attempt to reinterpret them as ideological functions because it is not applying extreme intellectual parameters to investigate the motives or rationalizations presented as theories. It does not serve for that reason as an instrument capable of penetrating in a universal and abstract form, if such a thing were possible, the genesis of literary creation. Neither does it serve to situate the literary project within the current world for its visible inattention of the writer as participant of a society and class structure. Finally, given his fixation on the individual function of creation, the thesis seems barely apt to attend to the demands of Latin American social sectors that have presented transformative projects.

That's why to the diverse notes that Mario Vargas Llosa provides I present other alternatives. When he says that the writer constructs their work to free themselves from their demons, I affirm that they are trying to serve a determined cultural project seeking to find through their creation a determined public. When he defines the writer as "dissident" of reality, wounded by it, attempting to assassinate it, I affirm that the writer is an interpreter of historical circumstances through a vision that represents a social group whose positions they share. Finally, and I repeat myself, "The work is not then the mirror of the author nor of their demons, but mediation between a writer joined to a public and a freely unraveled reality, which can only reach coherence and meaning through verbal organization." Needless to say—I have said it many times—that for this project I do not accept rules or programs, whether they come from the Council of Trent or the First Congress of Soviet Writers, given that the creative experience is always an experience of freedom whose reach, while it might not be explicit for the creator, does not cease to be anchored in a social structure nor to be less visible for the least compromised eyes of the public and critic.

Originating in Engels's distinction between Balzac and Sue, it has become traditional to recognize the possible incoherence between works and the ideas of the author. I believe that one can similarly see this with respect to Vargas Llosa and, disbelieving his thesis, benefit from the realist discernment of his novels.

5

The Two Latin American Avant-Gardes

Round numbers haunt us as if they were magical: fifty years have gone by since the start of Latin America's literary renovation; we have already celebrated half a century of those anniversaries. They make us long for that cyclical time Mircea Eliade sees as an undercurrent that tries to defeat the absolute linear time of our existence. Those key dates call upon us to critically re-examine a history that presents itself not as a linear period but as a cycle about to cancel itself out. And it is at that moment—when the cycle forces us out of its boundaries—that we begin to see more clearly its structure: we are finally able to approach it as another model.

Studying that cycle, its dynamics, the elements that form it and their functions, is not about understanding just Latin American literature but, at the same time, the society that established the cycle. From the collection of works, literary movements, artistic trends, and ideological positions, originating in overlapping time periods and coming from a wide variety of artistic regions scattered across the continent, we can reconstruct the struggles of a culture faced with the great task, inherited from the intellectual leaders of the wars of Independence, of searching for autonomy and identity.

1. Discovery of the Avant-Garde

These fifty years have been marked by the appearance of avant-garde groups, born out of an artistic break that writers intentionally registered in their literary texts as a representation of the changes they were experiencing in their societies. Their starting point was a discord between inherited literary forms and their Latin American reality. The former, in poetry, included Symbolism, which spawned the *sincerismo*[1] of the first two decades of the century, and, in prose, the realist mode, which, firmly established, produced the trend of the regionalist novel. The latter, emerged among those who spent their lives in rapidly growing cities, which after the First World War began an accelerated process of change, spurred by the imperialist regimes of the day (England, France, United States), cities where young, talented writers from the countryside were hoping to make their mark.

The disparity between the two planes—the artistic and the social—forced them to modify literary models so they reflected their new reality. What nature was for pre-Romantic artists, the modern city became for the avant-garde ones: it was the origin of their creations. Not only the technological city of the Futurists, which was barely a reality in Latin America, but also a city that inspired change because its new social structures made disparities among social sectors evident, that provoked a violent clash of traditions, and that kindled debates among members of the middle class, who were either on their way to consolidate their political power or about to demand it.

In 1922, with São Paulo's Modern Art Week, Brazilian youths' response to the official Centenary of the Independence celebrations, the avant-garde officially made its entrance in the continent. In attendance were musicians, painters, and, above all, poets—because, as always, it is in poetry where, quickly and with conviction, modifications spread in any established culture, and it is in poetic production where one should look for signs of changes that are still invisible to most eyes. However, Art Week was not the first manifestation of avant-garde literature in Latin America. In 1919, forty-eight-year-old Mexican poet José Juan Tablada underwent a literary metamorphosis and published a collection of "synthetic poems" in his book *One Day . . . Synthetic Poems*, and thus the "haiku" was introduced in the Spanish language. The next year, he followed that publication with *Li-Po and Other Poems*, in which Appolinaire-inspired ideograms made an appearance.[2] Even before then, Chilean poet Vicente Huidobro, who in Paris used to collaborate with Pierre Réverdy in *Nord|Sud*, had published *Horizon carré* (Paris, 1917) and *Tour Eiffel* (Madrid, 1918). Before leaving for Europe, Huidobro had expressed in *El espejo de agua* (Buenos Aires, 1916) the Ars Poetica of his creationist movement: "Why do you sing the rose, oh Poets! / Make it blossom in the poem."[3] In Brazil, in one very productive night, Mario de Andrade had fiercely written his *Paulicéia Desvairada* (*Hallucinated City*, 1922) declaring his rejection of the status quo: "I insult the bourgeois! The money-grabbing bourgeois!"⁴ Contemporaneously, on the Latin American pacific coast, César Vallejo was drastically transforming Spanish American letters both in prose (*Escalas melografiadas*, 1923) and in verse with *Trilce* (1922), a collection whose first line could be interpreted as a comment on these literary changes: "Who's making all that racket, and not even letting / the islands that linger make a will."⁵

All of a sudden, within the span of five years, from 1917 to 1922, a constellation of poets, mostly unknown to each other, were performing a transformation of Latin American letters and bringing it up to date with what was happening at the center of the artistic universe at the time (Paris, once again). Thirty years later, the same process of updating the local culture that in the 1880s *modernismo* realized in Spanish America, and parnasianism and symbolism did for Brazil, repeated itself. With the difference that time had not passed in vain, not only had Latin America's awareness of its uniqueness increased but this also exacerbated the process of rupture expressed by these new European artistic movements. The result was an avant-garde movement that focused and drew from Latin America's cultural stock while enacting an even more powerful break with the inherited poetic tradition than in Europe.

The existence of this wave of innovations throughout the continent, at the same time that a realist mode of writing—slowly and carefully developed—was gaining ground and undermining those projects of literary renewal, does not diminish the original impact of São Paulo's Modern Art Week. It was at that event where we witness, for the first time, the birth of an organic avant-garde movement that includes multiple artists; reestablishes links between different art forms that makes painters and poets, musicians and prose writers share the same adventure; and, finally, inspires a series of theoretical texts (from Menotti del Picchia, Oswald de Andrade, the recently rediscovered Graça Aranha) in support of these new works of art. The Brazilian movement, with its spectacular paraphernalia and the expected clash of personalities typical of these groups, perfectly exemplifies that characteristic of the avant-garde movements that appears to respond to the military origin of the term: that tendency to organize themselves with rigid discipline and align themselves with doctrines or manifestos, which, in the artistic field, may sometimes function as battle tanks to force open the doors of cultural fortresses.

Along with the Brazilian movement, in several other strategic places in Latin America, similar avant-garde phalanxes emerge, grouping themselves around manifestos, magazines, and outrageous public events, proclaiming their commitment to anything that is new. That naively dignified word becomes the watchword that brings them together, with which they recognize each other. Even though it is a word with a plurality of meanings, uneven levels, chaotic associations, they overcame that diversity with the only fact that seemed certain in the artistic horizon: the desire to be different from the ones that came before them, the joyous awareness of being new, of not owing anything to their ancestors (in spite of their growing debt to Paris), and having at their disposition the reality of what they were experiencing, which no one could dispute. The "new ones" (*los nuevos*) is a very explicit term in spite of attempting to be obviously vague: it is with this name that a magazine in Montevideo was baptized in 1920—in whose pages Ildefonso Pereda Valdez would discover, by reading Apollinaire, that there were blacks in Latin America too—or, in 1925, another one in Bogotá, around which a group of writers from diverse backgrounds (and perhaps with deep and "old" literary burdens) would gather themselves, although two of its youngest members, Hernando Téllez and Jorge Zalamea, would advance a process of cultural updating and fight against a stagnated culture. The word "new" is the one most frequently used to describe one of the mythical figures of Latin American literature, Ramón Vinyes, who in 1917 in a small regional literary magazine (*Voces*, published in Barranquilla, Colombia—at that time considered to be located at the end of the world) informed his readers of the adventures of Dormée and Réverdy, of André Guide's *Traité du Narcisse*, and of Chesterton's work, demonstrating that wonderful erudition about European modernism that compelled one of his intellectual grandsons—Gabriel García Márquez—to turn him into the "wise Catalonian" bookseller, a character in *One Hundred Years of Solitude* who "had read all of the books."[6]

Out of all the Latin American avant-garde groups, none, alongside the above-mentioned Brazilian movement, equaled in importance the groups formed around the magazines *Proa* (1922–1923) and *Martín Fierro* (1924–1927) in Buenos Aires. These publications, both of them edited by Evar Méndez and Oliverio Girondo, managed to attract older writers such as Macedonio Fernández and Ricardo Güiraldes, but above all they were capable of bringing together young writers (Eduardo González Lanuza, Leopoldo Marechal, Enrique Molinari, Norah Lange, Francisco Luis Bernárdez) to form a soft guerrilla against the late nineteenth-century generation, headed by the vilified and envied Leopoldo Lugones. From their ranks would emerge Jorge Luis Borges, whose work would internalize the group's contradictions, zigzags, and artistic achievements. We still have to add the "estridentista" movement with which Manuel Maples Arce (b. 1900), with the help of his friends Germán List Arzubide and Arqueles Vega, would bombard a Mexico convulsed by Carranza's assassination. The movement started with the publication of two books by Maples, *Andamios interiores* (1922) and *Urbe* (1924), and only four years later—time moves so fast during this period—there would already exist a memoir: List Arzubide's *El movimiento estridentista* (1926). There was also the Cuban avant-garde, which like the Peruvian would be dominated by social issues. With the *Protesta de los Trece*, led by Rubén Martínez Villena, the Minorista group began its bellicose participation in Cuba's public life, as can be observed in their contributions to the pages of the magazines *El heraldo*, *Social*, and of course *Revista de Avance*.

Latin Americans adopted a fateful custom of the French rationalists—proclaiming manifestos before creating the literary work they justify—and as a result we possess a multitude of words (including expletives) describing norms, edicts, precepts, numerous condemnations, and endless predictions. Throughout the nineteenth century in Europe, the future became the point of departure for artistic expressions, as if it were a wager on something that did not yet exist but must be imagined. It became a way to conquer not only the past but also the present. The interest in the future became a popular topic thanks to the influence of the Italians Marinetti and Pallazzeschi, the former having connections with South America during this period of origin. But from our present day perspective, that "futurism" has once again become the past, a past not exclusively found in editorials, manifestos, and polemics—which are a delight to the literary historian, who sometimes gives them too much importance—but above all in the works of art that emerged and created a historic cycle.

Those creations exploded like fireworks, brief and bright, throughout the 1920s. The first lines of the poem Huidobro dedicated to Pablo Picasso ("Ecuatorial") in 1918 could have easily been the beginning of any of them: "It was the time when my eyelids opened without wings / And I began to sing above unleashed distances."[7]

The authors' creative capacity increased as they enjoyed a feeling of openness and the giddiness of being the founders of new movements and igniting true reality. In the explosion of literary magazines that came out during the 1920s (in addition to the ones mentioned above), one finds that diligent search for any type of new intellectual endeavors in their environment. One can see it in *Contemporáneos*, the Mexican magazine Bernardo Ortiz de Montellano edited from 1928 to 1931, which included José

Gorostiza, Torres Bodet, Xavier Villaurrutia, Salvador Novo, and Gilberto Owen. It is also present in *Avance* (1927–1930), which brought together Tallet and Guillén, Carpentier and Roa.[8] One can see it also in Mario de Andrade's Brazilian magazine *Antropofagia* and in *La Cruz del Sur*, published in Uruguay by the Guillot Muñoz brothers, which tries to rescue the spirit of Lautréamont's work.

But one also can find the existence of other groups of intellectuals, other voices expressing their view of the "new" in the regular pages of those magazines or in their debates with other publications (the Peruvian *Claridad* vs. the Argentine *Claridad*). Over time the magazines' original search for renewal gave way to a revaluation of the diversity of their content. While at the beginning the members paid attention to coincidences that unified them as one, eventually a clarification of their artistic and ideological positions guaranteed that where there was once one force, now there were at least two. Mediocre literary critics, more interested in separating the new from the old without taking into consideration the meanings of those terms, are destined to write absurd literary histories omitting important narrative and poetic developments. They are blind to those moments that subvert hierarchies of the Latin American intellectual process and instead they focus on the latest critical fashions. Foreseeing this problem, H. M. Enzensberger warned in his essay "The Aporias of the Avant-Garde" that whoever distinguishes between old and new, or old and young, in some comfortable fashion, agrees by his very choice of criteria with the philistines. To him, the simplest dialectical proposition must remain inaccessible.[9]

2. The Two Latin American Avant-Gardes

Gertrude Stein's offhand remark to Ernest Hemingway ("You are a lost generation") has made her more famous than her unrealistic short stories. From the perspective of a "lost generation" (but recovered for art history) critics have reconstructed that period of North American literature as travel companion to the French avant-garde movement from the 1920s.

Contemporary history, told from a Eurocentric perspective (or "Yankee"-centric, which has replaced the former and complemented it), ignores that Latin America too had its lost generation. This was also probably true of many regions peripheral to Europe or, strictly speaking, to the belly button of the world (as Paulo Prado once called Paris and, specifically, "palace de Clichy"[10] in the preface to Oswald de Andrade's *Manifiesto Pau-*

Brasil), which gave us the right formula for the avant-garde, its universal paradigm, equally loathed and worshipped in all other countries, basically in the rest of the universe.

From the time of "Bateau-Lavoir" to the period of *Le surrealisme au service de la révolution*, Latin Americans have never stopped populating the banks of the Seine nor being hypnotized by scandalous artistic groups.[11] In 1916, Vicente Huidobro arrives in France with the intention of becoming a French poet. In the meantime, Jorge Luis Borges is studying in Switzerland from 1914 to 1919 and later on makes an appearance (which lasts until 1921) as a member of the Spanish "Ultraist" movement, where he left his mark. After 1923, a few more "lost" writers arrive in Europe: César Vallejo, who won't leave the European continent until his death on that foretold rainy day in Paris in 1938; Miguel Ángel Asturias disembarks there around the same period, where he will have personal discovery of the Mayan culture, translating the Popol Vuh into Spanish with George Raynaud[12] and publishing poetry (*Rayito de estrella*, 1925) and his first prose work (*Leyendas de Guatemala*, 1930) with a preface by Paul Valéry. There, he also begins his important novel *El señor presidente*, which he finishes in 1932 but does not publish until 1946. In 1928, Alejo Carpentier, with the help of Robert Desnos, flees to Paris where he collaborates with surrealist artists and writes ballet librettos. At the same time he is proofreading the second, definitive version of *Ecué-Yamba-O* (Madrid, 1933). It is there where Carpentier meets Venezuelan Arturo Uslar Pietri, who is working on his novel *Las lanzas coloradas* (1931). Around this time, younger writers open their eyes to Parisian art. In 1932, the only issue of Antillean writer Etienne Lero's magazine *Légitime Défense* comes out. Two years later *L'Etudiant Noir* brings together black poets from Latin America and Africa: [León] Damas from French Guiana, Aimé Césaire from Martinique, Léopold Senghor from Senegal. Also about to start his narrative work is Jacques Roumain, from Haiti, who has been studying in Zurich since 1919 and has been influenced by an important book about modern culture in his country *Ainsi parla l'oncle* (1928) by Jean Price-Mars.

It is an artistic movement that never stops, constantly renewing its positions and establishing a curious cultural continuity. It is not a reaction to the avant-garde, it has deeper roots. It was born out of a desire for cultural independence that the old colonies of Spain and Portugal developed since independence. They sought in France—which already was the capital of modernity—appropriate spiritual nutrition. From Esteban Echeverría's trip in 1825 to Julio Cortázar's in 1953, the flow of Latin American writers travelling through Paris has not been interrupted. But there are some dates when the exodus increased (such as 1900, 1925, and 1950), and they coincide with important moments within French cultural history; moments distinguished by a desire to break with the past that is then popularized around the world.

The Latin American artists were part of the avant-garde in "the belly button of the world," but they were never the protagonists. At best, they were third-rate actors who entered the scene to deliver a letter to the main character; at worst, they were mere spectators who hung out in Closerie de Lilas[13] and religiously bought little avant-garde magazines. They usually lived in that Latin American ghetto located at the heat of the Quartier Latin whose first bitter chronicler early in the twentieth century was Rubén Darío. When they tried to join the avant-garde, they experienced a tacit rejection from Eurocentric French writers who have not yet begun to travel outside their country. Later on, Artaud would go to Mexico, Desnos to Brazil, Breton to Haiti, but the experience of otherness Latin Americans felt explains why they unanimously rediscovered their place of origin in the Paris of the 1920s. They all say it passionately. In Paris they rediscovered the originality of Latin America, its specificity, its accent, its incomparable reality. Hence this group did not experience the turn-of-the-century alienation that made previous poets live in fake Versailles castles or narrators recount the "glory of Don Ramiro" or the "bewitching Seville." Instead, they devoted themselves to a living and contemporary Latin America that was situated in a specific political moment that inspired the anti-imperialist conference at Brussels. This meeting was a capital experience for the spiritual realignment of many Latin Americans, even if most of them already had long and tortuous stories of cultural persecution under dictatorship and represented them accursedly in their books. This rediscovery of Latin America via Paris, however, did not preclude other, more subtle types of alienation.

To understand it, we have to document the origin of this coincidence, which will have later misspecifications and will be questioned, without the writers being able to completely free themselves from it. From 1910 to 1930 the regionalist narrative emerges, a group of writers whose representative members—from Gálvez to Gallegos, including Monteiro Labato, Azuela, and José Eustasio Rivera—nationalize nineteenth-century-style realism. During the same period appear the avant-garde movements, which negate the underpinnings of this narrative project. While the avant-gardists consider the realist approach superficial, they do not cancel its themes or criticize its search for the expression of a Latin American reality. The regionalists, for their part, were concerned with the cosmopolitism that comes with avant-garde ideas, as one can already see in the manifestos that Gilberto Freyre and his groups (from which José Lins do Rego and Jorge de Lima got their start) presented in Recife in 1926. However, both groups had something in common. We are talking about issuing a call for alarm to Latin America, a zone particularly rich in original cultural traditions. Many years later in *Brazil-An Interpretation* (1964) Gilberto Freyre analyzed it thus: "Regionalism seems to us, Brazilian regionalists, as a sort of counter-colonization, a healthy tendency for the Brazilian environment, as well as for the environment of the entire American continent; a trend at the same time opposed to nationalist tendencies as well as to excessively internationalist or cosmopolitan tendencies."

We will find the same type of ambiguity expressed during the early years of the Argentine avant-garde, as can be perceived in the fluid relations between the two adversarial groups of Boedo and Florida. As early Argentine literary critics observed, these groups cannot be described as two perfectly parallel, coherent, and irreconcilable trends. One cannot accept the view that one of these groups (Florida) represents the outward-looking avant-garde and the other (Boedo), a nationalist populist attitude. The distinction would render us unable to understand the work of poets such as Nicolas Olivari and Raúl González Tuñón. Nor would we be able to study the place that Roberto Arlt occupies within the new porteña narrative. It would also preclude us from understanding the young Borges, who during this period wrote two books devoted to recovering the suburban neighborhoods (*Fervor de Buenos Aires*, 1923 and *Luna de enfrente*, 1925), his study about *El idioma de los argentinos* (1929), or his book *Evaristo Carriego* (1930) in which his nationalism invades with a minor dose of humor the enemy territory of populism. In this set of writings one could also include that short story, "Streetcorner Man," hidden in *Universal History of Infamy*, which became the first version of the myth of the knife-wielding man—a ghost that will accompany Borges's work for the rest of his life.

In fact, once the time of manifestos against old ideas is over and the writers' ideological or aesthetical orientations become clear, one can see that there are two juxtaposed debates. On the one hand, there is the battle over old and new artistic techniques, which is a common background of all avant-garde rebellions and relegates the regionalist novel being written at the time to the past. It is also a rejection of the simple, sincere, and transparent poetry present in the works of Gabriela Mistral, Andrés Eloy Blanco, Juana de Ibarbourou, or Carlos Pellicer, to mention only its most notable practitioners. On the other hand, there is another debate taking place inside the avant-garde. Two artistic positions about literary structure in general (and, by extension, Latin American society) battle each other. At least during the first epoch, the debate fosters temporary connections with other artistic currents. One sector of the avant-garde, in spite of its rejection of the formal aspects of realism, becomes interested in replicating the regionalist writers' interest for inserting themselves within social groups. Another sector heightens its connections with the European avant-garde to keep pure its artistic origins, that is to say, its break with the past and subsequent commitment to an unknown future reality. This forces them to assume the existence of a shared reality on both sides of the Atlantic, which, in turn, requires looking at this from a universalist position.

These two different operations are at stake when creating a two-front avant-garde. One could imagine similar problems found in the literature of other peripheral cultures, not only in Latin America. The arrival of the avant-garde forces authors from the periphery to find a way to accommodate themselves, a problem French artists did not have. Applying a model created in 1928 by Tynianov and Jacobson when trying to extend Ferdinand de Saussure's linguistic scheme, one could say that every literary work is a "parole" that enunciates part of the "langue" or expressed in semiotic terms, that it is a "message" that functions as part of a system that makes communication possible, even if the message is trying to introduce modifications to the system. The literary system within which a work of art is created is the "given" context, that which is handed down to the writer. Writers can easily mistake it for nature because it only becomes visible when their own work is rejected; they never become aware of it when the system validates and authorizes their writings. The literary work presents itself to the writer as the only thing that is new and original in the system, possessing the capacity to destroy it and reconstruct it. This capacity strengthens the illusion that the writer's work is the only one that exists and the one responsible for generating the system. The European writer, especially in France, has worked within a long established literary system, capable of self-regulating and adapting to the challenges introduced by new "messages." To achieve this, sometimes it must reevaluate the work of previously marginalized writers, for example the avant-garde writers' reconstruction of the literary pantheon when they called attention to the importance of Rimbaud and Lautréamont, Sade and Nerval, or how German expressionists were interested in Achin von Arnin and Georg Buchmner. Sometimes the literary system must appropriate trends that were considered disrupting in the past, and thus in the end they have served to strengthen the life and influence of the system.

No matter how much we think the Latin American literary system resembles the European one and how less developed it appears to us when contrasting them, there is no doubt that toward 1910 Latin America had already established its own entirely independent system. Within that system there was already an efficient interrelationship between the individual creations and the system. The abundance of possibilities and adaptations might look small when we look at them from a national perspective, but its importance becomes evident once we begin to look at Latin America as a single literary system.

The avant-garde writers found themselves in a paradoxical situation, one of the most slippery and tricky that any Latin American author had ever faced. Noticing the changes taking place in their reality and at the same time how the received literary forms did not reflect the new social situation, the writers accepted that rupture. But they saw it more as a confirmation of the close link between literature and life than as an example of pure destruction, which is how Octavio Paz will see it a generation later. This rupture in their universe was a reflection of a more general one. The root of this rupture is located in the European bourgeois societies. This social group's peculiar structure condemns it to experience successive and constant ruptures, each one deeper than before, with the intention of capturing the future by imagining it anew at every moment. These societies, because of the imperialist tendency to which their ever expanding economy propels them, force those countries in their orbit into a relationship of economic dependency. As a consequence they transfer their system of rupture and regeneration to all the regions in contact with them.

The Latin American rupture occurs at the same time and is affected by that other rupture, which, for the sake of convenience, we are calling "universal." But they work at different levels. The Latin American one involves an internal, local break that brings progress, straightens paths, and opens new possibilities. The break coming from imperialist centers to the periphery sits on top of the local rupture, distorting the process and appropriating it for its benefit. It does so in the name of a universalism that is only possible through dependency or, of course, destroying the original culture.

Latin American avant-garde lived with this duplicity. For some the avant-garde creation was a word, a work of art that required readers to apprehend the European literary system from which it took its models as they were consuming it. Two operations of appropriation had to be performed at the same time. Even though this appeared to avant-garde authors as a viable option, I do not think it was clear to them that adopting a European literary system imported with it other cultural elements. Those elements ranged from the obvious aspects of cultural dependency, such as the appropriation of a foreign language, to the passive acceptance of a set of values. It even included creating a foreign society whose demands or interests found their way into literary works, even those exclusively oriented toward investigating the Latin American universe.

Huidobro's French poetry is the extreme example, not so much because he wrote them, which is just an episodic event in his career, but because they indicate a "universalist" point of view. He will continue to cultivate it in *Altazor* and in *Tres inmensas novelas*, which he began to write in collaboration with Hans Arp at Arcachon and published in Santiago, Chile, in 1935. One could perhaps trace his antagonism with Pablo Neruda back to this. The latter places himself, beginning with his early work, within a national literary system whose influence is even more pronounced in another Pablo, Pablo de Rokha.[14]

The other example can be found in the notorious difficulty that begins to pervade Borges's work when he begins his narrative period with "Tlön, Uqbar, Orbis Tertius" (1938) with the purpose of controlling his environment and employing symbolic transposition, which will allow him to insert himself within the European literary system. At some point in his career, he encounters friction when trying to represent everyday life experience, which he can only depict through the sarcastic caricature of his secret writers. It would be a mistake to look exclusively in his themes for evidence of this desire to insert oneself into the European literary system (this approach has limited the critiques directed at Borges from Argentine nationalists). The use of Latin American themes was a dominant trend in the 1920s avant-garde movements, and, of course, no one can argue against the right of any writer to use any setting or character their imagination is attracted to.

Precisely for these reasons, it is interesting to study the process of becoming part of the European literary system in a narrator whose main works have focused on an exploration of the Latin American (especially Caribbean) region and above all in relation to the European presence.

I am talking about Alejo Carpentier, who since *The Kingdom of this World* (1949) has attempted to uncover the essence of the region's culture, studying the sources and remnants of a universality hidden within the shape of an endless memory of the movement of history. Nevertheless, it is a history that has never stopped being that of past or present conquerors. Carpentier's "americanismo," described in his collection of essays *Tientos y diferencias*, seeks to explain the Baroque style that he argues (obviously exaggerating) is characteristic of every Latin American writer. Carpentier uses a linguistic example that in actuality does nothing but confirm an unconscious dependence on the European literary system:

> Heinrich Heine speaks to us, suddenly, of a pine and a palm tree, objects known by everyone, trees that form part of the great universal culture. The word *pine* is sufficient to show us a pine; the word *palm* is enough to define a palm. But the word *ceiba*—naming an American tree that Cuban blacks call "the mother of all trees" cannot bring before the eyes of people from other latitudes the aspect of rostate column of this gigantic, austere, and solitary tree. . . . These trees exist. They are American trees that have the right to be present in American narratives. But they do not have the good fortune of being named "pine," "palm," "oak," "chestnut" or "birch." . . . So we must talk about ceibas and about papayos, but here we run into a writing problem. . . . This can only be accomplished through the apt deployment of various adjectives, or, in order to avoid the use of adjectives, by the metaphorical use of nouns to take their place. If one has luck—literarily speaking, in this case—the purpose will be achieved. The object will come alive; it will be viewed and hefted by the reader. But the prose that gives it life and substance, weight and measure, is a Baroque prose, necessarily Baroque.

According to Carpentier this aesthetic problem is so important that it determines the literary style of all Latin American writers. Hidden behind it, however, there is actually an appropriation of the European literary system, its values, and even the public for which it was created. In reality, Carpentier is not speaking to the Cuban public reading him (as Heine was doing with his European public) because for them *ceiba* and *papayo* are immediate realities, transparently expressed by their linguistic signs. Carpentier is addressing a European public who is not acquainted with those trees. It is the author, employing his Latin American (but also dependent) culture, who is trying to make them *see* those trees. Adopting an apparently universal literary system—in reality just a European system promoted to the category of universal because of its power—means accepting its public, the European society that created it. It also means to write, to create a style with that public in mind.

However, in addition to that avant-garde group there is another one. Its members were writers who might have also lived in Paris or who did not get to be part of the "lost generation" but whose works were created within a Latin American literary system. They drew from its structures and contributions, modifying and adapting them to new realities. They even borrowed creative elements from other peripheral regions around the world, from other "sunflower" countries that are always following the "belly button of the world," but they also borrowed those aspects of the center that could be appropriated for their own literary system. Going back to the topic of trees, César Vallejo writes with ease: "Undone knot of the sinamayera's lacteal glands, good for brilliant alpacas, for a coat of useless feather," without feeling the need to explain anything.[15] He is speaking within the complicity of a shared language and shared knowledge of a reality. The referential function of words is reinforced, as there is no need to explain them to foreigners, just like foreigners are not concerned with how their works are read in the periphery. César Vallejo was residing in Peru when he was writing *Los heraldos negros* (1919) and *Trilce* (1922), which marks a definite break with Latin American poetry, and his only contact with the avant-garde revolution was the information he found in magazines in Lima. Mariátegui still saw Vallejo as a regionalist when in reality he was already an avant-garde artist preoccupied with reshaping the local literary system. For Vallejo, that meant capturing in his work local linguistic idiosyncrasies, social and individual myths, the direction of [Rubén] Darío's late style. His innovation was possible because he was working within the structure of a written and spoken language as it had developed in the continent. This is why, years later, his writings could be compared to those of José Martí, whom he never knew (as Cintio Vitier has pointed out).

Even more singular is the similarity of Vallejo's prose texts from 1923 (*Escalas melografiadas*) with the narrative work that Roberto Artl (1900–1912) had been constructing in Buenos Aires beginning with *The Mad Toy* (1926). Arlt was another exponent of that avant-garde movement that worked within the Latin American literary system. There are points of contact between both writers that have nothing to do with their individual styles nor with the cultural area to which they belonged, but with their attempt to understand the crisis of the literary system in the region. Both writers face it, one of them grabbing the provincial remnants of Spanish *Ultraísmo*, the other learning from the traditions of another region in the periphery, nineteenth-century Russia, as they appear in Dostoyevsky's conflicting work.

The position of Roberto Arlt in the Boedo–Florida conflict is the result of a juxtaposition of the two sides of the debate: on the one hand, the renovation of literary forms in order to adapt them to a new reality—that of an urban petite bourgeoisie about to enter a crisis—and, on the other, the development of a literary system and its creation of a public (those readers to whom, for decades, the members of the other avant-garde tendency will have to renounce) and thus be able to establish a literary continuity.

6

Literary System and Social System in Spanish America

Critique of Literary Historiography

When we go beyond the national compartmentalization of Spanish American literature and judge it from an eventual superior unit, we organize this discipline and object of knowledge around two guiding methodologies, both reductionist in nature:

1. A consolidation of the plural vastness of literary material into the exclusive field of *learned writing* that was established by the aesthetic of the leading elites in the nineteenth century, even though this initial principle admitted later extensions that betrayed both aesthetic and social modifications of the value criteria.[1]

2. An evolutionary and gradual articulation that starts, generally, at the end of the eighteenth century and that, applied to this previous reduction within the field of letters, provides us with an apparent continuity. This can be based in the theory of genres (Alberto Zum Felde), in global aesthetic trends (Pedro Henríquez Ureña), or generational succession (Enrique Anderson Imbert), all three of which reveal the common use of the nineteenth-century historicist concept, depending at the same time on the idea of progressive and indefinite evolution with which these literary organizations

> tailor themselves, like imprecise shadows, to the lineal and gradualist model of the European literary histories from which they originate.

The most visible consequence of these operations is to have provided us with a lineal, progressive literary history lacking in density. It is structured like a lineal continuum because fractures have been concealed and rationalized by literary causalities (derivations, sources, influences); this constant going in circles through a single rigid channel, represented by the classist concept of learned writing, which has been furnished with an evolutionary progressivism that, in practice, is nothing more than the consequence of having merged together successive and obligatory value criteria (the children of social change) like the stages of a cultural project. This furthermore transposes to America the philosophies of history that European thought developed from Hegel to Comte. Additionally, an attempt to create structures parallel to those that organize European literature is visible: to this end, they are supported by the objective verification of external influences, which stress the transfer of identical names and from these similar ventures by which they conform to an evolutionary line, explicitly recognized or not as immanent: Neoclassicism, Romanticism, Realism, Symbolism. When, following the first historiographic models (like that of Calixto Oyuela[2]), they have been obligated to collect literary schools that did not fit within this outline (as is the case of the so-called gauchesque literatures) in the south of the continent. Historians were forced to create new compartments that they could not fit within the instituted methodological order, adding to them through heterogeneous criteria like language, theme, genre, and so on.

The European origin of this methodological repertoire is obvious and its transference evident—sometimes notoriously mechanical in nature—which at the time, however, signified real progress for literary criticism, even though it distorted the understanding of the continent's literary culture. It is also obvious that as long as we cannot detach adequate instruments of analysis and valorization from the culture and reality of Spanish America, we should continue to use foreign methodologies that have reached a greater level of development than ours. One can observe this in the most recent use of the hermeneutics derived from Marxism, the Sociology of Knowledge, or the approaches that come from New Criticism and French Structuralism, all of them indicating a modernization of literary knowledge together with the affirmation of a dependence that should be taken into account. More than a mere rejection of its contributions, our operative problem lies in considering ourselves as the target for the development of suitable methods for our literary material using foreign propositions as lucid awareness of their effectiveness on trial, specifically as instruments whose efficiency we should verify only to the extent to which they take us closer to a wider and truer understanding of Spanish American letters. This is evident when such instruments allow us to revise already consolidated traditions, discovering them as discourses that do not entirely reflect the cultural process. They would fulfill a liberating function and would bring us closer to a theoretical rediscovery of ourselves.

Literary Totality, Ruptures, and Sequences

The first critical task of this general revision would consist of recuperating (*re-submersing* ourselves) in the creative totality of Spanish American literary culture, without appealing to the interpretive grids established, in other words, to the aesthetic criteria we have inherited without subjecting them to critical analysis, and therefore breaking the already forged continuities and units within which evolutionary articulations are authorized. In a way, we need to operate with a virgin gaze (where, nevertheless, the situation of the observer is implied) that is necessary when one faces the flux of reality, which in this case we would call the flux of literary production, seen as the stubborn conscience of liberty. In a way it consists of situating oneself within the flow of a global, encompassing discourse to detect within it the discontinuous nature of the event, its unheard-of emergence: to break the preexistent connections to be able to direct ourselves from an amorphous stratum to a search for new articulations that recover for us a vision that is more coherent and at the same time more identified with literary creation.[3]

Such a return to the magma is necessarily temporary but beneficial in order to remake order. Working in a culture marked by dependence, which comes from the original colonial imposition, and later renewed by way of new imperial restraints, the effort of reordering will be situated far from the traditional tendencies to find American equivalents to the European artistic or epistemological periods, and instead it will try to find *literary sequences* that are capable of offering the largest degree of autonomy within the protoplasmic continuum of undifferentiated literary materials. That is to say, two simultaneous tasks will take place: discovering the ruptures that permit the demarcation of sequences and distinguishing among them, according to their diverse position with respect to the models to which they are subject.

These *literary sequences* correspond to historic periods but do not exhaust them. In each one of them (determining them is to make the same reading of the rupture and coherence of the separate segments, only in the vast field of history and not in the restriction of the word in its literary function), we will find diverse literary sequences superimposed, like true artistic strata that confer density to the period and provide it with a specific literary dynamic that duplicates the social dynamic typical of social stratification. They are different and autonomous literary propositions, sometimes opposing or simply adjacent, whose recognition thwarts the flat and linear system of established literary histories.

One must be able to determine the sequences (discontinuous, superimposed, and at times offset within the same historical period) from the restrictive angle of literary specificity that constitutes the *petitio principii* of the proposed field of operation; that is, one must be able to arrive at the demarcation and definition of them attending exclusively to their artistic manifestations and not to extra-literary reasons (authors, social classes, geographic locations, etc.). But as one could not categorize literary sequences without condemning them to an incoherent existence, they can only find their absolute meaning upon coordinating with other sequences (these ones cultural and not literary) through different degrees of mediation. The new sequences will be non-discursive in nature, but rather technical, economic, social, political, and so on, and they will be found forcefully linked with literary sequences by reason of the structural interdependence of an ensemble. For that reason, reflecting broadly about the place that the literary sequences occupy in the totality will lead us to a consideration of the relation between literature and society.

Before considering this point, we should add that in any historical period we find several literary sequences superimposed: it is difficult to find less than four strata since the beginning of urban development in the last third of the nineteenth century, and as we move forward in time we will detect a greater complexity. These sequences are not only founded in (explicit or tacit) aesthetics that are well differentiated and each one of them coherent, but they also manifest very clear linguistic preferences and preferences of artistic genre. They furthermore register internal evolutions that contribute to reinforcing their autonomy, but at the same time they maintain among them a relation that most of the time is one of conflict and results in literary debates.

The coexistence of different superimposed sequences can be registered in any other society, different from Spanish America, and one needs to make an adjustment to discern its functioning within the specific characteristics of the Spanish American social formation and take into account not only the characteristics of its internal dynamic but also the general state of dependence in which it was formed and from which it emerged with difficulty through the centuries. Therefore the links between the literary sequences and the rest of the social sequences imply previously revising the established concepts about the latter.

Singularity of the Spanish American Social System

Spanish American society entails a stratification and an entirely different dynamic from European societies of the last one hundred fifty years and the theoretical blueprints that interpret Europe are not applicable without serious deformations. Furthermore, Spanish American literature, like its society, always assumes the previous existence of European society, while it has developed at the margin of influential norms, through their own paths, expanding throughout the universe and responding to its intrinsic necessities and not to the zones that it encountered in its path.

Regarding the first point, one has to recognize that not many attempts of autonomous description of Latin American social stratification exist. There are even less that comply with two principles that we regard as obligatory: to not be limited to translating the distribution of classes elaborated along the models of nineteenth-century Europe based on Marx's concepts, with some corrections in the distribution of categories, factions, and layers within the middle class sectors, and to not be limited by the contemporary description of their structure, examining furthermore their development since the colonial period.[4]

Every analysis of literature and society would seem to propose a double and simultaneous reading: one of the literature and another of the society in which it is produced. From there, we recognize the initial correction about the concept of Spanish American literature, so that all productions, written or oral, that utilize language for imaginary constructions of a symbolic type are accepted (which configures an enormous body where together with *plaquettes* of poetry and high philosophic essays, newspaper serials, traditional songs, semi-theatrical representations, prayers and ceremonial repertoires, cordel literature, and the monumental combination of texts of *mezzomusic* from the radio and television are compacted). Even while the correction that tries to restore to us the real composition of Spanish

American society, which that literature has created, operates at the same time, we continue to contemplate methodological problems with respect to this parallel reading in dealing with heterogeneous materials (one literature, one society) that cannot be assimilated nor are they comparable.

The literary reading is always, basically, a textual reading, even in those cases in which the text comes accompanied by parallel expressive systems, like music or stage performance, that amplify the suprasegmental systems of intonation of any given form of writing. The reading of society, in contrast, is not presented as a text, except in mediation that is already offspring of a hermeneutics, of history or of sociology. Since our point of departure is that of literature, it is from their textual conditions that the conditions of adaptation with society should be aligned.

Three Discourses: Literary, Linguistic, "Social Imaginary"

The correlation of literary discourse can be attempted with two other parallel discourses, of a linked nature, because both pertain to the symbolic operations of culture.

The first of these is represented by language, whose functioning constitutes an essential point for the determination of the overlapping of literary sequences within the same historic period, since they correspond to different modes of appropriation of a language that in the continent was considered an external imposition, given that language itself and not only cultural values were seen as imported, even by the same descendants of the conquistadores.[5] Thus, we will not address the linguistic discourse only at the systematic level that characterizes current studies but above all the level of *speech*, which will allow us to descend to the *dialectical plane* that registers the high capacity of fertilization of artistic creations within Latin America.

Contrary to what seems to emerge from Spanish American literary histories, linguistic behaviors at the same point in history can be diametrically different, which points to contiguous and superimposed strata. In the same years when Leopoldo Lugones writes *Los crepúsculos del jardín* (*The Garden's Twilight*), we witness in the same Buenos Aires, from the stage of the Teatro Apolo, the apotheosis of the sainete that Los Podestá company presents.[6] Rodó's *Ariel* is strictly contemporaneous with Florencio Sánchez's *M'hijo el dotor* (*My Son, the Doctor*). If this occurs in a cultural area not at all hostile to imported language due to its nature as an immigrant community, one can calculate the specific difficulties of areas with indigenous or African cultural heritage. These areas had additionally experienced recent literacy and a late educational centralization, which translates into a greater difficulty for social identification and unification of the group through the functioning of language. That is why the assumed "speech" for the literary discourse in any determined text serves for the artistic structuring and simultaneously functions as a unique element that refers us to a social sector (and not all of society) and through it one identifies oneself, recognizing at the same time an organic community. At the lexical, phonetic, semantic, and even syntactic level, each one of the "speeches" superimposed in the same region operates as a unit of meaning that associates all of its aspects and gives the speaker a recognized identity.

If in the comparison of the same moment of learned poetry in Europe and America (e.g., that of Verlaine and Darío, to refer to strict equivalents) we can always recognize in the Spanish American writer a greater dose of poetic "orality," in opposition to the prevailing concept of "writing" in developed European society (the greatest example being Mallarmé), it is possible to infer how much broader this will be if we depart from the restrictive concept of high culture and we consult the lyrics of the habaneras or tangos, the innumerable lyrics of the music that was sung around 1900. On another level this can be translated through the astonishing capacity developed by Manuel González Prada to distinguish in the functioning of Spanish American poetic language a *rhythm* in opposition to the *meter* that had already conquered its positions in the functioning of French poetry of the same time period.[7] In fact, González Prada not only reconstructed a tradition, whose initial intuition belonged to another Spanish American, Andrés Bello, but he also recognized the particular idiosyncrasy of the prevailing poetic language of the continent. In one way or another, the modernistas arrived at the same point and that was one of the reasons that allowed them to found (beyond all of their fascination with the exotic bazaar of the moment) modern Spanish American poetry.

Literary discourse can also be linked to the discourse about society. As in the case of the linguistic discourse mentioned above, the discourse about society forms part of literature, but at the same time is different from it. In his suggestive study, Tynianov proposes the problem of the correlation between what he called *literary series* and *social series* and only considered this viable "through linguistic activity" to which, however, he attributed no more than a moderate genetic influence.[8] His problem consisted of discovering a common element with the literary series, which he could not find except in the verbal function, to thus distinguish it from the concrete political, social, or economic articulations that people live and that are obviously of a different (non-discursive) nature to the literary text.

Since I believe that the autonomy of linguistic discourse is evident, beyond its plural usage for all cultural disciplines that use the word as a tool, it is preferable to recognize the autonomy of two parallel discourses to the literary one: the linguistic one that we already saw and another that I would call the "social imaginary" and that is assumed by literature in a similar way that it assumes linguistic discourse: giving structural and at the same time indexical value to the group or class that in this "social imaginary" sees itself represented.

Literature generates a discourse about the world, but this discourse does not proceed to integrate the world but rather the culture of society, being one part of the vast symbolic net by which people know and operate in the world. In a similar way, a social class, beyond concretely living their situation, interests, demands, and problems, take all of this as a point of departure to generate an ideological construction that, following Lucien Goldmann, we can designate as a worldview. The peculiar thing about this construction is that it obeys a collective process, based on the group and not merely the individual, destined to obtain a symbolic instrument with which to act within history, to impose a collection of values, and to establish a series of common interests. Such a worldview is already a coherent discourse, and it is not merely a reflection of the social, political, or economic basis that gave birth to it. This discourse is marked by a more pronounced denotative inclination than literary constructions and thus maintains a concrete connection with the sociological or political approaches. It is part of this vast discursive stratum that is articulated at the same time as artistic creations but that can be recognized as autonomous and is composed of the thought of political leaders, popular allegories, religious precepts, ethical propositions, and so on. The theory of ideologies can apply to this "social imaginary" in an effort to reduce it to its bases and interests, but in the same way that the application of a theory of literature to reveal its hidden tendencies does not unravel the work of art.[9] In this case a theory of ideology will allow nothing more than to recognize the contradictions and thus more sharply demonstrate the imaginary function that has succeeded in transfiguring the basic facts of a worldview. It will simply contribute to demarcate better the exclusive traits of the "imaginary" of a determined social group.

The linguistic discourse as much as the discourse of "social imaginary" are both objectively and autonomously appreciable in the heart of society, consolidated even in documentary evidence. But we recuperate them in the literary text, in a synthesis that, having devoured them, returns them to society as an indivisible totality. From this product we can attempt another operation: to determine in what sense this text reinterprets the demand of the social group, which falls in the orbit of a sociology of the public.

The problems that this three-part distribution brings come from the binding of systems of equivalency between the three discourses. In having to do with the literary discourse, we recognize that it tends to reconvert the denotative discourse, of intentional ideological dominance, in another connotative discourse that has specific artistic virtuality. How is this conversion produced? And what role does language play? When Cintio Vitier detects the translation of an anti-imperialist ideology in José Martí's *Simple Verses*, in a poem sung "in the innocence of nature, sole environment untouched by ambition, only mediating reality between the two Americas," he is manipulating a system of surreptitious equivalencies that has not been founded nor clarified.[10] Apparently only through an amplified theory of symbols, in a fruitful approach inaugurated by Cassirer[11] but also counting on the contributions that the diverse descendants of psychoanalysis have elaborated with respect to the transpositions that operate among diverse fields of psychology, one could lay the foundation of a system of equivalencies and qualitative changes that allows for the narrow connection between the diverse parallel discourses.

The central concern in literary analysis of preserving the autonomy and specificity of literature demands caution with respect to any genetic dismantling of the text that would be limited to transferring the meaning to another text, frequently not formulated and only inferred from the literary text. The fundamental property of literature, of "being inhabited by a force that is originally shaping and not reductive" of which the image, by its impossibility to reduce itself into articulations or material components, would be the model, forces the recognition of the parallel discourses and their independence, even though it would be possible to detect among them a tense web of mutual interactions.

Dating, Duration, and Superposition of Literary Sequences

Autonomous literary sequences, within the Spanish American literary continuum, can be determined by attending to the appearance of the artistic *event* that determines a break. With that we can accept Octavio Paz's criteria of disruption specific to the letters of the continent,[12] as long as we can liberate it of its harmonization, more presumptive than real, with traditions and to which one would have to connect to the dependent behavior of Spanish American culture, a superstructural version of its economic dependency.

These discontinuities show different tonalities. The artistic elaboration (let's say, the coherence and autonomy of the work) shows itself differently based on the times and allows us to recognize the distance that exists between the emerging aspects that we designate as Romantic in the case of Echeverría,[13] and what we would later refer to as modernista in Martí's *Ismaelillo*, differences that we attribute to their different adaptations of the parallel discourses we defined earlier, more precisely the different rendering that they achieve regarding the community-based social reality to which they respond. In *The Captive* we recognize a rigid written language and conventional forms, while in Martí's verses we find a sensuously enjoyed language and a rhythmic freedom that gives witness to the full appropriation of the linguistic behavior of a wide social group.

The determination of the period in which a literary sequence functions is more imprecise, in that even besides those elements ahead of its time, it includes modulations that are produced within the generalized unity of its artistic functioning, being furthermore capable of prolongations that we habitually call epigonic and that can give us surprisingly extensive temporary measures. To take an example that corresponds to the first learned artistic movement that gains an original title, *modernismo*, critics like Iván Schulman or Manuel Pedro González begin it with Martí's renovating work from 1882 and confer to it a prolonged life until approximately 1930, something that can be attributed to the fact that they exclusively examine the movement and trace it to its final consequences. If one proceeds with an awareness of the "futurist" experiences of Vicente Huidobro or José Juan Tablada's first ideographic poems, they clearly mark a disruptive emergence within the same superior sequence.

These sequences can be associated with aesthetic styles or currents as Pedro Henríquez Ureña called them,[14] but they are also distinctive, not only by the specific artistic resources that they put into play but also for the unity that their "social imaginary" grants to them (from which their members partake) and which is revealing in the internal oppositions of the period.

The sequences coexist with others that are heterogeneous to them and it is this overlapping of artistic strata that confers density to any historical period and allows us to examine them as a representation of the normal social stratification. Thus, *modernismo* coexists with the development of *criollismo*, and in the same periods of expansion of the works of Darío, Lugones, and Tablada we sense the emergence of Manuel Vicente Romero García, Luis Manuel Urbaneja Achelpohl, Tomás Carrasquilla, and José Álvarez, who in different places of the continent construct an articulated thematic. They appeal to a more regionalized language than that of modernismo and develop a "social imaginary" that at times is diametrically opposed to that of modernismo, giving rise to confrontations where the aesthetic doctrines put forth become mixed up with more precise ideological petitions. But if we trace in zones less explored by literary histories (poems created to be sung, spontaneous theatrical manifestations), we will discover that the traditional rural forms that we designate as folkloric coexist with a different level to the forms in which a semi-urbanized restructuring of their forms is produced, generating a sequence that cannot be assimilated to any other of the period.

For all of that, the problems of naming and determining the aesthetic contents of this period that goes from approximately 1880 to 1910 could be avoided if we accept the literary density of each period, if we recognize that there are in these different strata a peculiar transformational dynamic, as there is also a relationship (nearness or rejection) between the diverse strata. The entire group of the diverse stratified sequences oscillates between two orienting poles that mark on one side the maximum adaptation to external impulses, originating from the imperial metropolises, and on the other extreme the maximum withdrawal that appeals to localism and the traditional repositories of culture.

This design of the literary operation, which I believe would allow us to recuperate a real, complex, and varied image of the dynamic that is its own in all moments of history, would also allow us, through the use of the discourse pertaining to the "social imaginary," to move toward an understanding of the social structure of that specific literary moment, of its diverse classes and groups, of the appearance of different operating layers, of their propositions that justify their interests, of their worldviews. And we would find that through the image of society that this operation of literature amasses for us, we would reencounter a similar image to that which sociologists and anthropologists arrive at, departing from the analysis of economic and political variables that conform to social structure and determine the function of classes.

THE LITERARY SEQUENCES IN DEPENDENT SOCIETY

It seems impossible to not see, Luis Alberto Sánchez's initial observations,[15] that modernismo inserted itself into what Halperin Donghi will call "the neocolonial pact," which for him starts around 1880 and enters into a decisive crisis around 1930. But in the same way in which this pact introduces a modification of Spanish American social stratification and in the same way in which it implies the development of these modifications, making them traverse diverse periods of mobility within the social pyramid, it seems impossible to not see its vicissitudes, which we can follow in the modernist aesthetic as diverse parallel steps that closely follow those that a social class goes through, with the advantage, for literature, of an operative freedom that allows it to detect social change much earlier than it solidifies in the orders of power, deploying thus an aesthetic worldview that can even be, initially, rejected by the same ones that will be represented by it. This freedom should not be understood as an essential trait of the writer but as the daughter of the situation that fits the period after Independence: it surges with a culture that begins to be determined by the rules of liberalism and the opportunities of the market, coordinates that will only continue to become stronger through the decades. This does not take into account that writers, because of their specific task, have a higher cultural leeway than the social group to which they are associated, which allows them space to find the aesthetic formulation that best expresses the "social imaginary," even when they have still not been able to clearly articulate it in a coherent discourse because it only exists latently.

Thus it happened that modernismo suffered from two different types of negative judgments. The first corresponded to its beginnings, between 1882 and 1900, when it was attacked not only by the icons of traditional styles but also by the spokespersons of the newly ascendant urban bourgeoisie, which came confronting its affiliation to received literary forms, which were still Romantic-Realist. Very slowly, through its ascension to power, they had to accept the new aesthetic, but not until they should face the demands of a lower middle class jealous for power would they willfully make this modernist aristocratism that began as an attack on bourgeois Philistinism their own. It is the time in which Rubén Darío celebrates General Mitre and writes the *Ode to Argentina,* and in which Salvador Díaz Mirón supports General Huerta in Mexico. At this time, modernismo is consolidated around the powers of the dominant class, even though it is progressively degrading, becoming anachronistic and obsolete. This period corresponds to the second series of negative critical judgments that are formulated; they are born from the cultural operations of a newly ascendant social group and from a new literary sequence to which we owe, among other things, the foundation of narrative regionalism in Spanish America. The modernista sequence by this time had already seen the three most notorious moments of the evolution of an aesthetic trend (ascension, apogee, and fall), but also those of a social class.

Even though the concepts of social change and social mobility could be inserted in a strictly functionalist sociology, their use is the object of considerable modifications on combining with the characteristics of a dependent culture where such a condition is not offered as a simple static situation (mere acceptance of colonial patterns) but rather as dynamic, moving between the reception of norms and their head-on rejection through an extensive period in which partial structural modifications take place. If the decline of the nineteenth-century patriarchy that is replaced by the "bourgeois king" is a recurrent subject of modernista literature, a subject whose artistic formulation required a mutation of language, musicality, vocabulary, and the forms of the imaginary, we simultaneously find in this time an abundant "libertarian" literature that includes writers like Carlos Pezoa Velis, Almafuerte, or Emilio Furgoni and Angel Falco in the countries of the Southern Cone (Chile, Argentina, and Uruguay, respectively), which drives a subject and an artistic formulation that is opposed to the modernista project, even though fatally and secretly contaminated by it.

Not in vain does every culture propose dominant and dominated strata, the former generating patterns that normalize society so that its governing action can be perceived, in differing degrees of acceptance, among the lower strata, even though with curious characteristics that reveal that it is not a simple acceptance but a transformative elaboration, and for that reason in opposition. In the lower strata the norms are received and incorporated to a directed force to break the cultural unity that comes from the upper strata to be able to then break down the artistic, or simplistically called "formal," resources from the content to which they look to substitute in an operation that generally results in hybrid and contradictory formulations. Thus, it is easy to sense, in the heart of the costumbristas and criollistas that form one of the dependent literary sequences of the late nineteenth century, alluded to already (1880–1910), the appropriation of aesthetic formulas that had been visibly extracted from the modernista sequence, which was the dominant one of the period and that are applied as mere "forms" to different "content," creating strange contradictions within the organic nature of the discourse. Even in a lower strata that corresponds to the epigonic continuity of the so-called gauchesque literature, as occurred with José Alonso y Trelles, the author of *Paja brava*, we can find the use of these same resources that pertain to the governing norms of society in literary matters applied to materials close to the folkloric levels.

The explanation of this internal dynamic of literary sequences responds to the global situation of society and, therefore, literary totality, regarding external imperial centers. Just as the upper classes originate from their modernization, this spreads as a norm through the social pyramid, generating partial acceptances and partial rejections that betray the internal necessities of other strata in their zeal for survival and progress. One should also confirm that at a certain height in the literary pyramid we find sequences that are subjected to processes typical of modernization, that is, an education that does not come from the culture of the power elites but that comes directly from foreign sources. This is the case for the libertarian literature mentioned earlier, of the contributions of turn-of-the-century anarchism—its ideology, its authors—all originating from Europe.

TIME FACTOR, REALITY FACTOR

The varied ways of exercising cultural dependency in the field of literature admits diverse manifestations based on what the literary sequences are, their situation, and the moment of the evolution in which they are found.[16] This demands that we manage the time factor and the reality factor as coordinates of the polygon of forces.

In the first place, it does not seem possible to affirm, by focusing on artistic categories, the oft repeated thesis that rejects outright works that form the dominant literary sequences, claiming that they are the ones that are situated close to the functioning of the controlling elites that, at the same time, are those that serve for the mediation of imperial interests. Without the work of Darío, the at least partial autonomy of Spanish American poetry would not exist, and this marks, with regard to the learned poetry that came before, a notorious qualitative leap, a discontinuity that establishes the literary modernity of the continent. It occurs here that, despite Darío's proclaimed affirmation that his success is due to "mental Gallicism," the more established critics (Federico de Onís) already took charge of recovering the multiplicity of his sources. For us the original note of his art is evident, where one attends to an appropriation of culture that is a recreation of a universal history from the angle that only a Spanish American man could possess, with its intrinsic virtues and foreseeable deformations. It is worthwhile to also recognize the plurality of contributions that any artist achieves and in particular the universality of their more specific contribution, which definitively conquers, spreads, and liberates itself from the restrictive ideological formulations that accompany them.

In the second place, the dominant classes, on spreading a foreign culture, fulfill a complementary task to the central one, which consists of restructuring society itself in the service of an economic project with which they confer progressive reality to a new structure of society, be that good or bad. They rearticulate the stratification for their benefit, promote necessary development for their own ends, and partially modify the social formation. This creates a curious connection with those dominant literary sequences that seem related to real and working forces in a transformation, whose function is not merely that of reflecting, obediently, an imported culture but of translating a new internal reality, a dependent culture that is forged within a national context, that forms pacts in differing degrees with some traditions and is trying, above all, to embed itself in reality. The degree of efficiency that is derived from this process will have its correlation in the level of authenticity of the literary sequence created and associated with it.

One can observe that at the other extreme of the density of literary sequences, we find that, having access to scarce intellectual resources, the creators should create a product that is one of opposition, responding to the abrupt modifications that have been decreed from higher up the social pyramid. This explains the frequent appeal that they should then make to the folkloric remnants, which are the only material they have access to, as occurred in the case of José Hernández's *Martín Fierro*. Regarding the intermediary strata, they frequently appeal to the contribution of a "social imaginary" as an explicit ideological discourse, which thus responds to their situation as one extracted from an external lesson; this is the case of the propagandist literature of the ascendant groups of the lower middle class.

The time factor and the adaptation to reality factor are present throughout the development of the diverse sequences. To the extent that they are able to precisely interpret the cultural process, the products that they present will boast this accent of authenticity and this clearness that speaks of an efficient harmonization of the diverse parallel discourses and of an efficient insertion into the demands of the social group.

The design of a literary structure should be the object of development, elaborations, and studies that make of it something more than the hypothesis of a work. With this in mind, one looks to contribute a greater approach to the functioning of Spanish American literature, one that makes it critically intelligible.

7

Literature and Social Class

Advances in Latin American Literary Criticism

Around 1910, one begins to see the progressive emergence of a Latin American cultural generation that would come to substitute nineteenth-century "modernismo," "symbolism," and "Parnasianism." This generation displays a belligerent behavior based on nationalist programs that interpret the demands presented by the ascendant middle class sectors. During a determined lapse, before a divide (and diverse conflicts) appears between the interests of the urban social classes that are developing in this period, this generation expresses the points of intersection between an industrializing national bourgeoisie, the varied strata of the middle classes, and the claims of the nascent proletariat.

This cultural movement would give rise to social-political changes, above all in the countries of the Southern Cone (Argentina, Chile, Uruguay) where it would accelerate the modernization process with a more firm urban domination over the territory of these respective countries. In Mexico, it would enable "Maderismo," continuing this action throughout the tumultuous revolutionary process that Francisco Madero's assassination unleashes. It would contribute to the nationalist climate with which these countries with Spanish heritage celebrated their centenary of political independence. In the Brazilian hemisphere it would generate the ideology of the League of National Defense as well as related ideas from the petty bourgeoisie of Rio and São Paulo. It would be expressed through the sweeping university reforms born in Cordoba [Argentina] that would spread, even to Cuba, throughout the entire continent. It would make European vitalist philosophies its own, fostering a new idealism imbued with a strong renovating impulse. It would put in motion a neorealist literature like the regionalist novel and "sincerist" poetry that would wring the neck of Spanish American modernismo's cosmopolitan rhetoric and would begin to reassess—utilizing modern tools—folklore, the embedded cultural traditions, beliefs, and local arts.

The members of this generation, which one could describe as "nationalist" or also of the "middle classes," make a considerable contribution to the study and framing of Latin American literatures, because they develop more efficient levels of research, creating the first reasoned attempts to think about literary production on the continent with a methodology derived from their specific historical characteristics. As is obvious, the superior level of research, as well as the attempt to discover their own methodologies, responds to the development reached at the time by literary studies and to the perspective in which they were situated, given that this generation of writers participated in the political conquests of the middle class sectors, the growth of the syndicate movement, and the climate of lively democratic demands that took possession of Latin American society.

This generation's methodological efforts (of which the well-known candor of men who believe that history always begins with them tends to be ignorant) did not pretend to cancel European contributions that had served to found the first organic structures of the literatures proposed by the best [critics] of the nineteenth century (the most significant ones, Sílvio Romero and Capistrano de Abreu, were in Brazil). Rather, these writers attempted to correct and reform them through additions born from their concrete studies and in some cases to relegate them to a second level. The most important literary critics of the nationalist generation corrected, through additions, the work of their predecessors, which on one hand clouded the general concept proposed by them but on the other hand recorded methodological outcomes that resulted from a detailed and concrete study that was more practical than theoretical of a few neglected periods of Latin American literature.[1]

This capacity to confront in an apparently spontaneous way the originality of the Latin American literary "event" to later begin to deduce a peculiar methodology from their attentive study is, together with the culturalist conception that marked their research, one of the considerable contributions of this generation of critics. The humility with which they achieved their tasks, the "practicality" of many of their contributions, and the cautious theoretical flight of their ideas have contributed to the fact that their importance has been ignored (their works, like the realist novels of the period, "blend" with the Latin American reality of their time). In the current period, marked by a feverish and many times inappropriate transfer of European "theories" about literature, their contribution is neglected. But their best contribution lies in this acceptance of the recognition of literary production, the singularity of its emergence, and the originality of its artistic conditions, which allows them to correct the theoretical baggage with which they had approached reality, trying to adjust it to what it told them. There is value in paying tribute to this lesson about humanity in a time in which the copy (if not the utilization) of Marxist or Structuralist categories turns out to be suppressing the effort to find a theoretical instrument that fits the literary peculiarity of Latin America, given this is not what is observed nor studied. The critics of the nationalist generation were also—as is necessary to recognize—docile transcribers of European models, above all with historiographic sequences and the concept of artistic value, but they contributed, through their patient investigation of the literary past, to the discovery of some specific literary behaviors of Latin America for which they were able to find their own critical positions. The balance of virtues and defects should be established with care, but I do not believe that the eventual results of this work not begun will shroud this assertion: we inherited from these critics the most comprehensive views of Latin American literature—the ones that have better served its internal composition.

The most prestigious names of this generation of critics correspond to scholars who were born in the 1880s: the Argentine Ricardo Rojas (1882–1957), the Dominican Henríquez Ureña (1884–1946), the Uruguayan Alberto Zum Felde (1888–1976), the Mexican Alfonso Reyes (1889–1959), and the Chilean Hernán Díaz Arrieta (1891–1984); to this list we can add the Spanish critic Federico de Onís for his constant and lucid attention to Latin American letters. In all of them the search for originality, uniqueness, the expression of an American culture through its literary manifestations is central.[2] The analytical tools that the philosophical renovation at the beginning of the century (James, Bergson) provided them was complemented with an effort at investigative systemization that is particularly high in Reyes and Henríquez Ureña.

This initial approach to the particular conditions of Latin American literary operations will be continued in later generations, who will accomplish a double task: the appropriation of literary theories disseminating in European countries and the expansion of the knowledge about the literature of the continent, these in the light of new creative Latin American circumstances in a necessarily historicist vision. Thus, the generation immediately after the nationalist, and which we tend to encapsulate under the title of "avant-garde" despite plural and contradictory orientations, begins to accentuate the global conflicts and ruptures resulting from the class over social interests in a critical period. This is a generation that will have to discover important literary avenues of the past that had been ignored (e.g., popular theater), folkloric or marginal literatures, political and social narrative, and so forth, along with the rudiments of a Marxist theory of art that responded to the debate that took place in Europe in the 1920s following the October Revolution. This group of critics is headed by the Peruvian José Carlos Mariátegui (1895–1930), in which can be included, among others, the Cuban Juan Marinello (1898–1977), the Peruvian Luis Alberto Sánchez (1900–1994), and the Chilean Ricardo Latcham (1903–1965).[3] These critics inherit the culturalist perspective that was initially forged by the Romantics, based on the scientific understanding of their time by the Naturalists, developed by the nationalists of the middle class sectors, and they will now appropriate socialist concepts within the specter of varied lights. At times they simply apply Taine's criteria about the influence of the medium or utilize a primitive sociology, but which in the most meticulous elaborations create believable equivalences between literary production and social structure. They do this with the intention of promoting literary precepts: Mariátegui's revaluation of Melgar complements his belligerent promotion of the indigenist literature of his time.[4]

Literatures, Subcultures, Social Classes

At the brink of 1930 the correlation between literature and social class had already reached common agreement, a fact that will have later and complex derivations primarily within the proposals of programmatic literatures. This present study does not look to specify the individual contributions of each one of the critics mentioned, but rather to show the evolution of literary criticism in the first decades of the twentieth century. This emphasizes that upon delving with greater understanding into the literary material of the continent, literary criticism establishes, over the course of two generations of critics, an interpretive trend (that, of course, is not unique) thanks to which literary production is considered as part of a broader Latin American cultural production.

The progress corresponding to these patiently elaborated assumptions has only been made possible contemporaneously, through a more rigorous culturalist grounding. This centering comes in light of the development of renewed literary creation and perceives the simultaneous and varied subcultures that developed in the different areas of Latin America (and that even within each one of them accepts autonomous superimposed constructions), with which we would not only have a map of cultural regions available but would furthermore within each one of them detect a series of distinct cultural layers that are tied notoriously to the pertinent social groups and classes. This progress in the best understanding of literary heritage and its methods of critical explanation (which has been accomplished in parallel and simultaneously with a better understanding of Latin American social structure that only in our time has reached a mature state) has been facilitated by the contributions of contemporary Latin American sociology, especially in those directions that come from a Marxist philosophy. Much is also owed to another science even more recently developing with Latin American scholars: anthropology. There is no possible comparison between the anthropological material that Capistrano de Abreu or Henríquez Ureña utilized and that which most recent literary critics had at their disposal, illuminating amply for the first time the culture of important sectors of society that until now had hidden behind generalizing stereotypes. It has been not only criticism but also the same creative work of writers that has benefited from this more advanced level of understanding, like what can be seen in the work of José María Arguedas.

Only by starting with the concept of culture that the main anthropologists in the world have continued to adjust (Boas, Sapir, Herskovits, Kroeber, Lévi-Strauss) has a design of the complete behavior of literature become possible. Furthermore, this design is amplified if one looks at the cultural uniqueness that Latin American anthropologists (Fernando Ortiz, Ricardo Pozas, Gilberto Freyre, Darcy Ribeiro, Juan Comas, etc.) have detected in the diverse areas of Our America about which they have studied, perfecting and correcting those general definitions. The placement of the literary product, as a coronation of the traditions and constant creative processes that have been achieved in the specific field of American subcultures, leads to a double intertextual reading to which criticism has begun to approach: that of the literary texts and that of the discourse that is forged in the inventions of diverse cultures documenting the collective work of men, to which a third reading can be added, critical in nature, about the loose connections that both processes show.[5] These are relations that will no longer be regarded as connecting, on one hand, a homogeneous block of works and styles and, on the other, a Latin American society seen as a whole indistinct as the critics of the previously discussed generations habitually practiced. It is seen, rather, as connections between precise and determined sectors of society (classes, layers, or groups that will be perceived not only as economic or socio-political associations but as representatives and creators of specific subcultures) and also precise and determined styles or artistic movements that operate in a particular and restricted manner within the social milieu.

This critical point of view allows one to access a vision of literature where the operation of the complex structure of Latin American society is evident. This vision perceives the dynamics of social classes, the confrontations, and the diverse instances of historical development that the conflict of class in American society has been producing. But it is not at the service of a series of documents, useful for the sociologist or politician, but rather as the expression of the best and most ambitious work of social groups that has been and is that of producers of cultural forms, which are manifested in the highest level to which their members can reach, through literary works. Thus the vision of literature, recognizing its autonomy and its own textual field, builds on top of another plane (the verbal and artistic, the symbolic according to Cassirer's concept, different therefore from the social or economic planes) a complex and dynamic combat in which diverse cultural conceptions, represented by diverse aesthetic conceptions, express themselves—they face and substitute each other. Any modern Latin American history or sociology text cannot but show evidence of, with greater or lesser interpretive refining, the class struggle that composes the core of secular development in the continent. It is incomprehensible, then, that literary history, which portrays the artistic production of these same peoples, is not capable of showing such a central and dynamic element of the historic behavior, nor is it capable of detecting the diverse cultural formulations that have been unique and that serve as support to literary creations situated in the superstructure.

Such a reconstruction can only be done through literary texts, making sure that it is the texts themselves that group themselves into movements, styles, tendencies, approaches, or differentiations, recognizing their own conflicts and periods of relevance. It would be risky to address this construction starting from the blueprints already prepared by historians and sociologists, forcing literature to adjust to them. In that case, literature would end up simply corroborating an interpretive discourse and would not be contributing itself to design the Latin American cultural framework. It would not make a specific contribution to generalized knowledge about a society. Likewise, it would be risky to depart, in such an endeavor, from a rigid doctrine, one of these codified hermeneutics that look for the mere confirmation of theories in reality without allowing reality to speak and correct their theoretical assumptions. Of course it would be equally damaging for us to restrict ourselves to a "content based" reading that took up so much space in the social criticism of literature as we would not be able to perceive in all its richness the construction of cultural and artistic forms that tell us, as much or more than the content, about the propositions that social classes and groups present within the horizon of Latin American society. This happens, above all, at a critical level where the traditional division between form and content has been surpassed and cancelled, recognizing one harmonic movement in texts when they achieve their most accurate aesthetic efficiency.

The Density of Literature

The cultured concept of literature that had ample and natural prestige in a society, like Latin America, that counted for many decades on incredibly reduced educated sectors that set the ideal norms of creation and the narrow radius of consumers for their written products, is responsible for the restrictions that occurred in the literary production of the continent. The highbrow focus where one wrote and published in periodicals or books, was very limited, only accessible to few social sectors so that the debate initiated by them seemed like a family debate. This contributed to fortifying the idea that literature was a unitary conglomeration where some discrepancies (that generated styles and works, contributing notable artistic differences) comparable to quarrels between fathers and sons could be produced. It is evident that we can reconstruct this debate and its very clear oppositions, which nevertheless only circulated within a track dominated by similarity. Outside of this enlightened circle, a great marginal zone spread, where there was not only persistent production of oral literatures but also a written contribution whose access to proper literature was banned by the norms established in the selective highbrow circle. With this in mind, one accepts what for Robert Escarpit is the distinctive mark of the diverse concepts of literature, even though, in this American case, and taking it to an extreme, it is possible to detect an exclusive trait of a colonized elite that resists, above all, integrating into its own cultural medium: "The only common trait that these various conceptions of literary nature have is the selection. It in fact concerns a closed system that draws its coherence not from the matter to which it is applied but from the selective attitude that is the fundamental cultural reasoning of all elitist societies."[6]

The historical expiration date of some norms of the elites (because of inefficiency or because they were replaced), the introduction of a methodological suspension with the objective of achieving an independent revision (with all the risks of relativism that it carries), allows the reconstruction of the density of literary production of any of the periods of the nineteenth century. This can most visibly be made in contemporary times, given the growing complexity of the economic and cultural system, which survives the homogenization that the economic system and its communication instruments are trying to impose. Such density is shown by the overlaying, in a same time and place, of different literary expressions that can have two extreme behaviors, which makes their relationship mutual: either they maintain scarce connection and they unfold parallelly, apparently without arriving at a collision, or they are capable of confrontations that translate into controversies whose igniting point deals with "the nature of literature" and its "function."[7]

The very fact that two literary productions can coexist without friction indicates the total separation in which they develop and, thus, the enormous distance that one is found in relation to the other despite both of them being contemporaneous with each other. Given that the synchronous structure of a determined literary period is organized around diverse superpositions where there are privileged forms that enjoy the support of the most important institutions and bodies (academia, newspapers, literary salons), while others do not count on such patronage, the entire disconnect between two simultaneous productions of literature reveals that they are found in the most distanced levels of the system. The lower one is ignored by the superior, which does not grant it estimable artistic status. Furthermore, as if this were not enough, the inferior is unable to present itself as a valid aesthetic alternative that defies the current norms established by the superior. A difficult overlap is added to this; the artistic texture of the lower, the principles on which it is organized, cannot be assimilated by the principles of the highest layer. The products that one or the other can circulate and that preferentially adopt a descent of superior forms to the lowest levels even though in some periods critics can invert the process, will depend upon very complex transformational operations, the majority of the time improbable. The lack of connections also indicates the fragmentation of the consuming public, separated from each other, bereft of bridges that can join them together, therefore working separately with their own distinct cultural baggage, whose uniqueness and value are not mutually understood with ease.

In Latin American literature there is no more notorious example of the disconnect between two simultaneous literary productions than the one found between the official cultured and urban literature of a period (products that have conquered the prestige of the instruments of cultural power even if it has already fallen into rhetoric and imitation) and the traditional oral literature of rural communities. This disconnect is even more notorious in nineteenth-century Latin American than in Europe of the same time period, given that the Romantic thesis about the creativity of the folk spirit that brought about a literature that would occasionally imitate ballads and songs did not gain an equal foothold in our continent. Here, despite their use of local color and national subjects, the Romantic poets showed themselves to be much more attached to learned writing (even when they imitated the European ballad or legend) than to the strictly popular or folkloric forms that were offered in their environs. With this, they fortified the progress of the learned trend, and its dependence on foreign models, when they claimed to reproduce the peculiar artistic forms of their regions. For the same reason, they strengthened the existing separation between the two extreme literary productions.

Being simultaneous, parallel, and independent, these productions follow tracks that seal their isolation, even though they accomplish similar operations that are typical of literary production. They settle into a determined course that is fixed by a linguistic variance that they appropriate, by a repertoire of unique literary forms, by a repertoire of subjects (even this is where they can overlap, occasionally), by a related textual repertoire, by a system of correlating author and public. Even though the inferior, folkloric approach presents itself as a persistent and invariable continuum, the numerous collections that we have (Juan Alfonso Carrizo, Vicente T. Mendoza, Augusto Raúl Cortázar, Luis da Camara Cascudo, Carlos H. Magis)[8] allow us to reconstruct their internal movement—with a different rhythm than that which moves the superior learned approach and with a constant productive process within which they are implemented, in particular to the process of a linguistic appropriation based on a person's environment.

Even though the disagreements between these two extreme literary productions are great and they are at the same time those that best define the limits of the density of literature, some of the differences noted between them can be the object of criticism and reduced to equivalent situations. This is the problem that their regime of transmission lays out, which also implies, in varying degrees, the mode of production. Learned literature is produced and transmitted through writing. It thus demands the prior literacy of the author and reader, which has value through the incorporation into a cultural circuit that works through more precise and also more limited codes than those exclusive to the regime of oral transmission that is applicable to folkloric literature. Although in this case the mode of production alternates orality with writing, the regime of transmission, as Jackobson has proposed, imagines, for all individual creation, "a group to accept and sanction it" and applies what he has called "the preventive censure of the community."[9] Starting with the theory of the genius developed by the Romantics, which the Surrealists in our century have taken to an extreme, applying it to new layers of creation that until then had not been incorporated into aesthetic values, it is easy to recognize that in both zones (the learned and the folkloric) the eventuality of the personal creator is possible, with the most varied levels of mediocrity or excellence, even though the constraints imposed by the regime of written transmission (newspapers, magazines, books) are less noticeable. Thus, many critics tend to underestimate this, not recognizing its great power, while they detect it easily in the regime of oral transmission. In fact, we have in both cases individual creators, whose relationship with the consumer is mediated within circuits: in one case it is the newspaper or book editor, in the other the transmitter or singer of poetry, who bring together supply and demand. These agents can be much more coercive in the regime of written transmission than in that of oral transmission, as the rebellion of the nineteenth-century *art for art's sake poets* demonstrates. Arnold Hauser, who includes diverse manifestations—among them the folkloric—under the heading "art of the people," underscores the weakness of intermediation to transmit this artistic message: "In folk art, producers and consumers are hardly distinguished, and the boundary between them is always fluid."[10]

Therefore, more than opposition, we find, in the aspect of transmission, equivalent forms of censorship. But we should immediately note the most disparate options between both literary productions. While learned literature responds to the existence of the educated cores in the cities and therefore is marked by the mental coordinates of the process of urbanization in its various levels, the folkloric spreads through the rural and provincial zone. It even invades the outskirts of recent rural migration to the cities, responding to mental mechanisms, associative forms, and ideological constructions that are the heritage of "rural societies," which have richest known tradition. Different literary behaviors come from this inclusion or exclusion of urbanization (understood as a system of different psychological adaptations to the forms of life of each zone), while the individual creator of the learned urban literature will operate an ample and versatile range of literary forms that grants a special conservatism in relation to literary forms. Once one adopts here a new kind of stanza, there a system of dialogue, whose origins will be found frequently in the vigilant and advanced work of the learned literatures, they will be inclined to remain attached to them and to extract from them numerous expressive possibilities to the point of exhausting them according to their own rate of artistic sampling, only then to move on to substituting them. This points to the advance of individualism within societies shaped by the bourgeois revolutions, which grows faster in urban centers depending on their dynamic: in Latin America the domination of the Neoclassic and Romantic styles in the learned sector reaches a very extensive scope that has been called anachronistic (in relation to the original European model, of course) but is a testament to the particularly restricted rhythm of cities in the nineteenth century. They enter into a process of substitution that will give us our first syncretic period—in which different approaches mix together because urbanization emerged as a mix in a tenacious attempt to keep up with the present—and then a rapid substitution of literary movements. In contrast, the more balanced reciprocity between the individual and their social group that remains in rural zones, the system of interdependence of the social nucleus, constrains this innovative work, even though it does not destroy it. It moves it, instead, to other aspects of the literary message, as can be observed in linguistic usage. Cultured literature appropriates writing and therefore the linguistic sign and is inclined to a greater capacity for abstraction over the substance of the content, tending to reduce the range of the vocabulary and to organize it hierarchically. In the cases of communication that Abraham Moles has studied, this implies a progressive compartmentalization of the public, which the transmitter addresses since, departing from a very reduced basic linguistic nucleus, it functions on knowledge and therefore the reception of information.[11] Folkloric literature manipulates a community-based language, with a wide spectrum and expanded expressive possibilities, a language attached to generalized creation of the symbols of its environs. While it does not cease to apply an interpretive hierarchy to its surroundings, as Amado Alonso has shown for the language of the pampas, it captures more freely the fluidity of speech and the creative linguistic work of the social group.[12]

There are also sensitive differences between the demeanor of the European and the American learned classes. The tactical awareness of the

American colonized creole (even more evident in the population inhabiting indigenous settlements) utilizing a language that was not their own but had been imported and, like the other aspects of American life, was governed from the metropolis, led to an excessive attachment to the learned norms of Spain or Portugal. The exaggeratedly cultured nature of Hispanic American literary language, which largely lived on past the revolution of Independence, is part of what Lipschutz has called the colonial "pigmentocracy."[13] An element of this considerable effort to approximate the external model, which, like white complexion, purity of blood, and militant Catholicism, serves to gain status by distinguishing oneself, on one hand, from the "inferior" indigenous or black races with their diverse mixings, and on the other hand, comparing themselves to the peninsular prototypes, trying to overcome the disdain for the "indianos" in Madrid or Lisboa. This hyper-culturism, which is still present in the writings of Eduardo Mallea or Caballero Calderón[14] in the middle of the twentieth century, liberated popular language and allowed its powerful creativity to be translated in the oral literatures linked to it. The exaggerated formality was a seizure of the established norm and in fact would generate the archaism that alarmed Américo Castro in the Buenos Aires of the 1920s (along with other absurd accusations), making it impossible to achieve the renovation that Alfonso Reyes recognized as more effective in the vulgar Roman centurion of the decline than in Quintiliano. Oral transmission, as rigid as it might be due to a conservatism, does not find itself subject to a rigid linguistic norm, but it tends to recognize the existence of dialects, adapting itself to phonetic, lexical, and morphological peculiarities and the fragmentation of rural social enclaves contribute to its autonomous restructuring.

Bordering Stratifications

If we were to recognize only this division of the literary corpus, we would rethink the known separation between learned and popular literatures, paying attention to their opposing characteristics in this exercise of binary thinking that undergirds our critical work. But that does not exhaust the density of literature. It is helpful to notice the existence, in a historical period, of bordering trends that therefore coincide in common notes but at the same time contrast in others. They are literary forms that are produced within the dominant characteristics of the learned or popular literatures, but that introduce breaches within their general norms. Clear differences and even confrontations are perceptible in them, debates that indicate how these trends belong to a literary family but with sufficient unique manifestations as to allow discrepancies.

This demarcation allows us to visualize at the same time the stubborn difficulty that even today literary criticism demonstrates by recognizing that literature does not circulate through one unique path, but rather it develops through diverse and parallel paths with greater or lesser affinity, with the capacity for domination or with regimes of servanthood, following paths and original organizations that have to be reconstructed through interpretive discourse. In this sense, some observations of the German critic Rudolf Grossman, in his very recent *Historia y problema de la literatura latinoamericana* (*History and Problem of Latin American Literature*), can serve as a point of departure to observe a concrete case of literary parallelism in bordering stratifications.

Referring to Manuel Antonio de Almeida's famous novel *Memoirs of a Militia Sergeant*, one of the jewels of nineteenth-century Brazilian narrative, Rudolf Grossman claims that this admirable novel comes "two years before Alencar's first Romantic novel" and that it is "one of these literary anachronisms that abound, especially in the nineteenth century."[15] For some time the best Brazilian criticism has already recognized the value of Almeida's work in relation to its socio-literary environs, his impartial decision to "remain in the Rio of the first quarter of the nineteenth century in the popular environment of barbers and neighborhood gossips in which our ill-defined middle class went about differentiating itself."[16] The incipient middle sectors had sketched out a peculiar worldview, they used a vast and flavorful language, they lived in a permanent fight to subsist, and they acquired an incipient rapid and objective realist attitude toward the culture and economy of the city.

However, the originality of Almeida's novel is not what allows for its recovery by the Brazilian modernists in 1922, which interests us at the moment, but rather the author's relationship with the literature of his time, his distancing from his contemporaries, and how his novel is produced, nevertheless, within a conjunction of dates, of regimes of literary transmission, and of common thematic and formal structures. Indeed, Manuel Antonio de Almeida is strictly speaking a contemporary of José de Alencar since the former was born in 1831 and the latter in 1829; their literary careers have contemporary initial developments and emerge within the urban culture of Rio in the middle of the nineteenth century. They both share the same journalistic profession, even publishing works in the same newspaper. In

1853, under the traditional form of the serial novel, *Memoirs of a Militia Sergeant* appears anonymously in the *Correio Mercantil*. It confessedly seeks to be a historical snapshot, within the penchant of the time for reconstructions, allowing it to be situated from the highest outside angle of literary forms within the narrative model introduced by Romanticism—the historical novel—which had wide diffusion in the periodical serial novels of Brazilian newspapers.[17] José de Alencar's columns (*Ao correr da pena*) had been published in the same newspaper since 1854, and his first novels and the famous work *The Guarany* (1857), which also follows and even typifies the romantic model of historical reconstruction, will appear in serial form in the *Diário do Rio de Janeiro*.

If the early death of Almeida cut his career short, while José de Alencar in contrast was able to extensively develop his work that, until his death in 1877 and despite his final defense, did not deviate greatly from his initial model, this does not stop us from recognizing the strict contemporaneity of both narrators. They share the same use of the regime of writing and diffusion through periodical serial novels, the same awareness of thematic orientations and models of the time, and the same utilization of the demand of an urban medium that authorized diverse stratifications, which were covered, however, by the same newspaper. Through these common elements the difference between their respective literary options becomes more evident, since the lyric, vocative model of the Romantic national novel that José de Alencar constructs directly contrasts with Almeida's realistic, objective, and ironic vision; José de Alencar's flexible, poetic, and learned language contrasts with the somewhat awkward language of a certain urban stratum that Antonio Soares Amora defines as "woven with the elemental resources of the common speech"; the idealism that permeates characters and actions drastically driving the dichotomous Romantic oppositions contrasts with a realism that focuses on customs and everyday life.[18]

It is not necessary to resort to the biography of both authors to find the causes of these differences: knowing that José de Alencar's family hails from Ceará; of the political notoriety of his father, a senator and great man who participated in the ascension to the throne of King Pedro in 1840; of his studies as a lawyer; of his conservative political activity, and knowing at the same time the humble origins of Manuel Antonio de Almeida; of his abandonment by his family; of his struggles in the heart of the small Rio de Janeiro middle class; of his poorly paid work as a journalist. It is not necessary to appeal to this information given that it is not in this, despite the insight it gives us, where one can trace the decisive literary orientation of a writer if we remember Marx's thoughts regarding the origins of ideologies. Differences are recognized in the reading of their respective works as a manifestation of two simultaneous and different worldviews, evidently destined for future confrontations, which unfold at the same time and give us, with the orientation that we have defined as learned and scriptural, two notoriously different tendencies. They are bordering trends: they possess common elements and at the same time utilize different ones that single them out. Such textual studies allow a reconstruction of the density of urban learned literature of the period, without looking for excuses in anachronisms, precursors, uniquely gifted creators, and so forth. Starting with their existence, we can attempt the reconstruction of this density within which they are born, that of the cultural forms that exist simultaneously in the same place and time and that are tied to social strata.

In the cited example, we have looked at two authors and their respective works exclusively, which offers us, thanks to the secular selection established by readers and criticism as possessing, a high artistic level. They have been extracted from a much wider group, separated from it through a system of values and fictitiously presented as isolated creations. If we return to the literary productivity of their time, momentarily suspending the selective principles that govern the establishment of literatures, we observe that they were born within the disjointed mix of a considerable production of serial novels where it is possible to trace, in diverse expressions and variable intensities, in intermediate levels, frustrated or even mediocre, the same trends that they represent with a superior artistic exactitude. It is then possible to deal with a reconstruction of the aesthetic axiology but starting with the recognition of the simultaneity and parallelism in which the distinct artistic expressions are produced.

This is what has led Alfredo Bosi to reorder the Romantic narrative of the period, paying attention to a type of selection that responds to literary excellence, even though, at the same time, doing this allows us to be able to recognize the simultaneous usage of both critical principles: detecting the parallel courses of literature and noticing in each of them a more urgent artistic task. Bosi states:

> One should prefer not so much a distribution of themes as the nerve of their literary treatment when judging works of art as such. We have, in the lowest plane, the romances that do not want to increase the literary expectations of the average reader, instead, they excite us so that we want the same basic model

to continue *ad infinitum*: this is the type of narration produced by Macedo, Bernardo, Távora and minor works of Alencar (*A viuvinh*a [*The Widow*], *Diva*, *A Pata de Gazela* [*The Gazelle's Hoof*], *Encarnção* [*Incarnation*]). Taunay's *Inocéncia* [*Innocence*] and some of Alencar's second level novels (*O Sertanejo* [*The Peasant*], *O Gaúcho* [*The Gaucho*], *O Guaraní* [*The Guarany*]) redeem themselves of their concessions to adventures and to their lack of verisimilitude by their descriptive breath and by their success in the construction of symbolic characters. Finally, at the level of texts created with the best intentions, as is to be expected, we have a few successful ones: *Memoirs of a Militia Sergeant*, prodigy of picaresque humor in the middle of so much banal disguise, and Alencar's two masterpieces, *Iracema* and *Senhora*, so diverse between them in their point of view but similar in the construction of precise tone and in the economy of means that the novelist writer values.[19]

On the other extreme that we have designed, that corresponding to the oral traditions of rural zones, we can also note the appearance of literary orientations bordering the folkloric literary sector but that cannot be confused with it. Within the Spanish American hemisphere, we find the paradigmatic case of the so-called gauchesque literatures, which approach the folkloric in their license in using regional dialects, even including learned vocabulary and archaisms this implies, for the use of metric forms common to the popular production of the rural zones, which they rapidly modified with their own adaptations (José Hernández's sextilla). In addition, they are similar to the folkloric in the linguistic irregularity that characterizes them (which gauchesque authors will soon restrain, however, following the learned norm from which some cultivators of the genre set off, as Amado Alonso's study of Estanislao del Campo's manuscripts has shown).[20] Gauchesque literatures differentiate themselves from the folkloric by the importance granted to the individual creator through their better insertion in the present historical circumstance, which implies a quicker pace of incorporation of artistic transformations and the incorporation of new circuits of communication, which complement orality with writing through the traditional use of loose-leaf paper and chapbooks.

The best criticism has reiterated that we are in the presence of a typical literary movement, with individual authors of a certain cultural level, with a creative attitude adequate for these levels, with a very notable choice of public.²¹ Gauchesque literature, which has been the object of diverse classifications, those that arise from its diachronic development and the incorporation of authors and trends that bring it closer to or further away from the folkloric stratum, also signals, as in the case of Almeida's and Alencar's narratives, to the existence of social classes with their own distinctive characteristics. If in the case of Almeida and Alencar it dealt with urban strata, in gauchesque literatures it deals with rural stratum where modifications that alter the original and uniform composition are introduced.

The stereotype of the historical account has presented the revolution of Independence as a confrontation between the creole people with their bosses, who came from the mercantile middle class, and on the other side the Spanish military with the few royalists of the colonial administration at its head. The real history was rather more complex: it recognizes that a profound division developed within the same people, regarding the rural worker, especially those dedicated to working with livestock. Boves's victorious royalist armies in Venezuela provide eloquent proof of this. In the revolutionary process a rupture within this abandoned social sector emerges, and although a majority rally behind the revolutionary flags responding to promises to attend to their demands, many stayed with the more traditional and conservative attitude. This rupture within a social class is what gauchesque literature exposes, signaling at the same time an incipient class consciousness that the revolutionary shake up promotes in the men of the countryside, situated in the most distant point from the socioeconomic structure that begins to develop in Latin America with the revolution.

In this way, Bartolomé Hidalgo's gauchesque literature refers not only to this vast popular sector where folkloric literature endured and developed but also to the more reduced sector that acquires a consciousness of economic, social, and political demands. Put another way, Bartolomé Hidalgo's gauchesque poetry is associated with Artigas's Regulation of Lands of 1815,²² like the "negrista" poetry that begins to flourish at the time without reaching sufficient autonomy. It is about the freedom of wombs and the emancipation of slaves that is decreed to obtain their incorporation into the revolutionary creole armies, which, initially, situates these sectors in a new social dynamic that distances them from the classes from which they originated: peasant or slave. The degree of rupture and the success of this enterprise will remain fixed by the capacity shown to constitute a new literary genre (which the cultivators of gauchesque literature achieve, but "negrista" literature does not) and by the persistence that it attains (almost a century for gauchesque literature). The problem of the relations with a specific literature is laid out, once their textual field is defined by their particular artistic characteristics, and the explicit or implicit social discourse of a social class, to which one must add its eventual self-consciousness.

In order to detect this connection, appealing to the social origins of these writers does not help because, as we have already indicated, this is not a rigorously determinant element (in fact, the majority of the first practitioners of gauchesque literature came from the rural or lower urban stratum, as is the case of Bartolomé Hidalgo to whom Castañeda reproaches for his "mulato" condition) but rather the appropriation of the thought and feelings of a social stratum that the writer achieves, no matter their education level. It is more productive to question, in the same text, the literary and linguistic operations. Regarding the latter, it is helpful to observe that the passage of a writer from the learned to the oral necessarily implies the perception of phonetic, syntactic, and lexical distance in which the regional dialect is found in relation to the learned norm, which can result in their application of a systematic spirit that in general is absent in the speaker immersed in their own dialect. When the rural speaker adopts a creative literary attitude, they tend to "speak well," that is, to assume the superior class's linguistic judgments: the anonymous poetry that Acuña de Figueroa compiles in his *Diario histórico*[23] is apparently written following this tendency. This would point to a producer from the popular stratum, as is also found in the ample passionately bellicose or patriotic revolutionary literature of the nineteenth century in Latin America. Its linguistic imperfections are not born from a stylistic choice but rather from the clumsiness in the use of learned norms. In contrast, the gauchesque poet takes the opposite path, going toward the dialectical speech and at times (like the case of Estanislao del Campo) subjecting it to a normative regime that is not typical of the speaker. The greater or lesser imposition of a normative regime on dialect, in order to transfigure it into literary language, is a good indication of the greater or lesser journey that the poet makes from their own language to one that is presumably rural. This is rather rare in the first generation of gauchesque literature and in the minor writers, toned down in Ascasubi, and in José Hernández conquers its best dimension because it eludes the obsession with a specific dialect and grants him the mobility inherent in a speech that continues to respond centrally to the linguistic current of the Spanish language.

Whatever the solution that the diverse poets give it, we are in the presence of a literary language and not a dialectal transposition. This language is a central part of the literary project and thus can be compared with that which the modernista poets adopt in relation to the learned speech of Latin American cities of the nineteenth century. As different as they might be, to the point of being clear opposites, both literary operations respond to the necessary construction of a specific linguistic environment (above all lexical, but also syntactic) to translate an artistic message. This reveals the foundational literary idea that the invention of gauchesque literature upholds and that distinguishes it from the unique forms of folkloric poetry. It corresponds to another aspect of literary density: the will of artistic composition, that demands the re-elaboration of language for these ends and then anchors the message in the ideological circumstances of the moment. Vigorously inserting language within history, the literary work reveals a modification of the rural social group that is incorporating itself into the social process in progress. The literary organization that it is able to establish serves as the self-awareness of its situation as a class because it is possible to define itself through that literature and open the path toward the acquisition of class consciousness.

The two cited examples do not exhaust the models of bordering literary stratifications and have been brought together only to show the appearance at both extremes of this literary density, of parallel and autonomous formations to those that we judge as furthest removed from each other. Another model would be represented by cases in which an intellectual group takes over the representation of another social stratum, considering (first argument) that it apparently lacks an artistic voice and an expressive capacity or that (second argument) even though it has these conditions, it lacks the instruments with which to project them into the heart of the dominant classes. It is an example of intermediation where we attend a masking of the deeper motives of artistic behavior that operate thus, which has been rather characteristic of the middle classes of society.

In this assumption, it is possible to infer a certain lack of transparency for the gaze that does not allow one to see into the lower stratum or, more precisely, it does not allow for the acceptance and appraisal of its unique and constant literary production, given that this is not found to be lacking in any sector of society. This lack of transparency translates in the conception of its traditional products as antiquated forms that tolerate the "transference," it is worth mentioning, a perfection to be incorporated into other cultural sectors, concretely that of the group or movement that lays out this task. Such an operation generates an internally contradictory art that has been rather frequent in those social groups that are looking to achieve social mobility within the global structure of society.

This has been the basic characteristic of "indigenista" and "negrista" movements in twentieth-century Latin American literature. These movements emerge in the 1920s and start as a project of social and economic recognition of these large, neglected sectors, plunged at times in the greatest neglect, for which they use subjects, linguistic elements, and literary forms that they understand are unique to them. But they "transfer" them within a strongly rationalized literature, whose internal characteristics point to a world view of another social class—the provincial middle class—which, in this instance, belongs to the lower part of the social pyramid. I have studied elsewhere the ambiguity of indigenism's literary products that reveal the internal contradictions between this inner artistic structure and the themes referring to indigenous people, bringing in the concept elaborated by the interstitial mestizo sectors of society, allied with the provincial lower middle class.[24] From Sabogal's art, and later that of Guayasamín, to López Albújar's or Jorge Icaza's novels,[25] we experience a production that installs itself in the lower part of the learned and urban sector, even though not in a parallel and independent way, but wildly confronted, in full conflict with the superior learned orientation whose relentless prosecution brings about and which it is able to replace with its own artistic propositions. For that, it begins to apply for the first time a coherent mode in Latin America, verbal terrorism.

That this is not the only form of opposing learned, Hispanicized, and artistic literature that the "colonidas"[26] had already begun to undermine is shown with Martín Adán's novel, *The Cardboard House*, which is at the margin of the central operation of "indigenismo": to assume the problems of the lower classes but not their art, even though their products are disproportionately idealized. This shows the eventuality of an urban literature that in the first third of the twentieth century promotes the aesthetic values of the middle classes as the first Ultraistas did in other contexts. But indigenista literature, in spite of its themes and declared objectives, does not border the folkloric stratum but rather the superior urban literature, visibly challenging it. If folkloric inventions are incorporated into it, it is because they are corroborating elements of this literature's presumed authenticity, when they do not fulfill the function of mere touches of local color, but they do not belong to the aesthetic concept that animates the "indigenista" production, which one more time brings us to the idea that the study of these problems does not restrict itself to a "content based" analysis but rather that it widens with the study of the plurality of artistic forms employed.

8

The Literary System of Gauchesque Poetry

The gaucho is one thing and so-called gauchesque literature is a different thing. This is a distinction that no matter how obvious it seems one still has to make. The relationship that for so long critics established between the two was confusing enough that before we can begin studying the artistic aspect of *gauchesque literature* we are forced to introduce a coarse division and propose that we dispense with the first term (gaucho) and focus on the second one (literature).

Since Leopoldo Lugones vindicated the genre at the beginning of the twentieth century, analyses of gauchesque literature begin, inevitably, with a chapter on the gaucho: his ethnic origin; the etymology of the name, history, religion, and philosophy; his customs, especially his use of written language as it can be perceived in songs; and "payadas," very few of which have survived and not enough to support the myths created around them. A good deal of these critics—focusing on accuracy of representation and employing positivistic criteria—tried to discover the degree of authenticity of the portrait of the gaucho given by diverse writers, treating literary texts as if they were documents or polished mirrors. A work like Martínez Estrada's *Muerte y transfiguración de Martín Fierro*[1] is exceptional because it finishes off and subverts this tendency. However, it does not diminish the need to avoid that route and forces us to look for a different entrance to this literature. Too much attention was paid to the adjective "gauchesque" and very little to the noun "literature," reasserting the ironic portrait of the (non-literary) critic as a policeman that Jakobson once painted: "Hoping to detain someone, they would acquire possession, randomly, of anything they would find in the room, even the people passing through the side streets."[2]

Gauchos obviously deserve posthumous attention from the inhabitants of the River Plate region (without any rhetoric, if possible) and justify undertaking well-documented historical research.[3] But the literature that has used the gaucho as a character and, mainly, as symbol carrying a message, is also deserving of research on its verbal characteristics and ideological structure without worrying about problems of verisimilitude that have preoccupied critics for so long. These studies reflect not only a mechanicist view of the creative process but, frequently, a lazy naiveté. To dispense with a historic or sociological chapter about the gaucho does not mean to undervalue him but to focus on the literary field, following the practical advice given by Borges: "To derive gauchesque literature from its subject matter, the gaucho, is a confusion that disfigures the obvious truth."[4]

In the same text, Borges argues that the type of person described in gauchesque poetry, with similar costumes and beliefs, can be found in other regions of the world that have not produced a literature around them like the "gauchesque": "Country life is typical of many regions in America, from Montana and Oregon to Chile, but those lands have energetically restrained themselves from creating a *Martín Fierro*. Hardened cattlemen and exile are then not enough." Carlos Alberto Leunmann agrees with the assessment. In one of his book chapters (bearing the long title "Outside of Argentina and Uruguay There Was No Equivalent to Gauchesque Literature"[5]), he establishes a comparison between the Southern Cone region and the plains zone of Venezuela:

> What my title proclaims becomes even more important when we realize that peasants in Venezuela were more rebellious and had more freedom than the gauchos in the great plains, also called pampas. They served admirably in the wars against Spanish domination and tamed wild horses (they call them *cerreros* over there) and they knew how to remain standing if the animal turned on its side. They were singers and at their celebrations they had poetry competitions very similar to the gauchos' payadas. However, in Venezuela there was never an attempt to create a national literature based on the systematic imitation of the old *llaneros*' language and style.

The origins of the gauchesque literature, therefore, should not be sought in the topics treated, and even less in the characters employed, but in the concrete literary operations of the authors that produced this literature.

This means abandoning the illusion that verisimilitude subtly creates (the idea that we are encountering spontaneous creations of folk singers) and ask ourselves who wrote these poems, why and for whom, and their reasons for doing so. In other words, we have to face this group of texts (focusing not on the adjective but the noun) as a "literature."

The Author's Function

It is worth repeating, even if well known, what Lauro Ayestarán and Jorge Luis Borges[6] have already said about the first authors of gauchesque literature: the immense majority of them were not gauchos[7] but city dwellers, with varying educational levels, though they could never be confused with the typical gauchos of the pampas. They lived in towns and cities alongside the River Plate from Independence (1810) to the early twentieth century and they wrote their poetic works paying close attention to the historical events of their time.

A legend has been created around Bartolomé Hidalgo's job as a barber (forgetting that he was director of the Casa de la Comedia in Montevideo and had positions in the Treasury Department) and Ascasubi's job as baker (but he was a rich provider to the Defense Government's army during the Great War). Both of them, as well as the other figures of the movement, were writers, poets, or simply verse writers, depending on the case, who were conscious of their social role as writers alongside the jobs they did to earn a living. Obviously, they became authors within the limitations that societies in the River Plate area presented for intellectual professionalization. However, they rose above the regular author category of their time as they possessed a systematic and coherent point of view not unlike that of the bourgeois writers in the Buenos Aires Literary Salon.[8] They were no less writers than their cultured counterparts just because they chose to devote themselves to gauchesque literature. If they were occasionally despised, and if critics in the nineteenth century ignored them or, rather, sympathetically placed them in a category isolated from literature properly speaking,[9] from our perspective they became part of the early national literatures of the River Plate region with a situation similar to that of other writers. One could even dispute the horizontal division that is still commonly made between the major literary currents of the nineteenth century and the inferior space assigned to writers of gauchesque literature and instead think of vertical divisions that would place each gauchesque author as belonging to different literary tendencies in that period: Hidalgo would be a Neoclassicist,[10] Ascasubi a member of the first Romantic period, Hernández an author within the mature Realist mode.

The function of a writer, the themes they must choose for their works, the ideology they must follow, and the public they will address were topics publicly studied and debated by the writers of the revolutionary period and even more coherently by the Romantics in the Literary Salon (1837). It is enough to follow Alberdi's reflections justifying his contributions to the magazine *La Moda* or review the polemics between Neoclassicists and Romantics in Santiago de Chile or Montevideo about literary styles to see how lucidly conscious they were as an intellectual group of those important topics. Authors of gauchesque literature had the same reflections except their options were much clearer and absolute. They did not justify them intellectually as abundantly as cultured writers did, but they applied them with precision, sometimes risking more, intellectually, than their lettered colleagues.

All the gauchesque writers emphasized the humble quality of their works ("humble production" is Hernández's slogan) recognizing beforehand that they were not trying to compete with serious or highbrow literature. When they talk about other poets, it is always about other gauchesque authors with whom they can compete ("I have seen many singers / whose fame was well won"[11]) but they do not mention cultured writers whose place they recognize as being higher in the literary Parnassus of the period. That a century later that valorization is turned upside down is another matter altogether. In that moment the gauchesque poets are located at the lowest level of literary production because they are addressing a practically illiterate public for whom the circle of arts and letters is foreign, employing this public's modes of expression and talking about their problems.[12] They are proud of their large number of readers and they are always mentioning the number of copies they have sold, but they do not extrapolate this fact to the area of literary quality—not even someone like Estanislao Del Campo, who came from a social level higher than his predecessors in the genre.

The fact that they accepted their lower status does not change their role as writers and the functions they had to fulfill. At the dawn of the new nations, torn away from the colonial viceroyalty in the River Plate region, the members of the small but skilled team of intellectuals faced problems characteristic of their function as writers. How to produce? Which genres and artistic styles to use? Which means to use to reach their readers or listeners? To which social group were they aiming their artistic or intellectual creations? All these points were considered and, for each one of them, they proposed multiple solutions, trying to discover their effectiveness. From poems written on public squares' ornaments, meant to exalt the fatherland, to speeches in theaters, not to mention traditional venues (publishing in loose-leaf sheets of paper, newspapers, or books), there was no media they did not try nor artistic formula they did not use, always modifying them for their public and according to the medium employed.[13]

A characteristic feature of this period is trying out different tendencies, traversing diverse paths. This explains abrupt modifications (with respect to previous products), or the coexistence of diverging models, due to an author attempting different solutions. In fact, all writers were searching for them. Some were copying the intellectual function of European models but discovered these models were useless for their time because, though cultured writers dreamed about it, only in the future could a literary system—like the one in France—be constructed. Other authors discovered the advantages of women's magazines as a tool to reach a potentially new public or the usefulness of reading rooms for delivering talks, and some authors even thought of singing poetry in those rooms or outdoors, accompanied by a piano or a guitar, respectively.

Searching and choosing an option was the norm. Writers urgently plunged into literary options, as they were plunging into other aspects of life, from politics to economics or military activities. They would try something to see if it was successful; if they failed, they would search again. Some options were richer and more gratifying than others.

The Creation of a Public

The reading public was the fundamental and basic option that gauchesque writers chose, the one that would define their aesthetics and politics (but much less systematically, their ideology), and that allows us to group them as a large movement. They chose to address a specific public adapting the diverse aspects of the literary message to them. Curiously, the choice of a public remained undetected, obscured by their chosen topic and only later was it slowly acknowledged as the basis of the movement, especially because initially the rigid juxtaposition of the elements composing the message obscured the impact of their choice of a public, which ruled all the other choices.

If we apply Jakobson's model,[14] his three functions (the ostensible addresser of the message, the context or referent about which the text is talking and singing, and the addressee or receiver of the product) are obviously performed in Hidalgo's poetry by the same gaucho. What is more, as if to internally echo this absorption of all the functions by the same representative, the work is built on a dialogue system that apparently makes communication an autonomous and self-regulating process taking place between gauchos, without ever making evident, as happens in the "cielitos" and similar compositions, that the addresser, supposedly a gaucho, is talking to a receiver outside the text who is also another gaucho.

When José Hernández in his preface to *The Return of Martín Fierro* (1879) says that he hopes gauchos read his poetry as "nothing more than a natural continuation of their lives," he is lucidly realizing that choosing a public conditions the other elements that make up the poetic language (characters, situations, speech, literary forms, ostensible addresser, etc.). In other words, he was hoping that not even the gauchos would realize they were reading but that they would believe that they were still leading their normal lives, just as happens with innocent addressees when they are unable to detect the texture of a message (be they images, words, or sounds) and can only see the actions or the beings represented. The illusion of reality reaches here its maximum artificiality because it is trying to make "literature" invisible to the chosen public. For that reason, as we will see, a gaucho almost always communicates this literary text, an addresser who is also talking about gaucho to other gauchos. In this way the desired reader is not aware that he is encountering literature, the literature produced also does not allow anyone to see that it has been constructed beforehand with a previously selected addressee in mind. In the preface to *The Return of Martín Fierro*, José Hernández explains:

> A book destined to awaken intelligence and love of reading in an almost primitive population, to be a profitable distraction, after exhausting tasks, for thousands of people who have never read, must adapt itself strictly to the uses and customs of those readers and present their ideas and interpret their feelings in their own language, in their own typical expressions, in their own general form, even though it may be incorrect; it must include their most important images, with their most characteristic idiosyncrasies, so that they identify with the book in such an intimate and close manner that reading it becomes nothing more than a continuation of their own natural existence.

We have to begin with the fact that it was a different kind of public. Authors identified with it to a greater (Hidalgo) or lesser (Del Campo) degree, but it was essentially different from them. It came from a social group to which writers do not belong. They were usually above that level. It was composed of gauchos who were soldiers in the army that fought for independence or disarmed gauchos who were wandering around the capital's suburbs; the members of the montoneras who participated in the civil wars that followed independence or simply the peasants who suffered with the liberal economic project, scattered around the countryside, in towns, in the outskirts of the city. Also, within it one could find cultured readers and city folks, discovering in their readings the gaucho side of them or, thanks to the Estanislao Del Campo's ingenious literary techniques, the ways in which they differed from the gauchos.

That public reflected a majority of the population in the River Plate region. They had rural origins, they grew up with the cultural production of the traditional and illiterate national sector, and they were scattered over cities and the countryside. A group that for a century experienced the most violent and, for them, incomprehensible unrest, they were torn away from their traditional habits to be incorporated into a dynamic, urgent present history.

But in addition, that public did not exist as such because, before gauchesque poetry existed, they were nothing but a mass of men foreign to the literary market, at least the way it was traditionally configured. The writers who addressed that market did not simply chose another option among many paths of potential listeners, but strictly speaking they had to invent a public, they had to create something where there was nothing. Thus, gauchesque literature began to create a public for their poetry, focusing on a social sector that remained tied to literary styles belonging to the rural traditions and that became a group of addressees that allowed them to develop their movement. Out of that mass they extracted a public, with the amazing result that it would become the largest literary public in the nineteenth century, much larger than the one cultured sectors of the same period obtained.

Because gauchesque literature develops over more than a century, when some truly cataclysmic social events take place, one cannot talk about the existence of a single and homogeneous public, unchangeable throughout the years. Each one of the gauchesque authors practically faced a different public or, at least, different circumstances of the same rural public: there is an enormous distance between the gauchos in the army that Hidalgo was trying to reach with his "cielitos" and the suburban, nostalgic, and idealistic public from the outskirts that Alonso y Trelles was addressing in *Paja brava* (1915). Throughout this journey they acquire, for the first time, an educated and urban public: Del Campo achieves this feat without losing his illiterate public. At the end of this period, the public will become national without changing its popular characteristics. That explains why pro-Perón intellectuals were able to use it during the 1940s and 1950s.

To address an invented public during the independence period required a series of skillful intellectual techniques with which authors had very little previous experience: it is possible to derive the originality of these texts from the originality of the enterprise of creating a public. Said in other words, for the cultured authors, writing *Triunfo de Ituzaingó* (Juan Cruz Valera), *La cautiva* (Esteban Echeverría), *Fragmento preliminar al estudio del derecho* (Juan Bautista Alberdi) meant expressing oneself within the same cultural group, hoping that it would grow larger; it was a way of talking to "others" as long as they were self-images. On the other hand, the invention of a public that gauchesque writers after Hidalgo achieve reveals a much more daring operation that also changes the concept of a writer. The writer becomes a man who produces cultural objects for consumption by a different group, as Hernández used to point out, to whose taste, expressions, and ideas he will have to adapt his literary product. He will become the spiritual provider of a coherent social group (which does not mean that he is obligated to serve them) and that helps establish the writer. The invention of a public results in the invention of the writer.

The Ideological Framework

As we mentioned before, choosing a specific public means choosing certain characters, themes, language, literary forms, poetic patterns, and so on. At the same time, the choice is informed by a previous intellectual project or ideology, which acts as its original cause. In very few literary movements is the priority of the ideological framework for literary production as visible. It makes Medvedev's dictum true: "Literary theory is one branch of the vast science of ideologies."[15]

The initial ideological framework, which emerges during Hidalgo's period and prepares the ground for gauchesque literature, does not remain the same throughout the years; in each one of the writers that comes after Hidalgo we will find a different ideologeme at work. This could seem contradictory because all of them are choosing the same public. But perhaps the contradiction is only apparent. Choosing a public is a move done as literary praxis and has several unavoidable artistic consequences, which, however, do not come from a coherent philosophy or defend a worldview. Addressing a specific public has been a frequent decision in what one could call canonical literary periods, without implying that there was a philosophy focusing on serving the desired public, interpreting it and in favor of its historical development. On the contrary, these decisions were frequently a reaction against the directions taken by the hegemonic groups, those in possession of the high culture of a time period and who manipulated the arts and letters addressed at the dominated sectors. The second period of gauchesque literature, corresponding to Rosas's regime, saw a prolific production coming equitably from the two quarreling sides. Not only were Pedro de Angelis and Florencio Valera intellectually directing opposite parties, employing for it their newspapers in Buenos Aires and Montevideo, respectively, but they also made sure that their ideological positions reached the illiterate public in the form of lively examples. Florencio Valera commissioned Ascasubi's poem "Media caña del campo para los libres" and "paid for it to be printed in great numbers to send as a gift to the Argentine Liberation Army" as the poet explains in the section of his *Paulino Lucero* where he collected it. Studying the "Unitarian" and "Federalist" productions of that period, Ricardo Rojas concludes that "they are alike in their vocabulary, their syntax, their passion, their poetic pattern and even the savage inks that colored their fantasy."[16]

The gauchesque literary production during the Rosas regime is a good example of the dissonance that can occur between choosing a popular public and ideology. Above all, it helps corroborate that writers found themselves in a dual position, between the freedom to respond to real and urgent demands from the public they were addressing (Hidalgo is an almost candid example) and serving a different social group (to which the authors belonged or another superior to themselves that was renting their talent) whose ideology they were in charge of translating, employing persuasive literary forms, for the dominated or inferior sector. In this last case, its function was not different from the tragic poets who served the Eupatridae of Athenian society during Pericles's century, as Arnold Hauser has shown.

In any case, it was ideology that propelled the idea of choosing a public to address (or inventing it, as we said before). The representational capacity that characterizes the work of art acquires additional attention in these cases because the message being transmitted is of utmost importance. The priority became literature's communicative function and its capacity to convey an idea, or sometimes simply a slogan, effectively. This desire to communicate creates a manner of working that will produce several combinations. There are several social levels juxtaposed, several different circuits—

each with its own idiosyncrasies—for the distribution of the literary product, and finally an author who is establishing correlations among different levels and circuits, transmitting a message that combines both levels.

On this aspect all gauchesque authors are in agreement. They were all clearly aware that they were at the center of a curious seesaw on whose sides there were two social sectors that were not only different but also opposed, without any communication between them, and only connected through gauchesque poetry. All the authors knew that they were bringing information to a socially inferior group that was in need of it, although a few also realized that they were transmitting pathetic messages to the superior group that was disconnected from the nation's reality, in spite of the small population, and they were especially ignorant about the gaucho.[17] One can follow both situations in their prefaces. Hilario Ascasubi, much more than the humorous Estanislao del Campo, represented the typical gauchesque poet at the service of a cultured elite (an exact replica of Luis Pérez), when he belatedly collects in Paris in 1872 the compositions for his *Paulino Lucero*, which had been published between 1839 and 1851 in newspapers, brochures, and loose-leaf papers. Ascasubi writes: "With the intention of educating the population of the countryside about the grave social issues being debated on both shores of the River Plate, I have employed in my writings their own language and their idiomatic expressions to get their attention, so it would be easier to spread those principles among them."

This was not different from Valentín Alsina's astute observation in 1848 about how it was eventually used: "As this genre has been accepted so well among the uneducated classes in our societies, it could become a vehicle that an astute administration could use to teach the masses and transmit ideas and events that otherwise they do not know or care about."[18] Or the parallel analysis Juan María Gutiérrez made: "The genre we are studying was given a purpose and employed in a praiseworthy manner. It was used to convert the souls of the people in our country to the dogmas of our revolution, it inculcated in them the gentle passions without which there is no independence nor fatherland."[19]

As for José Hernández, one can review the prefaces to *The Gaucho Martín Fierro* and *The Return of Martín Fierro*: the latter, written after the work was unanimously accepted among the rural population, explains the characteristics that make this poem perfect for people from that social sector to read; the former follows a logic that Arturo Lussich will imitate in his prefaces. Hernández addresses the traditional educated public, located in the city, ignorant of who the gauchos are, and asks them to accept the image of those unknown figures he is describing because it is faithful to reality. It would not have made sense to tell the gauchos that he was trying to "make a portrait, as faithfully as I could, and including all the typical characteristics or skills, of that original type from our pampas, little known because it is difficult to study him, often misunderstood and, as civilization spreads, he has almost completely disappeared."

In any case, it is obvious that the reading public has been chosen with a previous ideological motive in mind and it is not necessarily an ideology that represents the social or cultural demands of the public these poets are addressing. The ideological motivation appears during the independence period when the group leading the fight requires support from the lower gaucho classes, and, through Hidalgo, this group is integrated into the ideology of the revolutionary process. At that moment it was possible to combine diverse artistic proposals with different intellectual levels in a balanced manner. Hidalgo takes the norms he inherits from Neoclassicism and that correspond to the heroic period when the bourgeoisie fights against the aristocracy *in the name of all people* and combines them with ideas from early pre-Romantic works that were trying to capture local color, typical characters from costumbrismo texts, local slang, and contact with concrete nature.

Both tendencies represent a curious and never repeated balance between the ideological background that serves as the genesis of the literary project and the act of adapting it for a public who fulfills it. This means having to translate their circumstances, tastes, and expressive system, a balance that, at the textual level of literature, combines discordant elements that have an effect on the conscience of a social class in a specific time period and, for a moment, harmonizes them. The conflict the class is experiencing becomes evident in the literature addressed at them.

Lauro Ayesterán utters an efficient definition of this poetry that allows us to spy those discordant elements that come together in class consciousness and the literary text: "First of all, there is a poetic verb conjugated in the present tense."[20] The ideological message that a writer is seeking to transmit belongs to the historical present and to its most visible and urgent demands because it explains the armed struggle against Spaniards and Portuguese and justifies insurrection against recognized powers in the name of a set of ideas invented by the triumphant European bourgeoisie and imitated by the River Plate bourgeoisie. That is the conjugation of the verb in the present tense. But to the gaucho public, this message would be transmitted using an artistic structure from the past, creating thus the basis for a hybrid product (gauchesque poetry) that delivers the revolutionary message of the time using décimas, sestinas, and octosyllabic redondillas.

As I have tried to clarify in other texts,[21] to achieve its ideological purpose (the two steps forward that Latin American society is taking at the beginning of the nineteenth century), the artist must take a step backward artistically as he discards lines longer than eight syllables and the metaphoric repertoire and rhetoric of neoclassicism, which was the artistic horizon of the most cultured and advanced class of the time, the bourgeoisie, to return to the (epigonal) conservation of artistic forms from previous centuries in history, which were still valid for the rural sector of River Plate society. This double movement is illustrated by the work of Bartolomé Hidalgo: his first compositions, his "marchas" and "unipersonales" belong in style to Neoclassicism and it is not by chance that they emerge during the initial stages of the revolutionary process. However, when the battle is intense or dangerous, or when they are living in defeat, Hidalgo's poetry returns to traditional forms.

This contradictory situation, which combines an ideology from the present and an aesthetic from the past (but will generate, however, a new aesthetic and a new ideology, as the previous ones are sublimated when linked to one another) not only translates the intellectual operation of a writer moving from his educational level and social class to those of his public, but it also reflects the situation of the public he is addressing. That public comes from the rural social sector, it grew up with traditional literary forms in that tattered cultural margin of Latin American lands, but it has been violently incorporated into the present history, where it has received a protagonist role. Literature had to offer an explanation to a vast sector of society that was needed to defeat the Spanish army and that included gauchos but also black slaves and indigenous people.

This ideological motivation only applies to the first period of gauchesque literature, the one that revolves around the figure of Hidalgo. That will change with Pérez, Ascasubi, and Del Campo, who already belong to the Romantic period of factions and Romantic ideas and literary forms. The writer begins to "manipulate" his public and for the same reason he is capable of various adaptations that allow him to address different types of public, seducing them. Bernardo Berro was not wrong when, from his rigid Neoclassic point of view, he defined the Romantic writer for their new capacity to persuade without proving anything: "One who seeks to hurt imagination, who is only trying to present to our spirit shapes that scare it, confuse it, enrapture it, does not try to find out the truth, nor convince our understanding, but to move, to flatter our spirit, surrounding it with a splendid atmosphere, which introduces in the mind a sort of persuasion, capturing our will as if by magic."[22] The conquest of the pampas that will come later, the enclosing of fields with wire fences, the imposition of rural codes, laws against vagrants and crooks, and the energy created by an export economy oriented toward the European markets, all of these are events contemporaneous with the third period of gauchesque literature. It is in this period that we encounter Lussich and José Hernández, with which gauchesque poetry ceases to be political and becomes social. It employs an ideology of protest first, during its virile Realist moment, and later an elegiac and nostalgic ideology when gauchos begin to accept defeat and lament their loss.

Art or Document

Literary themes exist in close relationship with their own problematic history. They carry it with them and are traversed by it. They are themselves and, at the same time, they are the debate that took place before their time. One cannot summarize "gauchesque poetry" without restating again the question of its artistic value, which makes visible how recent and precarious its integration into the world of high culture is.

When one studies Leopoldo Lugones's 1913 lectures delivered from the stage of the Odeón Theater about *Martín Fierro*, which he later re-elaborated for his book *El payador* (1916), one's expected disagreements with his arguments and his main thesis are sometimes put aside out of admiration of the enormous intellectual task he is accomplishing. As in those intellectual projects, the "amautas," that Inca Garcilaso mentions, which were capable of transforming an entire society (even resorting to the same ingenious and magical steps), one can see Lugones founding the "noble lineage" of the Argentine race, its Hellenic antiquity, its greatness. These secure a future for the fatherland and allow him to face with disdain the immigration avalanche that had modified the ethnic composition of the nation. That historic crossroads ruled by a growing "mesocracy" not only was essential to majestically highlight the nation and oppose the rootless mass society that had modified the country's blood, but they also had to concede something to the lower classes, which were climbing the social pyramid by taking advantage of the economic development in the River

Plate region and were not able to feel close to the elitist culture that from Echeverría to Sarmiento and from Mitre to Lugones himself had dominated the nineteenth century, strengthening a highly hierarchized high literature.

Facing the oligarchical audience, headed by the president of the Republic, Rogue Sáenz Peña, and his cabinet ministers, the poet was clearly aware that he was achieving a cultural translation that would result in a transformation of the dominant ideas. Bidding farewell on the last day [of lectures], he told them: "I congratulate myself because I have been the agent of an intimate national communication between the poetry of the people and the cultured mind of the high class. That is how the spirit of the fatherland is formed." He was even was able to add with immoderate metaphoric repetition, "My word was the pollinating bee that took the message from the wild flower to the noble rose of the garden."[23] Undeniably, he had taken the best artistic product of that vast and confused movement challenging the nineteenth-century liberal project and whose trenches were among the battered rural populations (in spite of the coincidences on multiple topics that one could find between Sarmiento and Hernández) and transferred it to the urban oligarchy under the appearance of a milestone upon which they would found their right to guide the nation, displaying their commitment to preserve traditional virtues of the defeated rural population.

They had thus designed an important pact with the national society. The high class would accept the unrefined popular poetry and its worldview, they would make it their own, and in exchange the lower class (the gauchos, who according to Lugones were the founders of the national spirit) would recognize that they needed educated people to lead them. In that pact half of the population was excluded, they belonged to the first or the second generation of immigrants and they were already owners of the capital of the republic. About them, Lugones said in the preface to his book, "The riff-raff from overseas were marking noise in the halls!" The immigrants' shyness, their scarce and underdeveloped traditional culture, the abruptness with which the doors were closed to them stopped them from being creative. They were incapable of building the great national myths to which they were destined, and once they realized they were participating in the greatness of the nation, they limited themselves—and not even Lugones could foresee this—to accept the nationalist myth created by the poet, to accept the social pact underlying it, and to feel connected to any of the two sides signing the pact. They, the dark immigrants, their children and grandchildren, would accept the *Martín Fierro*. Beautifully bound in leather it would become their book, the new commandment tablets. Their acceptance was done to prove to the nationalist society, withdrawn and hostile, which, swamped by the immigration wave wanted to keep them in the hall, that those despised foreigners were not coming to change anything, only to validate the current situation and continue it. This is the genesis of what Darcy Ribeiro has called "ideological incongruence" that for him "is a sure sign that an ethnic-national process of maturing (for transplanted populations) is still incomplete."[24]

When Lugones compares *Martín Fierro*, a Realist poem of the second half of the nineteenth century, to the epic (starting one of the most useless debates about genres known, between those who supported the epic and those defending the category of the novel),[25] when he made its characters examples of the national virtues, erasing individual characteristics, depersonalizing them, understanding them symbolically, and when he reads it as if it were the sacred scripture because he saw in it *in nuce* the future of the nation and synthesized its dogma using the principles of justice and freedom, he started at the same time all the confusion and contradictions that would characterize the interpretation of this poem during the twentieth century. Before Lugones, the book had received scant attention by critics and the cultured public; after Lugones, they felt inhibited by the sacred qualities the poet ascribed to it. Every time, the aesthetic judgment was swallowed by other judgments (ethical, political, social). The situation of *Martín Fierro* is the same faced by the rest of gauchesque literature, because if Lugones once despised it only to praise a product he wished had been anonymous, later critics from Ricado Rojas and Martiniano Leguizamón to Lauro Ayestarán and Jorge Luis Borges, including Ezequiel Martínez Estrada and Vicente Rossi, restored in many ways the values that existed before José Hernández. However, the only thing they achieved was extending the original sin that Lugones detected to the entire movement, going back to its origins.

Because it was a literary production that did not have new followers in the twentieth century and therefore was not assimilated by any of the acceptable contemporaneous poetic aesthetics, "gauchesque" literature remains suspended, placed within a parenthesis, as a curious and sympathetic anomaly in the history of Latin American literature. We cannot consider it extinguished as it remains surprisingly popular among the vast populations in the countryside and the city, who keep it in the most intimate of places, their memory. But we cannot consider it "alive" either because those literary texts that can be associated with it have an imitative character that can be taken as a sign that modern society is incapable of developing this type of poetry further. The few who still believe in it must place their hopes in the future, turning it into a utopian solution, linked to utopian political or social beliefs. It is not a completely irrational position, when one remembers that one of the central topics of the gauchesque genre is injustice.

The first attempts at purely artistic appreciation, disconnected from political, social, or national meanings, came from Spaniards: Marcelino Menéndez Pelayo and Miguel de Unamuno said to a more attentive public what Juan María Gutiérrez had announced, and Pedro Henríquez Ureña summarized in a few words about Bartolomé Hidalgo that "his modest effort was, probably, the most revolutionary of them all."[26] All of these judgments are relative. They are born out of a reaction to the negative judgment of cultured poetry of the period. They use the latter as the opposite pole of the gauchesque poetry experience, making the gauchesque look more imaginative, more original. Surreptitiously, they are contrasting aesthetic positions but not closely examining the fluctuating artistic levels of gauchesque poems. What the critics were approving of was an aesthetic orientation that was not going to have descendants because modernismo severely suppressed it (except in Martí's lyric work) and was practically forgotten during the twentieth century in spite of scattered revivals (now with an urban character) in Ultraism and other similar movements. In the case of the gauchesque poets there is an overlapping and confusion among different levels: the principles of a school or style, the rhetoric specific to the movement, the succession of outdated aesthetic ideas, and lastly, individual creation. Virtues of their work belong to one or the other level, but not even the author is able to determine exactly their origin. For Hernández, his peculiarity was "singing an opinion," something that does not distinguish him from Lussich, but one cannot confuse his original artistic invention with the latter. When trying to determine the artistic value, beyond reading the content of these materials, we have to carefully review those levels.

The Rural Dialect of the River Plate Region

After the first general options (choosing a public to address, the decision to transmit an ideological message) come the secondary ones, the ones that correspond to the operations destined to produce the poetic text. Despite the fact that the first (or intellectual) ones determine the second (or artistic) ones, this does not prevent their partial autonomy nor their specificity. The second ones constitute the "ars poetica" of the gauchesque genre.

In very few occasions (in private letters, in the prefaces they use to apologize) gauchesque authors talk about their art. The norm was to focus exclusively, even submissively, on the characters and topics they were using, highlighting that they were mere reflections of real beings and situations or underlining the importance and social urgency of the topic as an excuse for the humble artistic quality of their works. That is why reconstructing the "ars poetica" of the gauchesque genre must be done with the poem as a starting place, with very little help from the author's opinions, even those who, like José Hernández, explicitly talked about these topics.

There is a very important first option: the language that this poetry employs. The writer abandons a cultivated language that was characteristic of the literature at the time and possesses a rigor and exclusivity unthinkable today. Their cultivated language, in spite of the exhortations to literary autonomy within the old colonies, was at that moment simply a copy of the literary writing styles predominating in Spain. The author replaces that language with a spoken language, which they incorporate into their creation in a free non-systematic way. This spoken language was imitating the rural dialect of the River Plate region, which has often been called the "language of the gauchos" (but without any arguments to prove it). Diverse authors, energetically interested in being faithful to reality, emphasized their efforts to imitate the spoken rural language, but it was also an excuse for daring to be unorthodox: Arturo Lussich, in his letter to José Hernández at the beginning of *Los tres gauchos orientales*, talks about "the special style that our countryfolk use" and in the preface to *El matrero Luciano Santos* restates his use of "the particular style used by our peasants." In his famous explanatory note to José Zoilo Miguens that serves as preface to *The Gaucho Martín Fierro*, Hernández is very clear: "I was striving to imitate that style full of metaphors gauchos use without realizing it or recognizing its value."

The importance of this option that we can describe as "revolutionary" can be measured if we remember Angel Rosenblat's statement: "Political independence did not mean cultural or linguistic independence."[27] In gauchesque poetry one finds a coherent effort, no matter how humble, to accompany political independence with a parallel linguistic independence, much earlier than the reforms attempted by Sarmiento or Bello. It is a decisive option. The gauchesque poetry is founded on it.

Critics have tried to define gauchesque poetry based on its content (gaucho-related topics), classifying them into two groups: one using a local dialect and the other using a cultured language. Among the latter we find most frequently mentioned Esteban Echeverría, Alejandro Magariños Cervantes, and Rafael Obligado.[28] Besides the fact that classifying literary works based on themes does not help define them, works with the countryside as a topic from those poets fits neatly into the different artistic stages of River Plate culture. There is no aesthetic difference between the compositions about the countryside and those dealing with urban topics. In addition, all of their works are radically different from the production of Hidalgo, L. Pérez, Ascasubi, Del Campo, Lussich, Hernández, and so on.

Martínez Estrada observed that "in its environment, scenes, actions, *La cautiva* is a poem as rural as any other, but its language (both in aesthetic and lexicological terms) opens a foreign abyss to the reader,"[29] adding that "in terms of national matter, rural, of that period, *La cautiva*, is not inferior to any gauchesque poem, not even *Martín Fierro*." With his usual courtesy, José Hernández recognized the legitimacy of cultured poetry about national and even folkloric topics as they were combining the independence and the romantic spirits. But he stressed clearly the difference between both fields: "There are among us poets with very refined and correct style saturated with the gauchesque spirit. We are not lacking in their kind of work, because it is a legitimate and spontaneous production of our Country and, to be honest, it is not exclusively present in the elegant world of high literature."[30]

What separates both groups is language that, artistically speaking, is a more important factor when classifying than topics. If one paid attention to these topics instead of artistic forms, especially poetic devices, one would conclude that there is an enormous mass of unrelated literary products to which one can assign the label "National–Rural." What makes possible grouping together gauchesque works and designating all these products as a distinct sector, different from other literary works of the same period, what gives them a historic continuity over the time and is also the origin of their artistic excellence, is the popular language they employ. These characteristics make it sound like a dialectal poetry (comparable to many of those that appeared throughout Europe in the nineteenth century, after Romanticism renewed interest in them), if it were not for the fact that the so-called gaucho dialect behaves differently than the European models, functioning within a framework of opposites that is not only linguistic but definitely ideological and social.

Peasant's language (or more exactly the slang of livestock ranching culture), also known as "the gauchos' language" was, during colonial times, a Spanish dialect. It was not a written language and nothing has been preserved of that language except for a few isolated words or occasional turns of phrase, especially those expressions for naming things speakers use. The language might have survived until the nineteenth century in rural areas until the educational projects started to corrode it. It might have completely disappeared under the attempts at national language unification had the poets not claimed it, after the War of Independence, to write their literary texts. In other words, its existence, its survival, is not simply linguistic but also literary. First, a warning: it is unwise to make the language of gauchesque poetry match the rural language of different periods, assuming they are the same, because that means confusing two different modes of language usage. We will come back to this point. But this confusion wouldn't even be possible if they had not tried to "write" a spoken language belonging to an illiterate population in loose-leaf papers booklets, and popular newspapers of the nineteenth century, just as the authors of this poetry repeatedly explained, calling themselves typists of the rural dialect. Since almost everything we know about this popular language, especially in the first half of the nineteenth century, we owe to gauchesque poetry, it was impossible to avoid the juxtaposition mentioned above nor others that followed.

The option of using slang from the River Plate region would yield the best fruits in the artistic field. One can consider it the origin (humble, as we have seen so many times, and perhaps for that reason, more promising) of their literary triumph (and not only with the public) that gauchesque poetry achieved against the cultured poetry existing parallel to it. It represented a radical position (although it lacked the theory to prove it) with respect to language in literature. It was one of the three paths that writers followed during the initial period after their country's independence, especially because of the influence of Romanticism.

Conservative Path. The Neoclassical style remained strictly connected to Spanish traditional high culture and defended the pure use of language, even though among its practitioners one can find some of the most rebellious anti-Spanish figures. But their political opposition, even their turning away from the rusty traditional Spanish culture of the time, did not influence their view of language, which they never perceived as a foreign cultural imposition. Andrés Bello himself, who was claiming an Americanization of poetry, as soon as he arrived in Chile, published his "Warnings About the Use of Spanish Directed at Heads of Household, Professors in Colleges and School Teachers" (1833) because he was alarmed at the corruptions of the Spanish language by South American speakers. Florencio Valera was angry about the first demands for linguistic independence and in a letter to Juan María Gutiérrez states: "All that talk about *emancipating language* simply means *let's corrupt our language.*"[31]

When one observes the linguistic opacity, the language insensibility with which a great part of the Neoclassical writers from the region use language, one can understand how it never became a problem for them. Neither in their poems nor in their prose do they try to capture the [popular flavor] of the Spanish language. They limit themselves to the official literary language of the epoch, originating in nineteenth-century Spanish high written culture, and some simple French vocabulary. They used a conventional language, a foreign language, copying Spanish models, which yielded different results depending on the chosen model: for the better when they used Larra's style of costumbrismo, for the worse when they created poetry imitating Zorrilla.

We must emphasize that high literature and all official uses of language during the independence period and a good part of the nineteenth century dominated by the Neoclassical style was not a reflection of the language used among educated people. It was the strict application of Spanish literary models, still indebted to writers like Quintana. The Spanish employed in salons or educational institutes was freer of Peninsular rules than the Spanish used for writing, or for oratory, a genre dominated by written models. Rosenblat has keenly observed that "in hymns and proclamations the old rhetoric was still dominant. No one was using *vosotros* (nor *os* or *vuestros*) any longer but in the Bolívar's or San Martín's proclamations that was the only way to address soldiers and citizens."[32]

That Juan Cruz Valera or Francisco Acuña de Figueroa use a "foreign tongue" is not because the Spanish they learned in the crib did not belong to them, obviously, but because they used it as if it were a borrowed tool following rules created overseas, without the familiarity or irreverence that one has with intimate things, created by oneself. No doubt they used it irreverently in their daily lives. But literature was, for them, something entirely different.

Romantic Orientation. The youth from the Literary Salon took an intermediate position when they affiliated themselves with a confused Romanticism emphasizing local color and the recreation of the environment. The writers who initially posed the problem were Esteban Echeverría and Juan María Gutierrez; the first one using the generalized thesis about national literature and the land, the second one taking an anti-Spanish stance, which, though outdated at the time, he and Alberdi would rejuvenate.

In his speech at the Literary Salon, Gutiérrez stated: "We are still linked by the strong and close tie of language; but we have to loosen it day by day, as we join the intellectual movement of the most advanced countries in Europe. To do this we must familiarize ourselves with foreign languages and study how to adapt to our language whatever is created in those languages that is good, interesting and beautiful."[33] One can find this thesis in *Cartas de un porteño*, his polemic against Villegas. For his part, Echeverría, in a note accompanying *Los Consuelos* (1934), justifies his imitation of Spanish poets using the notion of a national literature (he talks about nature, customs, ideas, and feelings but says nothing about language) and in the 1837 edition of *Rimas* warns that he uses "often common expressions and calls things by their name because he thinks that poetry is mainly about ideas and using circumlocution does not always achieve a clear image of the objects in front of us." However, in the first footnote in *La cautiva*, he quickly explains that "it has become necessary to explain some of the local expressions in case this book reaches the hands of a foreigner not familiarized with our things."

This intermediate position of the young Romantics could be described as an attempt to create an American cultured language, which would accept the inclusion of some local vocabulary to refer to new things unknown by the Spaniards. Above all, a progressive adaptation of foreign cultured writings (which, at the time, meant French culture) would polish this language and purify, as Echeverría said, the "brilliantly empty verbiage," "bombastic voices," "pompous speakers," and the "pretentious sound of grandiloquent words" from prose in Spanish. The creative limits of Spanish American Romanticism are partly the result of its dependence on a rigid, conventional literary language, a product of a backward Spanish bourgeoisie, which the addition of local expressions changed little. After going through an initial stage where Sarmiento used proper Castilian to face literary stereotypes, the idea of creating a specifically Spanish American high literary language will be achieved only with the great modernista prose writers: Manuel González Prada and his prose of ideas, Ruben Darío and his artistic prose; however, above all, José Martí will be responsible for the most prodigious renewal of prose in Spanish.

The reactions from the Neoclassicists to Gutiérrez's linguistic propositions are representative of this family quarrel (fathers and sons) that was in actuality a debate of Classics versus Romantics. Florencio Balcarce believed that it was an impossible proposal because they needed extremely high talent to modify a language (and this shows that he believed such modifications to be the prerogative of educated individuals, that is, writers without the rest of the speakers of the language taking part in it). With that, the options for creating in America became limited to "national literature." In other words, they could only aspire to represent "national scenes" with the expected local color. But he later adds this tasty comment:

> The notable difference between languages is found in everyday expressions and in the representation of physical nature, for the simple reason that these objects have existed simultaneously in all countries, they are different in each one and as a consequence, their relationships are diverse and multiply. The American language in this part is so different from Spanish that it deserves to be called by a different name. You can see proof of this in the language from the countryside, where the nature of objects and customs unknown in Spain has forced them to invent a language incomprehensible for a Spaniard.[34]

This already incomprehensible language for someone from Spain was that of the gauchos. This was a language so humble that it could not cross Balcarce's mind that it could be used for a literary creation because literature only circulated in an educated space, as was done in the European models. Although he could acknowledge that it was a unique and distinct language, he could not imagine it as the basis of a literary language. The option of using a dialect breaks forcefully with European models, be they explicit or implicit, and gives writers a dangerous freedom: they must use the dialect as a starting point to build something entirely different, a literary language for which they do not have any established formulas or traditions.

The cultured writers at the time (Neoclassicists) copied a literary language that had already been naturalized by a group of Spanish writers working on their own language and applying artistic norms to it. The new cultured writers (Romantics) limited themselves to polish, simplify, and eventually enrich with local expressions the language they received. The gauchesque authors had to build an entirely new literary language for which they only had access to raw materials, that is, a spoken language without norms or codes that existed as an expression created anonymously and collectively, not subjected to any grammar. To achieve this task, they employed solutions already constructed by traditional literature (expressions, sayings, traditional octosyllabic rhyme) as well as exploring original sources that they discovered as they immersed themselves in an unknown land, such as those metaphors and comparisons that dazzled Hernández, or the systems of enunciation of popular language.

In any case their main task (which they are achieving at the same time they are writing their concrete and particular work, though it may appear as if it came before) is the creation of a *literary language*, extracted from and based on the peculiar characteristics of the *rural spoken language of the River Plate region* during the period when they are writing. Let us remember Amado Alonso's observation: "Even in writers like Hilario Ascasubi and José Hernández, who lived for long periods with the country folk, gauchesque language is handmade, imitated, compacted, and if we eliminate the sense of mockery in the term, recreated."[35] More exactly, it is not about recreating but constructing a language for literature, which is never the same as the language used by determinate social sectors, even though it represents them.[36]

Class and Frontier Language. This gaucho language, as we said, cannot be compared to European dialects because it does not belong to a homogeneous community that has settled for a long time in a specific region and includes a variety of social groups. It is produced in a weak and confused linguistic zone, halfway between central linguistic locations, the incipient capitals (Buenos Aires/Montevideo), and a vast, dismembered ring of indigenous and foreign languages (Portuguese) marking the border line. The gaucho language is not merely a rural speech but also a language of the frontier, common to a population of people who do not belong to any class, and its strong persistence in Banda Oriental can be explained by these characteristics, which were prominent there. In between these two poles (small towns and "barbarians"), one finds the vast land that belongs to the King and to no one, populated with livestock, where gauchos, who comprise the majority of the marginalized sector of the society as so many eighteenth-century documents assert, exist.

It is enough to remember the terms used in Lorenzo Figueredo's report, made in Montevideo, on April 30, 1790: "Peons of all kinds who are called *gauchos* or *gauderios* and that without occupation or trade only are wandering and circulating through the towns and ranches of this neighborhood living on what they can steal on skinning expeditions, horse rustling, and other clandestine activities, without wishing to hire out to the *Estancias*, farms or cattle roundups."[37] Those are obviously socially marginalized people, travelling along the borders of civilization. According to some records, they might have been bilingual, employing Spanish and an indigenous language or Portuguese, not only because they had a bi-racial origin (Spanish father, Indian mother) but above all because they traded with both ethnic groups. To seek refuge in *Tolderias* like Cruz and Fierro was probably not unusual for many gauchos running away from the Spanish authorities and the national authorities that replaced them. Much more realistic than in José Hernández's poem was learning an indigenous language after five years alone amid an indigenous group, without being able to communicate in one's native Spanish tongue.

But Hernández did not live among indigenous people, and also, it bears repeating, the gauchesque poetry language is simply not the spoken language of the gauchos but urban writers' artistic appropriation, writers who apply a modification (creating an idiolect) that necessarily shows traces of the dominant language (Spanish) in their urban environment. Surely gauchesque poets themselves, in spite of their commitment to faithfulness, still represented their own expressive system, as Amado Alonso has subtly studied in relation to the original *Fausto* manuscripts.[38]

The difference (phonetic, syntactic, semantic) that allows us to speak of a dialect in the case of "the language of the gauchos," is expressed here, more than as a regional amalgamation as happens with the case of European dialects, as the opposition to the dominant language, a Castilian language that was the expression of the Spaniards. In the fury of the battle, Spanish was located on the other side of the trench, as can be seen in texts by Fray Cirilo for *Gaceta de Montevideo* or in the irascible reasoning of Father Castañeda in Buenos Aires. Using the gaucho language, as initially and with so much discretion was employed by Hidalgo, is taking a stance: it asserts itself against the mother tongues (like when they mock "gallegos" in *Los chanchos que Vigodet* or when they mock "falar" in Portuguese in *Cielito oriental*) thus becoming a legitimate expression of a social class. In the same way that the community faced Spaniards with weapons, they attacked them using a bastard language, happily accepted, because even more so than clothing and costumes it is possible to see that it was language that established the spontaneous association among the members of that community.

Martínez Estrada was alluding the class features of the gaucho dialect when he said that *Martín Fierro*'s language "was the language of a region (the plains), a class (rural workers) and a society (cattle fields)."[39] The gauchos Hidalgo or Ascasubi met were not farm's peons, but they did form a social class developed within the context of a ranching culture, the culture of leather as Capristrano de Abreu called it. Among the main components of that culture was language, visibly more important than songs, dances, and rituals that are mentioned so often when gauchesca literature is evaluated.

That language contained their worldview, and it is the origin of the artistic success of this poetry in opposition to the cultured poetry of the time.

To Find a Language! As is known, literary invention works within a specific linguistic structure that provides the necessary elements and, therefore, facilitates or blocks the creative process, depending on whether the latter finds the linguistic conditions favorable or must fight against them to achieve its purpose. The struggle between language and poetry, which Becquer saw when facing the heavy and cultured Spanish language, was the result of a disagreement between an already formalized language and a new artistic project clashing with it. One is reminded of Rimbaud's declaration in his letter to Démeny: "*To find a language!*" Taking a risky leap, the humble gauchesque poets established a convenient harmony between language and artistic project: they found a place in the veins of language, accepting its corruptions, vulgar expressions, archaisms, and so on and recognizing in them the peculiar expression of the an American community's worldview. Both of them, language and art, were coordinated with each other, and linguistic structure, lexicon, rhythm, and meanings supported the poem. They had found the right language.

Amado Alonso studied gauchesque language,[40] taking the Humboldian concept of "inner form" as point of departure, to observe the strict concordance between a speaker's experienced reality and the lexical distribution that language made of it, an idea that could be analyzed now using Hjelmslev's theory about "the form of content."[41] In the language Alonso studied, one finds the problem of transplanting and adapting: this was a language originally created by a European community in a determinate region during a specific period of time, within specific cultural guidelines, which is translated to another habitat, where the physical and environmental references change, to another type of society, to a different cultural order. In some cases language is kept rigidly applied, similar to colonial impositions, over the different reality in which it is used—it is the administrative, educational, religious, and military life of the capital cities—generating an obsession with being pure. In other cases, language bends intelligently to the speakers' needs, as happens with the gauchos. They mold it to their needs, their interaction with nature, their system of social relations, their work and customs. They "Americanize" it, so it adapts to their own culture, and, in that way, language adapts itself to their worldview, which at the same time is a manifestation of their particular cultural enclave. Analyzing four concepts, *pasto, cardo, pajas,* and *yuyos,* in contemporary gaucho language,

Alonso concludes by thinking, in William Humboldt-style, that "the words we use form a planetary system and gravitate towards the important centers of interest that shape meaning in our lives. When it moves away from the centers of our interest, every lexical system displaces itself and reorganizes according to new meanings."[42]

With his well-known precision, Edward Sapir gave language the central position cultures assign to it. In order to do that he needed to establish an inner relationship between language and culture:

> Human beings do not live in the objective world alone, nor alone in the world of social activity as ordinarily understood, but are very much at the mercy of the particular language which has become the medium of expression for their society. . . . The fact of the matter is that the "real world" is to a large extent unconsciously built up on the language habits of the group. . . . The understanding of a simple poem, for instance, involves not merely an understanding of the single words in their average significance, but a full comprehension of the whole life of the community as it is mirrored in the words, or as it is suggested by their overtones.[43]

The striking aspect of this linguistic option is represented by the new lexical repertoire: a large number of new words are added to language—and by extension to the literary products based on that language. Previous vocabulary is supplemented or replaced, or they respond to the appearance of new objects in our reality, thus establishing a new distribution and hierarchization of experience as is evident in the connection of meanings among the new words, which proves there is a "form of content." In the case of gauchesque literature, they present themselves as a variation of Spanish language, which gives them a relative autonomy that distinguishes dialects. But those new words, more than for their own value, matter because of the connections they establish between gauchesque language and the words it has preserved from the mother tongue, which are the majority. What is unique and original and productive about this contribution is a displacement within the system itself that takes place thanks to the new words incorporated. Then the image the system gives of them is discordant with the one that, from a linguistic perspective, give us the original language.

The union that comes out of the combination initially reflects the phonetic modifications present at the level of pronunciation. To an ear used to the mother tongue, perhaps that is the first sign that there has been a change. A new web of relations can be perceived in the phonetic change as it imposes deeper modifications than just the addition of new words. What changes the appearance of language is not just the insertion of new elements but a global change. Although without any strict rigor, each one of these phonetic changes points toward the laws apparently governing the modifications. Dropping the "d" in the past participle is simply a tendency, but it is not an absolute rule, as can be observed in Ascasubi or Hernández. Only when it is placed at the codified level of literary writing it becomes, as Estanislao del Campo explained, a "rule." Authors act as an academy or institution fixing uniformly what before was the free and arbitrary behavior of the speakers. They apply legal rigor to a phonetic tendency. In cases like these, Hjelmslev would talk about "phonetic zones of meaning."

But the best proof of the construction of a new coherent and specific system of language is not perceived so much in vocabulary and phonetics as in the changes taking place at the syntactic level, which reflect the other two but also underlie them (leaving aside for the moment the notable semantic transformation that accompanies these displacements and that like them seeks to change the language structure, thus showing the rigor with which the system alters and reconstructs itself).

At this level of speaker performance, we will be able to move from a strictly linguistic concern to a socio-cultural one, using the "sociolinguistic codes" that Basil Bernstein identified in his study of child development from different social levels. He asks us to pay attention to "the selective effect of the culture (acting through its organization of social relationships) upon the *patterning* of grammar *together* with the pattern's semantic and thus cognitive significance."[44] This is part of a rich group of sociolinguistic investigations.[45]

Within this culturalist perspective, Bernstein proposes an articulation of different structures: one that corresponds to language as representative of culture's various symbolic systems; one where language is mainly seen from the perspective of spoken language grammar; one that corresponds to social structure, according to the productive system, and the power and class relations that control it. Finally, the structure of personal experience, which even if it appears to be connected to the others because of individuals' social dimensions (especially language) possesses a notable degree of autonomy. In this web of connections it is essential to perceive the important role that language occupies (as *parole*) as a way of linking the social and the corresponding cultural systems, while being aware at the same time that the social system clearly includes different sectors and groups in accordance with the property relations of the production system on which is based, in the same way that there exists a varied panorama of subcultures manifesting this stratification. The variations among these diverse and equivalent levels bring with them language variations. In such a visible way that, by itself, this alone could be an index of which the social and cultural systems are being combined and interpreted. At the same time, it reveals whether those systems are harmonically linked or possess constraints that restrict their flow due to their place in the social pyramid's hierarchy or to historical circumstances.

Bernstein detects the functioning of different "sociolinguistic codes" according to the social classes in which he studies the socialization process of children through language. The lower classes, working men most of them, use "restricted codes [that] have their basis in condensed symbols" while the upper class employ "elaborated codes [that] have their basis in articulated symbols."[46] If the first ones draw upon metaphors, the second draw upon rationality. If the first ones are interested in particularistic meanings and tend to adopt collective roles, the second ones are universalistic and emphasize individual roles. If the first group cannot detach itself from the context in which language was created, the second group does not depend on this situation.

As this distinction is applied to two different subcultures characterized by their position in the social scale, it is possible to use this frame to study what happened to cultured writers in Spanish America in the nineteenth century when they employed a language from whose cultural system they were excluded. In contrast, gauchesque writers discovered the joy of expressing themselves in a language that had established a visible balance between the dependent group's social system and a cultural system that expressed it fully. The peasant's worldview was expressed completely in the concrete use of language, in its lexical as well as in its phonetic and syntactical operations, at the same time that this language became the most accurate symbolic system of the rural River Plate subculture.

A literary language constructed with those materials achieved a successful expression denied to the language of high literature at the time. With the latter, the rationalization employed to use a foreign instrument only allowed for a limited number of combinations: one can see this in the contrived and fake accent of the tropes they used. For its part, gauchesque literary language, while employing a limited code, established a rigid and conventional system of characters, situations, topics, and meters, but it encouraged greatly its proclivity for metaphors as well as the use of many privileged resources that form part of oral narrative. Ellipsis was one of them.

When one looks closely at the "clarifying letter," addressed to José Zoilo Miguens that opens José Hernández's *The Gaucho Martín Fierro*, one can disagree with the valorization of the gauchos and their philosophical and artistic expressions, but one must acknowledge that the precision of some of the descriptions shows a careful and rigorous observation of the linguistic behavior of the country folk. He founded on those characteristics the creation of his poetic language. Ellipsis is part of the restricted code Bernstein detected. It explains sudden changes in popular narratives due to their narrators' desire for faithfulness and their inability to translate completely their context into literary discourse.[47] It is to that condition that José Hernández is referring when he speaks of "the lack of links between ideas, which do not always follow a logical succession, frequently discovering between them a hidden and remote connection." His poetic choices are based on his appreciation of this linguistic behavior. Hernández's "sextina" unexpectedly connects terms that have not been linked through his discourse and are juxtaposed without including intermediate facts. This is especially evident in the original way the last two verses suddenly come together as if he had forgotten to develop them, because from one to the next, one can detect the quick ellipsis of a discarded logical development. Fina García Marruz has noticed a similar use of ellipsis in José Martí's *Simple Verses* when the author's usually balanced poetry is inserted in a popular tradition.[48]

Something similar can be said about José Hernández's often quoted observation about the use of metaphors in gaucho language. What Hernández registers is the attitude of the gaucho toward tropes in language, which they do not see or look for: "This style is full of metaphors, which the gaucho uses without knowing or valuing, and comparisons as frequent as they are strange." What he is noticing is that these metaphors belong to a language, not a speaker, or, a better interpretation, these are metaphors that go beyond the intellectual level of the person using them. Actually, they have nothing to do with analytical or rational capacities but with what Jakobson would have called a discourse's paradigmatic system of construction, which has nothing to do with educational levels. On the contrary, they apparently have more fluidity and variety among those who employ restrictive codes—just as in the twentieth century, in the same River Plate region, the authors of tango lyrics demonstrated.

Venues of Oral Tradition: Song, Narration, and Drama

Even though gauchesque literature since its origin had to go through writing, it used writing to recover orality, in whose bosom it was forged. For that reason, writing cannot be considered its specific mode of production, as can be witnessed in the work of many contemporary "payadores" who improvise over the skeleton of a traditional metric. Writing is only a register—necessary in modern times—to allow it to reach more people, again from within the orality that defines its conditions. The publication of loose-leaf papers was simply a mediation between one mode of production that, though using writing, was working using forms of orality, and a way of reaching the public, which authors also did through songs or performances in front of an illiterate public.

The metric structures that gauchesque poetry took as basis were not only part of the oral world but also, complementarily, part of a collective group of artistic manifestations: songs, dances, marches, with the participation of many performers and widely practiced in the River Plate region. When the poets of Independence and of the Rosas regime went looking for models for their works, they found an abundant repertoire at hand: cielito, romance corrido, décima, media-caña, and so on gave them the necessary matrices on which to work. These styles were very well known, sung or danced accompanied with guitars, and possessed a large diffusion ratio within a traditional illiterate culture that was largest in the region.

Some of the characteristics of gauchesque literature that are considered defining are actually the result of using traits of popular traditions: the octosyllable and in general the minor meters in various combinations of stanzas, from cuarteta or redondilla to décima, but also adopting the narrative structure of the romance corrido; the opening of the vowels typical of popular poetry, with strong stress and simple syllables, perfect for singing; rhythms and melodies that, even though they tend to be simple, show the beautiful versatility in the work of Hilario Ascasubi—he was a true master of the flirtatious rhythms of the caña and media caña dances such as his famous "Media-Caña from the Countryside for Free People."

We need to remember that we are at the beginning of the first half of the nineteenth century, when universally poetry was realizing, under the impulse of Romanticism, an ambitious recovering of oral diction, when the poem, enjoying its peculiar and rich narrative articulations, stressed simultaneously its vocation as song or as lofty discourse. We were still far from turning poetry into writing, something that will come at the end of the century with Stephane Mallarmé. Orality is then the general condition of the poetry at the time, whether it was Neoclassical or Romantic, even more so in Spanish America than in cultured Europe as it was frequent in America to continue using public singing or recitations, which in turn had an impact on mode of production.

But while the cultured part of poetic production, both Neoclassical and Romantic, favored a discourse that associated it with a bourgeois style of living typical of the high class circles in these small cities, which forced them to accept oratory expressions and dramatic tricks (Ea, Who dares? Listen!, See!, Oh!), the other part, close to uncultured and popular sources, associated itself with singing. Cultured orality signified the coming to power of the bourgeoisie, a minority and in its early stages in the societies of the River Plate. In the meantime, the gauchesque orality comfortably installed itself within the popular tradition of singing, dancing, and poetic narration.

Out of this tendency come two apparently contradictory notes (but they actually complement each other) that characterized the gauchesque for a century and on which a modern debate about genres was applied: the narrative note and the lyrical note. This poetry that sings in the wide field of orality is a poetry that is actually narrating. The same mixture we find in a good part of the Romantic poetry (Hugo, the literary father) also moves frequently into the lyrical and subjective world and dissolves its connections with the narrative, something that does not happen in the gauchesque to the same degree.

The gauchesque was always aware of its existence as a narration, whether it was as Hidalgo's *Diálogos* or the terrifying "stories" that Ascasubi gave us about mazorqueros or Hernández's majestic realist narration. The latter, who explicitly decides to sing the autobiography of a gaucho named Martín Fierro, creating the illusion that we are in the presence of a novel with a personal narrator, opens his poem, however, with a general reference to singing. It shows a high and delicate perception of the function of the poet to the point that he identifies his character with the Poet:

> Singing I'll die,
> singing they'll bury me,
> and singing I'll arrive
> at the Eternal Father's feet—
> out of my mother's womb
> I came into this world to sing.

The intimate relation between both functions—to narrate, to sing—is evident from the beginning of José Hernández's poem when Martín Fierro says:

> I'll sit down in a hollow
> to sing a story

To sing a story is a formula that, bringing together two poles, shows that singing (art) is subordinated to a narrative message (underlining its didactic function) Hernández would repeat with this "but give my opinion singing" in *The Return*. To be honest, the one who best expressed this idea was Antonio Machado. Years later, he would say:

> Song and story are poetry.
> A live story is sung
> told by its melody.[49]

This mix of apparently contradictory purposes (to sing a story, to tell a melody) also rules the gauchesque and that is exactly why in its case we talk about *poetry*. Such an alteration of trivial formulas (to sing a melody, to tell a story) is supported by modern critical theories. According to them, Machado was pointing to the correlation of two planes, expression and content, that poetic writing seeks. It shows their mutual necessity as can be observed in the use of parallelisms, repercussions, isotopy. The relationship between narration and paradigms is the same that one finds between prosodic structure and phonemic structure, which according to A. J. Greimas is the fundamental strategy for reading poetry.[50]

In the case of the gauchesque once can notice a separation of both planes because each one of them is advancing in a completely different direction whether it is toward narration or toward rigid forms of traditional poetry. On the plane of content, it contains a well-articulated narrative with different character-narrators, with a rich plot that sometimes imitates the novel or the comedy of adventures. On the plane of expression, it employs melodies that used to be sung with an accompanying guitar and employs typical stanzas: from octosyllabic quartet with assonant rhyme scheme, alternating a narrative stanza with one dedicated to repeating a refrain as happens with the cielito. Hernández uses a "sextina," which tells a story over four lines only to finish with a message in the last two. There are also the already mentioned examples of Ascasubi using caña and media caña with flexible vigor and also the noisy décimas machaconas used by Lussich in *Los tres gauchos orientales*. And when they need the romance form, as in those cases when, following the advice given by Lope in *The New Art of Writing Plays*, one must "narrate" using a dramatic structure (the model was established by Hidalgo's "New Patriotic Dialogue Between Ramón Contreras, Gaucho of the Monte Guard, and Chano, Overseer of Ranch in the Tordillo Islands" when he used the constant redoubling of assonant rhymes or ending his even verses in *Os*, which Ascasubi will copy exactly, a decade later in "Jacinto Amores") we find ourselves with a poetic solution that, once again, imitates singing. At least that is the way Pantaleón Rivarola established in the introduction to his *Romance heroico*: "To begin with, I write in *verso corrido* because this type of meter works better for the singing we do with our typical instruments and as a consequence it is the best one for people to recite and sing: workers at their job, artisans in their workshops, ladies in their living rooms, and common people around streets and plazas." The *romance* also calls for singing and it still survives in American lands in the form of Mexican "corridos."

If in spite of the obvious specificity of the autonomous tendency in each one of the planes we are able to see that they come together into a compact poetic structure, we mostly owe it to the moment of enunciation of the literary discourse in it, which can be considered one of the keys to its artistic success. It requires the presence of one or several "personal" narrators-singers whose voices are the ones we hear transmitting the message. The "personal narrator" is a rule of the gauchesque and this literature defines itself as a discourse the personal narrator delivers with an explicit receptor in mind.

We should probably acknowledge a realistic origin to this characteristic. To justify completely the use of local language, replacing the cultured language of literature, they use on the first plane of fictional narrative a character who represents popular culture and therefore could only speak in that language. At the same time, this validates the oral lineage of the poetic discourse as a way to transmit a message—reading aloud to illiterate gauchos, texts that are sung or recited with musical instruments accompanying them—presenting it as a discourse spoken, not written, so that the production of the text resembles its transmission to the public.

That realist origin explains the necessary presence of characters, although it would be more appropriate to call them "voices," who express the meaning of the text to a public attuned to it. The public can be represented with another character or another voice in the dialogue form so often used by the gauchesque genre. (About that literary form, one could say, according to Manuel Mujica Láinez, that "it is a more like a monologue, because the interlocutor is limited to feed the other person with questions and sarcastic observations.")[51] But the public could also be present within the discourse as a listener-gaucho who is located outside the text and is closer to a member of an audience than to a reader.

Very few literary currents have such a vigorous presence of a transmitter and receiver of a poetic message, whether one or both of them are present in the text. The transmitter could be the recognizable gaucho Martín Fierro, standing in front of an audience telling his life story, but could also be an obscure "soft old-timer [retired gaucho]," as they are called,[52] at a cielito, or could simply be the voice of a gaucho in a montonera summarizing the feeling of his comrades using cielitos attributed to Hidalgo. In all those cases, we hear "voices."

These are the ones that vividly show us the entire picture of their narrators. Borges pointed out the capacity of the voice to represent a character, noticing that in the first stanza of *Martín Fierro* "the entire man is presented to us through his voice."[53] In one of his texts, collected in *Discusión*, he explains: "In my short time as a narrator I have verified that knowing how a character speaks is knowing who he is; to discover an intonation, a voice, a peculiar syntax, is to have discovered a fate."[54]

To be exact, the voice is not enough; one also needs authenticity, truth, and originality. The dialogue between the voices of Brian and Maria, in *La cautiva*, looks like something out of a conventional and artificial drama and cannot be compared to the flavor and grace of the multitude of character-narrators Ascasubi creates, or to the strong and persuasive voices in Henández's poem.

All of those are "voices" registered within a text that is receptive to them. They leave traces of their worldview and also the circumstances from which their discourse emerged there, superimposing both of them on the linguistic act. But they rarely try to paint a typical psycho-realist portrait like those emerging as a tendency at the end of the century, out of the balanced lesson presented by José Hernández. The voices do not reconstruct psychologies. Usually, they translate prototypes and generic situations, thus its qualities should be sought in speech, in their lexicon, images, tone, rhythm, syntax; in other words, aspects that are not exclusive and different for each speaker but part of the totality. Of course, this totality is commonly engulfed by "a character's diction" who is the person singing and telling, as in the paradigmatic figure of Martín Fierro, obtaining the unification of discourse and stylistic homogenization, or that totality is distributed among two or three voices strictly similar from a linguistic point of view and only distinguishable from the point of view of history or of ideas.

The greatest virtue of the voices is not, for that reason, in the construction of realist characters possessing a rich individuality, but in a subtle and indirect contribution to avoid the presence of the author, a tendency abusively and noisily predominant in Spanish American letters. The author appears to disintegrate in this literature, replaced by the narrator who receives some of the author's best skills. With the disappearing author also disappear their superior education, cultured information, social manners, and the language forced on them during that period and that, as we have already pointed out, was only a copy of old literary models. Instead of being or "expressing" oneself in the literary text as was the norm in the nineteenth century, the author was forced to "represent," to "pretend" being another person. They withdrew from the first plane to which the Romantic impulse led them with its individualism and confessional form, to assume the function of a producer, more specifically, a professional author.

Their task focused on creating a literary language based on the contributions of the regional language, which authors used homogeneously in their artistic discourse. That homogeneity resulted from the use of narrators. But because this language originated in a dialect, and because they sought to appropriate it during the moment it was emerging and constantly transforming, this emphasized a third ingredient that must be added to the other two already named—song and narration—to complete a trilogy of orality: the dramatic element. This element comes from the same oral source and, like the other two, it contributes to solidify orality within the literary text.

The dramatic trait has been emphasized in relation to the dialogue structure that Hidalgo established and was imitated by his followers, but it is not limited to that theatrical form. Practically all the gauchesque texts are born with that dramatic tone because a character (in most cases clearly individualized) is directly narrating them: all the texts emphasize ceaselessly the existence of a conflict around which the argument turns; they all address in an explicit and intense manner an audience highlighting the conative function of the text. The "voices" give witness to the constant presence of the dramatic and (this is the best lesson learned from the dramatic authors) this implies a group of linguistic values that "realize" completely the text; they are the spirit of the text; they give words their authentic meanings and develop the text's beauty in a vigorous and open way.

A good part of the gauchesque can be invisible to the ears of those unaccustomed to the linguistic community of the River Plate, in the sense that they will be unable to reconstruct the tone of a linguistic period. In some cases, the metric form fixes it (as in the case of the decima) but in many others only the correct form allows an ordering and clarification of the syntax and meaning of a period. Much more than the meanings of regional vocabulary (they are accessible through a dictionary of dialectical voices), the problems of understanding are created by the level of what we might call "theatrical aspect" as it is indispensable to read the text aloud in order to reconstruct the measure of the verse and rhythms, but above all the meanings. As in the traditional and paradigmatic example from Anton Chejov, the written word is one part of the meaning and frequently is only visible when one combines the words' senses with the enunciation, which sometimes negates that sense and imposes a different or opposite one.

The creation of a text through "voices" includes not only orality but also the versatility and ambiguity of which it is capable. It is true that such a written message[55] possesses a margin of register but it also represents an ample system of oral communications, of the phonetic kind, with which it complicates the normal written literary message. Written language is easily decoded but it is complicated when a different regime of messages is incorporated, with other terms and codes. This is similar to what Barthes correctly named the "informational polyphony" of the theater.[56] The gauchesque poem, even though it lacks various theater attributes (scene, lighting, clothing) expresses the "density of signs" that is achieved when several codes are handled simultaneously and when one of them (which corresponds to intonation, that is, diction and meaning of texts) is far from possessing a specific register of its possibilities, existing in a constant fluctuation that is at the same time an arduous adaptation of the use of language by a determined linguistic community. Or, in other words, the semantic system must adjust to a phonetic system different from the habitual one, containing a greater number of variations with respect to the norm and at the same time characterized by a code constantly being elaborated and transformed.

The *voices* that narrate, sing, represent, within a linguistically homogeneous field, adjust the three components—song, narration, drama—absorbing and equalizing them. This regime eliminates the author and practically the reader or listener, who is simply peeking at the closed circuit that has been created between the transmitter and receiver represented in the text, both of whom can communicate with each other thanks to the correlation between phonetic and semantic systems, something that can only be completely achieved within the amplitude and expansiveness of orality.

A Rigid Literary System

The anthologies of gauchesque poetry and, more properly, any volume consecrated exclusively to its principal authors, when they emphasize an important writer or underscore the superior value of some pieces—something that is both legitimate and convenient—without intending to, deform a characteristic of gauchesque poetry that distances it from so many other literary schools: its codification into a rigid literary system.

The culmination and simultaneous extinction of the movement is marked by José Hernández's *Martín Fierro* considered by many to be the highest artistic achievement and whose publication date coincides with the defeat of the gauchos. Writers who came before were labeled precursors (as Borges studied in Ascasubi's case); the ones that came after were forgotten, without even recognizing them as imitative. That privileged moment reordered a long literary period and, one could even argue, social period. It is a typical example of the so-called history of literature by names—it is correct about the importance of José Hernández, but not about the essential characteristics of the gauchesque poetry.

Gauchesque is a *style*, to use a discredited term for which we have not found a replacement yet. Both Lussich and Hernández used the term broadly to talk about the expressive tool of a school containing the specific traits of multiple authors. That was a nineteenth-century notion that, because of the arrival of historicism, emphasized a reordering and understanding of the past creating collective formulas: groups, schools, federations, movements, styles. But the situation of the gauchesque poetry was different and particular with respect to diverse artistic styles of the nineteenth century. It was so to speak "restricted" because of the dialect it was using and the narrow repertoire of artistic resources available, but that condition had the effect of emphasizing the community aspects to which we are alluding when we are talking about "style." It allows us to recognize style as a "structure that cannot be derived from the qualities of the works that 'carry' it, whether by addition or by abstraction," as Hauser has explained.[57]

Beginning with Hilario Ascasubi's coherent and systematic production, where he clearly demonstrates what Juan Marichal has called "will to style" (to the point that of all gauchesque authors he is the most professional, the one that shows the greatest awareness of his creative role and the purpose of his poetic production), one can detect in the River Plate region a period—already one hundred years old—where they build, enrich, and preserve a literary style. Unlike the cultured styles replaced during the same period, it achieved a longer life because of its rigid codification: it handles a precise repertoire (not very large) of topics, it possesses a limited capital of aesthetic ideas, and it employs a group of artistic forms whose strict canonicity had no equivalent in any other literary movement in Latin America. Out of the two forces—individual creation and collective and historical norms—that battle each other in the creation of a style, it was the second one that imposed itself until it became empty academicism.

We begin with Hilario Ascasubi (and Luis Pérez) because they belonged to a second generation and they took the original proposals of Bartolome Hidalgo, a poet who was at risk of having no continuity and becoming an individual poet, creative and isolated, and followed them, giving his ideas a paradigmatic value and turning them into a model on which one could continue to build. In that way they founded perhaps not the gauchesque literature, which comes from Hidalgo (though its roots have numerous antecedents), but the River Plate school or style. Beginning with them until practically present day (though now in locations far from urban centers marginalized by the higher levels of society, but capable of inserting themselves in those levels of musical folklore) a style is created whose main characteristic is its concealed *literary* nature.

At the same time that gauchesque authors, almost unanimously, are trying to show that they are simply copying life, that in their texts one should look for reality transferred into words "those who truly know the original can judge if the copy do it justice," and there is nothing farther from their intention that the creation of artistic literary diction for which they consider themselves inadequate (even defects in their works are explained as resulting from their desire to "copy" as Hernández explains "the imperfections that art still possesses among them"), they see themselves as members of a literary movement, declaring themselves followers, refiners, simple disciples, and rarely disagree with past works or authors. In few occasions one can corroborate how literature comes out of literature and in turn engenders literature, in a succession that goes from fathers to sons, from teachers to disciples, and from texts to texts. Hilario Ascasubi signs "Jacinto Chano" to become the explicit follower and heir to Bartolomé Hidalgo, who created that character for his *Dialogues*. Estanislao Del Campo imitates Ascasubi's famous pseudonym (Aniceto el Gallo), signing Anastasio el Pollo and proudly confessing to be a devoted disciple of his teacher. José Hernández writes his famous poem in response to inspiration found in Arturo Lussich's simple and vivacious text *Los tres gauchos orientales*, which he never stops praising since receiving it. And Arturo Lussich, who learned from the poems he read in many "gaucho newspapers" during the Great War and the anti-Rosas fight, do not hesitate to rewrite and expand his book following the model provided by *Martín Fierro* to the point of plagiarizing with little imagination some of its scenes. Also Hernández would disagree with the humorous and purely ludic tendencies of certain gauchesque poetry (allusion to Estanislao Del Campo's *Fausto*, which, however, belongs to a tradition both Ascasubi and the founder himself Bartolomé Hidalgo contributed), and as a sort of literary opposition to vindicate a social and artistic truth, he writes his "opinionated" song as proof: "Perhaps it would have been easier for me if I had only aspired to make people laugh at the expense of their ignorance as has been the rule in this type of composition."

The poets from the magazine *El Fogón* (Alcides de María, Elías Regules, etc.) or the gaucho playwrights who followed the model created by *Juan Moreira* (1886), among them Orosmán Moratorio and Abdón Arózteguy, practically produce within the norms of the style, as if they were José Hernández's children, grandchildren, and stepchildren. Toward the end of the nineteenth century, we are seeing again the emergence of a community similar to the one characteristic of Rosas regime, where topics, forms, and artistic means were easily exchanged among diverse poets. Since José Alonso y Trelles's *Paja Brava* (1915) adopted the techniques of modernismo to the gauchesque, we witness a renovation of the assumptions of the movement, giving it a new vitality. Now in the present we possess a proliferation of regional poets and an abundance of successful folkloric singers. Among the first we should mention are Julián García, Guillermo Cuadri, Serafín J. García (with a large and successful work, also the author of one of the most important anthologies of the genre), Justo Sáenz, and Julio Migno; a second group includes the unquestionable master, Atahualpa Yupanqui.[58]

From one extreme to the other, the production that begins in the early nineteenth century reaches its zenith with Hernández's two poems (1872, 1879) and spreads thanks to specialized magazines, theatrical repertoires, and recognized artists until the twentieth century. It extends into different paths, some renewing it and others just imitative in nature, until the present day. What circulates during that period is, more than a copy of reality, the practice of literature. This is a literature shared fervently by several generations producing careful imitations of their venerated forefathers, turning them into masters, and inventing new solutions for their descendants, as it is only conceivable within a closed and rigid literary school composed of a disciplined confraternity. The "traditional" aspect of the gauchesque poetry is a product originally from its emergence within a rural culture, transmitted orally, using archaic models, which is highly conservative as is expected from this type of culture. But as the movement evolves, its "traditionalism" also comes from a complementary aspect: the rigidity of the rules of the school it has established. I am not suggesting that there are no aesthetic modifications throughout this extensive period: they exist and they are well known; they respond to the same epochal changes that in parallel to high literature create the changes that go from Neoclassical style to Romanticism, and later to Realism, and from the latter to Symbolism and Regionalism, and so on. But while these modifications, which originate in the influence of the European literary process, impose substantial modifications—though belatedly—on cultured literature, their effect on the gauchesque is weaker (though it is still stronger than on folkloric literature), and even if they add new literary resources, they do not alter the gauchesque's artistic principles.

If we take into consideration as criteria temporal duration and productivity, and establish a hierarchical list of Latin American "literary schools," we would give first place to the gauchesque poetry, probably followed by the *literatura de cordel* in Brazil. This shows the magnitude of the literary movements coming from the lower sectors of society, those that come close to being folkloric, but it is also an example of the "school" or collective characteristics of the artistic movements in the lower zones. They are frequently ignored by critics, perhaps for that reason, as in the upper social levels the "individualist" aspect of art began to gain importance, until it imposed itself explicitly with the emergence of modernismo, with Darío's anarchist manifesto in *Profane Hymns*.

Within the gauchesque poetry many times the "school" ruled over the "individual," the style over the work. Many factors contributed to this: above all, the low educational level, as both poets and those transmitting the poems orally initially belonged to a social group with little academic preparation. More importantly, however, was the idea and widespread conviction among writers that they were using a property with no visible owner. From them, they were employing popular "speech," musical rhythms from celebrations, traditional poetic forms used by everyone and with no known author, ideas being debated among gauchos themselves, all of which was common property, or, better said, it had no owner, so an illusion was created that the specific task of a writer was simply to write down everything that everybody knew and said or sang about.

The modesty of the literary horizon to which the poets aspired, as they expressed so many times, contributed too. This allowed the inclusion of an endless amount of verse writers, with little talent and who were only capable of offering variations of famous texts, many times without revealing their own names as it was common practice to use pseudonyms with sonorous peasants' names. Additionally, it was frequent to juxtapose creators and transmitters. In the popular side of the movement, the gauchesque poet was often the singer and he could modify the material received from other hands, applying to it the characteristic treatment of folkloric transmission. Finally, the immensity of the production of a genre that became the main contributor to nineteenth-century literature in the River Plate area, leading to endless copies, imitations, rewritings, and this unending game of variations on the same topic, was made bigger by oral transmission.[59]

Synthetizing, we have found the following characteristics in common: (1) a public to which this poetry was addressed; (2) a cast of creators and transmitters, with their functions sometimes juxtaposed, as we have just seen; (3) oral reproduction and diffusion; (4) an abundance of frameworks—metric, rhythmic, generic, thematic and specifically literary—that served as support for their work and came from anonymous and common sources. All this helped in the creation of one of the most rigid codes any literary movement has ever known, something similar to the Imperial Ballet School with its strict repertoire of positions, figures, and movements.

One cannot apply to all gauchesque poetry the "community censorship" regime that Roman Jakobson detects in folkloric poetry[60] because a great sector of it—which is, by the way, the most valuable artistically speaking—is the result of individual creators who employed the written word through newspapers, loose-leaf papers, and books. The popular side of the movement shows, both in the creation and the transmission, a collective note and an attachment to community norms that shows that there are no neat separations among sectors. Here we see *gauchesque literature* sinking into folklore.

The fact that the collective note reigns over individuality makes the most generalized and rigid aspects of the code stronger. One must reach a vast public transmitting a message with great clarity, a situation that encourages the use of conventional signs with stable or fixed meanings. The illiterate public, the regime of oral transmission, and the simplicity and clarity of the information contributed to the creation of a highly conventional system, using a set of simple definitions.

In this way, the gauchesque poetry became a specific literary style of a determined social group, combining the peculiarities of a determined use of language with those of an artistic expression, which corresponds to the second part of Charles Bally's project.⁶¹ The works produced in that stylistic tendency both feed on conventional norms and generate significant particular variations, which eventually also become new norms: the best productions reveal the typical conflict between "language-system" and "work-system" that Henri Meschonnic talks about when he highlights that the individual message, based on creativity, always opposes a group of values employed, which are truly "common places."⁶²

This conflict, which is the most desired trophy of individuality, on which its existence is constructed, does not function as a romantic opposition degrading the preexisting code. Without such an enemy, the work could not be produced, says Meschonnic. The code or literary system or style, in which the work is inscribed, when we are talking about a widely elaborated literary system, becomes constitutive part of the creation. As Hauser accepts at the end of his study: "There is no more a ready-made, unambiguous, entirely objective tradition than there is a convention of taste which has the same significance for all and sundry in all possible contexts. Equally, there are neither artistic impulses nor individual aims, but such as mark themselves off against the foil of some general stylistic trend and find their expression in and through a state of tension toward something else felt as alien."⁶³

Indeed, the style directs the author, without wasting any energy, toward the construction of his message, placing him within a specific field that is a literary structure with its basic resources; in addition, the system fixes in advance the form of communication; it orders its diverse channels to facilitate the transmission of information. At the same time, the literary system enforces its known restrictions, and it could condemn a writer who follows the code too closely and does not try to innovate within it. Without a doubt, there is a conflict, but triumphing in this conflict is achieved not by destroying one of the sides but by arriving at a dialectical resolution.

This style is essentially a signifying structure; because of it, we can put ourselves inside this literature and establish, more than a model, a "paradigm that cannot be found entirely in any concrete example." Its rigidity and conventions were not an impediment in the creation of masterworks and, on the contrary, one could argue that the latter were possible due to the existence of that structure patiently built for several generations and that can be considered a literary invention as great as the works of art that exist within it.

9

The Boom in Perspective

What Was the Boom?

With the same lack of solid arguments that in the mid-1960s people began to praise and consecrate the so-called Boom of Latin American narrative, toward 1972 several newspaper articles and interviews with writers became an index pointing to the supposed Boom's extinction. A public discussion of literary values lasting less than a decade can be considered among the most confusing and less critical in the history of Latin American letters and, after its initial impulse, became an object of warnings and even bitter battles foreshadowing a sort of general backlash against it. Because 1972 did not end the cycle of important novels being produced in the continent, nor did the public's interest in some of the authors decline, new writers did not stop being added to the group; in the so-called obituary, one could discover a strategic withdrawal at the same moment that some of the external features that characterized the Boom (advertising and commercial features) were beginning to fade in conformity with the laws of the market in which it was born. The Boom was after all a phenomenon of the consumer society to which many of the region's cities had only recently and partially integrated themselves.

Because of the well-known imbalance between the diverse Latin American cultural areas, that withdrawal did not stop the Boom from surviving by being translated from the capital cities in which it emerged and had declined to others where it arrived belatedly but with greater fury. It appeared originally in São Paulo and it contributed to strengthen the Brazilian's weak links with Spanish America. It expanded when it installed itself in Barcelona where a belated and confused information about the Latin American novel provided a first image of the arbitrary nature that would characterize the Boom. Mario Vargas Llosa became known before Julio Cortázar and the latter became known before Jorge Luis Borges. This contributed to a synchronic flattening of the history of Latin American narrative that only much later and with difficulty critics tried to fix.[1] Along with this arbitrariness, we have to highlight a positive feature that will reappear later with the reception in the United States: the insistence on globalizing Spanish America by collecting materials from different origins, some of which sometimes lacked internal circulation within the continent, giving these materials thus a distribution beyond just Spain, which was beneficial for Spanish America. Spanish Americans then received, brought together from the exterior, products created in isolation, from authors who did not know each other. Thus was reborn a publishing tradition that had been known during the modernista and regionalist periods and that because of the Spanish political conditions during Franco's rule, which were contemporaneous with the development of publishing houses in Spanish America, had not been applied to the productions of the avant-garde period; those were only edited by Spanish American houses and circulated almost exclusively within the continent.

The pomp of the Boom continued because of its transfer to other capital cities where signs of a consumer society began to appear such as San Juan, Puerto Rico, and Caracas. With predictable national pride these two places aspired to see their writers incorporated into the movement even if it was belatedly. This was partly achieved with Emilio Díaz Valcárcel[2] and Salvador Garmendia[3] from Puerto Rico and Venezuela, respectively, and it was reinforced with the local editorial business development that came with it. Much more important was the attention given to translations of these works—more than in the United States, France, Italy, and, much later, in the Federal Republic of Germany. This would become one of the principal chapters of its successful story, which is explainable given the feeling of being ignored by the foreign cultural centers that Latin America has experienced since emancipation. Here there are two different aspects: one pays attention to the reasons that led to the translation of Latin American narrations into other languages and this has to do not only with their artistic excellence or adaptability to other markets but also with the sudden curiosity for the region where the Cuban socialist revolution was born. The other aspect has to do with the effect that international reception had over the Latin American public, which saw its products being endorsed in the main world cultural centers, thus reinforcing the national and regional pride during the decade of the 1970s, a period characterized by great social unrest.

There was then a positive initial elation that had widespread backing and a positive critical consensus. But as the characteristics of the Boom became clearer, especially the reductive view that it brought to the rich variety of literary production in the continent and also the increased use of techniques of publicity and marketing that the commercial infrastructure needed to use when the traditional editions of three thousand copies were replaced with massive editions, this development led to negative views, to criticism and objections that acquired a bitter tone. The belligerent tendency of this critical reception did not limit itself to attack those increasing deformations of Latin American literature, those were inevitable consequences of the incorporation of the letters within the workings of a consumer society. Critics did not notice that there were two dissimilar fields: one of them represented by the high quality of splendid literary works and the other one by the way they were used when transformed into commercial objects (books) for the market. Critics tended to repudiate both the system and the writers the system was using, reinforcing the famous metaphor: they were throwing the baby out with the bathwater. Obviously, writers who were accused of conquering the public using publicity or commercial schemes answered back describing their critics as jealous, resentful, or bitter and after this the entire debate became a neighborhood quarrel. To take it out of that context and see it from a higher and more productive intellectual perspective is the urgent task of literary criticism.

The diatribes from that debate, which evokes passages from *Adán Buenosayres*,[4] are strictly symmetric. If the Boom reduces modern Latin American literature to only a few figures of the narrative genre on which it is focused, ignoring the rest or condemning it to the second row, their critics would deny those authors any artistic and social relevance, arguing that their works are merely copies of European avant-garde novels or mass media products or distorted images of the urgent reality of the continent, and so on. But when it is the writers who are speaking, they do not use that kind of reductionism and, within a legitimate range of preferences, they never cease to pay homage to their colleagues and they even use their prestige to call their readers' attention to those authors who are not very well known by the public but have written works of high artistic quality: Borges advocates for Macedonio Fernández, Cortázar for Lezama Lima or Felisberto Hernández, Vargas Llosa for Arguedas, Fuentes for Goytisolo, and so on.

To distinguish the Boom as a phenomenon different from contemporary Latin American literature in general, even from current narrative works, is to begin with a methodological *petitio principii*. Even though it is an equally legitimate question to ask about the reductive effect of the Boom and why the label applies to some products to the detriment of others, the candid notion that the Boom is a result of the artistic excellence of a few works is not acceptable. This would be like squaring the circle and existing in a panglossian universe where everything that is good becomes accepted and everything that is bad is rejected by the wonderfully knowledgeable reading public. If that were the case, there would not be any important work that would remain forgotten or any author who like Stendhal would be betting on becoming famous a hundred years later. It is legitimate to interrogate not only the options available to the Boom, understood as a process that is imposed on the literary production, but also its underground effect, its unmasked and subterranean effect on the production of new works and, in the same way, its effects on the behavior of writers as the public person they are. Studying in Baudelaire the emergence of art for art's sake tendencies, in one of his "illuminations," Walter Benjamin recognized the close link between the behavior of dandies and the situation of the poet in a new mass society created by the industrial revolution. In his rich analysis, writers were not isolated from society, they were reacting to its specific characteristics and impulses. Writers were adopting attitudes and developing forms that were personal responses within a field of forces already established. To understand the attitudes and forms it was necessary to reconstruct structurally the totality and that would allow one to appreciate to what extent the "frisson nuveau" was much more than a simple Baudelarian invention, it was one of the operative laws of the social medium and writers were taking it and turning it against that medium itself. To study writers and their works within the framework of present-day society is an equally legitimate and profitable critical task. It is even more urgent in a day in which the circulation of literary works has overflown the narrow circuit in which they used to move and have attracted the interest of economic forces that have been shaping the social structure and the workings of the market. These economic powers are much more decisive or important than the political forces that on occasion are nothing more than their rationalized transpositions. For that reason, it is more useful to consult socioeconomic transformations that have taken place in the continent since the Second World War than to spend time on the excessively ideologized political debates that have characterized more the 1960s than the 1970s.

Elusive Definitions

Before anything, we have to define the Boom; not an easy task given that its existence has been registered in thousands of magazines and newspapers in the last ten years, like a topic whose origin nobody knows but that is repeated as a password. It navigated with success in this medium almost as a wildcard standing for something undefined but known, which explains its ill-fated name.

The label does not come from the military slang but only remotely as an onomatopoeia of an explosion. It actually has its origin in a modern North American marketing term used to designate a sudden increase in sales of a specific product in a consumer society. It assumes the previous existence of such societies as it was perceived in the postwar period in the most developed urban regions of Latin America where there had already been a boom of cosmetics and it would soon register that of calculators and appliances. The surprise was its application to an object (books), which except for a few lines of production (textbooks) was located at the margins of these processes, even though previous to the Boom narrative the same phenomenon was perceived in the creation of a similar product that would contribute powerfully to the Boom's development: magazines of current events (weekly, biweekly, monthly), which since the 1960s were published in Latin America, after the European and North American models (*L'Express*, *Time*, *Newsweek*), but adapting them to the demands of the new national public.

The journalistic teams of those magazines included numerous young writers who developed an attention for the Boom authors, giving them the same type of attention that was previously only reserved for star politicians, athletes, or entertainers. This was not the only incorporation: businessmen received attention within innovative pages devoted to economic news and stressing the importance of that sector for national life, bringing it to the attention of the public. The magazines were an important instrument in the modernization and hierarchization of the literary activity: they replaced the specialized publications destined to a small, cultured public, basically composed of other writers, thus establishing a channel of communication with a larger public. Their readers discovered that the panorama of current affairs, which the weekly magazines were offering them, also included books, preferably novels or essays about general topics, and even a writer could be honored with a cover.

This transformation was especially noticeable in Buenos Aires, where big and small publishing houses sponsored a series of publications, among which one can highlight the weekly *Primera Plana* (1962) and later the newspaper *La Opinión* (Jacobo Timmerman), achieving an evident transformation of the journalistic style whose success certified the existence of a new receptive public—similar in this case to the one that in Paris was buying *L'Express* and *Nouvel Observateur* or *Le Monde*. That transformation found its equivalent in another one that was taking place in the literary field even though it was easier to detect in a popular literary genre like the novel, celebrating it as the arrival of a new period, more than in any of the other elitist genres, like poetry, where it had existed for a longer time. A sign of this way of appreciating the phenomenon can be seen in a note written by a cultural journalist who did a lot for the diffusion of the new narrative, the Argentine Tomás Eloy Martínez. The year 1967 could be considered a glorious one for the Latin American letters because it saw the Nobel prize awarded to Miguel Ángel Asturias and the publication of Gabriel García Márquez's *One Hundred Years of Solitude* as well as an abundant group of fundamental literary works:

> It is not improbable that within a thousand years, Güiraldes and Rómulo Gallegos and Azuela and José Eustasio Rivera appear as lost palimpsests in the endless history of literature; that Macedonio Fernández and Arlt and Borges be simply considered the original seeds of a world whose parents will be called Cortázar, Vargas Llosa, Onetti, Guimarães Rosa, Carpentier. This important parent who has definitely joined them with his *One Hundred Years of Solitude* is going to contribute a new flag to this adventure by himself. The novel he has just published summarizes, better than any other, all of those alternative literary currents.[5]

But to achieve a definition of the Boom, it is more important to gather the opinion of the writers who were selected to be in it, given that it allows us to visualize it from their perspective and at the same time we can see to what degree they were affected by it. In fact, we would be witnessing the reaction of those who were, willingly or not, protagonists in a sociological phenomenon entirely new in the continent, at least when it comes to the massive demand of literary works. I believe that the most complete public debate about this, but perhaps not the first, occurred at the *Coloquio del libro* conference that took place in Caracas in July 1972, organized by the Monte Avila publishing house.[6] It was significant that many of the most notorious figures participated and that it is contemporaneous with the first personal history of the movement, the one written by José Donoso.

Both the positions derived from this debate, as well as those adopted by some of the figures central to the movement, tended to underscore the positive aspects of the phenomenon. However, they also noticed discrepancies and confusions. We have to consider these actions as counterattacks with which the fiction authors reacted to public criticism—which had been going on for several years and had already generated polemics mixing artistic and political matters. The best-known one, because of the protagonists, was the one provoked by the publication in the *Amaru* magazine of the diaries of José María Arguedas, which would be included in his posthumous novel *The Fox from Up Above and the Fox from Down Below*, and Julio Cortázar's response to it.[7] Another polemic took place in 1969 in the pages of the weekly *Marcha* in Montevideo as a result of the article by the young Colombian narrator Óscar Collazos, to whom Julio Cortázar and Mario Vargas Llosa responded.[8]

Out of the three texts that, from my point of view, objectively represent the reactions from the Boom writers, the one that Mario Vargas Llosa delivered at the above mentioned *Coloquio del libro*, in which he expressed opposition to my views about those aspects of the Boom that I consider damaging, but that were in no way related to the polemic about the novel as a genre in which we both engaged in *Marcha* during the year of 1971.[9] Mario Vargas Llosa said:

> The so-called Boom, which nobody knows exactly what it is, I especially do not know, is a group of writers, we don't know exactly who, because each person has a different list. Those writers acquired, at more or less the same time, a certain amount of diffusion, a certain amount of circulation and recognition by the public and by the critics. Perhaps we could call this a historical accident. Now, it was never, at any moment, a literary movement sharing a set of aesthetic, political or moral ideas. That phenomenon as such is over. And one can already notice a certain distance with respect to those authors as well as a certain continuity in their works. However, it is a fact, for example, that a Cortázar or a Fuentes have very few things in common and many differences. The publishers took advantage of the situation, but this has also contributed to promote Latin American literature, and in the

end that is a pretty positive result. What happened at the level of the circulation of the works has encouraged young writers and it has led them to write and it has shown them that publishing in Latin America is a possibility; one can find an audience that transcends the national boundaries and even language barriers. The fact is that today there are many more novels written than a few years ago. I'm not asserting that the reason for that has exclusively been the success and large readership obtained by a group of writers, but without a doubt they have contributed to help young writers feel more secure in themselves and encourage them to follow their dreams.[10]

This definition focuses on the topic from the point of view of the individual creation ("a group of writers . . . that acquired . . . a certain amount of circulation") leaving in the background the unique social or economic aspects of any process of mass circulation, which are seen here as a "historical accident." Because such an accident of history corresponds to transformational forces, which in turn create new situations, the above-mentioned development or increase in the means of communication includes not only the magazines but especially the development of televisions, visual media and advertising, and the new cinema; those, I repeat, advanced developments in mass communications must also be seen in relation to those forces transforming society because they are the ones that generate their new public. Among those forces we must recognize the importance of an increase in the population, of urban development because of the evolution of the service sector, the notorious progress of primary and secondary education, and above all the industrialization of the postwar created in [Latin] America advanced regions that claimed for or required teams of people with better preparation than before. All of these were changes whose limitations and fragility are very well known.

Julio Cortázar's definition, instead, underlines the phenomenon of the expansion of the Latin American reading public and explains the attention that this public paid to the works of Boom authors as part of their search for an identity. This leads Cortázar to focus on the implicit political content that he sees in the Boom and which he studies from a leftist perspective. His opinions were originally expressed in the *Coloque de Royaumont*, which was convened in Paris in December 1972 by the Sociologie de la littérature section of the Institut des Hautes Études. Cortázar repeated them in an interview in Peru. There, he said, this thing that has badly been called the Boom of Latin American literature, it seems to me, represents a formidable support for the present and future cause of socialism, that is to say, to the advance of socialism and its future triumph, which I consider inevitable, and it won't take too long to happen. Finally, what is the Boom but an extraordinary awareness on behalf of the Latin American people of part of their own identity? What is this public awareness, but a very important part of overcoming alienation? . . . What is known as the Boom (it is regrettable that they needed to employ an English word to define it) has emerged as an indisputable and undeniable fact in the last 15 years. In the end, all of those who because of literary resentment (and there are many of them) or because their view is blocked by their leftist blinders, call the Boom an editorial maneuver forget that the Boom (and I'm already getting tired of repeating the word) was not made by the publishers, but by the readers. And, who are those readers, but the people of Latin America? Unfortunately, not all of the people, let us not be seduced by facile utopias. What is important is that there are sectors who have expanded with great speed and an incredible miracle has happened, by means of which a writer of talent in Latin America, someone who in the 1930s had with great difficulty circulated an edition of 2,000 copies (the first books by Borges only sold about 500 copies). All of a sudden this author becomes popular with novels like *One Hundred Years of Solitude* or *The Green House* or any of those novels that we are reading and are being translated around the world.[11]

Obviously, this text inscribes itself in an internal polemic of the Left, responding to criticisms expressed by intellectuals who, after the division the Padilla case (1971) created, were loyal to the Cuban cause, to dissident writers, and to the Boom movement in general. Julio Cortázar had to pay attention to that because, although possessing a significant degree of independence, he remained faithful to the cause but endured public criticism. To that one must add that he had been criticized because of his prolonged residency in France, criticism expressed not only by the Cubans but also by fellow Argentine writers like David Viñas.[12]

Cortázar answers persuasively the weak argument that the Boom was the creation of publishing houses and emphasizes the obvious fact that a new reading public has appeared, and that they are in search of their identity. The best members of the new public came from university campuses, which grew massively in the postwar era with students coming from the high and middle sectors of the bourgeoisie. They took a countercultural position during the 1960s, aligning themselves with Cuban revolution, promoting guerrilla groups, and encouraging attacks on conformity to the status quo, in accordance with the *foquismo* theory that Regis Debrais[13] elaborated from Havana.

This section of the public, which was the most active, did not constitute all of the public and not even the majority of it, although they had several characteristics in common with the rest of the new public, such as a high level of intellectual preparation, a specific view of social modernization and, above all, an idealist and even irrational attitude. Their attitude reflected the limits of their class education and authentic dissatisfaction with the deficiencies of the society that their parents had created. They replicated strikes or calls for university reform that took place in Cordoba, 1919, whose spirit had stayed alive throughout Latin America in the teachings of Rodó's *Ariel*, even though, in contrast, the different ideological circumstances and the lessons learned from the practice directed specific sectors toward materialistic and clearly social positions, toward a desire to establish contact, without success, with the working classes.

If we look at the overall constitution of this reading public, we are going find a wide variety of tendencies in which there are many different and even contradictory elements that are being brought and fused together. This search for an explanation is presented not as economic or social interpretation of Latin American history as it was the case with avant-garde thinkers (Mariátegui), but close to the metaphysical interpretations of the next generation (from Ramos to Martínez Estrada) as if it were a search for "identity." Encapsulated in that term, one can perceive the conflicts and even the struggles between tradition and modernization that became the backdrop of their existence. The preservation of that "identity," which they saw in danger because of a vertiginous modernization with the use of foreign models, motivated diverse cultural behaviors: from it stems an extraordinary and lively interrogation of the past, which even gave us schools such as "historical revisionism," but also founded an economic interpretation of history. From it also comes the study of a relationship with the exterior world that produced the theory of dependency but also reignited nationalist tendencies and even indirectly resuscitated folkloric ideals. From it comes the anxious attention for literary production, expecting from contemporary literature—more than they did from any of the previous social and realistic approaches—a sort of spiritual communion, both intellectual and emotional, open and free, philosophical of the idealist variety and, at the same time, focused on society, interested in realities and worlds beyond our own and, at the same time, focused on the concrete experience, urban and modern. That reading public identified itself with the narrative of Ernesto Sábato or Julio Cortázar in the South just like it did with the masterful teachings of Paz and the novels of Carlos Fuentes in the North. In all of them, they found that eager search for an identity that could not be defined with the interpretive models that they had inherited. The variety of political orientations that these writers represent, from liberalism to socialism, shows that politics was not nothing but a secondary element of this new and slippery demand, which was encapsulating the problem of a new generation in terms of "identity."[14]

A third definition of the Boom is also from 1972 and comes from the delightful book that José Donoso wrote, as some sort of personal confession, *The Boom in Spanish American Letters*.[15]

> What then is the Boom? What is there of truth and of fraud in it? Undoubtedly, it is difficult to define even with moderate rigor this literary phenomenon which has recently ended—if it really has ended—and whose existence as a unity is due not to the arbitrariness of those writers who may be a part of it, not to undying loyalties of friendship; but, rather, to the invention of those who question it. In any case, maybe it is worthwhile to begin by pointing out on the simplest level and prior to possible, and possibly accurate, historical and cultural explanation, there exists the fortuitous circumstances that on the same continent, in twenty-one republics where more or less recognizable varieties of Spanish are written and during a period of very few years, there appeared both brilliant first novels by authors who matured very or relatively early—Vargas Llosa and Carlos Fuentes, for example—and the major novels by older, prestigious authors—Ernesto Sábato, Onetti, Cortázar—which thus produced a spectacular conjunction. In a period of scarcely six years, between 1962 and 1968, I read *The Death of Artemio Cruz, The Time of the Hero, The Green House, The Shipyard, Paradiso, Hopscotch, Sobre héroes y tumbas (About Heroes and Tombs)*, and other novels all recently published at the time. Suddenly, there burst into view

about dozen novels, noteworthy at the very least and populating a previously uninhabited space.[16]

Donoso's point of view is strictly literary and he does not even take into account the most telling aspect of the Boom, which is the massive consumption of Latin American narratives. For him, the Boom includes books like *One Hundred Years of Solitude* as well as *Paradiso*, which only had a "success d'estime" [critical success] among readers, *Time of the Hero* as well as *El astillero* [*The Shipyard*], which is mainly a book for writers. This is therefore a perfectly good appreciation of what one could call the "new Latin American narrative," even though at this point it is no longer so new, which Donoso sees as a transformation of the narrative mode, beginning with Fuentes's *Where the Air Is Clear*, which he read in 1961 but was actually published in 1958. It is important to point this out because as Donoso offers a literary view of the phenomenon and tries to place it under the umbrella of the 1960s, he establishes a divisory line between what is actually new and what came before, which was a "deserted space," but where there are also books by Cortázar, Onetti, Rulfo, Guimarães Rosa, Lispector, and Borges's main works, which actually contain more connections to the new narrative than many of his contemporaries, like Carpentier.

For Donoso this "new narrative" is based on a generational renovation to which many "reservists" have joined. His definition is located at the crossroads between a new perception of the narrative structure and one of language usage. This is something that is evident both in Fuentes and in Donoso himself even though it is not equally important for other writers that for him form part of the movement. His essay juxtaposes and contrasts two approaches: according to one of them, the Boom is an "aesthetic," even if it is employed by people of different talents; according to another one, the Boom is a movement vaguely generational, where several aesthetic positions coexist that are as different and opposed as Donoso's and Carlos Martínez Moreno's or Julio Cortázar's and Mario Benedetti's. Donoso tends to favor the first approach when he tries to describe the characteristics of the Boom. From his literary point of view, and this is the reason why his essay should be considered a testimony (a personal view, which is how he defines it) that registers the subjective view of the process from the perspective of one of its protagonists but that adds very little, at least directly, to the examination of the sociological phenomenon in question. Indirectly, however, it adds information like, for example, when he asserts that the Boom of sales was not created by the writers but by their unnamed enemies, in whose mouths he puts simple accusations to which he can easily respond and in that way accuses them of being mediocre and resentful. One is reminded of that character from Chesterton who had hired someone to contradict him so that he could triumphantly rebuke him.

The Role of the Publishing Houses

To complement these opinions, it would be a good idea to summarize the testimony of those that have frequently been the accused: the publishers. The Boom authors have chosen not to speak about them, or have repeated in passing the old complaints about how it is the editors who are profiting while the writers are still poor, even though they are the ones creating the product. Both García Márquez and José Donoso, even though their positions in the market are very different, have said this. That accusation has not yet been proven.

The editors that helped the emergence of the new narrative were in their majority official publishing houses or small presses that have been called "cultural" in order to distinguish them from the strictly commercial ones. A partial list of the publishing houses in the 1960s is evidence of this: in Buenos Aires, Losada, Emecé, Sudamericana, Compañía General Fabril Editora, and, following behind them, smaller presses such as Jorge Álvarez, La Flor, Galerna, and so on. In Mexico, Fondo de Cultura Económica, Era, Joaquín Mortiz; in Chile, Nascimento and Zigzag; in Uruguay, Alfa and Arca; in Caracas, Monte Ávila; in Barcelona, Seix Barral, Lumen, Anagrama, and so on. From all of them, the most important ones were Fabril Editora, Sudamericana, Losada, Fondo de Cultura, Seix Barral, and Joaquín Mortiz, whose catalogs in the 1960s show a change from the foreign material that used to occupy a high percentage of them to an increase in the percentage of the national or Latin American production included. Some of them created international contests with attractive prizes, which allowed the public to know or learn about works of quality endorsed by qualified juries, this way assuring them a large readership. Thus Losada discovered Roa Bastos (*Son of Man*), Fabril Editora discovered Onetti (*The Shipyard*), Sudamericana discovered Moyano; though the most successful one was Seix Barral, whose award, beginning with the one given in 1962 to Mario Vargas Llosa's *The Time of the Hero*, showed a preference for Latin American narrative, with texts as important as Guillermo Cabrera Infante's *Three Trapped Tigers*, Carlos Fuentes's *A Change of Skin*, and, as conclusion, Donoso's *The Obscene Bird of Night*. Participating in contests became fashionable and the tendency only grew with the prize annually awarded by Casa de las Américas. This one had the purpose of discovering emerging new writers, even though in 1967 it recognized David Viñas's novel, *Men on Horseback*. Less fortunate were the contests organized in the United States. If in the past they had recognized, at the beginning of the emergence of a new narrative, an important product of regionalism in Ciro Alegría's *Broad and Alien is the World*, now they recognized a very conventional product of that new narrative, Marco Denevi's *Secret Ceremony*.[17]

When I call "cultural" the publishing houses that helped the new narrative, I am trying to highlight a practice that deviated from the normal behavior of a commercial enterprise and led them to publish books that they did not think were going to have a lot of readers but whose artistic quality was worth taking a risk. These publishing houses were directed or guided by teams of intellectuals who felt they had a cultural responsibility, and this is evident in their collections of poetry. They encouraged the publication of new and difficult works, no doubt thinking about the initial demand of a new public, which they thought was better prepared and more demanding, but they also did it thinking about the development of a literature more than about the profits for their business.

These publishing houses were successful, and even obtained some economic rewards, but from our current perspective it is evident that there were very few and they did not last. Many of those publishing houses disappeared while others survive but are ruined, and some others resurged by producing low-quality bestsellers. The case of Emecé is a great example: a publishing house in which Jorge Luis Borges, Adolfo Bioy Casares, and Eduardo Mallea published and included in Spanish some of the best English literature, becoming a modernizing guide for the Spanish American reader, has now become just another producer of cheap international novels. Fabril Editora, which gave impulse to the best literature of the moment, disappeared; Losada, after forty years of cultural trajectory, saw its founder retire and most of the actions sold, with great difficulty recovered later by Gonzalo Losada; Sudamericana has begun to follow the idea of bestsellers started by Emecé; Seix Barral alternates high culture books with those exclusively produced for the local Spanish American market; even houses such as Fondo de Cultura Económica had to battle economic difficulties and orders such as Joaquín Mortiz have limited themselves to the national field.

At the end of the 1970s a surprising transformation of the publishing market took place. The cultural publishing houses entered a crisis from which they could not recover and the multinational publishing houses have gained strength, whether through the acquisition of ruined competitors or through their development of massive direct-to-customer sales ("The Book of the Month Club"), or through sales of popular series in supermarkets. Latin America's editorial autonomy, which started in the 1930s, has been drastically reduced by the economic and political advance of multinational publishers. There is no possible comparison between what the multinationals publish and what, with a lot of struggle, the cultural editorials were trying to give to the public: the latter were trying to discover new talents, trying to help them connect with the public; the former are exclusively interested in profitability, and if it is true that they have incorporated in their catalog practically all of the Boom authors' successful titles, they have stopped helping new talent, they have stopped reseeding that indispensable nursery bed needed to plant a new forest. It is not because of some perverse anti-cultural position; it is the result of their own mass-oriented system that will only allow them to handle titles that produce a high number of sales.

This notable change in the editorial business responds to the evolution of the new public and the economic and political reality that Latin America is experiencing. The multinational publishers have focused on attracting this massive public that grew in Latin America beyond the boundaries of elite readers and now they are wooing them away from the cultural editorials that were the first to detect the group's presence and cater to it. At the end of the 1950s and at the beginning of the 1960s, before the so-called narrative Boom, there was another boom, which helped prepare the stage for the one to come. This boom focused on textbooks, especially university ones, but also on books about politics and historical books that recovered the national past. The two main publishing houses in Latin America supplied this demand: in Mexico, the Fondo de Cultura Económica and in Buenos Aires, Editorial Universitaria (EUDEBA), both directed by notable editors, Arnaldo Orfila Reynal and Boris Spivacow, respectively, who after being removed from their positions have continued their tasks with private enterprises: Siglo XXI and Centro Editor de América Latina.

Responding to this growing demand of a younger and educated public, Fondo de Cultura created its "Colección popular" (which extended the publishing strategies they had gradually attempted with their "Breviarios" collection to a larger reading public) and EUDEBA marketed to students several collections of brief books, manuals, and texts, which they also made available to the general public via direct sales. This is the beginning of the Latin American pocket book market and its two classic characteristics:

massive editions at low prices, in other words, directed at a large public with low income. One cannot compare the high cultural quality of Fondo's and EUDEBA's series offered with current commercial offerings from the multinational publishers, even though the former has obviously been forced to modernize its traditional approach. What is important is that both Fondo and EUDEBA, acting out of a genuine educational concern, contributed to give the new public a modern and rigorous intellectual preparation; they contributed to help them improve their levels of information and taste, on occasion above the levels of the university staff at the time. EUDEBA limited itself to reference books and classic literature, whereas Fondo incorporated into its Colección Popular authors from its catalog. It went from the small editions in its "Mexican Letters" collection to the large ones (usually fifteen thousand copies) of its educational series. The administration became alarmed by the houses directors' modern organization of the materials, their farsightedness and critical openness, and especially with the number of readers their projects attracted, which explains why they [Arnaldo Orfila and Boris Spivacow] were both replaced. The administration would have surely been content with editions of one to two thousand copies as was the norm. Their cultural success was the beginning of the end for EUDEBA and of Fondo de Cultura's stagnation, which lasted several years.

Simultaneously with the editorial expansion into new fields, publishing houses exclusively focused on literary texts begin to emerge. Their objective was to keep their exclusive readership updated about the newest literary currents in Europe and North America as well as about Latin American writers practicing similar styles. Among publishing houses with this orientation, one can find Compañía General Fabril Editora (directed by Jacobo Muchnik) in Buenos Aires and Seix Barral (directed by Carlos Barral) in Barcelona, both of them sharing similar characteristics. For example, they were important in the introduction of the French "nouveau roman," which generated so many debates among authors. They both were working for a minority public (hoping it would become the majority in the future), translating new material to be published in limited editions but reissued in pocket books as soon as the demand allowed it. They possessed an artisan character (one can clearly see it in *Años de penitencia*, the second volume of Carlos Barral's memoirs[18]) in spite of the care they put into the editions, their rigorous translations, and their search for new material. They were also aware of the need to function at the same level as the publishers in the most developed European countries. When Fabril Editora became bankrupt, Seix Barral remained as the only representative of this new tendency and moved to reconquer the Spanish American market that the Spanish publishing houses lost as a result of the Franco dictatorship. The notion, shared by Barral and Jaime Salinas (who later on was responsible for the success of Alianza Editorial and Alfaguara), that "the period of dominance of humanistic publications in Latin America was in its final stretch" was not entirely true, but the Argentine military dictatorship and its restrictions made it a reality.

Carlos Barral has clearly explained in his book the editorial concept for Seix Barral during this period:

> The theoretical basis of our businesses and hopes were very simple. We were trying to create a back-list of important very recent authors, which were unknown to Italian-French market sources where Argentine editors used to get their information, thus trying to cover a sector of foreign literature in which they didn't seem to be interested. . . . If we presented it intelligently and were able to convince the so-called captive minority, to impose that content of that literary stage on the Spanish speaking market was then a matter of time.[19]

This plan, however, was going to require a coordination of efforts with the European editorials in a sort of pool from within, in which Seix Barral tried to successfully represent not only Spain but the entire Spanish speaking hemisphere (the international awards were its external manifestation), but both the fragility of the Spanish cultural editorials and the arrival to the Spanish market of multinational publishing companies (especially the German ones), in a process of concentration of capital, would set limits to the efforts and lead to the same failure that had already taken place in Latin America. The cultural editorials yielded their autonomy to the banks that bought market shares or to multinationals linked to those banks, establishing the conditions of a new book industry market.

Both launching new narrative authors and marketing them to the growing public was done by these weak cultural editorials. Thanks to their youthfulness and skills, they also recovered the previous productions of these authors and extracted materials from that group to build their small growth. Commercially, they benefited more than the authors themselves, but they crumbled in the face of their stronger competitors.

In the debates about the Boom, Carlos Barral argued that any small or medium size editorial could not finance a big marketing campaign because the profit margins of the editorial business did not allow that. He also said that even with a strong series of ads in newspapers or magazines they were not able to secure massive sales of a book. In the previously mentioned *Coloquio del libro*, Benito Mina, who directed the publishing houses Alfa in Montevideo and Monte Ávila in Caracas, repeated emphatically, "We cannot pay for publicity for a product that doesn't have a mass circulation," adding that "when a book is known beyond its circle of readers then it is almost always for extra-literary reasons."[20] That is a convincing observation because there are other forces, created or not by the editors, that produced those extra-literary reasons, which in cases such as Sagan and Pasternak Papillon (to mention a dissimilar group) guarantees an enormous circulation for their books. Not even the cultural editorials of that time tried to create a book, as has become the norm in the North American publishing world, as James Purdy satirically described in *Cabot Wright Begins* (1964).

There are obviously forces at work within an economic market that sometimes coincide with artistic values (but are not moved by them) and during a short period of time, to maximize the impact of that coincidence, these commercial forces work within the means of mass communication, skillfully manipulating the imagination of the populations with ceaseless, devouring mobility. They sell gold and mud, mixed together as if they were the same, even though the former possesses a staying power that goes beyond the momentary splendor. It also means creators have to partially adapt themselves to some extenuating conditions such as the constant variations of topics and approaches, focusing on the attention-grabbing aspects of the present, keeping up with the latest fashions, adjusting to the international demands of circulation of products, and so on.

Catalog of Grievances

The chapter of complaints against the Boom is very extensive and it begins a little bit after its explosion. We have alluded to some of them, most of them political in nature, but they do not exhaust the broad range of stereotypical expressions. They come from multiple sources and even from opposite aesthetic positions.

Among the oldest ones, we can find the bitter accusations thrown at them by the critic Manuel Pedro González, who in his time was a strong supporter of the regionalist novel and especially of the narrative of the Mexican Revolution. From his aesthetic perspective he initially observed that there was a crisis within the Latin American novel,[21] a little bit similar to the position taken by another critic from his period, the Peruvian Luis Alberto Sánchez. According to him, that crisis took shape in a series of novels from the 1950s and the beginning of the 1960s that were showing traces of an artistic and cosmopolitan writing style, which he saw as an uneducated imitation of the avant-garde European or North American writing models. He attacked directly the authors of those books and in passing he also censured me and many other critics for having supported those products, which he considered frivolous and socially irresponsible.[22] A fragment of his indictment very clearly defines his position and that of a sector of the public:

> From my point of view, the generation represented by Juan Rulfo, Carlos Fuentes, Mario Vargas Llosa, José Revueltas, Julio Cortázar, Lino Novás Calvo and a few others, has gone too far in their desire to renovate literary technique and many of them have shown a mimetism that takes away from originality and vigor in their works. I realize that the last three, based on their age, belong to a generation previous to that of Rulfo, Fuentes and Vargas Llosa, and that the novelist task of Novás Calvo and Revueltas preceded by several years that of others in the group but, in spite of the chronology, I believe that they are all linked together by their desire to renovate, following imported models. Cortázar, Rulfo, Fuentes and Vargas Llosa are the four narrators most praised by Latin American critics today. *Hopscotch*, for example, has been proclaimed "the Latin American *Ulysses*" and a commentator as educated and talented as Carlos Fuentes has not hesitated to place the author at the same level as Rabelais, Sterne and Joyce, and he has even suggested that he has surpassed them. Such hyperbole, it seems to me, are both subjective and inadmissible because *Hopscotch*, in spite of the undeniable talent and culture of its author, is what the Mexicans call a "refrito," that is to say a potpourri of copies that become a real pastiche.[23]

His position plainly demonstrates the change in aesthetic perception that the new novel requires. It was favorably compared in the opposite direction by its defenders, who described it in contrast to the Latin American regionalist novel (Azuela, Rivera, Gallegos), establishing a gross dichotomy in which two completely different poetics—and, moreover, styles—faced each other, with that sleight of hand so typical of generational disputes in which the new, by its mere existence, is already better than the old and the style of a period is sufficient evidence of its artistic excellence. These are old fallacies that only come up during polemic times. Expressed differently, the excellence of *Hopscotch* has nothing to do with its new style but with its own narrative virtues, and the use of an outmoded style in [Rivera's] *The Vortex* does not take anything away from its inventive brilliance because he is not conventionally applying rules from an old style. But that polemic, which can be followed in the writings of Carlos Fuentes or Mario Vargas Llosa,[24] changes historical veracity and tends to present as exclusive invention of the 1960s what had already been developing in Latin American letters since the avant-garde generation of the 1920s and gave us fiction in which one can see artistic explorations that served as precursors to today's products. Let us remember texts such as *Macunaíma, Papeles de recienvenido, Leyendas de Guatemala, Tres inmensas novelas,* and *Novela como nube,* all of which challenged the then predominant regionalist narrative.[25]

A second type of criticism comes from one of the intellectuals who vigorously supported the new narrative, and even wrote a book widely influential in both Spanish and English. I am talking about Luis Harss, writer and critic who in 1966, in collaboration with Barbara Dohmann, published *Los nuestros*, which was translated as *Into the Mainstream* a year later.[26] Employing personal interviews with ten authors as point of departure, it is composed of critical and biographical essays that offered a careful panorama of the many faces of contemporary Latin American narrative. However, in the third edition in Spanish, from 1969, Harss added an "Epilogue with Retractions" in which he critically reviewed the latest work of the authors included in his book. He explained:

> As for the phenomenon now known as the Latin American "Boom"—a phenomenon, one can see now, that is more an editorial and marketing phenomenon than a real creative bloom—it goes on, not always brilliantly, but growing, with its quota of successes and failures, as in any diversified enterprise with a mix of talent and inertia. As it diversifies its plans, there are frauds and parasites disguised as competitors, and broken promises. The old web of interests, which in a moment of euphoria were thought to have been surpassed, has now been replaced by cliques. The actions have simply changed hands. Sudden fame and lack of criteria go together, putting in danger the critical sense a young

literature needs to judge itself. There are now plenty of false alarms, pseudo-events and overinflated egos, which uneducated popular magazines magnify.[27]

It is a very severe text that already in 1969 registers the wave of confusion and lack of critical attitude that surrounded the so-called Boom, looking at it as an environment perfect for selling any type of literary sub-product and, what is worse, establishing the idea of the bestseller as the goal any new author should aspire to. It is possible that the frivolous and derivative products in the late 1960s were blown up by what Harss calls "popular magazines," which explains his severe judgment. He is pointing out that during that moment we lived a sort of "fashion cycle of narrative" that was trying to launch every year "new literary trends" and simultaneously proclaim the artistic death of the ones that were dominating the market the previous year.

What gave the Boom its bad name was this type of diving into the nihilism of fashion unscrupulously playing with the aperies of the avant-garde, which caused the rejection by the younger generations.

The self-destroying force of this nihilism that comes from an unbridled avant-garde spirit is well known. An example can be found in the criticisms of the authors that Harss included, made by a distinguished writer who was not one of them. Only six years after the appearance of *Into the Mainstream*, José Dosono wrote, "brought together several years ago ten writers who seemed at that time definitive in the literary panorama but whose primacy in regard to fame and literary quality in several cases seems debatable only a few years later."[28] Those ten names that in "several cases" appear disputable because they have lost their "fame" and "literary quality" are Alejo Carpentier, Miguel Ángel Asturias, Jorge Luis Borges, João Guimarães Rosa, Juan Carlos Onetti, Julio Cortázar, Juan Rulfo, Carlos Fuentes, Gabriel García Márquez, and Mario Vargas Llosa.

A third type of critique comes from the narrators themselves, agreeing with some of the diverse critiques that were directed at the movement. Several of the narrators who were included in the lists of Boom writers distanced themselves from the phenomenon. These were Juan Rulfo, Juan Carlos Onetti, Gabriel García Márquez, and Alejo Carpentier. The latter explained himself at length during his visit to Caracas in 1976:

> I have never believed in the existence of the *Boom*. . . . The *Boom* is what doesn't last, it is noise, it is what's popular. . . . Those

who called *Boom* the simultaneous and relatively sudden success of a number of Latin American writers, didn't do them a favor because the *Boom* is what doesn't last. What happens is that the formula of the *Boom* was employed by several editors with more or less marketing purposes, but I repeat that there hasn't been such a boom. What has been called *Boom* is simply that a group of novelists coincide at a specific moment in time, more or less from the same generation, some ten years younger or older, the youngest ones are twenty years younger, but in general they are all men between 40 and, more or less, 60 years old, and some who are approaching that age.[29]

Thus, we have summarized objectively the different positions taken with respect to the Boom. A positive view, from some of the authors implicated; the view of the editors trying to reconstruct the situation in which they functioned and that of the critics or other authors who, at different times and looking at the phenomenon from diverse angles, expressed their concerns. They could be expanded with many others, but I understand that they are representative,[30] and I am also leaving aside my own critiques, which I have expressed on many occasions but which never stopped me from appreciating the higher artistic value of the works of many authors from this period, whether they were included in the list of Boom writers or not.

To better define the topic, there are two aspects we need to review. One of them is the names that form part of this public selection of authors, which is, as Donoso admits in his book, the most difficult task, and I will try to establish a list appealing to the most responsible sources. The other aspect has to do with the dates when it took place and I will try to fix them using objective data, detaching the process from any subjective views and from that confusing mixture (which goes back several decades) of the evolution of the new narrative and the explosive period of massive sales.

Who Are They?

In his declarations Vargas Llosa points out that "each of us has his own list" with which he is tacitly alluding to the selective principle that comes with this concept of a list and that one is trying to impose on the basic list that forms our object of study. From the moment that each one creates their own list we are accepting that this is a new selection, created from our point of departure, a list that combines all of the bestseller authors in Spanish America. We are thus in the presence of an intellectual operation that has at least three necessary versions, using a different "heterogeneous criteria" in each case, but which accumulate.

In the first version a distinctive function intervenes that establishes a division between different literary genres, implicitly accepting traditional definitions without paying attention to the enormous contemporary modifications. In [Latin] America, the poetry of Pablo Neruda or Marta Harnecker's *The Basic Concepts of Historical Materialism* or Octavio Paz's essays have sold as much or maybe more than novels, and none of these authors are incorporated into the Boom because the term explicitly rejects anything that is not narrative. This distinct function is reductive and impoverishing to Latin American culture, visibly deforming some of its strongest features, but this appears to be a methodological assumption needed to describe the concept of the Boom. The term will only be applied to contemporary Latin American narrative.

The second version appeals to an exclusively quantitative criteria, accepting only those narrators who have achieved the greatest diffusion, distinguishing between those who have "sold the most" and those who have "sold the least," ignoring the aesthetic quality of their works. This is the stage where one can find examples of writers, popular in their time, who are later rediscovered by posterior generations, such as the well-known cases of Stendhal and Kafka. The quantity versus quality predicament does not apply to them because now the fact that they are selling is surreptitiously equated with aesthetic quality. For this second version critics have not used rigorous quantitative methods, and instead of looking at the number of copies a book has sold, they have focused on the public's reaction, which is so difficult to evaluate objectively. If we were to stop our study here the members of the Boom would be determined based solely on popularity. But that is not the case. In most lists I have not found the names of Luis Spota, Mario Benedetti, Silvana Bullrich, Manuel Scorza, Miguel Otero Silva, or David Viñas, who are writers whose works have had great diffusion, but also not present of course are the names of Corín Tellado or Papillon, who have sold more than any other author.[31]

But also, this criteria is based on assigning value to sale numbers (possessing an ingenuous prestige defended using democratic arguments by progressives), and that is a very recent development within Latin American culture, traditionally associated with elitism. The five hundred copies of Darío's *Profane Hymns* or Rodó's *Ariel* were seen as normal at the time and most of those copies were given away, following the cultured customs in place around the 1900s. But even in the 1920s, when in Buenos Aires *Claridad* began to edit popular books, writers saw with disdain their great number of sales and that was part of the reason why the Ultraístas rejected Roberto Arlt even though their own magazine, *Martín Fierro*, was also a very popular publication. Borges has recalled with precision this distrust in an interview he gave to E. Gudiño Kieffer:

> I published my first book, *Fervor de Buenos Aires* in 1923: the edition cost me 300 pesos. It never occurred to me to bring a single copy to the bookstores nor to the newspapers. And one never talked about success or failure. My father was a friend of Arturo Cancela, who used to publish books that sold very well, but he believed that if other writers knew about this, they would think that his books were written for the masses and then they wouldn't have any value. So he would say "No, no, people are exaggerating. In reality I sell very little." He was afraid people would see him as a sort of Martínez Zuviría or something like that. No, he would sell his books and shut his mouth; nowadays, on the other hand . . .[32]

Of course this appreciation responded to an objective view of the phenomenon of sales. The person who overwhelmingly sold the most during modernismo was Vargas Vila,[33] not Darío, and Martí did not even enter the market with his books of poetry; the writer selling well in the 1920s was Hugo Wast even though by then Roberto Arlt would get from his popular success the uncouth pride needed to oppose the cultured elite.[34] Obviously, sales do not translate to the field of artistic values.

We thus arrive at the third approach to understand the concept of the Boom. This one is qualitative and argues that the selection should be based on merit according to the values intrinsic to the narrative works. If the first two versions were the result of apparently objective approaches, the third one responds to an aesthetic criteria, or at least a cultural one. This explains the plurality of the lists created that correspond to as many individual artistic perceptions. These are the types of critical judgments that are common when that distinguishing intellectual function is not limiting itself to describe but it is also valuing and establishing hierarchies, with some limitations because it is not about choosing freely the best playwrights from the Renaissance nor the best poets from modernismo but about replacing a hierarchy within a previously reduced field. It would be as recovering a spiritual aristocracy after a popular plebiscite.

To this one must add that in this third approach the selection does not frequently include the signature of the person responsible for the selection, but it is done as part of the informative and semi-anonymous task of popular magazines, employing for this the usual canons and taking into consideration the impact of that which is newsworthy. Maybe that explain why the usual lists of the Boom members does not include writers of the quality of Juan Rulfo or Juan Carlos Onetti who belong to the type of authors who shy away from public notoriety. For the same reason Jorge Luis Borges, who in these lists is assigned the ungrateful role of predecessor (something he has made fun of), has conquered in the press a position as relevant as that of the best known members of the Boom, on account of his controversial declarations.

If we consult reliable sources, represented by texts signed by editors or writers directly connected to the Boom, we could corroborate the journalistic material, but with the advantage of having utilized the sources more responsibly.

Looking at the two texts quoted above, Vargas Llosa's text mentions Cortázar and Fuentes, while Cortázar's text mentions García Márquez and Vargas Llosa. For his part, Carlos Fuentes, in his essay *La nueva novela hispanoamericana*, chooses five examples of new narrators, albeit without mentioning the Boom label: Mario Vargas Llosa, Alejo Carpentier, Gabriel García Márquez, Julio Cortázar, and Spanish writer Juan Goytisolo.

In his *The Boom in Spanish American Letters*, José Donoso establishes a hierarchy that looks like a carbon copy of a celestial one where there are thrones and seraphim and archangels, placing only four names to the right side of God the Almighty father: "If categories are accepted, four names make up the kernel, the gratin, of the famous Boom in the eyes of the public, and they were and continue to be the most exaggeratedly praised and criticized as the supposed Mafia bosses: Julio Cortázar, Carlos Fuentes, Gabriel García Márquez and Mario Vargas Llosa."[35]

This list—except for his own exclusion—coincides with Carlos Barral's. In a very curious book titled *Los españoles y el boom* [The Spaniards and the Boom],[36] which offers a view of Spanish American literature from a point of view that at the same time shares a common language but remains marginal to the process, the poet and editor Carlos Barral answers the question about who the members of the Boom are: "Well, I clearly think of Cortázar, I think of Vargas Llosa. I think of García Márquez, I think of Fuentes and I think of Donoso: the rest of them would be like second row, right?"

That second row, headed by Jorge Luis Borges, is basically the entirety of Latin American narrative. If this limited selection is made for precise aesthetic reasons, we would have to ask ourselves why Borges, who is the most daring renovator of fiction writing and the one who sells the most, is inferior to José Donoso or why Julio Cortázar or Carlos Fuentes cannot be equated to Juan Carlos Onetti or Juan Rulfo. If the reasons are not aesthetic, then we are giving credence to the vulgar comments already made against the Boom. In any of those cases, such a reduction of the rich Latin American narrative is an affront against it and a distortion.

Taking all of these texts into account, it might become understandable that I had satirized the Boom, defining it as the most exclusive club in the cultural history of Latin America—a club that restricts itself to the intangible principle of having only five seats, and not a single one more, to protect its elitist integrity. Of those seats, four of them are, as in language academies, "reserved": those assigned to Julio Cortázar, Carlos Fuentes, Mario Vargas Llosa, and Gabriel García Márquez. The fifth is free and it has been assigned to many from Carpentier to Donoso, from Lezama Lima to Guimarães Rosa. Extending this analogy, a second-class title has been created for a "consul" to the Boom, and it has been awarded to Salvador Garmendia on the front flap of his latest book, *Los pies de barro*, edited by Seix Barral.

Literary criticism, more interested in the evolution of narrative than in the noise of public overexcitement, has sensitively been setting the limits in which one or the other operate. John Stubbs Brushwood has done this with good judgment in his book *The Spanish-American Novel*,[37] one of the most complete attempts to encompass chronologically the narrative creativity of the twentieth century.

Brushwood thinks that overall the phenomenon has been beneficial because it has brought the high-quality narrative production in Latin America to the attention of both the internal and external public, in spite of the exclusions ("The boom is not four novelists, or even six or seven"), and believes that even marginal writers have benefited from it:

> Although the terms "new Latin American novel" and "the boom" sometimes appear synonymous, they really indicate two different

aspects of a single phenomenon—the maturity of fiction in Latin America. Specifically with reference to the Spanish—speaking countries, it is convenient to think of the new novel as dating from the late 1940s, the years of the reaffirmation of fiction. The boom, on the other hand, best describes the unprecedented international interest enjoyed by Spanish American novelists in the 1960s, and the spectacular increase in the number of high-quality novels they produced. Although nobody thought of it as a boom until several years later, the change is readily apparent in the years following *Pedro Páramo*.[38]

Once we recognize the different natures of each one of these two processes, we can date the one corresponding to the narrative properly speaking, as Brushwood has done, to the publication of *Pedro Páramo*, or go back even further to the short story genre where authors were designing new narrative modes and include Jorge Luis Borges's early books, written a decade before, or even go back to the narrative experiments in 1930s.

But the dates of the Boom are different: they correspond to the more recent period bridging the 1960s and 1970s.

The Boom Dates

As we have already pointed out, several accounts coincide in pointing to 1972 as the year of the death of the Boom, even though they do not have enough evidence to support this. It seems unimaginable that this announces that the expansion of the book market is over, or that there are no new narrators capable of conquering a vast audience. In reality, the book market continues its uneven evolution and massive editions are becoming common, but with growing interest in books about current affairs, imitating what is happening in the North American market, or in new books by those authors who have an established brand and have gained the trust of their readership because of a previous book, like an investment that keeps paying dividends without being affected by peculiar artistic changes. And youthful creativity does not seem like a reason for the death of the Boom either because it has not diminished, though, as Harss has noticed, because of the Boom's influence we are seeing a great number of improvised and confused imitations. Literature continues to be produced but we are at that difficult transitional period when it has become necessary to create a new style that responds to new situations, something that is not easy when the mass media has already imposed certain models on the market and, judging from some of the tangential reactions to the debate about the Boom, could lead to a new generalized parricide.

One can even argue that the Boom school closed in 1967 with the appearance of *One Hundred Years of Solitude*. By this date García Márquez had already published four works that critics had received favorably, among them his admirable *No One Writes to the Colonel*, but the Boom machinery was not in place at the time, neither for him nor for his literary colleagues. The amazing reception of his *One Hundred*, without equal in Latin America, fixed the number of members in the Parnassus and after that no new person was unquestionably incorporated into it. That book gave concrete form to the still fluctuating and indecisive Boom movement; it gave the phenomenon shape and even froze it in time so it could begin to extinguish itself.

Tomás Eloy Martínez[39] has provided another explanation for the importance of the year 1972 and, in the process, transporting the date to 1973, the dark year for South American democracies, and transforming that year not into the end but into a turning point: "Against the isolationism imposed by Power, historical discourse appears as a subversive recourse." In this case it is the Boom members themselves who would have made that transformation possible but everything that they have produced after that date does not support the thesis. The historical novelists continue the same line of work (García Márquez, Alejo Carpentier, Mario Vargas Llosa) with only the partial incorporation of Julio Contázar (*A Manual for Manuel*) and with a remarkable contribution by another historical novelist whom the Boom had forgotten, Augusto Roa Bastos, who publishes *I, the Supreme*; however, the rest of the group continues to distance themselves from history, not only in the production of Cabrera Infante, Sarduy, Donoso, Puig, and Sábato but also in those who started their careers using a historical discourse (Onetti or Fuentes) and are proposing a cancellation of that discourse (*Terra nostra*). A transformation has taken place, but unrelated to the Boom, in the process of the incorporation of a new generation of narrators who work toward the construction on a new type of writing. The group includes Osvaldo Soriano, Griselda Gambaro, Antonio Skármeta, Sergio Ramírez, Britto García, Héctor Manjarrez, Luis Rafael Sánchez, Jorge Aguilar Mora, Norberto Fuentes, Plinio Apuleyo Mendoza, Lisandro Chávez Alfaro, Libertella, and many more.[40] This is not the place to analyze this change, but one could point out a very curious feature: these writers come from the marginal intellectual centers because they either come from backward regions of the continent or they come from the diaspora, which explains their difference from those were following the Boom models that work in the metropolis.

If it is difficult to fix the ending date of the Boom, it is perhaps less difficult to establish the beginning of the phenomenon. I think one cannot go back beyond 1964, which would give to the whole process a minimum period of ten years, and then we could call it, as Roa Bastos did, an "explosion."

To determine the initial date, I will use the evolution of the book sales of Julio Cortázar, who is included in practically all of the lists of Boom writers. Sudamericana in Buenos Aires had published three of his books before he wrote *Hopscotch* and none of them had been republished: in 1951 *Bestiario* with a run of twenty-five hundred copies; in 1959 *Las armas secretas*, three thousand copies; and in 1960 *The Winners*, with three thousand copies too received early attention mostly as a result of cultural censure than market demand. *Hopscotch* appears in 1963, also with the traditional run of three thousand copies, but one can argue that its quality was a factor that led to sales and above all annual republications. The following statistical table visualizes that evolution.

After 1970, the re-editions of every title begin to average ten thousand copies annually.[41]

Table 9.1

Years	*Bestiario*	*Las armas secretas*	*The Winners*	*Hopscotch*	*All Fires the Fire*
1964	3,000	3,000	3,500		
1965	3,000	4,000	3,500	4,000	
1966	7,000	5,000	15,000*	10,000*	28,000**
1967	11,000*	10,000	10,000	10,000*	8,000
1968	8,000	16,000*	20,000*	26,000***	24,000***
1969	23,000*	10,000	20,000*	25,000*	10,000
1970	10,000	20,000*	10,000	20,000	10,000

*In two print runs
**In four print runs
***In three print runs

The highest point of editorial production during this period centers around *One Hundred Years of Solitude*. It is published in 1967 with an initial print run of twenty-five thousand copies and since 1968 the annual production is one hundred thousand copies, which represents a revolution for fiction sales in the continent. Much more than the other cases, we are witnessing here an overcoming of the expanded circuit composed of cultured readers and now we are incorporating the public from zones that were hardly touched by the book market or entirely virgin and even in some cases opposed to the book market. This authentic explosion is not repeated with García Márquez's books that come afterward; however, the sales of his previously published books reach high numbers.

In 1967 Sudamericana republishes *Big Mama's Funeral* with a run of twenty thousand copies, a number that remains the same year after year in subsequent editions. In 1968, the same thing happens with *Leaf Storm*, publishing twenty thousand copies that year and republishing the same amount year after year. In 1969 Sudamericana incorporates to its catalog *No One Writes the Colonel* with a small edition of ten thousand copies that a year later increases to fifty thousand copies, which is the amount it will continue to have annually until 1972.[42]

What happened in the cases of Cortázar and García Márquez repeated itself with other authors: although with variations, the publication of a new title, after several that only had one edition and very little circulation, generated new interest from readers and led to a re-edition of previous works and frequently moving from the catalogs in small publishing presses to others with larger circulation, getting an increase in the number of copies and, above all, being periodically re-edited.

The list of titles from the first five years of the 1960s is evidence of this type of editorial practice, which in some cases has increased in speed, both because the author is producing more and because of the greater circulation that the new publishing house affords, giving the impression of a snowball effect that toward 1964 impressed the general public. A selection of titles from the period of 1959–1964, where one can detect the new conditions for the narrative, gives us a faithful image of this editorial practice:

> 1959: Juan Carlos Onetti, *A Grave with No Name* (Marcha); Augusto Roa Bastos, *Son of Man* (Losada); David Viñas, *Los dueños de la tierra* (Losada). 1960: Julio Cortázar, *The Winners* (Sudamericana); Jorge Luis Borges, *Dreamtigers* (Emecé); José Revueltas, *Dormir en tierra* (Veracruzana); Sergio Galindo, *El*

bordo (Veracruzana); Carlos Fuentes, *The Good Conscience* (F. C. E.); Julio Ramón Ribeyro, *Crónica de San Gabriel*.

1961: Juan Carlos Onetti, *The Shipyard* (Fabril Editora); Gabriel García Márquez, *No One Writes to the Colonel* (Aguirre); Miguel Ángel Asturias, *El Alhajadito* (Goyanarte).

1962: Alejo Carpentier, *Explosion in a Cathedral* (Editora Nacional); Ernesto Sábato, *Sobre héroes y tumbas* (Fabril Editora); Carlos Fuentes, *The Death of Artemio Cruz* (F. C. E.) and *Aura* (Era); Carlos Martínez Moreno, *El paredón* (Seix Barral); Álvaro Cepeda Zamudio, *La casa grande* (Mito); Gabriel García Márquez, *In Evil Hour*; Juan Carlos Onetti, *El infierno tan temido* (Asir); Héctor Rojas Herazo, *Respirando el verano*; Rosario Castellanos, *The Book of Lamentations* (F. C. E.); Adolfo Bioy Casares, *El lado de la sombra* (Emecé); Guillermo Meneses, *La misa de Arlequín*; David Viñas, *Dar la cara* (Jamcana).

1963: Julio Cortázar, *Hopscoth* (Sudamericana); Severo Sarduy, *Gestos* (Seix Barral); Mario Vargas Llosa, *The Time of the Hero* (Seix Barral); Juan José Arreola, *La feria* (Mortiz); Miguel Ángel Asturias, *Mulata de Tal* (Losada). 1964: José María Arguedas, *Every Blood* (Losada); Juan Carlos Onetti, *Body Snatcher* (Alfa); Salvador Garmendia, *Día de ceniza*; Vicente Leñero, *Los albañiles* (Seix Barral); Juan García Ponce, *Figura de paja* (Mortiz).[43]

In this phenomenon of republishing previous works that adds to the growing narrative production from of this period, Leopoldo Marechal's novel *Adán Buenosayres* (1948) is paradigmatic. It originally appeared in 1948 and had very few readers as well as scant attention from the critics (famous exceptions were positive notes written by Julio Cortázar and Noé Jitrik) but in 1966 Sudamericana republishes it with an initial run of ten thousand copies, and with the same numbers they publish it again in 1967, 1968, and 1970.

Something similar happened in Mexico, as one can observe in the transference of the titles that initially appeared in the hardcover collection "Letras Mexicanas" from Fondo de Cultura Económica to the Popular Collection from the same publisher, which was using bigger print runs. Rulfo's *Pedro Páramo*, which since its initial publication in 1955 had been periodically republished as part of "Mexican Letters," became part of the "Popular Collection" in 1964 and has been republished every year since. In 1971 it reached a total of sixty thousand copies. That same year, fifty thousand copies Rulfo's other book, *The Burning Plain*, were printed. A similar situation happened to Carlos Fuentes. *Where the Air is Clear* (1958) was incorporated into the Popular Collection in 1968 and enjoyed successive re-editions. The 1972 expanded edition has a run of twenty-five thousand copies, to which one must add another eight thousand from the simultaneous republishing in "Letras Mexicanas."

A normal reader, having little experience with bibliographical references or literary generational divisions, was suddenly in the presence of a prodigious explosion of creators, which was both inexhaustible and rich. In fact, readers were not witnessing exclusively new production but the accumulation in only a decade of the production of the last forty years, which up until then was only known by the cultured elite. Two factors were influential: the size of the production was notably big and became very intense because of the demand and the previous titles of those writers were brought back to the market. The Latin American reader was exposed to the peculiar prodigality of the consumer mass market in which determined topics and treatments acquire the appearance of registered brands, defeating competition from other products, which following the laws of the market were trying to look like the successful ones rather than show originality. This side of the problem deserves to be studied in detail following the type of approach used by Escarpit in his work, but it is the other side of the problem, about the effect of these new mechanisms of literary consumption on the authors, that we prefer to consider.

Literary Productivity, Professionalization, and Market Laws

One of the first results of the recently created literary consumer market was the pressure exerted on new writers to increase their production, a topic closely related to the professionalization of writing. It was an old ambition of the Latin American artist, and the first coherent formulations of this idea appeared during *modernismo*. At the time there were a couple of concrete situations—like working in journalism or diplomacy—that allowed them to think of that possibility, but they imagined it more as an idealized version of what they thought was the paradisaical situation of the French writer than as the result of the public demand that was then almost nonexistent.

Modernistas did not analyze their professionalization from the angle of the demands of a reader in a free market to whom writers need to respond, thus conquering their professional autonomy, but the other way around, as a service that society should give writers so that they could create their work in accordance with their own methods and productive rhythms, which were very different, by the way, from those practiced by workers at any social level at the time, whether they were lawyers or laborers. Hence, more than private support, they used to address public authorities instead and ask for support from the State, sometimes getting it in the form of diplomatic positions or obscure jobs justified in the government budget. The fact is that society absorbed those writers in activities in which they needed their skills (journalism, teaching, administration), forcing them to duplicate their tasks, which limited their literary production: Martí's and Darío's journalistic work is more numerous than their literary work.

Literature as a second job was the way of life for writers during the early twentieth century and the fact that frequently their first job related to the state and therefore was closely linked to partisan politics brought them many difficulties; the best examples of this situation can be observed in the case of Mexico. Their persistent ambition was to gain autonomy through what appeared to be a free professional relation with consumers and it became really urgent when a gap grew between their political ideas and the positions of those ruling from the throne of the state. That autonomy seemed within reach (although only partially and after many personal sacrifices only known by those who worked for it) when there was a greater demand for books, when magazines that paid for collaborations multiplied, when related activities were established (conferences, university courses, appearances on TV) and decently remunerated. The joy in this possibility can be perceived in Roberto Arlt's arrogant texts when the populist "boom" of the 1920s made him think that a direct and autonomous communication with the public was already established. But it was only recently, in the 1960s, when the small national markets opened and began to constitute a continental market, at the same time growing through translations for an international market, that some finally thought the old dream could be realized.

Even though it was unjustly criticized by narrow minded people, the movement of Latin American writers to other regions within the continent (or to Europe or the United States) that presented better possibilities for the diffusion of their work because they possessed publishing houses, magazines, and large newspapers was the result of this attempt to professionalize. Authors were both realizing completely their vocation and simultaneously responding to a regional demand of the Latin American culture: writers were needed to build a rich literature. Faced with the impossibility of being professional writers in their own countries, for a variety of reasons (suffocating economically or politically, lack of time to focus on their work, lack of opportunities, lack of information, local narrow-mindedness), they moved to the best locations, regionally or outside the continent. It is the same thing that millions of people in Latin America have done, without having been chastised or morally criticized. And one must add that the vast majority of those writers have continued serving the Latin American culture from where they came and about which they continue thinking obsessively, splendidly, no matter in which city or country they are residing.

This conquest of professionalization is not perfect. Except for exceptional cases, the royalties of books and articles allow only simple lives and very frequently that income is complemented with other cultural tasks: courses, serving as advisor to editorials, translations. Still, there is already a group of writers for whom literature has become their first job, and in itself this marks them as notably different, adding a very distinctive characteristic to the phenomenon. The Boom was mostly composed of professional writers.

While following with tenacity a path that would incorporate them to the demands of an expanding world market, Boom writers discovered something that neither the modernistas nor avant-garde nor the regionalists (who in their time were the protagonists of a quasi-boom) knew: they discovered the need to have a work schedule in accordance with the new system. Not everything is flowers in this new world: the professional writer has to leave behind both the bohemian life and the "inspirational muse" to which we owe so many ingenious and fragmentary improvisations that were never continued, because writers now become producers like other workers within society. Strictly speaking they occupy a place in society similar to that of the independent business owner or entrepreneur who periodically brings objects to the market; even if their system of productions continues to be in most cases artisan, just like Valéry noticed, they work for a market, which means that they have to be aware of the market's rough conditions, tendencies, preferences, and disdains. It forces them to face the peculiarly competitive mass market, to register its basic orientations, and to detect its variables. Even though writers continue to be just individuals with a pencil and a block of paper, professionalization ties them indirectly to the market, which does not mean that it is making them merely servants but it forces them to accept themselves as producers who are working within a framework that has been imposed on them. Within this context, they must operate and succeed.

When this work regime was being designed, it appeared to contradict the essence of literature, at least the way writers who were part of the traditional system of letters, who we could call "amateur," saw it because it exclusively takes into consideration their productivity and not their artistic skills. That is the origin of the complaints Peruvian writer José María Arguedas directed at the professional writers while struggling to finish his last novel, *The Fox from Above and the Fox from Down Below*. He was talking from another time and from a position marginal to the market system. He was secretly envious of the new working regime and at the same times he hated its laws, which he saw as corrupting the sacred values he grew up with. Literature, for him, was still a priesthood that magically integrated him into the center of his community, giving him a heroic position. He couldn't accept being a writer as just another job among the many that the community needs, an idea that, at that transitional period, even professional writers wouldn't accept, at least in such dry terms, as they locate their profession within political, educational, or spiritual contexts that give them a reverential dignity. That is part of an ideological view of the writer that is still very strong within Latin American society, detecting its real circumstances, and it even provokes nostalgia in intellectuals belonging to more advanced societies. The loss of the notion of the "visionary poet" is still felt as an impoverishment.

The first and obvious difference between the professional and amateur is the high productivity of the former, which could be measured objectively looking at the number of works that the members of these categories put in the market and the frequency with which they are produced. There is no comparison between the production of Rulfo, Arguedas, Guimarães Rosa, Revueltas, and Lezama Lima and that of Borges, Cortázar, Fuentes, Vargas Llosa, Carpentier, Viñas, Benedetti, Donoso, and Bullrich, but of course one cannot extrapolate this to artistic value; it must be strictly appreciated in the field of production. The exclusive dedication of a professional obviously benefits his training and improves his ability to take better advantage of personal situations, but the need to satisfy an urgent demand can be detrimental to the process of artistic maturing, which does not necessarily follow the patterns of massive industrial production. After the readers' violent demand for works in the 1960s was solved with the re-editing of old books by their favorite authors, thus easily satisfying their appetite, in the 1970s the professional writers found themselves trying to fulfill the demand by inventing books or turning in works with which they were not entirely happy yet.

> The heterogeneous composition of Cortázar's *Octaedro* or his carelessness in the final version of *A Manual for Manuel*, uncharacteristic of his writings, seem to respond to the need to fulfill current demand. And this demand, let us be clear about this, is not only economic, as one could infer from the terms that were being used to describe it when talking about market operations, but the result of multiple types of urgent requests: to be present in specific places, to respond to political issues, to participate in circumstantial fights.

One could say the same thing about the construction of Neruda's poetry books at the end of his career or Borges's recent production, whose pace has increased even though, as it is well known, his faculties have diminished. In fiction this tendency has resulted in the composition of accidental books, getting forgotten manuscripts out of a trunk, sometimes placed there with good reason, or in giving permission to re-edit early work that a writer had condemned, or, in that custom typical of the 1970s, which consisted in compiling under a new title materials from previous books to give them new life or to introduce an author to new markets as if these were new works: they have done it with Fuentes, Cortázar, García Márquez, Vargas Llosa, and Viñas, among others. These are legitimate editorial practices. What is in question is their role in detecting the problems of the field's recent professionalization. On the one hand, the professional writers seem incapable of permanently supplying the public's demand for novelties, in spite of their desire to do so, because even a writer as prolific as Fuentes cannot shorten the time it takes him to produce a book to less than two years. On the other hand, as always happens when there is a sudden expansion of the market, it has been proven that there was only a very limited quantity of producers, well below the number initially expected. This is evident in the editions in Spain: after Seix Barral produced a brilliant series of entirely new Latin American titles in the 1960s, in the 1970s Seix Barral, Alianza Editorial, and others have begun to re-edit old books that had little circulation in the Peninsula, thus repeating the Latin American production of the 1940s and 1950s. It safe to say that the market has expanded beyond the limits of the offer. And they have been unable to normalize it incorporating new titles, which points to a conflicting situation that must be studied because it is the obscure origin of some of the prejudices against the Boom writers.

No work (or author) from the 1970s has been able to dominate the international mass-market even though many of them have been—or are—very interesting and in spite of the efforts of their cultural editorials, which have been chasing that illusory success, editing night after night without getting anything in return except books in storage or on the half-price sale tables. The surprising situation has a lot to do with the behavior of the mass public (applied now for the first time to serious literature) and also with the mechanisms of commodity production that are part of the industrial infrastructure: these reasons are more important for creating the typical reductive impact of the Boom than the so-called authors' or publishers' tricks.

We have gone from a literary market for the elite to one for the masses and we have not paid enough attention to how their inner workings are diametrically opposed. While the elite are offered a high and, above all, diverse number of titles but always in small quantities, the masses have very few titles available to them, but in large quantities. Two images give an objective example of these two contrasting sales strategies: one is represented by shelves full of titles, usually one or two of each, characteristic of stock bookstores, the ones frequented by writers and scholars who are part of the same elite (Oxford's Blackwell Bookshop is a good example) and the other is represented by the tables with large piles of the latest bestsellers that regular bookstores make available to everyday consumers. If modern bookstores have introduced a modification, it has been the progressive reduction of traditional stock, replacing it with books destined for instant sales. In modern bookstores, the staff only restocks the bestsellers, the ones their clients are looking for, denying those clients any opportunity to come into contact with young authors, and, when facing a demanding client, limiting themselves to order directly from the distributor or the publisher a copy of the book requested because it has already been sold beforehand. In countries with a highly developed information structure, booksellers have catalogs of the published material, which allows them to accommodate unusual requests; in others, the clients must content themselves with whatever is on the tables. This has led to new types of bookstores because at the same time that the number of bookstore chains has increased, duplicated by supermarket locations, and stock libraries have disappeared, in the big cities, to counterweight to the current situation, new small businesses have emerged for niche buyers, such as, for example, poetry lovers.

In any case, it is noticeable the limited selection in regular bookstores, which is a response to the decreased capacity among their everyday consumers to select products. For them, several modern systems have been developed to guide them in the bibliographic jungle (that for niche readers is a delightful field), like automatically generated bestseller lists. To the impact of the limited selection, we have to add the consumers' habit of returning to the products that have satisfied them, choosing that which is being offered with enough guarantees or buying the book of which public knowledge has made, even non-specialized readers, aware. Public knowledge thus becomes one of those "extra-literary" reasons that makes common readers—or even non-readers—buy a book.

This explains the popularity that industry brands have acquired in the mass market in general where they act as a sort of guarantee: they conquer the loyalty of the client through the early success of a specific product in the market. It is symptomatic that in the moment our literary market is larger, there is a return to the strategies employed centuries ago, first in England, then in France and later in the US, when the popular book entered the market in the eighteenth and nineteenth centuries, respectively. At that time, the success of a product used to lead to the creation of a "brand" that made future products trustworthy. The cover of a book would frequently mention that the author had published a previously successful work in case the common readers were not aware of the connection to a title that they had enjoyed and that now was presented on the cover as a guarantee. The same thing happens now when a new work "by the author of *One Hundred Years of Solitude*" is announced, transforming that title into a brand that certifies a line of products with the same construction. In other cases, the cover would appropriate a title already registered in the collective memory because it belonged to an impressive work, or because the author had accomplished a notable action outside the field of letters. I doubt that Pablo de Olavide was the author of the seven moralizing novels that thirty years after his death appear in Spanish in the United States (and that now have been re-edited by Estuardo Nuñez), but for the conservative public at the beginning of the nineteenth century, it was enough to know that those novels had been written "by the author of *El Evangelio en triunfo*," a work that not only defined an anti-Enlightenment position but also registered the most famous conversion of an eighteenth-century "freethinker" held as an example by the Catholic church.

Within the economic market, a fixed value remains unchanged, absorbing the maximum number of buyers, for a more or less long period of time (depending on the fabric of the society) to the detriment of what a new value could get. It would require a series of proven failures, because of the violent emergence of an extraordinary novelty, to displace it. There is a collective understanding that plays in its favor and solidifies in these "industry brands." These brands survive as long as they satisfy buyers and, at the same time, are capable of attenuating a desire for novelty operating in the market that threatens their supremacy. Once a brand has obtained loyal consumers and it possesses a permanent influence on a market sector, competition becomes more intense and new products encounter a stiffer resistance—new brands trying to displace it must appeal to daring inventions or rapidly take advantage of propitious situations. The established brand can counterbalance the competition with success if it is capable of adapting itself to the endless cycle of renovation so characteristic of the lively, sensual, and restless strategies of the contemporary market. Put differently, the empire conquered with the first invention is only able to reinforce its position through constant adaptation to variations, combining its hard fought prestige with its willingness to adapt to change.

But even in the cases when it is not obvious (and rarely is it in literature), the book industry continues to have at its disposal an instrument of power that corresponds to the industrial and marketing infrastructure necessary to move objects (books) within the market. Modern technology has never stopped emphasizing, whether in the production of cars, computers, or books, the connection between systems of productions and mass demand. The production as well as administrative and marketing costs go down in proportion to the increase of each successive print run until it reaches an optimal point (Gabriel Zaid has examined some of these cases in his research) so that to improve an enterprise's earnings it becomes necessary to limit the number of offerings in favor of a small number of products with a greater probability of success. The catalogs of cultural publishing houses have a larger number of titles than the commercial ones, considering the readiness to invest of each one. In addition, the latter are always trying to avoid paying the lowly and legendary 10 percent of the copyright royalties when faced with the need to lower the unit price of an item as their operations depend on the massive production of a few titles. Let us not forget that books connect two productive activities, one literary coming from writers and the other industrial coming from the editors. There are links between them, sometimes harmonious and at other times chaotic, especially when the industrial side takes precedence: I have witnessed books created by request to meet an expected market demand, a phenomenon so common in North American publishing houses.

When the narrative Boom started, the sudden expansion of the market had in its favor a very unique situation: for thirty or forty years a number of works had been accumulating. These were works that although born from an amateur system, and exposed to the selective influence of literary criticism, were created over a long span of time and reached a considerable number. Not to mention that during that period several writers adopted a heroic attitude that led them to sacrifice everything just to produce literature. They wrote, continuously and stubbornly, even though they did not know if they were going to be published and their readers proved elusive. Onetti's essential work, to which he adds very little later on, is created between 1939 and 1964, with a total of twelve titles or an average of a title every two years; Julio Cortázar, in only ten years, publishes two collections of short stories and two novels and writes many other texts that will appear later; the same can be said about Borges and Bioy Casares, or Asturias, or Carpentier, who think of themselves as professional writers, and they are with regard to production, and even during periods when they were not professional in terms of the reading public's demand.

There was then a stockpile of works that the Boom massively distributed in just ten years, using a qualified selection of authors and titles, counting on a team capable of responding to the growing demands, a team strengthened with the emergence of young professional writers such as Carlos Fuentes or Mario Vargas Llosa, and having at their disposal the best possibilities available in Latin America. However, they proved to be insufficient for an increase of only a few degrees (and it was fairly timid, if one adds all the copies of an author during that decade and contrast this with the population and the number of potential readers), and even though the Boom encouraged young authors, it also created harsher conditions for the profession that led to establishing more restrictive norms for the dissemination of their works.

Alongside this transformation from amateur to professional narrator, there is another one that duplicates and reinforces it and sees the artist/writer replaced or counterbalanced with the intellectual/writer. That change is a good indicator of the demands of the time and writers were not the only ones affected by them. Other intellectual disciplines underwent a similar change; "amateur" sociology and economy have begun to be gradually replaced with their professional versions. In a discipline closer to letters, the transition from classical philology to modern linguistics was an impactful example; Carpentier has illustrated this with examples from musical analysis: "The best musical journal I know, *Musique en jeu*, . . . is absolutely incomprehensible for someone without very advanced and up to date musical knowledge," something he says did not happen with the musical magazines in the decade of the 1920s.[44]

In all the literary periods in Latin American history there have been intellectual/writers, if we understand by this, creators who do not limit themselves to invent literary works but are also capable of developing a coherent intellectual discourse about the multiple aspects of life during their historical period. There are many examples in the nineteenth century, from Andrés Bello to José Enrique Rodó, though their fame did not obscure the group of artists/writers who saw a resurgence among self-taught members of the modernista movement. However, the growing specialization that forms part of the urban cultures in the capitals exerted its influence on the writers' academic preparation. This is not a regional but a universal revolution. It was the issue that sparked a well-known controversy between two of French Nobel Prize winners, François Mauriac and Albert Camus. The former recognized that the differences between his generation and the generation of existentialist postwar writers were not going to tip the creative scales in favor of the intellectuals and against the artists. Indeed, the difference has nothing to do with art, even though intellectual/writers are better at certain types of literary finishing, while artist/writers have a greater capacity to communicate at a national level.

In Latin America this transformation dissolved certain sharp divisions that had become commonplaces in literary life: the opposition between writers and critics, who sometimes were seen as "the enemy," or the idea that one person could not hold both jobs as this could seriously damage one's creative spirit. The high-level critical capacity that European avant-garde writers developed let [T. S.] Eliot consider it necessary for a writer's progress to reach a level of intellectual reflection based on a systematic cultural knowledge. The academic preparation that became frequent among writers, their subsequent participation in diverse professional activities, all of this exerted an influence on the Latin American region, dissolving prejudices tinged with provincialism. The narrator was no longer afraid of publicly using his intellect, nor was he afraid that such an action would damage his creativity. With reliability and more frequency than his predecessors, he applied himself to other intellectual fields. I am not talking about politics, which, like religion in the past, has been public hunting grounds, and it has not always been beneficial neither to the writer nor to politics. But in other intellectual fields connected to arts and letters he was able to use his knowledge, analytical capacity, and soundly based reasoning.

We had, then, narrator/essayists or poet/essayists, who with the same dexterity created from both sides of this diptych divide of the letters. The cases of Otavio Paz and Julio Cortázar are exemplary and in a way they help to date the parting of the waters, even though other narrators preceded them like Alejo Carpentier, who possesses insatiable intellectual curiosity and a keen capacity to penetrate issues of modern culture, or Jorge Luis Borges, who demonstrated not only spectacular knowledge (chaotic, no doubt, just like any self-taught hedonist but always very interesting) but also the flexible talent of an essayist that connects him with illustrious predecessors like Antonio Reyes. It would be a mistake to argue that contemporary authors who do not practice the essay alongside poetry and narrative lack a solid intellectual formation. Juan Rulfo's or Juan Carlos Onetti's literary knowledge causes envy and José María Arguedas, who left a large and respected work, was a professional anthropologist, but none of them employed essay writing as a parallel path to narrative that was worthy of the greatest dedication and effort. For their part, Lezama Lima, Mario Vargas Llosa, José Emilio Pacheco, Carlos Fuentes, David Viñas, H. A. Murena, and others[45] dedicated themselves to intellectual discourse, whether interpreting their own work or that of their colleagues, or examining contemporary cultural problems, solidifying their reputation as intellectuals.

Because of their skills, they had access to cultural jobs where they performed educational tasks, such as university teaching positions or giving public talks, but it is even more interesting to see how all this contributed to a sort of intellectual autonomy. They were the first critics of their own work, they observed the evolution that for them was happening in the contemporary world, they aspired to be guides of an intellectual movement. They were, above all, cultural theorists with a passion similar to that of Sarmiento, González Prada, or Vasconcelos in the past.[46] They re-started a Latin American tradition, placing it within the framework of a modernity with which they were obsessed. The essay genre that Montaigne supported so much found in them very skillful writers, but in addition to their suggestive proposals and literary fame, they brought with them sweeping generalizations based on intuitions that provoked distrust from specialists working at the professional level. However, it was rarely their intention to behave as researchers; they were more like interpreters, like great mediators between the literary public and the global problems of their time.

Their intellectual capacity gave them a greater audience and allowed them to have social influence in several ways. They were asked their opinions about different aspects of national life and their answers became attached to their literary work as if these were the basis of their creations (here and in almost all the rules that apply to the new group of writers that appeared in the mid-1960s, we have to make an exception for García Márquez. Being an author of unparalleled success among the public and occupying for that reason a visible position in the renovation, his behavior, however, does not follow the general pattern: he is not inflexibly professional nor does he express an intellectual discourse, and neither do his works, albeit their technical innovations. In fact, he is proof of the arbitrary nature of the criteria that has been applied to the Boom—he belongs to the group only because of his publishing success. This is also the best argument for reorganizing the narrative production of the last couple of decades differently, paying attention to intrinsic characteristics and acknowledging the assistance of parallel developments, autonomous from each other).

Public visibility was greater for intellectual/writers, another example of how global culture has moved from the old Latin expression "Hide your life" to propose a new one that says "Show your life" or "Publish your life." The twentieth century has added a debatable stage to his evolution that Harold Rosenberg has explained as the public attraction for the writer more than for his work.

All kinds of writers, intellectuals or artists, amateurs or professionals, became objects of a public curiosity that emphasized the personal and did not hesitate to look into the authors' private lives. The literary interview suddenly became a fashionable genre. It had been used in other periods but only now gained an unstoppable popularity. It is not a Latin American invention either, but the imitation of an old practice that had dominated the market in the most developed countries during the postwar period, especially in those places like North America where individual images are more important than static or philosophical concepts: see, for example, the series of interviews published in *The Paris Review* since 1953 and that have already been compiled in at least four volumes. An international literary figure like Victoria Ocampo had previously developed under the label of "testimonials" a transcription of conversations with foreign intellectuals, narrating her encounters with them, describing their way of living, their spontaneous opinions during their conversation, thus contributing to that vague and dangerous idea, believed by some readers, that writers say the most important things in informal conversation and not in books.

It was, however, the new press that voraciously developed the literary interview, photographed the writer at home, requested opinions about current events, pried into his private life, and offered publicity in exchange for that information. It was what in journalistic slang is called "an exchange of services": satisfying the curiosity of the public at large, frequently giving them insignificant details about the author's private life and, at the same time, rewarding the writer by disseminating his name among a group of potentially new readers.

More serious was the work of several critics who decided to try the new genre and proceeded to interrogate writers too; their questions included literary topics, cooking secrets, explanations of political and artistic ideas. The results became part of books or were published in specialized reviews. Added together these interviews already form a considerable corpus never seen before. In it one can frequently find contradictions and improvisations, as could be expected, but through those channels writers widened the scope of their intellectual teachings and they made their presence felt among wide public sectors. This attention intensified as newspapers began to ask intellectual/narrators to collaborate as columnists: they acted as witnesses of current events, reviewed newly published literary works, explained political or social events. These developments intensified a connection between mass media and the narrators that did not exist before, when authors only appeared in a death notice. Also, those communication channels had strengthened because of technological progress and population growth, so they became the obligatory mediators for the public.

When one takes a look at the forms of communication that Latin American writers had utilized throughout history (from the traditional book to a talk or recital in the theater, or the avant-garde's wall-paper newspapers in the 1920s, or the radio in the 1930s and 1940s), one can measure the jump that this moment represents, and one can understand how this is the result of the absolute domination that the mass media possesses and of how distant from their public writers saw themselves. To reach a mass public that had replaced the elite, writers needed to go through mass media, something that in one way or another almost all authors did, even those who were shy when talking to crowds like García Márquez or Onetti. Not everyone was happy to do this, even though there is always someone willing to do whatever it takes, or there is always a Borges who answers any question in any place, but most of the time most writers try to use the new means of communication to convey their own message.

One does not have to agree with McLuhan's theories to know, however, that the medium imposes its own rules on those who are working with it. During his life, Darío would evoke with humor how his newspaper's director would ask him for a page in the style of "Claude Bernard," or some other famous figure, to say nothing of the techniques that popular magazines, TV, and occasional interviews put in practice now and create results that writers cannot foresee. Filming a literary meeting, Solana presented in his film *The Hour of the Furnaces* a couple of sarcastic minutes about the frivolity of writers.[47] And the simple use of montage allowed a Venezuelan filmmaker to put a narrator (Uslar Pietri) who was seriously talking about a part of the history of his country in an unattractive situation.[48] There was a variety of answers to the emergence of the mass media and its norms, but all of them found different ways of accepting it, and we had those who adapted to its requirements, no matter how extravagant or scandalous, and those who tried to establish a dignified pact. The authors' interest came from their legitimate desire to transmit their personal message and, in no small measure, their desire to obtain publicity to conquer the public they wanted for their messages, that is to say, their literary works in the form of books. Here the multiple jobs that this entrepreneur must realize are visible and one can see that it is neither the publishing houses nor the agents who take over their obligations. They are in charge of not only the production but also of procuring for it at least an indispensable amount of publicity so that the distant public learns about its existence. What the editorials call with grandiloquence the "launching" of a book is a task that, at least a good part of it, falls on the shoulders of the writers, who must give interviews, appear on TV, autograph copies, and fulfill ten commitments, nine of which they would have preferred to avoid. In other words, these "independent entrepreneurs" are not really that independent. They not only pay attention to market fluctuations but also look for new ways of penetrating it. On the other hand, their recently conquered professional autonomy, so desired or coveted from afar, means a visible restriction of their freedom and their integration into a mechanism whose wheels could easily crush them. The best example comes from one of the central figures of the new narrative. This man, who appears to be an anarchist, whose statements—because of their ludicrous exaggerations—are useless even for the right, to which he belongs, has easily adjusted himself to all mass media manipulations, from his wedding, broadcast from church directly by all the TV channels in Buenos Aires, to his passive acceptance of all questions, no matter who asks them. This absolute surrendering to all kinds of publicity and manipulation is like something foreign to him but within which he floats adrift. His capacity for witty replies, for the dissonant comment, for playing with the topics of general interest (soccer, politics, religion, blacks, the military) have transformed him into a desirable prey of the distorting means of communication, and he has happily lent himself to their requests, as if he were an actor performing in a theater of his time period, without feeling contaminated by this. One could argue that he does not need this publicity and he is merely amusing himself and one could also argue that it has helped to extend his fame to sectors of the population foreign to books and literature. These dissenting interpretations have little weight. What is impressive about Borges is how well he has adapted to the system, without any resistance. Of course, one could see all this as a reflection of the solipsism of his literature, but it also allows us to notice the separation of two spheres that used to be fused together, public knowledge and influence. Traditionally fame was perceived as a recognition of one's social virtues but that view has disappeared from the modern horizon where fame has been equated to the impact of an accident, unconnected to ethics. The constant presence in the public eye has made authors better known to the public at large and their names carry some meaning for the distracted listener who is the usual target of the instruments of mass communication. This has possibly contributed to adding to their number of readers, but that has not increased their concrete influence nor to a more precise transmission of their message. The generalized diffusion of their work has dissolved their connections with the small social groups, which, working as vanguards, could have carried forward his thought or art, take it as a banner. Mallarmé's snobbish austerity resulted in a devoted follower writing the famous article "Je disais quel-quefois à Stéphane Mallarmé . . ." predicting that he would have young provincial followers killing themselves over his verses. The general noise that authors have achieved rarely has been accompanied by this type of fervent trust from groups interested in their field. On the contrary, it has neutralized and disfigured the authors, and one should make note here of the corrosive effect of the means of information advancing its own projects, not conveying the specific message of the writer. It takes from writers the elements that are useful for its task, fragments with which it constructs a different discourse, suitable to its objective, and in the process destroys what was original about the writer's message. The effort they have put into reaching homogeneous groups, especially in their political ideology, define their effort to preserve the specificity of a message that mass media dissolves. What makes the task even harder is that followers are usually recruited among the youth, who are distrusting whatever messages they receive via mass media. These disintegrating tendencies of mass media fit Borges's solipsism and skepticism like a glove. He is not trying to fight them and simply swim in their waters. Those writers who see the dangers but are forced to deal with these powerful intermediaries sustain injuries, and they try to develop parallel channels through which they can save permanent values. In any case, I have never seen the Latin American authors lonelier than now, when they have mass audiences. They belong to everyone and to no one.

10

A Research into Ideology in Poetry

(The Diptych Series of *Simple Verses*)

1. On the Ideological Framework

Martí wrote his *Simple Verses* during August of 1890 in the Catskill Mountains (New York), destination for "those who have a thirst for nature and want water from a waterfall and a roof of leaves."[1] It was the summer that followed "that winter of despair, when due to ignorance, or fanatical faith, or fear, or courtesy, the nations of Latin America met in Washington, under the fearful eagle,"[2] an occasion in which Martí became physically and spiritually ill, causing the doctor to send him to the hills. On December 13, "in a night of poetry and friendship,"[3] he read his verses at home; the project of publishing them was born there, conquering Martí's resistance to making poetry an object of the market. The book appeared in October 1891.

In the very short period between 1889 and 1891 some fundamental events for Martí's life occur: some personal (the definitive separation with his wife), some professional (he is named Consul to Argentina and Paraguay; he rejects these positions as well as the Consul of Uruguay and his news correspondent post for *La Nación* in Buenos Aires), some political (the formation of the Revolutionary Cuban Party and activities leading to the War of Independence), some doctrinal (his experience at the International Conference in Washington, from which his Americanist speeches and "Our America" originate), some economic (his participation as a delegate in the Monetary Conference), some religious (his abandonment of *La Edad de Oro* due to not sharing the editor's demands regarding religious education), some literary (notes, articles, and a progressive aesthetic transformation that culminate in *Simple Verses*).

"The agony that I suffered," as he describes the Conference of 1889–1890, will have transfigured into a book without equal, *Simple Verses*, which in the prologue he defines as "simple, playfully written"[4] and which has to be read in light of the Nietzschean aphorism: "A man's maturity: having rediscovered the seriousness that he had as a child, at play."[5] Not only there "but in all of Martí's poetry, the little space that political and social struggle as a theme hold is surprising" as Cintio Vitier has said. He explains it thus: "The revolution of expression in him connected intimately with the historical and political revolution."[6]

To research ideology in *Simple Verses*, where it does not appear as the explicit discourse of Martí's doctrinal prose, nor as the subjective, reasoned and at times rhetorical expansion of his *Free Verses*, implies questioning the specific capacity of poetry to express ideology and the appropriateness of critical methods to investigate it, without thus abandoning the central purpose of studying poetry autonomously, that is, its singular artistic invention, its poetics and aesthetic. It implies asking, furthermore, about the place that ideology holds in poetic production as a constructive instrument of the work (and not only as detector of the complex doctrines that act in the author, in his social group, in his cultural era), as the crucible where the work is molded, acquiring tendentious lines that we will find registered independently in the textual crux, which means attributing to ideology not only content but also form and furthermore an operative mode that adapts to the conjoint treatment of multiple disparate contents. Finally, it implies asking about the generating capacity of ideology that is revealed in the productive process of the text, considering that the text does not unambiguously proceed from the will of the author nor even from unconscious discourses that operate in them, but that it uses a plurality of concrete and real materials that belong to outside systems preceding the author—from ideas to language, from melodies and rhythms to regimes of tropes and images—all of which are combined in the service of an original invention. This invention obligatorily assumes the existence of plural extra-individual fields of knowledge: linguistic territories, concepts of history, aesthetic principles, forms of emotion and the place granted to eroticism, distributions of political thought; in short, the plural praxis of everyday.[7]

The sociological, psychological, and cultural boundaries proposed for ideology when the concept is interpreted as distorted truth do not appear in poetry as separate and contradictory options but as parallel and equivalent levels, between which ideology makes a connection responding to the totalizing vocation that characterizes it and that has already been recorded in Dante's famous letter about the plural symbolic reading of his work.[8] Given its notable capacity for multiple radiation, poetry appears to us as an "aleph" where the various levels of cultural reality and the fields where individual psyche operate are unified by structural more than content-based equivalencies, thus presenting an integrating and regulating process of collective or individual discourses in which we traditionally divide praxis.

The various discourses that make up reality, and can only be grasped through separated delimitations, are concentrated in a point of dynamic and unstable equilibrium. Through that point they are dispersed as focal points that establish the convergence. This convergence responds, in large part, to ideology understood as function, allowing for the discovery of structural equivalences, which—*illusorily*, obviously—are analogously associated. Ideology's capacity responds to some of its defining traits: in the first place, its astonishing energy, only comparable to that of hunger or the libido, which leads it to impose apparently absolute solutions in a drastic and irresistible way because they are authentic "vital reasons" of which its very existence within the social consortium depends. The principle of mutability that governs and allows it to adapt to the same diverse impulses that also originate from diverse sources, operating with an enormous mass of vital interests to those that it should justify and legitimate, connecting them within explanatory synthesis that flirt with rationality, but to which reason surrenders. Finally, its amazing adaptation to disguise, its method of promptly and comfortably endorsing masks, passing from one to another without impediment nor loss of identity, with an agility that denounces its instrumental function, to make from the ghost an operating reality.[9]

In the same way in which ideologies work on vital realities, they cannot be reduced exclusively to distorted realities. It is possible to recognize in any of them more or less subconscious, frequently collective discourses—classist, sexual, cultural (linguistic), political, and so on—just as false rationalizations that reveal repressive social systems but also objective representations of reality and higher levels of awareness and rationality derive from the fact that the author as well as language and the very literary system are producers of meaning that function within the social framework. This recognition brings us closer to a culturalist perception of ideologies, which sees in them symbolic structuring of reality, with a variable degree of legitimacy, responding actively to the impulses originating in supra-individual discourses, subjecting them to the proof of the praxis.[10]

From the moment that we perceive the poem as a symbolic structure where very different impulses and discourses are regulated and balanced, responding to a unifying effort whose inherent rationality is presupposed in accordance with an interpretation of reality, it is necessary to specify if this synchronic vision leads to pushing history out of the way. This point has had a lengthy debate that does not merit reconsidering here, but it does establish within what conception we are working: here I propose that an accumulation of the past acts upon the component elements of the poem, which are updated in light of the concrete circumstances of the historical moment, through which its behaviors are determined in the juncture of these forces.[11] The past continues to be seen as a stone that weighs on society and, more visibly, on the cultural products with which they create the literary work, to such an extent that even the most apparently neutral word ends up being an accumulator of potentialities in which humans, their time, their group, elect and update some and reject others in light of their circumstances.

This working thesis signals that, more than the prose of essays, even more than narrative, and only giving way to the "informational polyphony" of theater, as Barthes defines it,[12] poetry is a privileged productive system where the most varied conscious and subconscious levels combine, just like the diverse discourses that come from them, through a positive effort of options, rejections, balancing of forces, and inventions. It does so in a way that surpasses contradictions and responds to them through an aesthetic proposition in which the acting totality, past and present, is accepted, ensuring that this position gives it meaning, a task in which ideology fulfills a main function.

The advantage of using Martí's *Simple Verses* for this research comes as much from the enigma that this mutation of Martí's aesthetic holds (which with his habitual astuteness Darío had already recognized as the feat of difficult simplicity) in a crucial moment for his political, doctrinal, and emotional life as it does from the enormous body of intellectual works that Martí produced in his articles, explaining experiences and proposing interpretations, which function as the framework or correlative needed to read this original and almost unexpected artistic invention.

2. The Serial Diptychs

The forty-six compositions that make up *Simple Verses* can be classified in distinct ways within the general homogeneity lent by the unusual recuperation of metric matrices, the "hirsute hendacasyllable," rebels of the rhythmic order, which Martí undertakes. Even in 1890 he denounced the "comedies in rhyme, for absurdly painting truth with a false language."[13] Months later he wrote rhymed octosyllables distributed in stanzas, preferably quatrains or polished redondillas.

The most extensive poems develop narrations under Antonio Machado's emblem of "song and story is poetry"; the less extensive ones reduce narration for the benefit of "illuminations" of a speculative type; still more reduced in extension are the poems of only eight verses, distributed in two stanzas, that we will take as a guide for our analysis. There are, furthermore, three initial poems where "each stanza constitutes a closed unity," according to Cintio Vitier, who sees them as "apparently unconnected summaries of a wisdom where the personal and the anonymous merge,"[14] a definition that applies to content but also governs what traditional rhetoric has called the "redondilla," recognizing the autonomy and spherical nature that has made it especially apt for transmitting popular wisdom in a brief and concentrated way, by way of self-sufficient sharp and clear illuminations.[15]

Halfway between these poems made with "closed unities," constructed with independent and disconnected stanzas and the more extensive ones, where these unities are articulated between them through narrative sequences that link them and suppress their autonomy (as if they were weaving necklaces of beads or rosaries), a combination of twelve poems is situated, that is, more than a fourth of the pieces of the volume. These poems are constructed through two stanzas that face each other in the way of diptychs. They are the most enigmatic of the book, and I think that Fina García Marruz refers to them when she says that "in truth *Simple Verses* are truncated ten-line stanzas, to which the connection of the two central verses has been eliminated to allow them to be converted into quatrains revealing not a visible link, but a transcendent connection."[16] This critic astutely perceives the obligatory nature of the tie that the author proposes between the two stanzas, aspiring that this not be narrative in nature in this case as in the extensive poems, but intellectual. But it is this same proposition that claims that they are effectively two visibly independent quatrains, even though they are placed in forced contiguity. In this way a tension between the disparate elements is created so that they transform in favorable places where the problem of difference and similarity, the one and the many, rupture of the autonomous parts and the harmonic reinstatement is communicated, making the understanding of the poem revolve on an opaqueness, that white space that separates both stanzas, as obsessive as the "white page" that electrified the French Symbolists and the Spanish American modernistas.[17] Like them,

Martí saw this white space as a challenge because it sets limits of what can be filled with respect to emptiness, it sets the borders and appears as the negation one must conquer in order to establish the "juncture" that will be able to defeat it. In fact, Martí restores the medieval metric form of the "copla de arte menor" and makes modern use of its particular norms.[18]

Except for poem XXIII, which narrates a desire, the remaining eleven (XII, XIV, XVI, XX, XXV, XXVI, XXIX, XXXV, XXXVI, XXXVII, XXXIX) are built through two heterogeneous series, placed in discordant relation of contiguity. In some cases (XXVI, XXXV, XXXVII) the heterogeneous series responds to a causal law that makes one an antecedent and the other a consequence, which introduces time in the opaqueness of the white space and a structure of logical derivations, but the predominant use underscores the independence of the series in relation to each other, using temporal and spatial simultaneities and establishing thematic disconnections so that the series coexist in parallel with null or scarce connection.

This autonomy is accompanied, in half of the compositions (XIV, XVI, XXV, XXVI, XXXVI, XXXVII), by the integral reduction of each series to a stanza, in such a way that they develop separately within the "closed unity" of the quatrain, which at the same time emphasizes the forced nature of its contiguity within the composition. This has its equivalent at the level of the metric matrix because all of these poems function with the rhythmic model ABBA/CDDC (or its combinations, like ABAB/CDCD), that is, four pairs of consonant rhymes for eight verses, distributed in a way that reinforces the autonomy of the quatrains, since none of the rhymes in one stanza are repeated in the other, except under the opaque form of assonance. There would be in these six compositions equivalent operations that are produced in different planes: in the plane of content they develop independent series ruled by the model: Series A, verses 1–4; Series B, verses 5–8, with minimal points of verbal contact (i.e., terms that repeat in each of the series). In the metric matrix separated rhyme schemes are applied on the model ABBA/CDDC, which regulate the melodic autonomy of the stanzas. In the expressive plane, heterogeneity is also emphasized, even though without the same rigor, it accepts intermediations, more minor and thus distinguishable from those that are produced in other diptychs.

The remaining five diptychs (XII, XX, XXIX, XXXV, XXXIX) equally develop two heterogeneous series, but instead of referring them independently to each one of the component stanzas, as in the previous cases, they intersperse and alternate in both quatrains, taking advantage of their heterogeneity (fixation of series), at the same time they put into practice a combinatory principle. These five diptychs correspond to three characteristics that distinguish them from the previous six even though each group obeys the general norm that establishes the double serialization. These three traits are (1) the two series are distributed within the poem alternating with each other whether it be according the model Series A, verses 1–2, 5–6 and Series B, verses 3–4, 7–8 or according to the model Series A, verses 1–2, 7–8 and Series B, verses 3–4, 5–6, respecting, thus, the integrity of the verse; (2) the verbal elements that constitute the links between both series increase their importance, having come to be represented by an entire verse, like in poem XXXIX, where the verse "I have a white rose to tend" repeats in both series; (3) in the metric matrix the rhymes are reduced, they pass from four to three in order to serve the eight verses, such that a rhyme is necessarily repeated in each one of the quatrains, in accordance with the model ABBA/ACCA or its variants.[19]

The three traits can be associated by their functional equivalence; they are distinct in nature but all come together to reinforce the ties between the two component stanzas, laying out bridges that operate on diverse planes. In the expressive plane this is complemented with the importance that homophony acquires, which comes to be excessive with respect to the scarce dimensions of the composition, intensely manipulating the interior rhymes that make sounds reverberate in a way that crosses between the two series, as a dialogue that exclusively takes place among signifiers, a sonorous dialogue that, however, does not destroy the semantic autonomy of the series but constructs a web of almost erotic attractions where the semantic "juncture" captures greater tensions and even repulsions.

> I. Ideology initially is revealed to us as a function of rare and skilled mobility, responsible for an integration of different zones through which they can be seen as authentic mortal leaps between disparate orders whose connection is procured by being, in the words of the poet, a "state of confused and tempestuous spirit" whose power and energy overlaps with that of the very mind, "placing and taking away, until *what comes from outside it* is translated into music" or, in other terms, finding a system of equivalencies that the poets frequently attribute to a "daimon" that they called analogy, but that here, far from associating concrete loose terms, establishes ties between structures à la Lévi-Strauss, recognizing the heterogeneity of the materials that participate in the creation of the work and its necessary harmonization.[20] The

vigor, availability, and masking that we anticipate as unique to ideology allow it to invest music, as ideas, or eroticism and its also recognized capacity of rationalization that we attribute to the tenacious effort of unification, by equivalencies, of the different orders that are brought together in the poem.

3. Structuring Function of Ideology

Simple Verses is not where Martí practiced the diptych for the first time. A year earlier, in the youth magazine *The Golden Age* (no. 1, July 1889), he published a poem of two stanzas that combined heptasyllables and hendacasyllables with pairs of independent consonant rhymes and developed two strictly heterogeneous series, each one of which integrally occupied one stanza, under the very revealing title "Two Miracles":[21]

Iba un niño travieso	7-A ┐
Iba un niño travieso	7-B ┤
las cazaba el bribón, les daba un beso,	11-A ┤
y después las soltaba entre las rosas.	11-B ┘
Por tierra, en un estero,	7-C ┐ (a)
estaba un sicomoro;	7-D ┤
le da un rayo de sol, y del madero	11-C ┤ (a)
muerto, sale volando un ave de oro.	11-D ┘

(A mischievous boy went by
Hunting butterflies
He caught them, the rascal, and gave them a kiss,
And then let them go among the roses.

On land, in an estuary,
Sits a sycamore tree;
A ray of sunlight hits it, and from the wood,
Dead, a golden bird takes flight.)

What is unique with the poetic form that appears here is the heterogeneity that the terms, which together compose each series, show, responding to a double orientation: in contrast to the basic differences among terms employed, there is in each series an analogous narrative structure at work, in such a way that difference and similarity function at the same time. No term of a series repeats in the other, even though some could be located in the same paradigmatic axis, but the articulation of terms, in each of the narrative series, is similar. If there are differences at the level of distinctive features, at the level of structure there are, in contrast, similarities.

For that reason, there are few poems better suited to Lévi-Strauss's observation, "it is not the resemblances, but the differences, which resemble each other" than these. His productive observations in *Introduction to the Work of Marcel Mauss*,[22] which Lévi-Strauss developed frequently through his major works, can serve as a guide to investigate this uniqueness. So can the contribution to philosophical thought and the interpretation of literary texts that Gilles Deleuze proposed in his initial contributions,[23] though one would need to modify them so that these operations can be also applied to the social field. The utility, here, of this critical tool derives from its correspondence to the uniqueness of Martí's intellectual project as these diptychs decisively illustrate.

This project is born from the initial verification of the divided, fragmented, sliced, different (what Foucault would have called "the categories of discontinuity and difference, the notions of threshold, rupture and transformation, the description of series and limits"),[24] which was made concrete in Martí's praxis faced with what he perceived as the cataclysmic collapse of a historical order that had not come to be replaced. Truly a child of an era of transition, he posited the tenacious inquiry for a unifying structure for the dispersed parts, an intellectual effort that should be concentrated on this emptiness that had been opened in the previous *fullness*, procuring through it what with a jubilant word he called "juncture" in contrast to this perception of rupture: "I notice the threads, the juncture" he said in his poem "Every time I sink my mind into deep books." The reading of a deep thought, he says, allows him to watch the link that would tie together what is divided, something that he sees as "the flower of the Universe," as it establishes the conjunction of idea and reality. The *juncture* of this divided reality operates through the idea and not through decorative ornamentations, which he explicitly condemns in "My Poetry" because he sees them being used "to hide the juncture with judgment" and not to resolve them. The *juncture* of the biased, the unspoken, the broken, is an intellectual operation that confers meaning, which explains that once they are perceived the "junctures" can announce "the impending birth of an immortal poetry," born from thought, a concept that he reiterated in the imminence of *Simple Verses*: "The flower of thought is poetry and newness in the world."[25]

The definitive difference between the series of "Two Miracles" recognizes, however, a point of contact, even though it is partially extratextual, which is that provided by the title: it is an interpreting rationalization of the poem, perhaps motivated by the juvenile public to which it was destined, indicating that not only in one but in both series an exceptional fact that violates objective laws is revealed, a miracle.

The diptych XIV of *Simple Verses* seems to be modeled on "Two Miracles," for not only its serial structure but also its themes, except the two series are linked at a point that is now intratextual, even though not direct: a temporal simultaneity establishes that both series cross the same "Fall Morning Long Ago."

> Yo no puedo olvidar nunca   8-A
> la mañanita de otoño   8-B
> en que le salió un retoño   8-B
> a la pobre rama trunca.   8-A
>
> La mañanita en que, en vano,   8-C
> junto a la estufa apagada,   8-D
> una niña enamorada   8-D
> le tendió al viejo la mano.   8-C

(Ne'er will I forget, I vow,
That Fall morning long ago,
When I saw a new leaf grow
Upon the withered bough

That dear morning when for naught,
By a stove whose flame had died,
A girl in love stood beside
An old man, and his hand sought.)

The assimilation of the terms of both poems is flagrant: Series A: (1) a withered bough/a dead trunk; (2) in Fall / in an estuary; (3) gives a new leaf / gives a golden bird; Series B: (1) a girl in love / a mischievous boy; (2) in a morning / in a field; (3) kiss butterflies and let them go / give her hand to an old man (even though now in vain). The articulation of the terms of the narrative sequences as much as the deep themes, and in part the characters, are in both poems mere variants of a type of composition model. Martí's known capacity to construct homologies making a same profound idea reverberate around distinct concrete surfaces remains illustrated in the oppositions he puts into play.

The heterogeneity of the series, in both poems, is fixed by the disparate realms in which they transpire: one pertains to the natural world and the other to the human, for which we are faced with the traditional model of oppositions: *Nature versus Culture*. The "miracle" to which the author alludes is ostensibly produced in the series of Nature, because it alters the rigid laws of the natural order: death gives life (new growth, a golden bird). In contrast, the series of Culture develops trivial or emotional stories (letting butterflies go free, giving an old man one's hand) with children (innocents) as protagonists, and as singular as they can be considered, they do not reach on their own a precipitous meaning until we incorporate a supernatural meaning to them, displacing it from the parallel series of Nature.

The Nature series stands out as signifier through its unique excess (the miracle, the *floating signifier* as Lévi-Strauss says), which finds room in the relative lack of the same that the Culture series shows, which appears as signified, which fits the perception that Nature can only provide series of signifiers, while series of signifieds are distinctive of Culture. As Martí argued in one of his *Notebooks*: "Seeing does not serve me at all if the explanation of what I see is not there, if my understanding does not become an element of judging vision. The object was outside myself, but the intelligence of the object is within me."[26]

Thus, the meaning of both poems can only be born of the link that is established between its component series. Nature and Culture are presented as independent and separate worlds that generate heterogeneous series, but the categorical difference between them opposes the similarities of their formal structures. This similarity, however, is not complete, due to an excess (and what more excessive than the miracle?) that destroys verisimilitude, altering the functioning of the eternal and invariable, moving to what, with respect to this excess, appears as lacking in the parallel cultural series, in order to fill it.

Summarizing this development, we can conclude saying: the outline of two parallel series is the basic condition in the construction of a structure; to define them as heterogeneous is to decree the difference as inherent to reality, designing the contours of the divided parts; to attribute them to Nature and Culture, respectively, is to accept a prototypical dichotomy in whose connection one is obligated to find man; to design them with analogous formal structures implies overcoming the particular differences through a similarity of a second, abstract level that is the obligatory condition to proceed with the *juncture*, which would no longer function at the concrete level, but in that of the diagram. We are circling, thus, around one of the crucial points of the modernista *episteme*, which some saw as the problem between the one and the many (Darío, in "Colloquium of the Centaurs"), but that imposed an intellectualization of art on all of them in order to confront the contradictory modernization of society underway, which demanded a coherent interpretative discourse. In Martí this will center on the problem of difference, which is the result of the privileged and ragged experience of having lived his adult life on the borderline between diverse cultures and diverse eras of humanity.[27]

> II. Ideology does not operate as simple content inserted into poetry, but as a structuring force of the work. It thus dissolves all adjectival character that it could have within the composition to appear as the generator of the productive process: it determines its structure, governs its operations, gives the key to its meaning, and, because it austerely abandons all overlapping explanation, it sends that meaning to the autonomous work of the reader who correlates series in the poetic text as they would do on any other reality, as long as it overcomes the confusion of appearances through their intellectual organization.

4. Objective Construction of Meaning

Poem XII in *Simple Verses* goes a step further. Here Nature splits into two paths in conformity with an aesthetic, emotional, or hedonistic division so that within it both the beautiful and the ugly, what exalts as well as what depresses, what pleases as well as what displeases, fit. Likewise, Culture also splits thanks to the fact that the conscience seems to assimilate natural beauty and reject natural ugliness.

The organization of the two heterogeneous series becomes more complex, given that each one is partially associated with Nature and Culture, one time according to Beauty and the other according to Ugliness, these being the appropriate name for each series. The connection is found here in a repeated element in both series that is no longer temporal as in XIV, but spatial: the "boat," to which the task of opening and closing the poem is given, laying out the situation and ending it symmetrically, just as also occurs in poem XXXIX. This element assumes a principal role in the elaboration of meaning thanks to the semantic displacement that is produced between its initial and later appearance.

En el bote iba remando	8-
por el lago seductor	8-A
con el sol que era oro puro	8-
y en el alma más de un sol.	8- (a)
Y a mis pies vi de repente	8-
ofendido del hedor,	8-A
un pez muerto, un pez hediondo	8-
en el bote remador.	8-A

(Once I was sailing for fun
On a lake of great allure,
Like gold the sun shone so pure,
And my soul more than the sun.

Then suddenly I could smell
Before I saw at my feet,
A foul fish, with death replete,
At the bottom of the well.)

Each stanza is occupied by a series and in each one of them Nature and Culture are refracted internally around Beauty and Ugliness, respectively. Both series, furthermore, are distributed on a vertical axis, which Martí shared with the Romantics and even the modernistas, making the spatial distributions that religion introduced in culture transparent: *Above*: the sun so pure / my soul more than the sun; *Below*: a foul fish, with death replete / "I" offended by the stench. The dichotomatic presentation evokes that of his first poems ("Pollice verso" and more clearly, "Contra el verso retórico. . .") and would even lead to Romantic outlines if it were not for the objectivity of the enunciation inherent for the modernistas (the description of the "sacred jungle" in *Songs of Life and Hope*[28]) and, above all, the heightened functionality of the connection: from the initial verse "I went rowing in the boat" we pass to the final "in the rowed boat," following a technique that Poe proposed for the modern manipulation of the refrain, introducing difference within the repetition.

What is lost in this passage from the first to the last verse is the agent of the action. The entire poem being a confession of experience, the active "I" that sails the boat and crosses the two antithetical states, refracting them in an equivalent way in the conscience, passes to a passive element at the conclusion of the two series and is carried by a "rowed boat." Inversely, the *boat* assumes the agent function and attains an immediate symbolic resonance.

This movement had already been signaled in *Flowers of Exile*, a collection that chronologically holds an intermediary place between *Free Verses* and *Simple Verses*. When the metric matrices and rhyme schemes emerge suddenly in it, the poet is who is first surprised: "Who . . . anoints me with the bland stanza?" Looking for an explanation of this enigma, he detects the appearance of a superior force above / within him, with respect to which he stops being a subject: "Who thinks of me?"[29] he asks himself. He finds the key in the appearance of a "giant and benevolent hand," but, above all in the integration with a Totality that has been lacking and now returns: "From where I came, there I go: to the Universe" ("Cual de incensario roto . . ."). This singular experience culminates in poem XII.

In this poem the two series touch in one point (*the boat*), which corresponds to what Deleuze calls "a paradoxical element, which is their 'differentiator.' This is the principle of the emission of singularities,"[30] because being in both, it moves through the field of meanings, even though only in the sense in which it has crossed, in only eight verses, the exposed contradiction. The categorical design of this poem using two natural elements ("sun of pure gold" and "reeking fish") when only three years earlier Martí had already recognized in Whitman's worldview, with one of his symmetrical formulations, that "sacred is the sweat and the entozoan is sacred," reveals the exemplifying voluntary nature of the opposition, a principle that he had learned from Emerson: "Contradictions are not in Nature, but from the fact that men do not know how to discover their analogies,"[31] which serves as a reference of all value judgments to the exclusively restrictive field of culture.

The contradiction is resolved in the poem through the dissolution of the "I," or stated a different way, in the cultural consciousness, given that this is where Nature is considered beautiful or ugly—conditions that would not exist outside such classifying forms. The completed double experience (natural beauty and natural ugliness due to refraction in a consciousness that has been invested by the culture of selective values) gives rise to an unexpected solution: the dissolution of the "I." This intellectual proposition is what explains the dual composition of the series, where the natural objects (sun, fish) are accompanied by a conscious refraction (exaltation, repugnance), thus proving the valuing operation that the latter has achieved.

The loss of individual conscience, of the "I," austerely transmutes the natural elements put into play, situating them outside the cultural value systems, making them simple objects of reality, neither beautiful nor ugly. This affirmation leads to the eviction of the "I" or, at least, the loss of their confidence that it is the "I" who sails the boat. In concluding the poem, the boat is the agent that not only sails but also connects, indistinctly, the two antithetical elements that governed the series: man ends up being a natural object also.

The excess of one series with respect to a lack in the other is encoded in the duality of the term *boat*, that is in the two series: in the first it is manipulated literally as means of nautical transport ("I went sailing in the boat / on the seductive lake"); in the second it is exaggerated by means of its symbolic opening, emphasizing the eventuality of any word, making of it, as Lévi-Strauss thought, a "simple form, or to be more accurate, a symbol in its pure state, therefore liable to take on any symbolic content whatever."[32] Certainly, any word can be charged in a symbolic, more effective, way even when, as in this case, it is not reduced to a univocal meaning that would link with the sign but that floats, moved by a potentiality that refuses to be restricted or fixed. But a word's capacity to symbolize responds to the accumulation of previous materials contained within its sign that in the end realize themselves in the phrase (sintagma), which becomes their conclusion. It is worth saying that it cannot assume any content but that which responds to the articulation of the two series and of each one of its respective terms, all of which converge at the end of the poem. In this moment, the known iterative tendency of Martí's writing takes on the form of a paradoxical or derailed symmetry: repetition is the condition of the ostensible difference, which can be exclusively semantic like in poem XXXIX, through symbolic allusion to the same initial signifiers, or can lead to modifications, like in poem XII, to fully consummate the symbolization.[33]

> III. Thus, Martí's thoughts in his *simple* poems are also content and not only structuring force. It is not thought as an intellectual discourse, but, in the way that Whitehead understood it, as meaning. The meaning of words and images tend to or

are explained by this thought. These are forms of thinking that explore what is concrete and unique in the reality that they mention, they are materials suppressed by a rationality that was central in the poet and that led him to combat rhetoric and the ornament as supplemental and non-essential to showing ("put words as the bone, instead of clothes, for the idea")[34] and to progressively disdain, under the influence of Whitman, methods of comparison.[35] The image is justified, in this demanding doctrine, when an objective declaration of the world, perceived as structure, attains meaning. It is obvious that the rationality of the universe is still assumed, at the margins of its apparent confusion, since "art does not have to give the appearance of things, but rather its meaning."[36]

There is a sort of excess in the process of symbolization. The semantic intensification exercised on a determined term of the phrase moves to the expressive plane through homophonies with the signifiers of that term. The symbolized word infects, bristles sounds, spills through them, summons them to a generalized phonetic redundancy. This is probably more evident in *Simple Verses*'s diptychs for their accentuated brevity, conciseness, and precision.

Even though this poetry maintains the percentages of consonants and vowels of spoken language, it is the vowels, thanks to grammatical and rhythmical accents, that construct the echo of the symbolized word. The vowels of *bote* [*boat*] mainly occupy the poem fixing the norm of a medium opening, as much in the *aguda* accents as in the *grave* accents,[37] of the *e-o* sort (in contrast to what happens in poem XX, governed by *e-a*, or poem XXXIX, governed by *a-o*), and they are the ones that appear in order in the words that sustain the only rhythmic connection of both stanzas, which, in this poem, is governed by the liberty of the blank octosyllables: *seductor/ hedor/remador*, and also in the opaque assonance of the fourth verse: *deunsol* [*of a sun*].

The rhythmic structure of poem XII is rather exceptional, within the generalized polyrhythmic tendency of Martí's verses, since it is attached to a visible monorhythmic dominant, with fixed pauses and fixed accents in the third and seventh verse. This monochord base is interrupted by a unique alteration in each one of the stanzas, to construct two verses with successions of trochaic verses, through accents in 3, 5, and 7: "y en el *a*lma m*á*s de un s*o*l"/"un pez mu*e*rto, un p*e*z hedi*o*ndo." In this way what in the semantic plane are two opposite situations in each series are rhythmically associated, agreeing thus in a crossed fashion: exalted cultural conscience (before the sun) / repugnant natural object (the fish). Let us remember a statement by the poet: "What is said is not expressed with thoughts alone, but in combination with the verse; and where the word fails to suggest, by its accent and extension, the idea that goes in it, there is where the verse sins."[38] In the use of the field of homophony and rhythm for the construction of meaning, as a zone of high sensibility and high freedom, where the unconscious discourse can be expressed negotiating the rigors of intellectual censorship, we will have to more fully see it achieved in those poems that, like poem XX, are constructed by the impulses of desire. Here some of the paths that this discourse traverses in the text remain simply indicated.

5. Transposition of Society in Nature

If the concept of Nature's harmonic equilibrium in Martí can admit influence, it is alongside the religious tradition and philosophical formation of the North American transcendentalists, in particular of Emerson (and it is useful to not forget that Martí is the first Spanish American who builds a literature accepting two so disparate influences as North American and Spanish language literature, distinguishing himself from the modernista norm that conjointly referenced French and Spanish language literatures). In contrast the neutralizing dignification of "uglyism" is inherited from Whitman, as well as the realist school of literature and art, with which Martí had ample and fertile dealings for which he has been recognized as having been pigeonholed alternatively as post-Romantic or modernista and for being furthermore a school that in Spanish American literary studies tends to not be seen. Even more than in such artistic sources, that dignification derives from José Martí's experience as a sacrificed worker in New York with the masses of poor immigrants that accumulated after the American Civil War and conferred their unique "populist" note on the city.

More than the direct experience of Nature, Martí's concept is born from the lesson that art provided him (in particular [Jean-François] Millet, who he admired above all, and about whom he said "that he found what is beautiful about ugliness and sadness"[39]) and of the experience of a shared alluvial society such as can be traced in his articles from his entry into the United States, with the one he wrote about Coney Island[40] starting a long series about popular life in the lower neighborhoods of New York, where the workers and their families, immigrants, and the poor like him were piled on top of each other.[41] This can be traced in the poems with which, at this same time, he was composing for *Free Verses*. It is the emergence of "popular culture" that is produced in the United States and had been predicted since 1871 by Walt Whitman in his *Democratic Vistas* that serves as the experimental field to dissolve the dichotomy of beauty-ugliness that, de facto, was constructed on a social and class-based hierarchy. What practitioners of art for art's sake like Baudelaire, Rimbaud, and Verlaine were able to do in France while the Naturalist artists paradoxically could not, prisoners of bourgeois cultural systems, is what in Spanish language the conservative populist Spaniards, from Ferrán to Bécquer,[42] partially achieve and, with a progressive sense, José Martí does for Spanish America.

In the poem mentioned earlier "Contra el verso retórico . . ." from *Flowers of Exile*, the opposition (*there, here*) is designed with analogous terms to those of poem XII, fixing a contradiction: "golden bird" in the upper section of the poem, "fetid and viscous track of a worm" in the lower. This vertical line, however, is duplicated by another, more extensive one that touches on one extreme the "star" and on the other, "oven," through which the defective forms of social life—crocodiles, serpents, gozques[43]—are incorporated into the poem, even though it requires a laborious intellectual discourse. In an apodictic verse reminiscent of Ducasse,[44] Martí had already stated his conviction: "I know man and have found him to be evil," pointing out that the guide to his search was made on the basis of the social experience. In it he establishes not only a new appreciation of values but even the viability of poetry. What is revealed in the title of a poem he calls "New Stanza" is "a new social class," in such a way that the new art all writers in his era were exploring appeared to Martí as imposed by the emergence of a social class, the urban proletariat, that nowhere in Spanish American could be observed with more clarity than in New York of the 1880s. The poem "New Stanza" makes an enumeration of the members of this class ("a sooty worker; a sickly / woman, with gaunt face and thick fingers," etc.) whose unique "ugliness" is completed in the poem "Bien, yo respeto" (also from *Free Verses*), where he outlines the objective series of the "uglyisms": "the wrinkle, the callus, the hump, the sullen / and lean paleness of those who suffer." Those enumerations at the same time must be seen from the unique perspective with which in these years of hard work Martí became aware of from his own life: it is the experience of frustration, given that social structure impeded the free expansion of energy and vocations, which for Martí, who aspired to be a poet, will be fixed in a repeated image that I believe appeared for the first time in the prologue that he writes for Pérez Bonalde's[45] *El poema del Niágara* (1882): "But now the poet has changed labor and walks about drowning eagles."

But if his knowledge comes from social experience, in *Simple Verses* these facts are transposed to Nature. There, the "uglyism" appears as a mystery to resolve, like an alteration of a mysterious order like the miracle, as a signifier that looks for significance, or, better still, like a sign that creates what is real and that can only be incorporated into culture if it becomes symbolic, something that Martí undertakes in his last poetry because "all mind of true power in its maturity tends towards the vast and symbolic."[46] This eventuality converges on the establishment of a "universal term," only through which it begins to be possible to trace the web that makes up the disparate or heterogeneous elements of experience, providing them with meaning. It is what Cassirer perceived when he noted that "each particular is mediately or immediately referred to a universal and measured by it."[47]

The degraded circumstance in which the face of the proletariat emerged into human history alters not only multiple political and social concepts accepted until then as absolutes but also the concept of beauty. It is the judgment received on beauty that is suspended, within this generalized objective pairing of the facts of reality. What is unique about Martí is his transposition to Nature, where one can detect the search for the absolute, the "universal term" that allows an entire resizing of the completed experience, saving in this way the reassessment that is made (which is not an exclusively new aspect but the totality that by way of this new graft has entirely been modified) of the possible relativism to which a solely social basis would be condemned. "From the ugliness of man to beauty / of the Universe I ascend" is the refrain of the poem "March," such that the injustice, disorder, and ugliness of human society can only be measured (and, thus, rescued) thanks to the *universal term* that Nature now, and not God, provides, similar to Darío's "ideal forest that complicates the real."[48] He had seen this in Emerson: "Nature prostrates itself before man and gives him its differences so that he perfects his judgment. . . . And man does not find himself complete, nor revealed to himself, nor sees in what is invisible, except in his intimate relationship with nature. . . . And in this entire multiple Universe, everything happens, as a symbol of being human, as it happens in man,"[49] which indicates that Emerson as well as Martí continue to work on common traits that for Marx make the unity of production ("which arises already from the identity of the subject, humanity, and of the object, nature"[50]), without recognizing the historical variations that, however, are those that surreptitiously engender his thought.

We could say, with Marx's words, that "here we ascend from earth to heaven. . . . We set out from real, active men, and on the basis of their real life-process we demonstrate the development of the ideological reflexes and echoes of this life-process."[51] Even the process of transposition to Nature evokes the work realized by the eighteenth-century intellectuals (Rousseau), who Marx saw as a "purely aesthetic appearance" that masked the "civil society" that was underway. The tie Martí maintains with eighteenth-century interpretative rationalism, whose economists and political scientists laid the foundation and supplied those of the nineteenth century, is perceptible in the use of this "illusion," which leads him to project on nature what he has discovered in history, in the reality of a highly evolved civil society like that of North America, in which he participates as a worker, making his the same paradox that the transcendentalists had cultivated. They also worked on the isolated individual who had created the new productive system, what Marx had already astutely perceived as another of the masked forms through which thought takes possession of novelty, but returns to the past (origin, coincidentally, of *Angelus Novus* with the head turned backward, in which Benjamin symbolized the modernizing attitude of the twentieth century) so that this "illusion" allows him to claim for himself the enormous modification: "As the Natural Individual appropriate to their notion of human nature, not arising historically, but posited by nature. This illusion has been common to each new epoch to this day."[52]

> IV. The experience of the degraded class, with whom he coexists and to whom he is able to *serve*, modifies Martí's concept of beauty, establishing a new aesthetic; it only becomes noticeable through a reading of the absolutes of Nature, which are presented as real, immovable signs, capable of growing, with a new symbolization "so that what is real can be better seen in a symbol."[53] This facilitates the surreptitious incorporation of history through the symbolizing process, without thus destroying and taking advantage of the absolute values that would watch over Nature. By belonging to a superior order, it is capable of giving legitimacy to the demands that natural-men present it. In the same way, the dissolution of the restricted individual "I"

is, simultaneously, as much the result of the incorporation to the natural macrostructure as taking on the principle of *service* to another macrostructure, that of the destitute, since this is also given legitimacy in the first: it is not simply personal and historical will, but the application of a superior, invariable, eternal, and just order.

It even bears recognizing that Martí was not completely estranged from the hidden tie between "civil society" and nature, within his known sociological perception of literature. He at least notes in one of his articles: "That love of the natural is the aesthetic consequence of the regime of the Republic,"[54] which seems to come directly from the Walt Whitman's essay "Nature and Democracy-Morality," published in *Specimen Days and Collect* (1882).

6. The Discourse of Desire

In the cases examined here there is a margin of exteriority that facilitates intellectual speculation. Others more relentlessly implicate intimacy: they have to do with emotions, with customs deeply rooted in traditional culture, with a sentimental and erotic worldview.

Poem XX of *Simple Verses* unfolds two different series at the same time, but instead of confining each one in a stanza, as we saw earlier, it places one within the other. The first occupies the exterior verses (1, 2, 7, 8) and we can name it "Eve" because it deals exclusively and repetitively with her. The second occupies the interior verses (3, 4, 5, 6) and we can call it "Cloud" because its actions speak of this. From this series the word *Eve* has been excluded like *Cloud* in the first set.

Mi amor del aire se azora;	8-A
Eva es rubia, falsa es Eva:	8-B
viene una nube y se lleva	8-B
mi amor que gime y que llora	8-A
Se lleva mi amor que llora	8-A
esa nube que se va:	8-C
Eva me ha sido traidora	8-A
¡Eva me consolará!	8-C

(The wind my love terrifies:
Eve is blond, but Eve is not true:
A passing cloud takes to the blue,
My love as she moans and cries.

It takes my love as she cries
The cloud that passes from view:
Eve has betrayed me anew,
Eve consoles me with her lies!)

Each one of the series entails a succession of terms that are not only between them different but furthermore organized in a different way, such that the component elements are distanced as much as the structures. This is an obvious difference from "Two Miracles" and poem XVI, even though in these and in poem XII the series are classified in the order of Nature and that of Culture, respectively. The "Eve" series belongs to the former, which deals with the behaviors of the woman; the "Cloud" series to Nature, which refers to that natural element.

The two cross at a common point that both repeat: "my love." Through "my love," which is the same as saying for the feeling individual, the two pass, or perhaps it would be convenient to say, given the disparity of terms, subject and structure, that they intersect at this point. The crossing of Culture and Nature in a human being, in what the poem calls "my love," is obvious, but such a term ends up being ambivalent: it has two faces, which allows it to perform a role in each series without reaching in either of them, taken independently, entire significance. Its meaning, therefore, derives from its own duality.

The introduction of a series within another comes accompanied by a variation in the metric matrix with respect to the earlier examples. Instead of using a rhyme scheme ABBA/CDDC of four rhymes, it is reduced to only three, which in this case are distributed ABBA/ACAC, chaining the two stanzas together through the repetition of sounds and tying, in the plane of expression, what is untied in that of content. This intervention by the metric matrix, capable in its own right of fulfilling a significant contribution, and despite the neutrality that distinguishes it in poetry, can help explain Martí's brusque conversion of the "hirsute hendacasyllables" without rhyme to rhymed poetry, more so even if, as we will see, it is connected to the functions that homophony carries out in the expressive plane. As he gets further into measured and rhymed poetry, Martí better adjusts the matrix components, as can be seen when one reviews "The Pink Shoes" (from 1889) and "The Girl from Guatemala" (from 1890). A modification in the rhyme scheme that responds with linked rhymes that reverberate alternatively from one to the other series integrally connecting the composition corresponds to the insertion of both series, in which one goes on to occupy the central position externally circled by the other. And the discrete and surreptitious approximations that the rhymes carry out and that, in belonging to pure signifiers (*ora, eva, a*) do not seem to affect the independence of both, correspond to the function of "my love," which in the semantic field signals the point of intersection of the two series.

The drumming quality of homophonies is especially noteworthy in this poem, with an excessive note, as a sonorous spilled redundancy. The first series, in only four verses, repeats the word *Eva* four times; the second, also in only four verses, includes four terms that repeat: *cloud* in the extremes (3 and 6, which open and close the internal period) and *takes, my love*, and *that cries*, concentrated in the interior verses 4 and 5, which, except for one term, are practically the same verse. But both series double the homophonies in different ways: the first uses one single and invariable sound, *Eva*, with intervals that impose their function of subject of the successive phrases: the same sound, repeated periodically, always as subject. The second, in contrast, uses a multiplicity of sounds that repeat in symmetrical pairs and are, grammatically, nouns as much as verbs or objects, distributing them so that they reflect like a mirror, mating verse 3 with 6 and 4 with 5 so that the empty space between stanzas serves as a hinge over which the four verses of the "Cloud" series can turn symmetrically, two by two, to overlap.

Such distinctive traits are reinforced by the verbs of each series. In "Eva," departing from the present of the love that is terrified, we have four phrases that develop a linear story: the first two define the character in the present, the following two alternate and contrast brusquely a past ("has betrayed me") with a future ("will console me"). In "Cloud," however, all of the verbs are in the present, marked by two contrary actions, but both in the present, which signals the entrance and departure of the cloud: *comes, takes, moans, cries, passes*. A special redistribution shows the contrary functioning:

Eva es	viene Nube			
Eva es	se lleva	mi amor	gime	que llora
Eva ha sido	se lleva	mi amor		que llora
Eva será				Nube se va

The structural circularity of the second series is reinforced by the series of present tense verbs, while the linear structure of the first is sustained by the use of lack of limits that the past and the future provide. In fact, there are two clearly different times (two labyrinths as Borges would have said in "Death and the Compass"): one lineal, unceasing, which diminishes the present for the benefit of the undefined extension toward the past and toward the future and what is the time of the "event" where the facts, causes, and effects act; and a circular time, also unceasing because in this time things revolve within an inexhaustible present that makes them pass time and again through the same points, which is the time, let's say, of permanency. According to this, we should agree that *Eve* exists in history, as it was fully understood from the nineteenth century; it exists in the becoming, which jumps from the past to the future with the least section of present; it exists in variation, in novelty, in change. While *Cloud* exists in nature, in permanence, in repetition, in a sort of eternal present, in a disappearance of time, in a search for its cancellation. Linearity and circularity, historical time and eternity, dizzying culture and constant nature, cross in only one point: "my love."

It is not necessary to delve too much into his work to know the conflict in which both concepts are situated in Martí's emotional life nor how, in his concrete experiences, he understood that this differentiation corresponded to two worlds: the United States in which he suffered and the Spanish America in which he dreamed, nostalgically, idealizing it and, even more so to the problem of modernity that placed a new era in opposition to the ancient one, openly showing itself in the United States of his time. No one (and this no one is unfair for Darío) like Martí quite lived in the center of the problem of modernity because he suffered it entirely, he experienced its confrontations, he measured the advantages and prejudices that came with it, and in a huge effort he tried to overcome its dilemmas.[55]

His advice will be governed by the law of equilibrium and moderation, as a way of counterbalancing the negative effects that the forces in conflict generated. But this intellectual lucidity, this continuous rescue of positivity on one side and of the dividing line of two eras on the other found its most inhospitable place in the irreducible zone of emotion and eroticism. The apostolic character that certainly should be recognized in Martí has made it difficult to explore this secret region, that of potent sexuality that distinguished it, that of his eroticism subjected to so many moral constrictions and at the same time so angrily rebellious. To the view of Martí as extremely loving father and son one would have to add the

Martí of sensual feminine portraits, of "Much, my lady, I would dare / If down your back I could drape / Drape your wild hair from the nape, / Let fall your golden-red hair,"[56] that which he petulantly confesses in 1880 "in all parts a woman's soul has come to bless and sweeten my exhausted life,"[57] recounting his conquests from Liverpool to Guatemala.

When this young man of twenty-seven arrives in the United States, after living in the provincial and familiar environs of La Habana, Aragón, Mexico, and Guatemala, the first thing that he notes is movement and women within it: it was his initial contact with modernity, perhaps the origin of the dual relationship that he will maintain with it. Another young man from Central America was the same age when he disembarked in cosmopolitan Buenos Aires at the turn of the century, having the same experience: this was Ruben Darío. Both were "passionate Latinos" and carried with them the constrictions of the traditional education of their original environment. What to do? Given his rigorous ethics and the most modernized society to which he descended, it is likely that the most difficult experience fell to Martí. Of the three articles he writes to cover the "Impressions of America by a recently arrived Spaniard," the second is devoted to women and the topic reappears in the third. Confessing that he carries on "like an inconsolable widower, waiting for the first strong emotion," he explains his bewilderment with women that seem nothing like those he knew in his lands:

> But, why should women look so manly? Their fast going up and down stairs, up and down the streets, the resolute, well-defined object of all their too virile existence, deprive them of the calm beauty, the antique grace, the exquisite sensitiveness which make of women those superior beings—of whom Calderon said that they were "a brief world" . . .
>
> Young women in America are remarkable by their excessive gaiety or excessive seriousness. Their control over themselves, their surety of being respected, their calculated coldness, their contempt of passions, their dry, practical notions of life, give them a singular boldness and a very peculiar frankness in their relations with men.[58]

To judge this provincial attitude one would have to recur to a novel that this same year Henry James was writing, *Portrait of a Lady*. Those women are already of modern society, those that have passed on to actively make up working society on par with men, confronting them in daily life with autonomy and even curtness, fighting for their place in the world, alienating themselves in a spurious environment. They are Ibsen's Nora, who Martí will slowly learn if not to love, then to respect.[59] They are those who study, work, reclaim their civil rights, and aspire to be, in love, subjects.

The "mystery of the eternal feminine," as people still said then, had entered the circuit of variation and constant novelty to which the new time had summoned it. As in Baudelaire's sonnet, the woman had become "a passerby." She begins to exist in the movement of society like man, she is no longer the fixed point situated in the family home and the outline of paths and encounters automatically becomes immensely more complex (and also more fleeting) because man as much as woman come from the movement that sweeps them along. If Martí maintains the indivisible unity of the unique woman in his poem, under the mask of the woman, of women in general, of the primordial Eve, then the verbs that regulate her should establish the change and the accident: *is, has been, will be*. Parallel and inversely, Darío in the poem "Heralds" from *Profane Hymns* keeps the verbs in the present tense ("announces her"), on establishing the incessant succession of women under their multiple and changing appearances. While they are different *they are* always in the present of the encounter. The mystery of the eternal feminine is being replaced, as Hoffmansthal argues, by the mystery of the encounters.

The short erotic series (poem XVI to poem XXI) to which poem XX belongs deals with disagreement, trickery, treachery, misunderstanding of appearances, revolving around the dilemma: the woman of one or woman of all, eternal and invariable woman where repetition corroborates identity or always changeable woman where the difference sharpens desire? His whole being aspired to the first one, the "virgin bride" and the "faithful spouse," paradigms of the Latin American worldview from which he came, the second was the one that appeared, disturbing, as a condition of a dynamic society. He related their confrontations and his spontaneous rejection of the new woman in the poems of *Free Verses*. "Oh the displayed woman! Oh cups of flesh!" he said in "Iron," and corroborated this in "Love of a Big City": "The city frightens me! Everything is full / of cups to empty and hollow cups!" It is in this poem, dated April 1882, in the recently debuted New York where he confirms: "Love happens in the street, standing in the dust / of saloons and public squares: the flower / dies the day it's born," recognizing that this mode of love implies its fatal transience, it makes and unmakes itself like the event, in its own incessant movement: "And love, without splendor or mystery, / dies when newly born, of glut."⁶⁰

In his sarcastic exhortation to the "despicable wine-tasters" to quickly drink those offered cups, his consternation is left imprinted: "Drink! I am honorable and afraid!" The clear benefits of modernity that he advocated so much for the stagnant Spanish American countries revealed to him, barely arrived in the United States, other effects that for his cultural conscience were not equally positive: "Because it is not worth taking away some stones and bringing others nor to substitute a stagnant nation with a prostituted nation."⁶¹ Rubén Darío will fully accept the new situation in which he sees the future of the society whose germination he is witnessing: "Passing love has a brief enchantment / and offers an equal end to pleasure and pain." Martí will suffer from all temptations, but he will not try to save the "tremulous virgin" or the "beautiful woman," spouse, and mother, the one that he sees in the "salon of the painters" but not in reality, and to whom he dedicates the poem of *Simple Verses* that immediately follows poem XX and closes, with an apparent answer, the short erotic series.

But in poem XX, the effort to register the objectivity of the universe that animates his quatrains collides with his ethical discourses. In the rococo movement of poem XX, *Eve* and *Cloud* oppose each other in a compensatory fashion from their respective autonomous series. If Eve is the woman, implying all women that are substituted under the name of their sex, who is Cloud? It is also a sign of what is general, not particular, but in contrast to Eve it is situated in Nature, from where, as we saw on examining its transpositions of society, corroborates what is human. By its use in the era and even more in the twentieth century from marginal regions to the central empires, it was a useful symbol for the problem of the one and the many with which Spanish American modernistas (and before them Europeans) were able to confront the hemorrhage of plurality that characterized modernity and placed in doubt the unity and stability in which they had grown up. It allowed the recognition of a thousand forms and ways certifying at the same time unity and permanence, certifying that plurality was nothing more than the apparent succession of the one, that this one persists unscathed under what was established as mere forms.

It is the theme of Proteus, to whom Rodó⁶² dedicated his principal work in "a book in perpetual becoming, an open book about an undefined perspective," but where the study of the transformations of personality did not stop conserving its uniqueness unscathed. Departing from the perception of an undeniable but difficult to apprehend force of power, he saw it as generating the "figure" through "movement" and "change" in an unending cycle ruled by modernity's new Dioscuri.[63] Rodó found in Proteus a perfect symbol:

> Always elusive, always new, he passed through the whole range of appearances yet fixed his most subtle essence in none. And in this infinite mutability, as a sea deity, he personified one of the aspects of the sea: he was the multiform wave, intractable, incapable of stability or repose, the wave that now revolts, now caresses, that sometimes lulls to rest, and at others thunders, that has all the spontaneities of impulse, all the vagueness of color, all the modulations of sound, never rising or falling in the same way, lifting and dropping back into the sea the liquid which it takes from it, imparting to that inert levelness, form, movement and change.[64]

The hedonism of this entry to a becoming where permanence reverberates under the apparent mutation, in such a way that the voluptuous excitement of what is new did not contradict the enduring identity, is frankly revealed in Rubén Darío's erotic exultation, declaiming to woman, where both symbols (cloud and sea) are yoked together: "Love me sea and cloud, foam and wave."

That *cloud*, which for a madrigal reading of poem XX serves as a metaphor or dispute, jealousy, traditional "dépit amoureux," witnesses another feminine presence, even though it is situated in the realm of order and justice that for Martí is that of Nature. It is timely to point out that Martí's thought always rests on an unconscious dichotomic matrix that with complete clarity plays out the opposition *masculine / feminine* with its rich weave of mutual attractions, which in him is transcribed in a very precise use of gender in language itself, perceiving with extraordinary acuity the difference between feminine and masculine words, making one suspect that he transferred it, synesthetically, to the opposition of *aguda* and *grave* words on the model *él / ella*. Sexual pairings are frequent in his literature (we will see them in poem XXIX), which can be seen as a linguistic transposition of the oppositions confirmed in the natural world, in conformity with a function of the mind that he noted in his admiring study of Emerson: "Nature gives man its objects, which are reflected in his mind, nature which governs his speech, in which each object becomes transformed into sound."[65]

The femininity of Cloud does not seem casual, as its reappearance in other poems that confront the same subject certifies (XLII).

The vowels *e-a* rule the entire poem over the expressive plane, invoked by the name *Eve*, spilling voluptuously through both series. While in the first series they solidify in the feminine name, serving to give presence and roundness to the cultural woman, in the second they resound covered up within other words, as an echo that fleetingly takes shape within the sonorous torrent, but impregnating the totality as an unfixed remembrance; that is, eroticism without an object. Twice it is heard in "se lleva" [takes away], both as part of the exterior rhyme as well as the interior rhyme, and more especially in the sixth verse of the composition, which closes the second series: there, a minimum alteration of the accent allows one to read, substituting "esa nube que se va" [that cloud that passes from view], a verse that had defined desire: "esa nube que's Eva" [that cloud that's Eva].[66] Martí provides allusion and elision that the sonorous game tolerates, revelation and concealment that can act beyond the conscious will, imposition of a buried truth that speaks with more force than the explicit intellectual discourse when it can do so over the sonorous weave that unfolds signifiers, free from strict univocal meanings.

In this rhyme of the sixth verse the order of grave accent that the rhyme scheme regulated is interrupted by the introduction of the *aguda* accent; in it the irregularity begins in the model of the first series, since there the tridimensional rhyme of the poem opens up; in it the underlying sound, which repeats *Eve* obsessively as the dominant object of desire (like how in poem XVII the poet hears what in nature the buzzing bee that "*Eva* dice: todo es *Eva*" [says *Eve*: and all is *Eve*]), suffers a modification or registers an ambivalence that is linguistically the mildest of the language. It comes from a minimal displacement of the accent on top of a similar phonetic background, which, if it cancels the possibility that *Cloud* is *Eve*, does not cease to associate them by a path that is not semantic and that underlies the intellectual discourse.

The protean reminiscence of *Cloud* suggests more an energy than a form, a potency that would be established as performative if it were not the case that it is already a form, even though one capable of assuming without ceasing other new forms without thus losing its identity; a form furthermore that, in the context of the series, is in movement, that comes and goes taking with it "my love," that moans and cries. The movement of the "Eve" series is, similarly, in the "Cloud" series, except in this one it revolves around itself in an eternal presence, which allows the gods of movement and change to generate a new figure as Rodó expected, installing in the end thus a gratifying peace, the reunion of the repetition of difference, order. If Darío took advantage of the relation of Ixion with the Cloud to endorse the formal plurality of the centaur, Martí, in contrast, makes the Cloud a sponge that seizes cries and tears conceding peace. But the meaning of the poem does not merely come from the opposition of the series as separate and alternative options but in the contamination that regulates its distinct levels and that when it is contained in some is introduced in others where the repression is less effective. In fact, it is denouncing how the transposition of civil society to Nature cannot be accepted in its final consequences when it descends to eroticism, just as Whitman attempted with his erotic pantheism, because the cultural reading of Nature that Martí makes incorporates an ethical principle that restricts it.

We know little about this intimate zone of the poet's life. Various compositions in *Simple Verses* point to a visible tension: the poems of the small erotic series (in particular poem XVII) as much as other from the book; poem XXI; the discouraged poem XXXIII; the symbolic poem XLIII, which has been tied to his conjugal frustration, having recently reached its conclusion; poem XLII, of untethered sensuality. They are children of desire, that word infrequently used to talk about Martí,[67] about whom momentarily one could say he converted to the "celibate machine," even without suspecting the voluptuous intensities of which he can be capable.[68] To avoid the obvious Freudian quote, we remember one of Nietzsche's phrases: "The degree and type of a person's sexuality reaches up into the further-most peaks of their spirit."[69]

In poem XLIII, which by belonging to the most extensive and narrative poems in *Simple Verses* makes incursions into explicative zones, we find again the two female figures placed on the problematic axis Culture / Nature like in poem XX, which here they not only oppose each other but initiate the dialogue around the theme of love. It is easy to begin this conversation because the poet establishes that "love's strange bazar" is situated "by the seaside," with which Culture and Nature (bazar / mar [bazar/sea]) are contiguous and oppose each other and resemble each other through the link of the consonant. The feminine figure of the cultural series is concretely defined with a proper name: *Agar*. The feminine figure of Nature is no longer *Cloud*, but as Rodó and Darío would have appreciated, is *Mar*, such that the consonant associates them clearly and also, as in the case of bazar / mar, distinguishes them. The dialogue that they maintain refers to the possession of "a sad pearl bright as a star" ("my love" from poem XX), which *Agar* moved by the demons of change, of novelty, of difference, has disdained and thrown from herself ("Too long to her breast she pressed it / And too long her eyes caressed it, / That soon she came to detest it") while the *Sea* that is defined as permanence, fixity, continuity, treasures it ("the sad pearl you spurned I guard"). But it is that same *sea* that for Rodó changed its figure without ceasing, even though Martí visualized it clearly as feminine, just as Rodó, due to the sought after interjection of Proteus, masculinizes it, which in each case has its own persuasive explanation.

Clearly and explicitly, the two women are made corporeal here as participants of the opposition, making the natural protean form triumph over the cultural historical form. The ideological scheme is superimposed on the poetic material and transmits its meaning. One could not say the same about poem XX, where there is not a repentant Agar nor a feminine Proteus that triumphs, where times elude and distance each other as the straight line with respect to the curve, where Eve lies beneath the Cloud but Eve is only granted a complementary consoling function, where desire certifies the force of novelty and the force of its rigorous laws.

> V. Poetry reveals itself to be capable of expressing an articulated thought, but also its vacillations and failings, the darkest zones in which ideology gestates, gathering the conflicts and contradictions of its task of interpreting a concrete reality. More than the law of realism that Lukács will make his, that would illusorily impose an objective solution, without leaving a residue, what we note is the capacity of poetry, derived from the multiplicity of levels and planes in which it simultaneously develops, to detect the unique conflicts at the heart of which an ideology is forged, collecting its productive process and not just the conclusions to which it arrives. Similar to oneiric elaboration, poetry manipulates diverse and even contrary impulses, with which it traces a compound product where the tracks of the sources remain in diverse intensity and profundity, but also the concrete functions of the field of forces, not only those that have to do with the complex operations of the psyche, but also in the not always resolved relationships between the ideology of the author and that of the social medium in which it is carried out.

7. The Dilemma in Society

When the outline of the series is not supported in the classic dilemma of Culture and Nature but wholly belongs to the orbit of the first, the subjects become social but more arduous. There is no "universal term" on which to base them. In the case of poem XXIX of *Simple Verses*, the series alternates in the two stanzas based on the model A, verses 1–2, 5–6 and B, verses 3–4, 7–8, and this rhyme scheme like in poem XX is reduced to three for the eight verses, fixing thus the norm of connected stanzas, which will be complemented, as we already saw in poem XX, by the extension of homophonies that will reverberate through both series.

Series A-I	{	1	La imagen del rey, por ley,	8-A
		2	lleva el papel del Estado	8-B
Series B-I	{	3	el niño fue fusilado	8-B
		4	por los fusiles del rey.	8-A
Series A-II	{	5	Festejar el santo es ley	8-A
		6	del rey: y en la fiesta santa	8-C
Series B-II	{	7	¡la hermana del niño canta	8-C
		8	ante la imagen del rey!	8-A

(By law the king's face appears
On all the instruments of state,

And the king's own volunteers,
With his guns sealed the boy's fate.

It's the law to celebrate
The sainted namesakes of kings,

And the boy's sister sings
In front of the royal portrait!)

Rhyme A encompasses the entire composition and opposes equally the rhymes of the interior verses of each stanza (*ado, anta*), forming a triangular system: on one side they are composed of *aguda* rhymes against *grave* rhymes and on the other side they consist of single vowels against combinations of vowels and consonants, but even exclusively considering the vowels, these are distributed in an opposite way on the vowel triangle, while rhyme A develops progressively on the *aguda* vowels *e-i*, rhyme C remains fixed in the neutral point *a* with an extension due to the nasal resonator and rhyme B ascends through the *grave* vowels *a-o* with affrication of the *d*. The dominant is fixed by A (four rhymes), opposed equally by B (2) and C (2) due to the noted characteristics. To this is added the uniqueness of A, based in a monosyllable with decreasing diphthong that, as is the norm with Spanish, is not monophonemic, diminishing the difference between the words that maintain the opposition *r*/*l*, consonants that occupy a peculiar phonological situation: both belong to the fluid category, passable for vocalization, which makes the difference between vibrant / lateral sounds rest in the opposition interrupta / continua.

The choice of rhyme is narrowly tied here to the choice of the key words *rey*/*ley*, where the similarity has been supplied in the deterioration of the difference. This word-rhyme ends up supported by an interior rhyme repetition that signals it and establishes, in each one of the stanzas, another phonetic triangle whose dominant is *rey*:

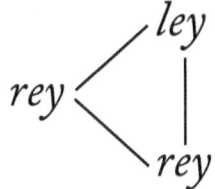

In this triangle, *ley* appears as a mediating term between the repeated *rey*, which, as much the consequence of mediation as of its reappearance in distinct contexts, registers a gradual modification that authorizes the second to not strictly repeat the first.

This semantic transfer is perceived most clearly if one substitutes the reading of the stanzas for the reading of the series, independently, which allows one to see that in Series A its first term (verses 1–2) affirms that it is *law* that imposes the image of *king* in the currency of the state, just as its second term (verses 5–6) unmasks this primacy of the legal agent affirming that it is the *king* who imposes the *law*, which makes honoring the saint obligatory; in Series B, its first term (verses 3–4) affirms that the power of the *king* is directly that which orders the execution of the boy, just as its second term (verses 7–8) reveals that the girl sings not before the image of the saint but in front of the image of the *king*, practically repeating thus the first verse but inverting it and excluding from it a word: *law*. In summary, if Series A initially affirms the primacy of the *law* to then contradict it, showing it as simply an instrument of the *king*, Series B initially affirms the brutal and direct action of the *king* without any form of legal intermediation to then show him ascended to the image (legal, that is) in front of which one should give reverence, due in fact to its direct imposition.

The function of the *law* is unmasked to uncover the despotic action of the *king* through a sarcastic contradiction, but the whole process cannot develop, as we saw already, without appealing to the concept of image. The triangle that governs each one of the stanzas (see figure 10.1), travels by the distinction *r/l/r*, thus allowing the passage of the ceremonial *king*, magic image of power, to the repressive governing *king*, which can only be achieved through the intermediary character of the *law* as generator of images, in which we can discern a sharp and interior perception of the forms of power by Martí. He already pays attention to those that were very recent and unique forms of domination imposed by the bourgeois regime of the nineteenth century, which had replaced monarchic absolutism (even though it preserved the monarchs), developing an abundant legal apparatus that offered itself up with a neutral appearance, as if born from the consensus of citizens. Let us not forget that for Martí the point of departure of the history that he lives is the overthrow of the old regime. Furthermore, he was witness, in his privileged New York viewpoint as in his punctual and suffering knowledge of Spanish American *caudillismo*, to the distance between the meticulous legal apparatus of constitutions, regulations, and legal codes (that he had to study to graduate with a degree in civil and canonical Spanish law) and the real function of power at the margins of this paper maze that the bourgeoisie brought to the world. Through this context, one could measure then the comparison and simultaneous denunciation of *king* and *law*. But this simple diagram is not able to account for all the problems in the poem because it leaves out too many component elements. What it proposes as interrogation of the function of images as instruments of the current symbolic social system will only become perceptible through the separate consideration of the series, before combining them.

Series A is built with two terms (verses 1–2 and 3–4) apparently deflected from each other and even loosely extemporaneous, as are the figures used in paper currency and the worship of a saint on its day, which do not seem to have a spontaneous tie. In one case that gives us the civil life of society through the instrument that fixes the value of exchange and, therefore, rules the production-consumption of its economy; in the other case it proposes to us the religious life through the official ceremony in which homage is given to the image of a saint. For the same reason, this is about a representation of the economy and the church, or, if we risk using a more technical term, which Martí visibly avoided, we would say bourgeoisie and church, powers that in the poem complement each other and balance through a third term that literally crowns them, which is the state represented by the king. The triangles obsessively function within the poem, and here we are before a type of saintly masculine trinity (*el rey, el papel, el santo*) that comprises in fact the totality of power. But it is not a lesson of political economy that Martí provides, but rather something else that has to do with the function of power through the singular pairing proposed by the bourgeois regimes of the nineteenth century, *the king, the law*, which constituted its original formulation, effecting its action on the economy as much as on religion as an institution. About this last point it is useful to not forget that in colonial Cuba the regime of patronage of the Spanish crown established in the sixteenth century still ruled, and that only thanks to the wars of independence had the Spanish American republics been liberated, establishing direct ties with the Papacy, such that in the island, flagrantly, the state ruled both the economic as well as the religious institutions.

At the time that Martí writes, paper currency still had not come, as in our time, to be confused with nature: it was a still disconcerting invention. There were few more curious experiences of the way in which wealth seemed to become a volatile symbol than the introduction of paper currency, which put in the hands of citizens a scrap of paper substituting gold and silver. This gold, about which Marx noted, "all the physical wealth evolved in the world of commodities is contained in a latent state in this solid piece of metal," "functioning as a medium of circulation, gold suffered all manner of injuries, it was clipped and even reduced to a purely symbolical scrap of paper," in the middle of the century.[70] At the 1891 Monetary Conference in Washington, the delegate José Martí speaks without ceasing of gold and silver and not "of the merely fiduciary and conventional character of paper money."[71] But this symbolic paper, like others even more incontestable (stocks), experienced the difficulties of private banking notes, with their fraudulent collapse and the unrestrained speculation of an era of big businesses, some of whose scandals were reviewed by Martí in his *North American Scenes*.[72] The patrician image or the monarchic image on the official bills could appear as a mode of bestowing confidence to a simple paper, but above all it fixed the connection between the economic market and the validating state system for legality: businesses operated under the protection of the images that symbolized the maximum power of the state. This translated into images that assured the exchange value.

Would Martí have seen in the worship of saints, these statues-paintings-images to which the people offered reverence, in which potentiality was coded, disturbing thus the perception of true reality, the same illusory way as those who guaranteed paper currency? The Martí who writes poem XXIX exactly a year after he had abandoned the management of the juvenile magazine *La Edad de Oro* by not wanting to obey the editorial mandate of teaching "the fear of God," was the same one who in it had explained (even talking of the Greeks) that people made the gods in their image and likeness, reiterating a conviction that accompanied him in life and that he evoked autobiographically in 1888:

> Which brings to mind the teachings of a young professor of History and Philosophy in Guatemala, some ten years ago, when, passing with his disciples through ancient towns, showed them how the gods had not made man in their likeness but that man had made the gods in the likeness of himself.[73]

It is the Martí in whose vast works the saints have faded, just as the personal god of an exclusive church had faded, giving way to a religiosity that he called natural ("in these times in which natural religion dawns"),[74] together with a sharp deviation with respect to the diverse dogmatic religions: "Man will look outside the purely human historical dogmas for that harmony of spirit of religion with free judgment, which is the religious form of the modern world, where the Christian ideal must flow, like the river to the sea."[75]

Martí did not write his promised letter to Manuel Gutiérrez Nájera[76] to explain to him his religious ideas, but through his articles his faith can be recovered in a "natural religion," his rejection of Catholic dogmatic forms and, above all, under the impact of the multifaceted religious life in North America, which he studied in detail in its ups and downs, its drastic opposition to the servitude of ecclesiastic institutions with respect to temporal power. Writing about the inauguration of the monument to the Pilgrims, he exalted the religious independence of the founders of the United States:

> An even this was a spiritual thing, that for its dignity and nobility was outside and above the intervention of man, without the minor art of governing the terrestrial interests of the community becoming arrogance like a child taken under wing at the house of the creator, nor its usurpation to the point of presuming to feed and care for the Church, which should not

be at the hands of anyone, because it is like putting God in the manger and giving him one thought in the afternoon and another in the morning.[77]

The "law of the king" imposes the royal figure not only in paper but also in the worship of saints, dealing with in both cases the reverential imposition of images that substitute, cover, and mask true power. The verbs of both terms of Series A, *llevar, ser*, signal the mere existentiality of these procedures: these are the symbolic manifestations of institutionalized life. The articulation of the poem divests the law of its second and fictitious nature to common eyes, proving thus the imposition of images as the principle function of power, to which magnificence and value for the exchange is attributed per se (since the saints are intermediaries in relations with divinity in the same way as money in the circuit of production, allowing the comparison of both as values of exchange).

If it is possible to establish such an equivalency between the two terms of Series A, it is not possible to accomplish the same operation with those of Series B, governed by action verbs that oppose each other (semantically and through their tense): *was executed, sings*. Furthermore, their protagonist characters, even though associated by law of kinship, oppose each other by their denomination (*the boy/the sister*) and by the contrary actions that they carry out. We already noted that Martí uses matrices that rule the genre constructing clear pairs of sexual opposites: the two principle pairs of the poem are *the king/the law* and *the boy/the sister*, but while the first is traced with the greatest phonetic similarity to then identify both parts semantically, the second maintains, under the tie of fraternal relations, the difference, which the opposing actions signal. We are thus in another triangular system, parallel to those already signaled in the poem, for which the unity *law/king* opposes simultaneously two different entities, which brings it to submission thanks to the alternative use of its dual nature, fixed by the opposition interrupted/continuous *r/l*, which pairs it to a revived Janus: when he confronts the child with his bare face, marked by the *vibrant* and *interrupt* characteristic *r* (*king*), he destroys him; when he presents his masked face to the sister, which is ruled by the *lateral* and *continuous* phonetic trait *l* (*law*), the reverential celebration conquers. We are not assuming significance to the fluid phonemes in question, assuredly, but lifting up that their phonological opposition is designed in parallel to that which governs both words semantically and to the opposition in the actions that, in both characters, provoke within the narrative sequence. The contrary responses that they receive are, furthermore, regulated by the relations of gender within which they are initiated: on the masculine side, the opposition *king/boy* results in the execution; on the feminine side, which connects *law/sister*, the consequence is the song.

A semantic triangle remains constructed, which crowns the other triangles detected in the poem. Its original function revolves as much in the duality of the guiding term (minimal difference over an expected phonetic and semantic similarity) as in the tie that connects the other two terms: effectively, to close the triangle, giving contour and pathos to the combination, it provides a blood tie to the young characters (which at a maximum difference of behavior adds a minimal similarity). This emotional note is incorporated to the text only through intonation; the dry declaration does not register it but in the exclamation points that mark the final two verses within which the little girl sings. The opposition between the agent term and the two patients rotates, therefore, on *similarity/difference*, through displacement of the positive charge of one to the other: in the agent it falls back to the similarity and in the patients to the difference.

As we say, only in Series A the pair *law-king* acts explicitly, while in Series B we exclusively find *king*, even though they occupy narratively inverted positions that grammatically derive from the opposite verbal functions: past/present, passive/active. Given that the two terms of Series B occupy chronologically successive positions in the linguistic chain, the sister in the second responds to the king who executes the child in the first by singing to him, through the intermediation of the legal imagery. However, the connection of the two series is not reduced to the dual term *king/law* but, as in the diptychs XII and XXXIX, extends to an entire verse that is repeated, introducing in this pairing of power a singular alteration that brings us to another that we can understand as homologous: *king/image*. Reproducing the model that we already saw in the diptych XII, there is a verse that repeats itself with an alteration: it is the first and the last of the composition and, furthermore, that which opens a series and one that closes the other, closing the entire development of both. "*The image of the king, by law*" it states initially and concludes "*In front of the image of the king*" with which it returns to work on the subtle dissociation that can be introduced between signifiers and signifieds when the same words are placed within different linguistic contexts (which the poet effectively does in poem XXXIX, where he strictly repeats the same verse, which then comes to mean something else) and on the variation of meanings, which are achieved with minimal alteration. As minimal as in poem XII because it works on absences and not on presences, the one that speaks is lack, the hole that has been demarcated when all the other linguistic terms repeat (En el bote iba remando / en el bote remador), and which in this case is represented by the disappearance of *law* between one and the other repeated verse. In such a hole another feminine association of the masculine king is located, reconstructing a pair that is overlaid on the previous one examined by the poem: *king/law* is now *king/image*, substitution of autonomous signifiers that, however, tend to coincide in a single and exclusive signified, according to which *image* is *law*, losing thus its autonomous meaning and assuming that of the iconic sign that represents the king. We have lost the masking intermediation of the law to recognize the startling imposition of power through a "consort" that simply represents it.

But it is not just "the image of the king" that thus remains demonstrated. If in a poem of such austere enunciation we can risk saying that, beyond demonstration, it remains stigmatized, denounced, combated, it is because in it we find a belligerent action against the *image* itself, against all the possible images, and, in the first place, against those of literature, a position that can only acquire its true magnitude relocating the poem in the era of its composition, which corresponds with a new consecration of the linguistic role of literary images, deifying the function of metaphor.[78] How to explain that the poem so notoriously does away with figurative images and abides by a direct and precise diction of characters, actions, and things, using simple and even trivial words, as if extracted from an administrative report or, like Flaubert, from the penal code. How to explain what in the entire book appears as a severe reduction of comparatives (already observed by Vitier), that earlier inundated his poems, the visible elision of metaphors and the pompous constructions of metonymies that populate his newspaper articles, even the retraction in the use of the qualifying adjective, which was an obsessive commonplace in his writing? It is obligatory to recognize that a compensatory law exists in *Simple Verses* through which the incorporation of the metric and rhyme matrices is counterbalanced with a reduction in the use of tropes, which even could extend to a compensatory law of poetry itself if one thinks that, starting with Huidobro, these matrices are archived and lyricism evolves to revolve around the metaphoric cell.[79] This does not disappear in Martí but lowers its importance for the benefit of a dry enunciation of actions where he pretends to refer objectively to the terms of reality with more precise words.

In this questioning of the images the eventuality of an apparently realist poetry remains planted, something that can also be perceived in another poet that pertained strictly to his generation and was rationalizing in his disposition and vision (Manuel González Prada), contributing to what I believe is a recessive line of modernismo but linked to them by the common problem that the multiple operations of modernista poetics confront. Well before Huidobro would exhort poets to not declare the rose but to construct it, the modernistas had already become aware of the challenge that the modernity, which was underway, would offer to them, before the avant-garde. Darío resolved this through "artificial roses that smell of Spring";[80] Martí hoped to do it assuming himself to be a natural being and proceeding in the field of language and of poetry, belonging to the cultural symbolic orb, in the same way that nature did. This explains the impersonality (despite the insistent "I"), the acceptance of "uglyism," the social transpositions to nature to legitimize them, and also the dissolution of the image parallel to the incorporation of song. It explains, above all, that Martí depends on the structures of the composition for the creation of the poetic effect. Focusing on structure allows equivalences of thought and of poetry, which in one of his last writings he noticed in Tejada's painting, praising the "natural message," "the form of expression of painters of reality" through the "gift of composing" that made "the pain of the world" visible.[81] The *gift of composing* works by tying things together and at the same time making them objective, which responds to an effort of understanding the function of the universe that can only pass, obligatorily, through a conscience. The *images* will appear then as illegitimate associations that distort or cover what is real or as corrosive of the unity of the object, with which, paradoxically, the language of this poetry should take a denotative inflection, throwing them from its heart and approaching the combinatory system of judicial languages. Poem XXIX is written with a succession of sentences, like a legal text, that alternate the enunciation of general dispositions with their concrete particular applications.[82]

The effects of such objectivity on the senses can be unsettling. Gabriela Mistral's[83] unease with poem IX for Martí's light impassivity to relate his beloved's suicide suffices. Martí is not always faithful to the principle, and among the extensive poems of the book there are those that are weighed with doctrine, but in the diptychs, laconism helps to suspend the expressed judgment because it defers to the conscience of the reader working on designed oppositions. It is obvious that Martí had done so in his own conscience, to show "the pain of the world" through structural agency, but to the extent that a poem places the plane of content in opposition to the plane of expression and to the extent that Martí has stripped it of images to leave it confined to sounds and rhythms, the acquisition of the totality of meaning can only be made by the concurrence of these sounds and rhythms, for which as is known, we do not have precise codes as those of language, even though poets have traditionally manipulated improbable subjective codes that for them established clear equalities, sometimes through synesthetic correspondences and, at a higher level, through equivalencies with meanings. The "subliminal linguistic structures" that Jakobson has tended to see as signals of significance can be recognized as free operators that bring with them other information, not necessarily corroborated but amplifying, complementing, even contradicting the meaning.[84]

When we approach poem XXIX and we believe we have traced the path that ideology takes in it, we perceive nonetheless, that something continues to escape shielded by its very objectivity, which has dropped all images to show the cruel derision of the image. Because what is presented as denunciation of the operations of power through the image does not extend to a denunciation of the suffering that they engender, classifying it as a spurious and unnecessary element. I suspect that it is the creating function of *pain* in human society, as so many times Martí argued and lived and justified and came to love,[85] what is at play in this lack of condemnation that in content is merely absence (even though by that meaningful) and in expression constructs the two series in a different way, overlaying them, contradictorily, with those that we have seen structured by significances.

As much based on vowels as on consonants, the poem's tessitura is aguda, a general tendency of Martí that, however, allows for curious variations, but among the vowels, the paired distribution of the aguda vowels (*i-e*) has an accumulation of grave one in the central verses (3–6) through the reiteration of *o-u* that is accompanied by a diminishing of the neutral *a*, concentrated in the exterior verses (1–2, 7–8). Likewise, the consonants are distributed in such a way that the exterior verses register the greatest number of occlusive and nasal consonants, as the internal ones triplicate the number of fricatives (*f, s*) with respect to the remaining ones. In other words, the phonetic design of the composition would seem to divide it in two different series to those explored: one includes verses 1–2, 7 and 8, and the other groups together into a coherent sonorous succession verses 3, 4, 5, and 6. If we were to be regulated by this distribution, it would end up that the expressive plane tends to associate the execution of the child with the saint's festival and the image of the king on paper money with the song of the girl. We do not try to give a meaning to these sonorous singularities but show that they contradict the design of the content series. It is this contradiction that we think can be reasoned, which we make by connecting it with the absences of content that have cleaned the four actions that are enumerated in the poem of any assessment or adjectivization.

Cognizant of the slippery nature of the terrain, we are able to see if the expressive operations that we note in the rhyme triangulation or in the construction of the pair *king/law* does not extend to the totality of the poem, if the painting of the "pain of the world" that would be achieved through the "gift of composing" does not also include the subliminal uncoded structures. Like we pointed out, this would not lead us to end up in the function of *pain*, that without a doubt exists in the poem, within the objective recognition of the charges that are obligatorily inverted in the general function of reality as indispensable parts of its general economy. In other words, the *pain*, that Martí reclaims as a value in numerous texts is not recognized as such, positively, in the poem.

This suggestion responds to the fact that Martí was fully a member of the "civil society" installed by the bourgeoisie, which had reached such a high degree of development in the United States at that time as to rule the thoughts of its main theorists. Martí's worldview uses an economic concept of the function of Nature that obviously comes from the civil society that he had adopted as his "second nature." Like the transcendentalists, he remits it to Nature, but instead of designing it exclusively with merchandise within the circuit of production and consumption through the values of use and exchange, he amplified it with a number of psychological contributions and with spiritual elements, inclusions that do not affect the structural function of the system but that, on the contrary, fold in the laws of production, of efficiency, of exchange, of use, of value. Nature remains visualized as a market: in it one buys and sells, except that these exchanges imply an ungovernable surrealist air: one gives blood in order to get freedom or receives suffering in exchange for beauty. The relation between *pain* and *poetry* that the Romantics (the first to arrive at the economic market) had established before him is described in *Simple Verses*' diptychs (XXXV, XXXVII, XXXIX) and is frankly associated with the productive task: as much for friendship as for cruelty, it proceeds with a "cultivation."

None of this can surprise us, even if we allow ourselves to see the internalization that had already been achieved in human conscience, of the economic market that triumphantly ruled social life. A few years after Martí writes, Sigmund Freud will proceed in a similar manner to elaborate a theory to explain the deepest part of the human psyche, which will be seen as ruled by charges of energy, productions, and rigorous laws of economy, making the subconscious a landscape of bourgeois industrial society.[86] For Martí, pain is a human product that has value in the market of exchanges. Its capacity to insert itself into the circuit of sales and consumption, just like the currency that gives it value, is not much different from those that Marx visualized for the economy, but the value that Martí confers is diametrically opposed to that which an era recognized with a class-based vision, which made pain and ugliness homologous, rejecting them. Inversely, Martí will dignify both, such that what "uglyism" represents in his aesthetic is equivalent to what "pain" represents in the spiritual economy of society. Both can translate into poetry with words, even though he will tend to select them from among the most simple and less aristocratic, but pain, furthermore, mobilizes an emotionalism that sometimes Martí (in *Free Verses*) is able to transfer to an explicative intellectual discourse, but that in these rare peak moments of *Simple Verses* lets itself run through the recently recuperated and sensitive phonic skin of language, in this crossing in which like Machado "one sings a lived history telling its melody": "and something that is earth in our flesh, feels the humidity of the garden as praise."

> VI. We see ideology pushed by a totalizing ambition, probably derived from a rationalizing capacity scarcely immune to truth, which accepts scarce concrete restrictions when it elaborates its coherence and dominates and unifies the different orders of reality that it should realize. When it constructs structures, it tends to repeat them in distinct fields, corroborating this desire, and when it conceives of an interpreting idea (e.g., an anti-imaginist thesis) it will tend to transfer it practically to the specific poetic texture (rejection of tropes, assumption of a denotative inflection, selection of simple words). Its free and super-rationalizing intellectual work will tend in poetry to systematize linguistic contributions (in which, with a Freudian scheme, could be understood as a tie with the preconscious that collects mnemic verbal remains) working in parallel fashion signifiers and signifieds prevailing against the re-elaboration of signifieds that allows the fluidity of signifiers but definitively will have to tolerate a greater opening of this phonic zone by impulses of emotion, of the highest energy and most complex composition, even though it submits them to the global function of the system it constructs.

Among the same phenomenon of unifying totalization, those derived from the extreme mobility of ideology can be included, capable of surreptitiously transforming themselves, when we see it transpose the entire economic system that rules society to absolute, universal, and invariable terms of nature, through equivalencies of structure. The structural transposition facilitates corrections and amendments within the social model, which respond to the perspective of the lower class that lives within it and suffers it and that is able to introduce the values that are their own (pain, uglyism), even without attaining with this the modification of their global function, that definitively accepts or surrenders to it through Martí's difficulty in accepting a third value inherent to the class (violence).[87] The ideological ceiling thus created reflects the social floor with an aggregate of some components, without affecting its general function. Here too men make gods in their own image and likeness.

11

Narrative Technification

The International Impulse: Techniques

It has not been said enough that the new Latin American narrative is a movement, more than an aesthetic, which allows for plural orientations within a rich artistic and ideological spectrum that is structured around two axes that order the literary production of the continent: a horizontal one that registers the action of diverse regional cultural areas in which Latin America is divided and a vertical one that allows the visualization of socio-cultural stratification produced in each one of these areas. This new narrative has its origin in the avant-garde of the 1920s when it formed in opposition to the patterns of the regionalist novel. It was consolidated in the 1930s and 1940s, protected by the strong urbanization that saw the imposition of cultural publishers that design a first circuit of internal communication. It reaches its full emergence in the 1950s and 1960s by counting on the support of a new public accrual that seeks answers to the conflicts that the continent witnesses in the transition to its greater integration into the world market—economic, technical, social, and ideological. This new narrative continues the development curve of the new society and witnesses its increasing complexity, its varied propositions, and its tensions and conflicts. Its sign, therefore, is this same complexity and this variety of solutions, which translates into a plurality of aesthetics that compete among each other and that will be defended in an exclusivist manner, as the only acceptable ones, by those who practice them and the critics that support them, even when they are, for a totalizing view of the phenomenon, only segments with greater or lesser influence, within the group as a whole.

These opposites will coexist within the movement in extremely varied doses, singling out factions: the realist and the fantastic worldview, the attention in its content to history and its negation, the manipulation of learned language and the recuperation of popular speech, existential expressivity and objective impassiveness. Some of them are more capable than others in expressing the sharpest points of the new situation, but even in this case they should be seen within the general functioning of an extraordinarily dynamic structure, dialectically related to other factions.

The whole structure functions between two opposite poles that from the origins of Latin America have been fixed in their support, and which have continued to evolve according to historic circumstances: the internationalist, which registers a variety of successive external impulses, and the nationalist, which capitalizes on the integrative forces and traditions, whether they are autochthonous or creole with a long tradition. These are modernized and conventional designations of energies that have been categorized very diversely through the centuries but that we do not cease to find always formulated: creole versus Spanish culture, civilization or barbarism, conservatism and liberalism, Catholicism and positivism, cosmopolitanism and nationalism, and so on. The history of such a dichotomy is varied, sometimes it feigns an isochronous pendulum rhythm, sometimes it mixes its characteristics, and in the last century it continued an accelerated development that corresponds to the planetary expansion of the external cultural metropolises, which has reinforced the action of the internationalist pole whose impact on our America has been abrupt on two occasions: starting in 1870, when European states restructured themselves, a few years after the United States unified the economic power of the North, and starting in 1945, upon the start of the long postwar period that has generated a redistribution of the Western empires conceding supremacy to the United States.

The external push acquires greater strength in this second moment due to the work of the technological revolution that replaces in incomparably superior terms the industrial revolution that fed the impulse of the first moment at the end of the nineteenth century. To use an example from the communications field, there is no comparison between the effect that the invention of the linotype, the expansion of underwater cables, and the advent of international agencies had on Latin American journalism at the end of the century and that of the conquest by television, the transmission by satellites, and the direct expansion of illustrated magazines after 1945. The international influence, which had its first field of action in the economy, has been favored by the conquests of the technological revolution, and even though it had different degrees of penetration in the distinct areas of Latin America, it did not leave any untouched, provoking enormous removals.

Such encompassing power has an equally global equivalent in the literary field where it manifested in a requirement of the technification of letters, parallel to that which began to be fulfilled in other intellectual disciplines. It was a basic and general influence that touched all the factions of the new narrative and that therefore can be seen as one of the defining marks of the movement and not simply as a characteristic of some of the aesthetics in which it is subdivided. On the horizon of the narrators, the techniques appeared as a possibility of renovation and better adaptation to the messages that they hoped to transmit, and (from ecstatic presentation to cautious use) we had at our disposal various answers to a single impulse, as much admired as coveted. The important thing about this new element was the breadth of its action that allowed an overall revision of the movement to search for its deeper meaning, even though one has to see it above all in the sector that gave it supremacy, operating an authentic sanctification of techniques. Likewise, it was this aspect that more forcefully claimed the readers' attention and around which the definition of the *Boom* revolved, as much for those who accepted it as for those who rejected it. The extreme mode in which the new narrative techniques were absorbed meant that they acquired an exorbitant importance within literary works and thus had a greater impact on readers.

A writer who at the end of the nineteenth century, in the first period of strong international influence, evinced his uniqueness through the use of tools learned from French poetry, Rubén Darío, very quickly discovered that this resource, which provoked indignation, rejection, and contempt was precisely the one that opened the doors of popularity to him because it had a strong influence on the imaginary of the common people, establishing the path through which a poet of the minorities could be transformed into a poet of the majority. In the prologue to *Songs of Life and Hope*, which he published at the height of his fame, Darío gently says something that has not been adequately noted: "Form is what primarily touches the masses."[1] He then began what he would call his "sincerist" period, where his formal methods would acquire a smoothness and greater harmonious adaptation without completely disappearing, but they had been the ones that in his furious manifestation opened to him, through a clamorous scandal, the doors of the masses' imagination.

The attention to techniques from the beginning meant, in the second period of international influence of this century, the interest in the works of the European avant-garde of the interwar period, where they appeared as the original structuring of an equally original worldview. Contact with this material began among the few writers who understood foreign languages (from Oswald de Andrade to Vicente Huidobro)[2] and increased among those who coexist with the European movement as a type of Spanish American "lost generation": Miguel Ángel Asturias, Alejo Carpentier, Jorge Luis Borges. This impulse expands through the 1940s when the recently established Argentine publishers, Losada, Sudamericana, Emecé, begin a systematic series of translations: Aldous Huxley, Virginia Woolf, André Gide, Franz Kafka, and the first Spanish edition of Joyce's *Ulysses*, together with William Faulkner, Ernest Hemingway, and soon after Thomas Wolfe, Carson McCullers, Truman Capote, and so on. Disconnected from the original European works, the techniques were used as simple systems of composition, enduring therefore as a general and indiscriminate use. Far from the etymological significance that turned "tecné" into an epistemology for the Greeks, they became literary resources that were extrapolated from a European or North American work to another Latin American one and that subsequently authors developed with a highly inventive spirit, working in the same trajectory and proposing new solutions. The initial application of techniques to any issue or focus contributed, unavoidably, to fetishizing them and, more curiously, to seeing techniques as neutral elements, without forced ties with the material, a type of parallel field of universal applicability and, thus, an unclaimed good that even though it had recognizable parentage, lacked a patent.

It does not consist simply of a behavior unique to Latin Americans but one that has long antecedents in European thought if we consider the reasoning of Arnold Toynbee about the initial failure of the Jesuit project in China. This project introduced the cannon associated with the need for religious change in contrast to the system applied since the nineteenth century that limits itself to the introduction of the cannon and the remaining technical implements separating them from all apparent doctrine but using them in the service of a restructuring of colonized society that is welded marginally to the central governing powers of the metropolis.[3] The success of the technique in all the universe since the nineteenth century obeys this apparent neutralization that did not cease to establish conflictive imbalances in the remote regions over which it acted. And at the same time this success was confirmed by the conduct of the colonized populations that accepted this situation as a matter of fact and used technology for their own gain. In 1870 in Uruguay there was a rural revolution called the "revolution of the lances" because on the same date in which German cannons bombarded Paris these revolutionaries were still using a weapon predating the Spanish conquest; the government put an end to it with the introduction of Remington rifles, which were to be used by the rural sectors in their next insurrection.

In the prologue that I wrote in 1964 for a brief anthology of new literature (narrative and poetry of Latin America), which I published in the newspaper *Marcha* in Montevideo and that I believe is the first attempt to unite a collection of this literature's important contributions at the time, I noted as a principal characteristic the technical preoccupation that distinguished it within the international avant-garde underway at the time:[4]

> The period begins with a distinctly experimentalist attitude gathering in Latin America for the first time the European and North American avant-garde . . . which explains the techniques of composition of *Things and Delirium*, the first book by Enrique Molina, or *Pedro Páramo*, Juan Rulfo's only novel, or *No Man's Land* by Juan Carlos Onetti, or the creations of the Chilean "Mandrágora" group, in particular Braulio Arenas.[5]

This experimentalism coexisted or obtained a pact with a tendency that we will call "Latin Americanist," responding still to the proposition made by the greater artists of the continent (Pablo Neruda, César Vallejo) of mixing the artistic avant-garde with the political avant-garde, a proposition that had already effected a considerable schism in narrative with the uniquely experimental and fantastic option that Jorge Luis Borges assumes and that distinguishes him from the joint tendency that Miguel Ángel Asturias and Alejo Carpentier cultivate contemporaneously. But it would be this later one that would govern the narrative and more in the climate of commotion of the 1960s, through the work of the new narrators emerging around 1955, among them Rosario Castellanos, Carlos Fuentes, García Márquez, Cepeda Zamudio, Salvador Garmendia, Martínez Moreno, José Donoso, Adriano González León, Mario Benedetti, Mario Vargas Llosa, Augusto Roa Bastos, and David Viñas.[6] Their initial works justified the combination of avant-gardes, in greater or lesser degree, that were not seen as opposites. Hence, I said then:

> We already pointed out the new North American influence, that intensifies in all of America after 1939, and that corresponds to the entry of the great avant-garde writers, combined with

European avant-garde that in America begins to function later. Simultaneously, an awareness of human and social responsibilities exists, which was inherited from the rosy period of antifascism of the 1930s, but without the overflowing and naïve confidence in good feelings that also marked this movement.[7]

In the fifteen years that have passed, this interest in literary experimentation has continued an accelerated evolution and has contributed to the schism of the narrative movement, above all in those cases that, within the Borgesean lineage, effect a rupture with history and employed a hurried and somewhat simplistic adaptation of the ideology of structuralism for their composition exercises. This process has been seen with skepticism and even with sarcasm by those authors who were part of the beginning of the technical renovation of narrative. Already in 1973 some fragments of a novel that Ernesto Sábato was writing, *El ángel y el abismo* (*The Angel and the Abyss*), had come to light, something that did not shy from irony regarding the methods of composition of the most popular writers at the moment.[8] Juan Carlos Onetti has expressed perplexity and consternation, referring concretely to Latin American authors in several interviews:

> It is very curious what is happening now with Latin American writers. Ninety percent of those who attract interest are left-leaning and one has to assume that they advocate for a better communication between writer and reader; however, with this absurd abuse of techniques, they are creating—or there is the danger that they might create—a literature of non-communication.
>
> By way of technical exaggeration one arrives at non-communication and I think that the writer should fundamentally communicate with the rest of humankind. On the contrary, their work loses all real interest.[9]

It is possible that, if he were still living, a critic like Manuel Pedro González, who already had taken on the technical nature of *Pedro Páramo*, would claim that that dirt led to this mud and faced with the criticism of those who opened the path of renovation would evoke the history of the imprudent servant with the magic broom. More so if one considers that in the initial proposals in favor of technical renovation at the end of the 1930s, the same Onetti argued with the commissioners of the left who defended a focus on social content ignoring all the remaining aspects of artistic writing. Onetti has probably been the first to expressly think about the problem of technical incorporation in terms that show his point of view of the concept, which has been subsequently imitated by the other writers of his generation and by those of the next one, with the addition that in these same dates the greater writers (Asturias, Carpentier, Borges) who were in loose communication with European sources, were putting it into practice.

A Lengthy One-Sided Dialogue with Europe

Before exploring different uses of technique, it is helpful to remember that all modification of society translates into a parallel modification of literary products that adjusts to a renewed worldview that forcefully moves through adequate expressive mechanisms. Except in authoritarian regimes that impose strict aesthetic canons—the case of the Soviet Union—the stylistic mutations are in tune with the history of the culture, habitually being those that detect in advance the changes within society. Thus, the freezing of any "literary form" results in the end in an archaism or mere imitative manifestation, but furthermore, in any period of history, diverse solutions coexist uneasily. These solutions represent the contrary propositions that operate within society, with greater abruptness in the current century thanks to the incessant focus on the future that the avant-garde proposes.

Hence, it is evident that in the developed urban centers of Latin America one cannot write like Gallegos or Azuela[10] did, and perhaps not even like Asturias or Carpentier, without this assertion diminishing at all the excellence of these authors' works given that they are not merely illustrations of past aesthetics. Art is not measured by its location in a chronology. In the moment of renovation writers that hoped to express the new circumstances of Latin American existence found in European techniques an efficient aid and in regionalist models an enemy to conquer. They defined themselves against the latter and in favor of the former, seeing techniques as neutral instruments of work.

I wrote in detail about the "curious imitations and curious disagreements between Latin American writers that make the effort to pick up the foreign lesson" in a lengthy essay from 1964 whose terms could be repeated because I believe they have been confirmed in the intervening time.[11] I depart from the idea that techniques are not neutral, nor mechanically separable from the so-called content of the works, but rather they are systems of significance that writers makes use of to elaborate this "expressive" unity that is a work of art. This does not prevent me from recognizing that determined technical resources, created in European countries or the United States around precise situations of their worldview, end up meeting their real equivalents in Latin American countries, legitimizing themselves this way with a significant basis within the continent. No matter how much their incorporation obeyed the reading of solutions found by a foreign writer, one could say that the passion of this reading by the Latin American writer led to their awed rediscovery of their own situation, thanks to this passion, which acquired a mode of expressing oneself precisely in a renewed technique that foreigners had developed. This is how Carpentier recounts that Stravinksy's rhythms prepared him to perceive the rhythmic richness of the black music of Regla that he had at hand, in front of him in La Habana. And in no other way did a distinguished group of Latin American authors discover in William Faulkner the appropriate mode of expressing a situation that was extraordinarily similar to that of North American Southern society that did not in vain have essential points of contact with Latin American societies. By 1956 James Irby had discovered the presence of Faulkner in Lino Novás Calvo, Juan Carlos Onetti, José Revueltas, and Juan Rulfo,[12] and if he had written a few years later also would have traced it in Gabriel García Márquez, who had made of Faulkner his mentor in interpreting the decadent estates of the tropics.[13] In the same way one could have followed the trail of John Dos Pasos from Onetti's *No Man's Land* (1941) to Fuentes's *Where the Air Is Clear* (1958), in authors who hoped to encompass the urban totality of their new macrocephalic capitals.

Outside this eventuality, in which techniques appeared as good conductors for local circumstances, the vast danger zone could be found where the attraction of forms leads to vacuous mimetism, scarcely significant for a lack of authentic experiences that justify them. From there comes the cautious exhortation, that in the cited essay I formulated thus:

> The acceptance of an adult attitude on the part of the Latin American novelist would reside in the subtle distinction between their own values, independent of the techniques or systems, as an expression of determined historical-cultural—and, as a result, economic-social—situations, and the possibility of adaptation of the elements of those techniques that can become the vehicle of their own situations, which does not mean exclusive, but the result of an insertion of the writer in a determined social context.[14]

While the avant-garde fearlessness that bets any form on the future does not aspire to find confirmation of the situations of the moment but rather in the eventuality of its future attainment (which, strictly speaking, means betting on a determined socioeconomic structure whose model has already proven successful in some current metropolis), the dissociation of techniques with respect to the components of the work, replacing largely controversial dichotomies like that of "form" and "content," appears in the literary field as the representation of a development option that attributes to technification, on its own, the capacity to lead to the concomitant social change or that extends to the whole community what is produced in a restricted sector of society, often to the detriment of the majority sectors.

The evolution of this problem in the literature of the last century, from the first great international push at the end of the nineteenth century until the current one of this delayed decline of the twentieth, illustrates its difficulties and the tenacious effort to put this problem into focus. Darío's initial jubilant discovery aimed at frankly incorporating the themes of the millennial tradition of European culture, as he acknowledged in his anti-manifest in *Profane Hymns*, stating that there was no poetic theme in the America of his time. The thematic assimilation obligatorily led to a technical assimilation for which the reconversion of language and instruments of composition was indispensable, reflecting the image of European models from Romanticism to Symbolism, from which he ingeniously revised the literary tradition of the language, returning to the code of the Baroque.

The second moment, *postmodernista*, implies an initial rift, if we recognize, as the publication dates of the works show, that the regionalist as well as the avant-garde novels are strictly contemporaneous and that both respond to a central attempt at internal historicization of the continent, and an appropriation of the social context. They are divided by the different artistic methodology that reflects the first contrast between rural culture and urban culture: while the first is equipped by the combined heritage of Naturalism and Modernismo, the second employs Ultraism and Futurism. Both confront the same historical project, representing it at different levels. This unity is what facilitates Alejo Carpentier's transition between *Ecué-Yamba-O* (1931) and *The Kingdom of This World* (1949). Continuing in the historical field he moves from what we could call intrahistory—as defined by Mario de Andrade[15] in *Macunaima*, or even in Roberto Arlt's[16] dosteivskian *The Seven Madmen*—to the universal historical events where there would be space for Latin American participation, building his narrative as a cultural bridge between Latin America and Europe thanks to the progressive integrative communication resulting from the European expansion. These are not just exclusively the themes of the thousand-year-old European culture like in Darío, but rather the historical facts that the author manipulates, that were caused by them [Europe] but that counted on participation, generally involuntary, on the part of Latin America. What is curious about this lies in the fact that this development, despite being historical and referring to Latin America, demands that one keep in mind the European culture from where the impulse originates. It transfers from the thematic field to the stylistic field and affects the central operations that technically construct the text, making even Carpentier return to the code of the Baroque.

In his essay "Problems of the Current Latin American Novel," Carpentier affirms that "the legitimate style of the current Latin American novelist is Baroque."[17] More curious than this statement, only true for a sector of contemporary narrative not for all of it, is its basis—it originates from the idea that assumes a foreign reader who does not know the component elements of American reality. The need to incorporate Europeans, North Americans, and the entire world as readers of the Latin American novel, avoiding at the same time the "glossaries" that used to appear in the final pages of regionalist novels, leads Carpentier to propose a Baroque writing (even though he likely wants to say detailed) that provides "the sensation of color, the density, the weight, the size, the texture, the aspect of the object" unknown to foreigners. Perhaps few texts better illustrate that minority in which the Latin American writer has felt with respect to the self-assured mode of operating that a dominant culture like the European has enjoyed. A European culture that has developed by itself, independently, and has not bothered explaining itself to the marginalized of the world. The examples that he uses are transparent:

> The word *pine tree* is enough to show us the pine tree; the word *palm tree* is enough to define, to show, the palm tree. But the word *ceiba*—name of an American tree that the black Cubans call "the mother of trees"—is not enough for people of other latitudes to see the appearance of rostral column of this giant, sullen and solitary tree, as if displaced from another time, sacred by its lineage, whose horizontal branches, almost parallel, offer the wind a handful of leaves that are unreachable to man as well as being incapable of any rocking.[18]

Faced with this depreciation of a culture that is only regional and not universal like European culture in which one can talk about pine tree or palm tree, the narrator should undertake a technically painstaking task so that the foreign reader can feel, value, and weigh the things in their own right:

> This is only achieved through an accurate polarization of various adjectives, or, to avoid the adjective itself, by the adjectival use of certain nouns that act, in this case, by the metaphoric process. If one proceeds with luck—literarily speaking, in this case—the purpose is achieved. The object lives, is contemplated, lets itself be weighed. But the prose that gives it life and consistency, weight and measure, is a Baroque prose, forcedly Baroque, like all prose that clings to detail, repeats it, colors it, emphasizes it, to give it prominence and define it. . . . Our ceiba, our trees, dressed or not with flowers, have to be made universal through the use of exact words that belong to the universal vocabulary. The German Romantics arranged these words to allow a Latin American know what a snow-covered pine tree was when that Latin American had never seen a pine tree nor had a notion of what the snow was like that made it snow-covered.[19]

The Romantics didn't have to say anything more than simply "snow-covered pine," because they were writing within the semantic environment that they shared with their readers, which simply repeated the environment of the experiences of the same community. Dozens of Latin American writers did the same thing when they wrote within this shared environment, because José Hernández[20] never explains what an *ombú* is and even mentions it very few times because it consists of a well-known element for his circle of readers. Only the desire to universalize the reception of literary works, originating from a marginal culture to the great metropolis, explains the foundation that Carpentier makes of Baroque writing (which could be found with more precision in other causes) and reveals to us how sharply the international pole influences the specific techniques of narrative writing.

Within the second moment corresponding to the regionalist avant-garde period and within the same effort to equally coordinate what is native and what is foreign, which is its distinctive trait, another solution is noted that avoids this path of historization that Carpentier practices and finds harmony appealing to the concept of archetypes. Instead of appropriating concrete materials from European culture similar to the modernista Darío and instead of looking for the tie to Europe through common historical points, it recognizes the existence of archetypes, presumably universal ones according to European anthropology and psychology, which would have their own unique incarnation in Latin America. This incarnation would be as legitimate and as dignified as the European one. This use of archetypes had a version that was highly rooted in American circumstances in the work of Miguel Ángel Asturias. His theoretical basis is found in the anthropological concepts of Lévy-Bruhl and above all in Jungian psychoanalysis that would continue to supply diverse authors from Julio Cortázar to Carlos Fuentes, which operate with these assumptions despite the corrections introduced by Lévi-Strauss, even if they try to partially employ some of his structural proposals. Within this context, the one who reaches the paroxysmal version of archetypes will be Jorge Luis Borges, who will rid himself radically of history and will operate with complete freedom in the field of universality. Abandoning a period that sometimes is described as "folkloric," he will elaborate images supplied by the unconscious without worrying about its local incarnation, believing that this emerges in addition as an equally preconscious eventuality and abandoning himself to an unrestrictive and enjoyable use of techniques developed in Europe and a reinvention through them. The note of freedom that distinguishes his texts, bordering the playful range in which he designs them, recalls Darío's solution that had achieved harmony between discordant elements, even though no longer dependent on an admiration for millenary culture but rather on its use within an indiscriminate totality: the compadrito and the lottery in Babylon.

The third moment of this evolution will witness the schism in which technique fully assumes its neutral character, of an indistinct use, with the simultaneous preservation of a unique thematic range that is exclusively Latin American. We will have two sharply differentiated planes, one of a universal bent and another regional, and the narrator will act simultaneously in both, the resulting work of art being that which mixes them.

The Operative Model

I believe it was Juan Carlos Onetti who initially developed this concept and did so within the debate during the decade of anti-fascism in which the advocates of the new artistic writing opposed the supporters of socially conscious art.²¹ Onetti's observation is from 1939 and is not casually contemporaneous with his discovery of the cold systems of perks in Latin American cities (Buenos Aires) where the "men without faith" to whom he dedicates his novel *No Man's Land* will emerge

> to import from there (Europe) what we do not have—technique, purpose, seriousness—but no more than this. To apply these qualities to our reality and trust that the rest will be given to us in addition. Of course this whole careless critique does not apply to the leftist writers who—by right of their nobility, disinterest, and modesty—have disdained byzantinisms of style and technique. No fault falls to them. It is true that they could have given us some *Salambó*, one or two *Hamlet*s, three or four *Crime and Punishment*s. But they preferred to put their pen, Underwood typewriter, and their minds in the service of race, class and oppressed peoples.²²

The economic terminology with which it is expressed seems indicative of the general predicament in which Onetti's proposition is inscribed. He refers to "imports" that are strictly reduced to the essentials that are not found locally to apply them to one's own reality, optimistically trusting in positive results from this crossing. It the equivalent of the widely proclaimed doctrine of import substitution that was developed in various points of the continent in the shadow of the Second World War, when the metropolises encountered difficulties in furnishing necessities for Latin America like before and the balance of exchange was temporarily inverted in favor of Latin America, a situation that lasted until the economic boom of the Korean War. The optimism of this period of accelerated development made possible the nationalization of important foreign businesses (from Mexican petroleum to Argentine railroads) and opened sources of more technological labor contributing to emigration from rural areas to the cities. It thus extended from the war for a long decade that helped alleviate the underground crisis that from 1930 had settled in Latin America and whose emergence in the 1960s gave sustenance to social unrest. From the current melancholic perspective, the period is defined as one of great illusions.

In fact, import substitution was a first step, taking advantage of the international situation, toward autonomy. The desire and confidence in Latin America's own strengths obscured the view of the limitations coming from the dependent period in which the continent was functioning, the delay of the Latin American economy and the dizzy advances that imperial centers would achieve, through already superior levels, upon unleashing the technological revolution. This placed imbalance in other levels, increasing instead of diminishing the power of the structured world economy. In the 1930s the problem was still situated, for the River Plate region where Onetti was writing, in the in situ processing of virgin wool that constituted one of the important productive markets for the country, creating a light industry to supply the internal population. Ironically it seemed to reproduce a situation as old as that of Spain with respect to England around 1700, the date in which Spanish wool was dyed in England and subsequently was bought back for the necessities on the peninsula and in the colonies. Substitution was carried out combining the purchase of factories, produced in England or the United States, with the establishment of protectionist laws that in fact involved the financing of industrialization by the whole of society. The change seemed positive and became a flag of liberal and progressive thought, even though the edge of the advance quickly showed its limits and the previous inequality reappeared at a new level.

It is instructive that such a modification reinforced one that the same area of the River Plate had seen at the end of the nineteenth century, when the development of the refrigerator industry of meat and the expansion of literary modernismo coincided simultaneously, corresponding to the first great global industrializing impulse. Its terms signaled even less Latin American autonomy, given that the refrigerator industry and commerce almost exclusively answered to foreign investments, all of the technological equipment came from outside the country and the combination established the typical "operative model" that ruled the development of the marginal zones of the planet, which linked, in a dependent position, with the "productive model" that corresponded with the industrial centers. In the first instances of a co-participation that would become increasingly greater within the universal economic systems, some produced the industrial advances and also operated them, to then give way to a second solution in which the metropolises produced industrial advances and marginal zones operated them using their own raw materials. As Onetti would say, the technique came from Europe, the raw material was ours—with the addendum, which should be highlighted, that the manufactured product thus was destined for the consumption of an exclusively regional society, even though it aspired to enter in the exportation circuit, at least with respect to the less advanced zones in this process.

It is obvious that economic and artistic fields cannot be seen as equivalent, nor can one posit that the first genetically governs the second, but both face similar situations, marked by the ambition of autonomy, so obvious in the series of articles that Onetti wrote in 1939 and 1940 under the pseudonym Periquillo el Aguador and under the revealing title "The Stone in the Pool."[23] It is also visible in the expectations of Latin American politicians of the time. Achieving the efficiency and the peak of foreign production was necessary, becoming independent of its domination, and the moment of confluence seemed favorable. A synthesis of the failed hopes that Stanley and Barbara Stein have expressed in their book helps to show the vision that at the time was held:

> From 1930 to 1945 temporary reduction in the capacity to import consumer finished goods provided a domestic market for national manufactures; added factors were tariff protection and population growth. Europe's post-war reconstruction and the demands of the Korean War fostered the belief that it was tenable to expect that the gains from international trade would provide exchange to finance long-delayed projects of industrial development and by mechanization to raise productivity in agriculture. The recession of British economic influence after 1945 led some to conclude that the long struggle against the "imperialism of free trade" for economic sovereignty would shortly be achieved. How else to interpret the results of Péronist economic nationalism or Mexico's appropriation of foreign-owned oil companies? In sum, during the immediate post-war years changing international and national conditions indicated that Latin America would in the foreseeable future attain an appreciable degree of economic autonomy, by creating on a national scale a capital goods industry, developing and processing local sources of fuels, reducing foreign investment and raising local savings and investment rates, stimulating productivity not only in traditional export sectors but also in production of foodstuffs for internal consumption. Taken as a bloc these developments augured the achievement of economic autonomy, the end of economic dependence of the periphery upon the industrial core.[24]

This is not the place to follow the frustration of these hopes; it is only necessary to consult the series of publications from the Economic Commission for Latin America to measure their social effects and their limits in terms of the search for autonomy. The last document by date is the official report by the accountant Enrique Iglesias in the Eighteenth Session of the Commission in Bolivia from April 1979.[25]

For our purposes, it is important to see how this schism between technique and raw material in the theoretical conception of authors has continued. Since then the introduction of foreign techniques has not stopped nor has it ceased to contribute new inventions in the same path, which has already produced descendants. The schism continues to be perceived, however, even though technique is no longer affiliated with a concrete external center but is seen as a modality of intellectual work, typical of common international rights. In contrast, materials conserve a sort of privacy or interiority that even seems to elude programs of rational thought to collectivize them.

The Peruvian Mario Vargas Llosa, a self-confessed fan of Flaubert (and it is not pointless to remember that Flaubert inaugurated the attention to literary techniques in the contemporary novel), appeals to one of these dichotomies of which he is fond: the opposition of rationality to intuition as a way to explain how the two paths through which his work is constructed are combined:

> The rational element in reality does perform a dominant role, but only at the technical level of style, of writing, but in the domain of material it does not. In the domain of material there is an intuitive element that is what should entirely prevail so that the literary work might exist, so that the literary work might be authentic.[26]

Vargas Llosa has operated a theoretical framework that frequently relies on marked antithesis, seeing the literary work as a tense and conquered equilibrium between opposites that the writer harnesses, as if overcoming their centripetal tendency, at the service of creation. The contrasted use of both elements (rational and intuitive) is incredibly noticeable in his narrative where a new type of realism coexists with an extremist technical creator, author of these "traps," as Onetti has labeled them, that give structure to the material. Despite the convergent effort of the author, the operant forces preserve their autonomy in *The Time of the Hero* or in *The Green House*, even though they found a more amenable integration in *Conversation in the Cathedral*.

Julio Cortázar has been even more explicit. The representative of a fully avant-garde attitude, according to which the artist is a permanent conqueror of the unknown, always open to the quest and to new prompts, always available. In a 1969 text he affirms the complete internationalization of literary techniques that would have constituted a sort of great common market of letters, in which both Europeans and Americans, Asians and Africans would meet with the same rights, making use of the same sources and the same inventions, creating through them new ones that would pass on to form part of the common heritage, being both influenced and influencers in conformity with the force and originality of their contributions.

Even though Cortázar sees it as a recent development, the mildest recounting of Latin American letters shows the permanent use of European technical novelties, to which a lineage of artists has been particularly inclined since the beginning of our culture, using them as a common good, without a recognized owner, which sometimes has come close to plagiarism. What in Cortázar's text seems new and recently acquired is the awareness that this market is truly common, that writers of the oldest marginal zones participate with equal footing in it, that thus they have gained autonomy. Darío at the end of the nineteenth century said, in French, "Who could I imitate to be original"; he lived many years in Paris without being incorporated into the international market (although he did break into the Spanish market in a first conquest by Spanish Americans) and without his considerable contributions, based on French technical sources, reverting to their market. Cortázar who in the middle of the twentieth century lives in Paris feels that he is already incorporated, certified by translations to European languages, and inventions like the structure of *Hopscotch* can operate in French or German authors. He states:

> *There is no longer anything foreign in literary techniques* because the shrinking of the planet, the translations that almost immediately follow the original editions, the contact between writers, increasingly eliminate the stagnant compartments in which the diverse national literatures had been produced previously. This does not mean that a novel by a Mexican author resembles the novel of a French author, given that each one is born of a particular experience, of a unique "reality" . . . ; but the formal mechanisms that propel these experiences have ceased to be the privilege of certain cultures; the experimental field is one alone and its resulting individuals propagate with a velocity directly proportional to their importance and efficiency.[27]

What is interesting for our reflections is that the schism between one and another order continues to exist within Cortázar, one of these orders being international and the other regional, one common to all writers in the world and the other only to Latin Americans, who thus achieve their specificity. The techniques derive their universality from their extraordinary mobility within the interconnections of the present world, for which one does not even have to wait, as he indicates, for immediate translations, because the increased knowledge of foreign languages by current authors allows Spanish Americans, above all when they are installed in important locations for foreign publishing houses (in Cortázar's case, for example) the instantaneous awareness of new technical contributions that bring challenges to literature. This changing situation has impacted the field of academic criticism that has been forced to substitute its search for sources (something that was easier before, because of the temporal imbalance between foreign production and Spanish American adaptations) with comparative studies. The universal circulation of literary techniques is merely an individual case in the very restricted sector of literature of a generalized behavior of the industrial era that has carried forward modern empires and has assured them planetary domination. It consists of the diffusion of technical inventions born in the heart of determined societies in accordance with its particular cultural evolution and scientific-industrial levels, which are offered to the marginal cultures in the system in the form of neutral factors that are available for absorption by any of them and that apparently assures them the conquest of the goal of development similar to the producer society. These incorporations reveal their limitations if one relates them with the line of technological progress: the marginal societies that can produce old looms remain plentiful; fewer, but still plenty, can produce cars; fewer can produce thermonuclear plants; even fewer can build supersonic airplanes; and incredibly few can build satellites. The science and technology that need a highly developed infrastructure tend to be concentrated in a few countries. Literature could avoid that, given its artisanal character that sets aside archaic productive models, even though by being situated in contemporaneity it cannot avoid being affected by the universal circulation of techniques.

What in these and other opinions about technical universality does not get mentioned, provoking certain bewilderment, is where these literary techniques have come from, which since Flaubert to the European avant-garde of the twentieth century, passing through Mallarmé and the Symbolists, brought a rich combination of inventions that were chronologically prior to those of Latin Americans, who added their own contributions, installing themselves in this common international market. It is obvious that such inventions had occurred before the ones from Latin America. It is also obvious that they were the ones that were inspiration, and the only novelty that has been claimed, within a climate of exaltation that has left little space for objective proof, is that the contributions made in recent decades by Latin Americans are entirely original with respect to foreign models and influence universal literature instituting models to follow.

Since Europeans did not count on the preexistence of those inspirational models, it is obligatory to agree that they created for themselves the technical inventions, as Flaubert's correspondence from the nineteenth century abundantly proves. If we were to obtain a genetic trial we would possibly not find any other possibility than to resort to what Tynianov has called the social series (that consequently is economic and industrial) whose evolution is strictly parallel to that of the technical enrichment of the last century, allowing us to see, therefore, that it had been in the experience of their own changing reality that the authors found the inspiration that led them to a growing technification of literature so that in them material and technique would not appear to be divided, but rather that this would be the only viable way of expressing a particular material. They apparently extract from themselves, from the historical-social lessons that they receive, the necessary impulse to confront as obligatory a technical search that provides models of universal acceptance, parallel to the equally accepted models that English, French, or German factories produced for themselves and for the entire world.

Simultaneously, neither does one finds a contemplation of why Latin American reality did not find itself to be capable of the same high motivations, why its lived experience did not give off the technical inventions that instead should be found in the international field, why this reality is simply "raw material," "intuition," "subject matter," "mishap," "problem," "enigma," showing itself incapable of also being "technique" to generate a formal order that translates this so persistently defended uniqueness for what is Latin American, and arranging thus a harmonic theory of the parts that make up the insoluble unity of the work of art.

What is unique to the greater part of the passionate defenses of literary techniques (there are considerable exceptions that should be valued) is not in the recognition of its obvious importance nor its presumed universality, but in this perception that separates them from the sources where the material, the specific, the interior springs up, establishing two differential entrances that supply artistic creation. It is an incomprehensible explanation if we do not recognize that this schism (and also the contradiction that resides in it) is nothing more than the transposition to literature of the functioning of a sector of current Latin American culture that, by the imposition of economic and regional social circumstances, works on a *technical operative model*. The progressive incorporation of marginal societies to the world economic system has been made through the acquisition of its technical tools that were initially operated directly from the outside. Gradually they passed into the hands of the natives, who developed evolutionary capabilities to look after, as simple "operators" and "maintenance workers" for the external machinery with which they process their raw materials. Even though always at the rear of technological advances, they were then capable of producing, in some parts of the continent, the machines needed for these processes. From then they have lived in a double tension as they also incorporated new technical inventions: that of producers of outdated artifacts and operators of modern ones, which I believe defines the levels of partial development that characterizes the Latin American situation within a global system, but also the situation of the smaller sector that is in charge of technical operations, about which two lines that intercept there, the external and the internal, exercise influence, consecrating the demand for higher technical efficiency at a universal level in order to operate fine-tuned manufacturing instruments for regional materials. Literature is not split off from this sector but rather accompanies it—it expresses it in its complexity, its tensions and contradictions, and one could even add that in the way in which it goes out searching for a wide public (as is the case of recent narrative), it adjusts to the average dimensions of the sector, inclining toward one or the other side of where the impulses come but without overtaking the limits of the space in which the two disparate spheres overlap. The issue is definitively the correlation between technique and culture, which appear to be forcefully linked but in uneven hierarchies because contrary to prototypical evolution, culture, which is the legitimate producer of techniques, is dominated by techniques originating from another culture, something that for multiple reasons the global system established. Among the insightful theoretical suggestions of Immanuel Wallerstein is the displacement of cultures conceived as occupations to cultures as places that lead to planetary reshaping:

> While, in an empire, the political structure tends to link culture with occupation, in a world-economy the political structure tends to link culture with spatial location. The reason is that in a world-economy the first point of political pressure available to groups is the local (national) state structure. Culture homogeniza-

tion tends to serve the interests of key groups and the pressures build up to create cultural-national identities.[28]

The fact that the greater complexity of modern society and of advanced technology has relegated the majority of the world population to the state of operators of artifacts that are produced by a small minority does not however allow confusion of the characteristics of both types of societies. The existence of the *technical productive model* contributes to strengthening the concept of the nation-for-itself and generates a significant amount of benefits that extend to society and influence its development, but above all works within the particular cultural orbit whose tendencies it cultivates, in such a way that assures the conservation of identity even in cases of abrupt jumps and incorporates wide groups of the population to its new modalities, if not all groups. The *technical operative model*, in contrast, works on the basis of an illusory autonomy. It makes use of fragile bases that expose it to insecurities or complete destruction and tends to disperse the harmonic evolution of the social body, fracturing it and separating some sectors from others. Above all, it suffers from a fatal identity crisis because it lives through contradictions and opposites, the members of the directing group seeing themselves obligated to rearticulate the whole local cultural system. They achieve it with enormous difficulty because the social majority lacks a real basis to secure these transformations and moves toward an extreme and strained ideology.

The technical operative model has an almost secular development in the continent. It goes back to the modernista period (and if we do not limit ourselves to its technical expression and we see it under the lens of cultural contact it would go back to the origins of Spanish America), which has allowed an evolution, which we partially synthesized some pages back, that has opened up to rich illusions but also considerable frustrations. Perhaps even the greatest illusion, because it settles in an old aspiration of the continent, is that of autonomy, which has been envisioned as a form of competitively bringing itself on par with the developed metropolises. Each time this seemed close, it implied an advance on the path of technification and at the same time an advanced breach within the social body. The situation of Latin American production mimics another general situation that has exacerbated the conflict of the literary field in the current industrialized world, where the system of literary production faces insurmountable difficulties inserting itself in the system of social production and surges toward entrenchment that seems appropriate to protect identity and autonomy. Certain paroxysmal forms of making the literary text autonomous with respect to all its contexts, avoiding the referential capacity of language and writing, belong to this position adopted by European and North American literature (even though to a lesser extent for the latter), which has already had an influence on Latin American letters.[29]

Illusions and Realities of Technification

Techniques appear within the literary text in various ways, such that their practice is not always in line with explicit theory and sometimes even invalidates it, above all in the universalized sector of Latin American culture that so assuredly practices syncretism, the free collection of the most diverse and even contradictory influences and its improvised and subjective manipulation. A cautious mistrust is convenient for these manifestos and an independent examination of the works that they protect.

If it is normal that techniques appear as functions and, in the most visibly emphasized cases, as operators, contemporary literature has witnessed its ascension to objects, behind which one can perceive the sanctified vestige that has accompanied its use in diverse writers, in the end part of the contemporary bedazzling by the "bella macchina" that seems to be unhinged from its utility and functionality and considered an autonomous reality. All Latin American authors of the recent quarter century have been supplied by this new technical arsenal but have made use of it through diverse modes that fit their greater or lesser confidence in the referential capacity of literary discourse and the diverse moments of its production because, as is common, initial fascination with the technical resources gave way to a usage linked to the material being addressed. There have been those who used the automobile for the more rapid and efficient transfer from one place to another; those who polished it in order to make it a symbol of modernity, ceaselessly changing from one model to another; and those who decorated it with family portraits, diverse labels, children's toys, images of saints, bedroom curtains, and twinkling lights like an adolescent "garçonnière."

In all of the cases of elevated absorption of new techniques, the norm was that the "form" would label itself, presenting itself ostensibly as an independent object that named itself and occupied the first level of the work. This is evident in one of the first texts that Alejo Carpentier writes when he converts his narrative from a regionalist style to avant-garde writing that emerges in the 1920s: *Journey Back to the Source*, published in 1944, which he collected with other pieces that deal with temporal displacements in his volume *War of Time*.[30] The inverted narration that he practices there, possibly inspired by Lumière's cinematic "shorts" that at the turn of the century humoristically projected the arrival of the train to the station in reverse, shows a flagrant imbalance between the technical resource with which the literary discourse is organized and the history that is told through it. Not only does the discourse adhere to the highest visibility, reclaiming the attention of the reader and guiding it toward an appreciation of the unusual solutions through which the author faces the challenge that has been imposed, but at the same time, inversely, the story being told is relegated to a secondary level through the reduction of interest in the actions and opacity of the characters. Such a story, told in chronological order, lacks the virtues of Carpentier's normal narration. It has been devoured by the main role that the discursive technique assumes, thus bringing attention to itself and making itself visible.

This situation does not constitute the norm for Carpentier's literature, not even in the experimental period that the texts in *War of Time* represent; it defines the extreme point of the excluding attention of technique and its secondary effects on the order that the story brings to the narrative. More than signaling that both terms—discourse and story—are forcefully situated in literature as inversely related participants within a work, which would be refuted by their evidently successful combination shown in some of the great works of European avant-garde (Joyce, Kafka, perhaps to a lesser extent Woolf), this would indicate an initial discordant functioning within Latin American narrative, child of this duplicity of sources that we have seen registered between technique, derived from its European origins, and material originating from the region. We could argue that upon producing the collision, it is technique that takes over the driving force in deteriorating this internal story that contributes its own sometimes traditional elements that are expressed with difficulty within modernized structures.

In an appreciable number of cases, the initial conflict gives way to more equal adjustments that diminish the imbalances. Onetti's use of the point of view narrative technique, which in contemporary use goes back to Henry James, is the origin of what one critic has called his "traps," which consist of hiding information or overlaying intermediary planes that ambiguously twist the perception of facts, but the roughness and even failures that *Goodbyes and Stories* (1954) travel far when they arrive at *A Grave With No Name* (1959). In the case of Mario Vargas Llosa, a similar trajectory is noted, within an always sharp attention to the technical elaboration of discourse, but between *The Green House* and *Conversation in the Cathedral* he abandons resources derived from imitations or false information used voluntarily, to attend to the course of the story with a sustained attention.

It would consist of a process of adjustment between the opposing impulses, but there is room to ask whether it is achieved through a comfortable equilibrium or through the conquest that one of the poles exercises over the other. It is difficult to say as it is a process in development. Furthermore, the panorama of authors shows very diverse modulations of the treatment of technique in their works. In the same way, as we have already pointed out, the introduction of an apparently neutral technique in the peripheral regions of the planet is the beginning of a rearticulation of the society that connects and partially brings it closer to the society producing this technique. One can also suspect that universal techniques that are adapted to narrative and applied to a Latin American content subtly drive a transformation of this content within equally universal patterns. At least this is the conclusion one would reach from Alejo Carpentier's observation about the characteristics that Latin American themes would have in the narrative works of contemporary renovators. He perceives that there has been not only a technical modification but also a modification in the treatment of the narrative "character":

> [This is] a group that emerges in a determined moment, with deprovincialized works and works that have a universal validity, because they are technically good, technically interesting, technically modern and because they deal with American themes in almost all cases. American themes, with a window on the world of ideas, on the world, on things in general, with a universalization of characters that makes these characters understandable outside the Spanish speaking context.[31]

In the same way, on the level of style, for Carpentier, Baroque writing would be the consequence of the internationalizing effort of the Latin American author. On the level of content it would be the discovery of the universal man that there is in all Latin Americans, with which the incorporation of apparently neutral mechanisms of technique would end up revealing their true nature, namely, universalizing and homogenizing, even though this is within a gradual and nuanced evolution that would allow all types of intermediate states. Many authors would continue to identify themselves with these intermediate states, together with their public (thus the defense of their own internal, singular content) while others would fully adopt the resulting futurism of the adopted rules of the game.

In this first group of authors who adopt the intermediate situation in the process of universalization as much as, paradoxically, in the second who are absorbed by their future, multiple resistances are noted that act below their confessed doctrinal positions, which more clearly testify to the conflict in which they live, the opposing forces that fight over them, and the limits that find and trace the spatial borders within which it is possible to act. These involuntary behaviors are revealing of their exact place in the universalizing process, and in them the Latin American situation that moves them is transparently revealed.

It is, above all, the concept that they have about literary techniques, not according to how they theorize them but how they apply them in their works. Miguel Ángel Asturias has declared that his first books (*Legends of Guatemala*, *The President*) use the resource of "automatic writing" that was the delightful discovery of the surrealists in the 1920s, a date in which Asturias resided in Paris and had direct knowledge of these explosive heterodoxies of French letters. The reading of both books does not entirely corroborate his assertion: the will of poetic style that is manifested there, the careful associations of meanings to create a sonorous music, which end up closer to the experiences with "jitanjáfora" that Mariano Brull[32] practiced than the French products of "automatic writing" where irrational meanings were constructed. Even when these disconnects of meaning are addressed the appeal to psychological tricks that allow a realist justification are perceptible: it is the description of dreams, of oneiric states, that, given its uniqueness, allow the associative disconnects, forms that the Mexican Ortiz Montellano[33] also used when he produced the first adaptations of Surrealism in American lands.

The same realist excuse is perceptible in the use of another surrealist resource, the "marvelous," by Carpentier, which he even renames as "real-marvelous," contrasting it with its stagnant formulation in French poetry that is born from a willingness in which, for him, "the miracle workers become bureaucrats." Beyond what can be true in this critique, it was evident that the French Surrealists tried to "live" the experience of the marvelous, taking on "liminal states" that in some cases bordered on insanity and death. Carpentier's behavior is something else as he does not take on this experience but limits himself to describe those who integrally possess it, that is, the superstitious populations of Latin America, those who authentically believe that it operates in the world, who are willing to accept the irrational, magical, or marvelous elements. The sympathy that he shows for these investigations into reality that avoid the rationalist parameters of industrialized society and that are the rich heritage of marginal societies does not affect the realist narrative articulations that he puts into action in his writing, which relegate him to the critical realist and even the nineteenth-century tradition of the European novel.

It consists of a double position with respect to literary content that can be extended to modes of reading. This is the case of the "table" of double reading that Cortázar proposes in *Hopscotch* and that he will abandon by the time he publishes *62: A Model Kit*, which given its unique porousness could benefit from guides for its many possible readings. If the individual use of the "hopscotch" is to jump from one segment to another, the permission to read it in order seems to be a concession to the "female reader," to use Cortázar's terminology, that is not found in *Eyeless in Gaza*, even though Aldous Huxley dates the chapters to allow the lazy reader to reorder them before reading. Even the splendid discovery in the title, *Hopscotch*, a substitution for the initially considered *Mandala*, is a referential nod to reengage the complicity of the Latin American reader and revive their freely associative capacities related to their memory of childish games.

One can explore the resistance to abandon themselves to the plurisemantism that the new narrative writing technique so tenaciously practices in another way. Juan Carlos Onetti has created an enigma around his novel *Goodbyes*, based on a reading by the critic Luchting, who argued that below the system of intermediations instituted by narrators' systematic use of the point of view technique hides an unambiguous significance that challenges the reader to discover it, and it gives the legitimate key to its creation.[34]

Perhaps the most curious and enlightening resistance is that represented by the rejection of some technical inventions that are extremely characteristic of European letters. There is no more typical case than that of the French "nouveau roman" that has motivated the only unanimity that can be seen among Latin American writers. The analysis of the works by authors from the last quarter century certify the plurality of aesthetic and ideological paths that they follow, even within the reduced group that habitually make up the so-called Boom, but all of them, with the partial exception of Cortázar, who is explained by his willingness to try all possible experiments, have come to an agreement to jointly reject both the worldview and the corresponding technique that French narrators put into circulation guided by Alain Robbe-Grillet. This radical attitude coincides in general with that of elite Latin American readers, thus making up a homogenous panorama that is not unrelated to the scarce reception that an excellent narrator, the Argentine Antonio Di Benedetto, has been given, who through very different paths has coincided in the use of some objectivist techniques.

This unanimity has provoked surprise in the German critic Günter W. Lorenz whose interviews with many Latin American authors are characterized by a decided inquiry into literary techniques, finding in all the same frank opposition to the "nouveau roman."[35]

> Hence, perhaps, the scorn, the anger, that talking about the "nouveau roman" provokes, this "syllogism of European decadence" (Sábato), "the only thing that Europe is still in a position to give" (Vargas Llosa), "the ridiculous manipulation of language" (Guimarães Rosa), "this literature that abandons man, that betrays him" (Roa Bastos). This critical position towards the "nouveau roman" produces a strange impression, above all when one considers that some works that are precisely an illuminating example of the search for "new" narrative forms have emerged in Latin America.[36]

Lorenz's inquiry could be extended, with the same results, to almost all contemporary authors. Some of them, like Ernesto Sábato, have dedicated long essays to refuting Robbe-Grillet's proposals in which they have seen a dangerous path for Latin American literature;[37] others, like Carlos Fuentes, have ascribed to the "nouveau roman" an extension of middle class realism and its methods, characteristics of the neocapitalist stage. By 1966 Onetti was already reacting to my critique of Uruguayan literature for its lack of experimental interest, in contrast to what was happening in the visual arts, by "giving a warning cry" against "the stubborn will to complicate things, to complicate the novel through easy means of chronological confusion, to unnecessary glimpses of dialogue and thoughts," and in an interview he directly opposed the school of the "nouveau roman":[38]

> They (novelists like Robbe-Grillet) don't interest me. I believe that they work literature like a laboratory discipline and in a totally intellectual sense, trying to make an objective novel, almost photographic. What is curious is that through the path of supposed objectivism they have only arrived at a complete subjectivism. They have made technique the most important

thing and it is necessary to keep in mind that technique is only an instrument of which one should make the best use, without converting it into the central focus of the creation.[39]

This term—objectivism—even keeping in mind its ambiguity, is what moves his opposition and is what he thinks is dangerous for the free expression of subjectivity, and seems to trigger the emotional resistance of Latin American authors. It would restrict one of the most visible and rooted tendencies of new narrative: the hedonistic emergence of a subjectivism that takes possession of the world, translating it in terms strongly steeped by personal experience, and the accompanying emotionalism or sensualism that infuses the subject, characters, and situations, giving them to the reader within a fraught existential atmosphere. The influence that some incredibly personal poets have had on young writers, which through them have constructed elaborated lineages (in Cuba it is the legacy of Lezama Lima in Cabrera Infante, Pablo Armando Fernández, Reinaldo Arenas, and even Severo Sarduy;[40] in Chile the heritage of Pablo de Rokha is seen in Carlos Droguett, Alfonso Alcalde, Enrique Lafourcade, and even José Donoso[41]) signals the reign of lyrical subjectivism that has absorbed narrative, folding its expressive waves into it. The hedonism that governs this "pleasure of the text," which circulates through Fuentes, Cortázar, García Ponce, and Donoso or which in a visceral and almost painful way erupts in Revueltas, Vargas Llosa, Viñas, and Sábato or feeds the Mexican "new wave" in Sáinz and Agustín,[42] reveals a tendency widely cultivated by new Latin American narrative that extends beyond the different generations, tying them all together. It was already in the original masters, in Asturias giving himself to the sonorous sensuality of language, in Carpentier giving himself to the lustful sensuality of the flavors of the world, in Marechal[43] who breathes the pleasure of the apprehension of recently discovered reality and even in the intellectual Borges who builds constructs at whim in which for fleeting instances the entire universe bends to his will. It is now in the ardent writing of the youngest, who consider themselves children of Revueltas, Arlt, or Cortázar or who return to the lesson of the poets. The discovery that throughout the period was made of frankly displayed erotic themes is simply the application of this tendency rooted in hedonism that lays waste to all dams and exudes the unrestricted expansion of subjectivity that is dominant in all. It is possible to think that this has been one of the reasons for its success within a sector of society that has split from traditional normative constrictions that penned it up and that, with the strange extreme of the recently discovered and long desired, it has thrown itself into the enjoyment of sensorial impulses. There is something like a liberation of the subconscious and a sensuality in all of this narrative, and the pleasure of the game that runs through it is not out of place, enjoying its quota of irresponsibility, the fresh incorporation of humor, with its sudden pleasure in the joke, the *calembour*, the diversion of satire and the intense translation of eroticism into writing that appeals to hyperbolic techniques (in Fuentes, García Márquez, Reinaldo Arenas) or oblique modes (Cortázar) or ardent impregnations of writing (in Viñas, Vargas Llosa), and so forth.

Subjectivism without restrictions is the law of new Latin American narrative and it is understandable, therefore, that the enemy is represented by an objectivism that seems to suspend judgment before the world to be able to fulfill the work of writing it, something that Italo Calvino interpreted in a structural fashion, as a response to "an eternally problematized world that exudes meanings, which is at the edge of being the allegory of itself." If it were that way, the subjectivist answer would signal a much simpler world, with clear and intelligible options, something that could be based in the extremely schematic form in which Latin American political discourse is formulated, in any of its versions, frequently brushing against the caricature of itself. However, its grounding in the difficulty that the majority of the time society has to see itself in objective terms due to the absence of suitable systems of measurement ends up being more legitimate. These systems set limits, determine real possibilities, establish obligatory benefits, determine mutual concessions, look for favorable levels of efficiency, and are articulated based on a realist project for the community. From the unscrupulous and personalist use of state administration by politicians to the idealist voluntarism of their critics, an unstoppable subjectivist wave dominates public behavior, suggesting the movement to the social order of private modes that direct personal conduct. The peculiar texture of a marginal society, like what Faulkner detected in the traditions of North American Southern society, where honor, passion, sin, humiliation, resentment, desire, and hate play a vital role, is infiltrated even in those sectors that, brushed up against industrialization and technified structures, would seem to escape their devouring empire. The rejection of the forms of the "nouveau roman" from even the boldest supporters of literary techniques seems to be born of these painful and rich intimacies of Latin American society. When a writer that has such a plentiful and fervent audience as

Cortázar attempts an investigation connected with these objectivist paths in *62: A Model Kit*, it is immediately abandoned by his readers, who feel lost in this cold universe.

For compensation, the Latin American author appeals confidently to fantasy. A burning imagination that constructs universes that are not disconnected from reality but charged with illusory and dream-like eventualities ignites readers' fervor. This pleasure in imagination has had its own field in the fantastic that, initially developed by a true Buenos Aires school (Borges, Martínez Estrada, Bianco, Wilcock, Cortázar, Bioy Casares, Sábato, and their many descendants[44]), took root in similar terms within Mexican narrative and in all areas put its mark through diverse doses. The most successful were those that combined a realistic use of everyday facts with a plausible and startling break with them, establishing that sudden insecurity that splits the firm ground on which we normally walk. The pleasure of imagination also counted on another fertile territory, that of the marvelous, which authors from the Caribbean and its surroundings used, from Carpentier and Asturias to García Márquez, passing through Cardoza y Aragon, Jorge Zalamea, and Jacques Stephan Alexis[45] and extending into distinctive younger writers like Reinaldo Arenas, Luis Britto García, and Germán Espinosa.[46] It is the freedom of imagination that unfolds without hindrance that here seduces readers. The thunderous success of *One Hundred Years of Solitude*, with Remedios the Beautiful's excited delight at ascending suddenly into the heavens while she tried to attend to drying the sheets, marks the ideal point of this passion for free fantasy, even in this peculiar articulation that was the key to the novel's success, transforming the trivial realist note (Fernanda complaining about the loss of her sheets) with the sudden and unexplained invasion of the marvelous that invades everything and upholds the readers' jubilation, which is the joy of the recuperation of their total and unrestricted freedom above any imposition of reality. Such hyperbolic cultivation of imagination, such reunion with the full universe of fantasy, sharply shapes the specific composition of Latin American society and the strength that the subjective tendencies that supply it reach.

It is instructive to revise a private comment that this tendency motivated in Elio Vittorini, who discarded it as "telluric trash," according to the statement that José María Castellet gave in his interpretive essay on Latin American narrative. He emphasizes, as one of its ostensible characteristics, "fantasy as beautifier of reality" and opposes the pejorative judgment of the Italian writer trying to explain the different coordinates in which

Italian postwar authors operate with respect to those that originate in Latin American societies.[47] Even though one can debate this foundation, certainly in Vittorini's unjust perception there is a distrust that comes from a different view of the problems of contemporary society. The resources of the fantastic and marvelous have been practiced by multiple European writers and in the United States single out some tendencies of Southern authors in contrast to realist and behavioralist New Yorkers, such that they can be seen as elements of a line that also operates in developed societies. Except that they do not reach the splendorous magnificence that this genre has achieved in Latin American narrative, singling out a historical stage and serving as a tie to a new part of society that has emerged as readers.

Latin American authors trace the limits of the incorporation of techniques and thus construct the underlying map of their cultural land (which involuntarily permeates them and ends up defined in a unique transitional historical circumstance) as much in the rejection of objectivism as in the adherence to the marvelous. Discarding Vittorini's disdain (trash) there is no problem in recognizing that there is a tellurism present here, except in a more distinct way than the one practiced by regionalists because instead of using the concrete content of an American reality like they did in adjusting to symbolic schemas, now they aspire to translate their mechanisms: instead of contraposing nature and civilization, so visibly excessive in Rivera or Gallegos, they explore the cultural conceptions that these excesses generate in the view of reality. It takes on subjectivism and the overflow of fantasy as the procedure of narrative technique, above all in its best example, García Márquez. That which in other cases might come masked under modern techniques extracted from external lessons, at times mimetically and awkwardly incorporated, only reaffirms a very Latin American enjoyment of the costume of the masked dance.

Perhaps where this surreptitious betrayal of imported techniques becomes flagrant is in the use that is given to them suddenly within Latin American narrative. They are manipulated outside their original strict functionality, in an almost picturesque demonstration of the way in which the *technical operative model* is implemented.

Let's be clear, to say that the technical operative model intensified in narrative from the 1930s and 1940s does not imply a depreciation of respect for the works produced in it. As in the famous Prague debate about decadence and literature, it is a question of correctly situating artistic creation: just as the works of Picasso, Musil, or Kafka as much as they elaborate the problems of society with signs of decadence cannot be assimilated to this decadence, neither can the works of recent Latin American narrative, whose artistic splendor is beyond discussion, be compared as mere imitative operations. They work within the technical operative model, as all of society, and play on its risks, virtues, and collapses as an imposition of the circumstances of the moment, but they are not examples of passivity and surrender. Above all, because it helps to not forget, the writer is not an operator but a producer and all artisanal notes that can distinguish them do not lessen in the least this essential quality of their work. Such a producer can operate the technified instruments that they have discovered, but within a productive project: they undertake different and original constructions and obey internal forces (personal and cultural) that are more powerful than the same techniques, through which they can derail these instruments from their own function, subjecting them to unheard of adaptations. Those automobiles transformed into rolling bedrooms, causing scandal for the modernizers at any cost, communicate the creative circumstance and willingness better than those who passively and in a bourgeois way sanctify their impeccable use of the latest model without noticing that they operate in another type of lack of focus.

The comparison cannot be pleasing, but the operations that Lévi-Strauss has detected in the "bricolage" of primitive societies can be found, transposed to another level, in the literary composition of Latin American authors. Perhaps none exemplifies this better than Jorge Luis Borges because of the unscrupulous freedom with which he moves within the jungle of international culture, only comparable to Lezama Lima. Borges has taken control of the fine-tuned resources of the essay and contemporary erudition as a brute, forcing them to perform unlikely burlesque pirouettes, taking them out of proportion and transforming them into narrative resources. He has compared historical literary research to political inquiry, has derailed it from its specific function, has even ridiculed it, introducing mundane elements, and with the irresponsibility (and freedom) of a savage he has put it in the service of a production that contradicts it. Starting with the conviction of his narrative deficiencies, he has constructed essays, bibliographic notes, or source research and transformed them into stories. At the same time he and Lezama Lima have enacted a joyful confusion in the field of cultural objects thanks to a free mode of applying associative analogies, which has allowed them to find the "aleph" in the basement of the house of a ridiculous provincial poet or the mystery of the "Greek cups" in Cuban culinary practices, respectively.

The immense reading of both, along with their inclination for enjoyable erudition, is not up for discussion, but rather the particular use of European mechanisms intermingling them with their materials because in one or the other case their concrete reality is what remains portrayed. It is not an exclusive novelty. Going back a few steps, to the years in which the colonial pact was forged from which we now live an intensification through technified masks, one can remember the joy of "artifice" that intoxicated Rubén Darío and the modernistas in general. It led them to a risky adaptation of nineteenth-century French metrics, but paradoxically, more than adjusting our poetry to the strictly metric regime that French lyricism had arrived at, they proceeded with liberating the hidden rhythm of the Spanish language. In the thematic field, it led them to poeticize their own colonial incongruency: what Darío had in front of him was not the graceful youth of Giovanni da Bologna's statue but a poor product of industrial trash that had added an industrial artifact to the delicate raised hand of the Roman god in order to light up the room: "With a lighted candelabra in his right hand/Giovanni da Bologna's Mercury was in flight."[48]

The success of the Latin American novel abroad has been justified by its ascent to universal technical patterns at the same time that a presumed decline in the novels of other European regions was happening, in particular France. Perhaps this reasoning that Vargas Llosa has proposed and García Márquez accepted could be turned around and we could say that it has triumphed thanks to the fact that it continues to be connected to traditional operations, despite modernization, even connecting it to folkloric contaminations that can still respond to the common reader's appetites.[49] These readers in turn are not satisfied by avant-garde narrative products that conform to the most rigid process of technification followed by developed societies. One could then say that the relative success of Latin American narrative is not only in its evident modernization, but also, paradoxically, in the presumed archaic nature of its worldview, of its subject matter and its operative modes. The reproach directed at the most successful novel of the movement, *One Hundred Years of Solitude*, and beyond it to another prime example like *The Green House* for showing archaism with respect to the position of the narrative that at the time would be marked by books like Fuentes's *A Change of Skin* or Cortázar's *62: A Model Kit* (both of which are the leaders of the universalist modernizing tendency), responds to a naive deification of the technical operative model whose deficiencies it does not perceive and thus misunderstands the purpose of the literary work.[50]

Lost Illusions

The decade of the 1970s begins to look like the decade of lost illusions, with a succession of political and economic failures that did not seem foreseeable in the hopeful dawn of the 1930s. The limits of the technical operative model have been made clear, questioning the entire industrialization project. In the book cited earlier, the Steins talk of the "present impasse of industrialization in most of the area, a condition which some observers have described as 'the end of industrialization via import-substitution.' "[51] And even though there have been less pessimistic and still hopeful evaluations,[52] Raul Prebisch's intervention in the plenary session of the CEPAL conference in La Paz (April 1979) sounded like a funeral march. The bottleneck to which it has led, generating wider social inequality with the implantation of small nuclei of consumer societies in the center of vast underdeveloped populations, the impossibility of supplying their demands, the increased prices of finished products that cannot be competitively exported, and the progressive transfer of the same factories that process raw materials to multinational corporations has created a state of skepticism, has enriched the arguments of the structuralists who propose enormous economic-social modifications, and has established a generalized revision of the paths travelled during the last forty years.

The evident and successful expansion of narrative, which appeared in the upper plane of culture as its best expression, has emerged as an exotic and above all isolated flower. Its products began to be seen as exceptions that did not accompany a global transformation of the structure of Latin American culture, and frequent critiques of related sectors of the phenomenon appeared. This happened with the closest sector, literary criticism, and one could already see that what critics were proposing was the late absorption of "new criticism" or French "structuralism," even though embracing the latter would be the equivalent of Latin American authors accepting the "nouveau roman." The cultural shortfalls were made evident. At a time when literature faced the problem of language up front, allowing it to free itself from the restrictions of a purist and academic writing, it was necessary to recognize that two hundred years from its political independence, Spanish America had still not produced its "dictionary of American Spanish," like North Americans had through Webster. It is worth recognizing that the prevailing situation in the period before the *primary productive model*, when numerous dictionaries of Americanisms were edited as complementary materials to use with the dictionary of the Royal Spanish Academy, given that this institution ignored Spanish American lexical inventions and semantic modifications, did not give way to the greater productive work that consists of producing the dictionary that would cover the global function of the language in distinct linguistic zones of the continent in the technical operative model period. The almost 250 million American Spanish speakers could not complete a work accomplished by 30 million European Spanish speakers. The obvious difficulties of such a project do not have to be resolved within that mode of functioning since it implies an immensity of intellectual resources and a technical infrastructure that writers might not need when they produce their works but that clearly mark the limits within which these writers work individually. The absence of great encyclopedic and American dictionaries, of critical appraisals of our intellectual legacy, of developed investigative organisms, show the model's deficiencies.

Even within the same narrative movement, the disillusioning awareness with respect to the substitution of imports that demanded foreign techniques for national raw materials and trusted that the rest would happen in addition, a lovely individualist perception, is an example of the enchanting arrogance of youth that in adulthood recognizes that there are other human beings to whom one has to attend to, there are problems derived from the cultural environment that cannot be ignored, and there is a governing law of intellectual discourse: communication. Since we take Onetti as a guide for the period, it is with his words that we can define this new situation:

> In the first stage of that time we adopted a position, a spiritual state that can be summarized in the phrase or slogan: the one who does not understand is an idiot. Years later, a form of serenity—that could perhaps be called decadence—forced us to modify the faith, the slogan, in summary: the one that does not make themselves understood is an idiot.[53]

This text is from 1966 and belongs to an alarm that various established authors made theirs, in particular those authors placed within the processes of narrative transculturation that would have to be considered in detail (Rulfo, Arguedas, Guimarães Rosa), faced with an allegedly experimentalist incursion among the youngest writers who followed the impulse from the masters of the avant-garde, above all Cortázar and Fuentes at the head of an incessant "plus ultra." They were witnessing thus the typical avant-garde behavior. As is well-known, avant-garde operations share the improvement of already acquired stages as well as their own internal cancellation. By definition, they are offered as perishable articulations, even though the work they engender cannot be so by virtue of other systems of validation that, even though they are disdained by the avant-garde impulse, meet together to rescue the product when the temporal wheel has turned and has discarded the novelty over which it was based. Such a self-destructive system is more evident in those who have put greater expectations on technique, its dizzying cancellation and replacing confers a nihilistic note to its productions that not only determine subject matters and themes but also affect the basic system of communication of any literary work.

The culminating point of the avant-garde incursion corresponds to the two-year period of 1967–1968, which at the same time signals a decisive crossroads. The accumulation of a series of investigations that clearly broke with the known earlier works of authors and penetrates into unknown lands comes championed by two works by Fuentes (*A Change of Skin* and *Holy Place*) and one by Cortázar (*62: A Model Kit*) and is strengthened by the production of various young authors: Néstor Sánchez (*Siberia Blues*), Guillermo Cabrera Infante (*Three Trapped Tigers*), Salvador Elizondo (*El hipogeo secreto*), Alberto Duque López (*Matthew the Flute Player*), Héctor Libertella (*El camino de los hiperbóreos*), and José Balza (*Largo*).[54] Curiously it is in the same two-year period headed by García Márquez (*One Hundred Years of Solitude*), that signals the presence of an abundant production that points toward another path, deviating from the avant-garde excess without ceasing to work within modernization: David Viñas (*Men on Horseback*), Carlos Martínez Moreno (*With the First Lights*), Vicente Leñero (*The Code*), Carlos Droguett (*El compadre*), Salvador Garmendia (*Hard Life*), Adriano González León (*Portable Country*), German García (*Nanina*), and Manuel Puig (*Betrayed by Rita Hayworth*).[55]

We witness a split at the same the time in which the avant-garde realizes a drastic penetration of the advanced guard. This penetration leads to the reflux of elite literature that the Boom had overcome, the reconstruction of the experimental laboratory that had already found its home decades ago. It is a foreseeable result, but it serves to show to what extent the technical modernization that takes its searches to the extreme finds as support in the narrow circle of consumer society, represented by the cadre that accompanies the process. The opening that in these dates *One Hundred Years of Solitude* forms is strictly contemporary with a narrowing of the field that in fact abandons the perspectives of the public, expanding for the benefit of an advance of the technifying trend, this one being what begins to seem exhausted in the Latin American panorama.

Even more, those who provide the continent with this rich variety of searches do not continue them all on the same path. While some persistently follow the same path, as Carlos Fuentes proves better than any other in the production of *Birthday* (1969) to *No Man's Land* (1975), others stop. The brake seems to remain marked by *62: A Model Kit* (1968) after which the author withdraws to his early expressive systems, publishing various books in which he urgently reworks them, still within the fantastic orbit as well as in that of socially committed literature (*A Manual for Manuel*), explaining the reasons for the public failure of his novel in an intelligent article in *Último round* where he reflects on the advantages that the research completed in said novel would have in his subsequent creations.

This withdrawal is also perceptible in Mario Vargas Llosa. *Conversation in the Cathedral* (1969) shows it balancing with contrasting methods with which he had composed his previous novels, and after a critical excursion that makes him return to his Flaubert-inspired origins, he adds two texts, *Captain Pantoja and the Special Services* (1973) and *Aunt Julia and the Scriptwriter* (1977), which points toward a clear distancing from the technical experiments and a period of sedimentation of his contributions signaled with the same voice of alarm that Onetti expressed: communication.

The incorporation or development of authors that go back to the mechanisms of critical realism, above all in a time of political upheaval like that of the 1970s (Antonio Skármeta, Luis Rafael Sánchez, Griselda Gambaro, Plinio Apuleyo Mendoza[56]), just like the revival of populism that has its greatest supporter in the tetralogy of the indigenous in Scorza, served to strengthen this type of careful revision of the state of Latin American narrative.

Two Modernizing Avant-Gardes

In an essay written at the beginnings of the 1970s, I shed light on the prejudices that the simplification of the avant-garde concept that critics were bringing forth, established in contrast to traditional or regionalist trends, and what this implies for the strict appreciation of Latin American culture.[57] If critics were able to give clarity to it by fixing a categorical black-and-white opposition, they paid for these advantages with a diminishing of the view of the avant-garde, whose plurality of paths was erased, unifying them all under one common denominator: *modernization*. I argued then that even though they share the same modernizing sign, one cannot equate paths so categorically different as those followed by two contemporaries who were the initial renovators of postmodernista poetry, Vicente Huidobro (1893) and César Vallejo (1892). For that reason, I proposed that we accept the possibility of two parallel avant-gardes within Spanish America. I understood that this hypothesis allowed us a more precise visualization of the differences that exist among Latin American cultural areas but above all would make evident the existence of two simultaneous cultural dialogues that are plotted along different terms: one, internal, connects to uneven zones of the continent's culture looking to reach modernization without losing traditional constitutive factors, through which it is able to link such disparate terms as Trujillo—Lima—the world; another, external, established direct communication with foreign centers that were the origin of the transforming impulses flowing through already modernized points of Latin America. The latter translated into the link Santiago de Chile—Paris—the world.

Both are authentically American dialogues, with a many times secular development, and even though its operations are connected because of the clear modernizing option that governs them, their products are distinguishable by different content and different circumstances in which they work, by the worldview they reflect, by the language they choose, and by the artistic resources they put to work. But from the moment in which both depart from the persistence of an instability that should be resolved, in both the work of art appears as a dynamic combination of opposing forces to which they are obligated to coexist. Their stakes are what vary: internal dialogue is conciliatory, recognizing the weight of the past; the external is futurist, opening itself to a universal perspective.

If we go back in time to the beginning of this cycle of Latin American life, which was accomplished under the terms of the neocolonial pact established in the last third of the nineteenth century and which has correctly been labeled "modernism" because it witnessed the violent entrance of Western modernization, this time being therefore pristine and original in which options are manifested with freshness and clarity, we will find both avant-gardes coherently formulated in the work of Rubén Darío and José Martí. There is no doubt that both propose modernization but the circumstances and terms in which they plot the negotiations are different because the historical situations in which both writers live and formulate their programs are very different. Between them are obvious ties and also flagrant discrepancies, which are captured not only in the subject matter of their works but conjointly in the technical resources used to present them. They knew this, something that did nothing to cloud their mutual esteem. The long and sterile controversy that their followers have kept in order to disagree with each other could be resolved with the recognition of the diversity and authenticity of the two modernizing avant-gardes that cross through history until now, detecting the plural cultural situations of Latin America.

These two avant-gardes are determined by their placement with respect to the two guiding poles that dominate the field of forces in a time characterized by the fact that modernization is pushed from outside and constitutes the unrejectable nature of all cultural operations. The external has been called "cosmopolitan," picking up the name that European intellectual society at the end of the nineteenth century adopted for itself and that the famous English magazine *Cosmopolis* used as a banner; internally I have preferred to name it "transculturating" because even though the two respond to the absolute modernizing power of the time and in both the basis of behavior is the capacity for adaptation, in the latter it is achieved at the level of cultures deeply rooted in the historical life of the continent trying to attain the greatest preservation of its values in the transformational process. Of the difficulties and abruptness of this work the best illustration is Arguedas's cry "I am not acculturated," proclaimed by one who fulfilled the authentic, subtle, and delicate work of transculturation and died due to the internal conflict that this caused.

We find the same polarization that repeated itself in successive generations again in the new Spanish American narrative that emerges in the 1930s, that is after the definition of the two avant-garde paths that are tracked in the poetry of Vallejo and Huidobro. Even though the solutions contributed individually display a varied range, with different doses of the impulses derived from guiding poles, it is possible to classify the optimal, extreme, and emphatic positions with different names. Accepting the classification by generations every fifteen years that Enrique Anderson Imbert applies in his *Historia*, and copying from Julián Marías's propositions, we can trace a diagram of oppositions in each one of them: in the first generation the cosmopolitan pole is represented by Jorge Luis Borges (1899) and the transculturated by his contemporary Miguel Ángel Asturias (1899); in the next, the first is occupied by Julio Cortázar (1914) and the other could be represented by Juan Rulfo (1918) but also by Arguedas (1913); in the third, cosmopolitanism has its defender in Carlos Fuentes (1929) and the trasculturating pole is assumed by Gabriel García Márquez (1928). It is clear that this classification, obeying lines of cultural tendencies, intersects with the most varied political, religious, or doctrinal positions of the authors in their public life, but in contrast it sets coherent fields of the worldviews of the concrete works and allows interpretation of the technical and artistic options that they form in a joint and organic fashion.

The cosmopolitan line responds to Rubén Darío's intensely longed for expectation when he establishes his dialogue with European (French) culture and spies in the future the eventuality that the most developed urban center that Latin America could count on would be able to compare to international centers: "Buenos Aires! Cosmopolis!" he exclaims in the conclusion to his prologue to *Profane Hymns*. He did not count on the American fatality of this perception that would become visible to him quickly from his residency in Europe, revealing the inherent Latin American condition of his cosmopolitan project.[58] On the exact same date in which Darío's text *Azul* . . . appears, José Martí judges the strange position of the Latin American writer as "painful." He sees them as having two sides, one external and one internal, because in fact the writer participates in both. In the same way that one has a head and a body, likewise the writer acts on two dissimilar cultural fields. More than proceeding with censorship, Martí witnesses an authentic anguish, given the discordant situation that in his time was shown as much more contradictory than it is currently and that placed the writer in an impotent situation to be able to fully expand their capacities. It is an admirable text that makes Martí's own pain transparent but that he brings up to define Heredia's situation:

> Because it is the pain of Cubans and all Spanish Americans, that even though they inherit through study and assess with their natural talent the hopes and ideas of the universe, as the one that moves under their feet is very different from the one that they carry in their head, they do not have their own environment nor roots nor rights to have opinions about things that most move and interest them, and they seem ridiculous and intrusive if, from a rudimentary country, they pretend to enter into the issues of humanity with a loud voice, which are those everyday issues for those countries where they are not just beginning like us, but in all of their animation and force. It is like going out crowned in lightning and shod in laced boots. This is truly a mortal pain and motive for infinite sadness.[59]

Martí does not extract more considerations and limits himself to recognizing the painful situation. He could have recognized that these two vast cultural worlds are not entirely separate from the moment in which they coincide in determined individuals, thanks to the work of those whose "hope and ideas of the universe" are made legitimately American as history has abundantly proven, with the incorporation of doctrinal "corpus" that gave rise to enormous modifications of the continent's societies and also with the incorporation, at this intense moment, of the contributions of European and North American science and technique that would revolutionize the conditions of life. Writers, and not only them but numerous intellectual and professional groups, are situated at the intersection of two cultural fields that, even though they cover vast, entirely dissimilar, extensions, also count on a space in which they overlap. A diagram would represent this as two great circles that intersect, allowing the people that occupy this common sector the double option: either incline themselves toward the external center achieving a cosmopolitan modernization or incline themselves toward the internal center achieving a transculturizing modernization. Both movements do not imply equivalency with unambiguous political or social positions, like sometimes has been claimed: in cosmopolitanism both the proponents of development who are in favor of the free reign of multinationals as well as anti-establishment revolutionary groups advocating for a violent modernization have been able to coexist; in transculturation, retarding conservative sectors have been able to coexist with revolutionary nationalisms.

The evolution that this diagram, which we represent graphically with two intersecting circles, has followed has been that of a constant intensification in each one of its three component parts, through the stages of increasing development. If the external and increasingly more highly technified impulse has been increasingly greater, the progress of the internal circle that has demonstrated ample cultural plasticity has also been accelerated. The most noteworthy has been the increase of the middle sector in which both circles overlap, which has grown proportionally in a more rapid way. It is there where most of the Latin American cities lie, it is there where the industrial centers lie, it is there where the educational institutes and complex administrative apparatus lie, and it is there where the public for new authors that the Boom has assured through sales numbers lies. Even though the overwhelming success of the works of García Márquez with respect to the considerable success of Carlos Fuentes is indicative of its basic tendencies, this points to its greatest problems and to those affected by these problems.

This amplification of the middle sector can provide a deceptive image. In fact, it conceals the original imbalance between both poles of the field; far from tempering and dissolving, they have increased through the years, and this constitutes the heart of all Latin American conflicts. The distance between the extreme points of both circles is currently much greater, for which the option that literary modernization has made in any of its orientations and that basically tends to equalize the parts within the margins that the overlapping sector allows has found an extreme tension that puts the system itself in danger. Its effect is to push avant-garde tendencies toward one or the other side so that they more strictly enfold the discordant impulses of the poles or they are replaced with other forces, which can be even more harmful: cosmopolitanism can give way to direct foreign presence; transculturation, to the traditional conservative strictness. The entire system has acquired a screeching quality that does nothing less than copy the operative contradictions. At the same time, writers, these revolving plates that adjust to parts of the system, find lesser margins for maneuvering and greater difficulties in achieving the processes of transition.

The cosmopolitan pole has had its master in Jorge Luis Borges, just as Etiembe provocatively celebrated him in his article "Un homme a teur: Jorge Luis Borges cosmopolite" in 1952:[60] "I don't see anyone venturing to study in Borges, what seemed to me one of the most seductive aspects of his work: the perfection of the cosmopolitan spirit."[61]

The effects of this position can be investigated in the two faces that it presents, derived from its unique installation: the one that looks toward the interior, that is toward the problems that it can generate in the elaboration of the literary work and the one that looks toward the outside, toward its reception in the world. The very same Borges has examined the first situation in a brilliant text, "The Argentine Writer and Tradition," in which he responds to the salvos of the nationalists. Given the orientation of these attacks, where they argued over local color, like in the Romantic period, or over social commitment, like in the Regionalist period, Borges could easily defend the right of the writer to the culture of the entire world and to the most varied dioramas. In his works exotic themes coexist with not only national but also folkloric cultures. More important and noteworthy is the result of his analysis of a concrete example, his short story "Death and the Compass," because if he emitted a norm from there, it would signal his perception that surrounding reality happens in symbolic or oneiric, and in either case masked, terms. Given the frequency with which this solution is found in the writers of his lineage, more than a particular example of the filiation with Nietzsche's aesthetics of the mask, we would be faced with an operation of which the emergence of cosmopolitanism that characteristically unfolds a web of entwined values that are more dreamed than real is the constitutive element. We will never repeat sufficiently that cosmopolitanism is not a transposition of the foreign but the establishment of a universal order within which factors are extracted from the most diverse cultures to serve a project that originates in each of them and creates connections between them. It is a project that, furthermore, is fatally marked by the restrictive culture within which it is concocted.[62]

The other situation is that which attends to the reception of the work in the world. Silvia Molloy has explored this point in detail in her study of the incorporation of Spanish American authors in French culture, arriving at the conclusion that Borges's case is exceptional and distinct from that of all others (Rulfo, Carpentier). Being the least French of the Spanish Americans, he is who best adapts to the intellectual coordinates of the country:[63]

> Borges's books seem unique in Hispanic American letters, because they all bring something new—that irreverent lucidity where the author claims privilege for the inhabitants of all Spanish America—they fit perfectly with the most recent European literature, and particularly with French literature.[64]

The cosmopolitan spirit is easily detectable in multiple texts by Julio Cortázar who belongs to the generation that follows that of Borges. In Cortázar's case, he has defended cosmopolitanism from a personal (and on occasion emotional) standpoint as he has been the victim of many attacks given his almost thirty years of residence in France. As we already stated, he shares the schism between international techniques and Latin American raw material that Onetti established in his younger days but, in contrast with the latter, has not diminished his penchant for exploring, his confidence in the avant-garde search for new territories, and his bet on the future, having renovated the intellectual proposal of the 1920s that conceived of the conjunction of aesthetic and political avant-gardes and having firmly established his move to France as one of the components of his artistic creation. The deep meaning of this move can indubitably be traced in a magistral story, "The Other Sky," that is almost a statement of his poetics, based on the concept of "passages" that serve as transitions between cultures and in his narrative writing translates into the sovereign art of transition. This would not be possible if it did not depart from a confidence, as unlimited as unproven, in the analogy, to which he dedicates an enthusiastically complimentary juvenile text.[65] Without the fruition of this analogy, Cortázar's narrative would not exist, but without it his cosmopolitanism would not exist either. Supporting himself with the theories of Lévy-Bruhl he defined analogical design as inherent to the magical concept of the universe, practiced by primitive communities, to experientially and internally dominate the world. This desire to associate that had been restricted gradually by science flourished in the literature inspired by the surrealist movement that saw in it a uniqueness of artistic creation at the base of this freedom to establish relationships and correspondences that do not require of proof and basis and very frequently operate based on primary data. Nothing facilitates better the establishment of cosmopolitanism's web of connections than this associative freedom, but if at the same time we accept that it deals with a perception in which the focal point of which it departs counts, one should keep in mind the aggressively formulated declaration of the author because the topic, as he says, "irritates and exalts me": "And Cortázar left his corner and made a work that anyone can judge as they want, but that is based, precisely, in the fact of having left his corner, of having gone to the other side and from there made his own stuff."[66]

Carlos Fuentes has been the one in the third generation who has argued about the advantages of cosmopolitanism, tying it expressly with the circumstances of the Latin American culture of the time within his global perception of the changes that have been happening in the world. His affiliation with the trend intensified through the 1960s, when he destroys what he had written of the trilogy begun with *The Good Conscience* and begins the novel that will carry the symbolic title *A Change of Skin*, the foundation of a new cycle of investigation into narrative forms. This declaration is also from 1966:

> I believe that North American literature is what it is thanks to the perspective gained through immigrants, and Latin American literature in general will be so too. But so called cosmopolitanism keeps getting criticized and using Darío as an example. We forget that there is an aspiration very much ours, very worthwhile, very true, very concrete in cosmopolitanism that is that of not weakening ourselves in isolation, that of breaking this isolation that diminishes us and finding a whole series of correspondences and affirmations in the open relations of culture.[67]

Behind these three generations one finds young authors that practice the same coordinates, probably with a greater poise than the cited examples had initially, but at this point in its evolution cosmopolitanism can no longer be enclosed in the simple appropriation of techniques, in opposition to content that for the majority of authors continues being private and regional, because its particular tendency for universalization of values offers as a logical consequence a full and mature installation in a universal theme, in a universal plot, in universal characters. Carpentier's already mentioned reference to the "universalization of [Latin American] characters" opens the door to use equally "universalized" characters that now originate from any point on the planet, an eventuality that was implicit in the cosmopolitan program of "modernismo" of the previous century (Darío's French stories, the evocation of French landscapes in José Asunción Silva's *After Dinner Conversations*, or Carlos Reyles's *Castanets*[68]) and that now acquires an unrestricted sovereignty in Borges's inventions. It will allow for memorable tales like Cortázar's "The Pursuer" and a good part of his short stories and novels; it will involve vast historical reconstructions like Manuel Mujica Láinez's *Bomarzo*,[69] Alejo Carpentier's *The Harp and the Shadow*, Carlos Fuentes's towering construction in *Terra Nostra*, books that in other levels and circumstances repeat Enrique Larreta's[70] effort in *The Glory of Don Ramiro*; and it will extend to Sarduy's texts among the younger writers.

If the ascendancy of techniques as neutral and universal instruments constituted the point of departure, the later evolution gave proof of the intimate tie that they manifest with an international perspective. The use of backgrounds, characters, and themes from any place in the world, the use of an international raw material, was merely the logical and legitimate consequence of the absorption of foreign techniques. The legitimacy of this free incorporation of content cannot but call attention to the force of attraction that the external pole emits in a period of increasing tension in the literary system, which only reproduces the tension of the Latin American social organism.

It is an evolutionary bend that can have even bolder and risky instances because of the application of the attractive force that central empires exercise over marginal zones, in both economic and cultural fields. In previous centuries there were various examples of full incorporation of marginal writers in the metropolitan centers but in our time this has increased: the best example comes from Vladimir Nabokov, who in the novels of his North American period substitutes his original language, Russian, for English. It is a profound transformation of which until now we only have one example in contemporary Latin American narrative, represented by the Argentine author Juan Rodolfo Wilcock, who forms a part of Italian literature.

The cosmopolitan tendency, which had in Buenos Aires more than in Argentina, one of its privileged enclaves, for obvious and well-known reasons derived from the alluvial and recent composition of its society that developed in close contact with European sources, reached its culminating point in the work of this excellent author of the generation of Borges's successors (Bioy Casares, Bianco, Cortázar). Through this bridge he travelled toward his integral incorporation, I would not say to a type of international literature but to another culture of the many in which the universe is divided. The Spanish language was made the object of criticism and affronts in the ranks of cosmopolitanism, initiating a true judgment that differs, in level of intensity, with that which the modernistas began. Many of the latter would have preferred to write in French (and they have left some clumsy examples of this) but they were clearly conscious that "my spouse is from my land"[71] and proceeded with the renovation of the language, returning to the accumulated riches in its long development, especially in the inventions of their "Manierist" period to which they added a not excessive number of French words and syntactic forms. In this second revaluation of language, which was led by Borges, the linguistic ideal was represented by English, which had already left its quota of anglicisms in Spanish but above all operated in the path of purification, agility, and expressivity that were already foreseen in learned and disciplined language of a great American Hispanist, Alfonso Reyes. This is an extensive and complex chapter in which the arguments forwarded in the 1920s about national American languages continue to resonate, but where they mix with the protests for the hardened forms of the literary use of Spanish, visible inabilities to completely take possession of the language in all senses of the word: the capacity for reworking and invention that is a constant of its standards, in accordance with regional imaginaries. Carpentier, having the ability to pass to French, opted for keeping his native language; like the vast majority of Latin American fiction authors he recognized the existence of blueprints for national languages that are capable nevertheless of continental intercommunication, which work within an obvious Hispanic system.

Curiously, the desertion of the native language that has always served to establish borders within which a specific literature is forged allows for seeing cosmopolitanism as the product of a specific culture, as a supranational dream fed from a restricted national region. Without a doubt, one can continue to dream from the heart of another culture and can even be recognized as an instrument ready for the traffic of languages, but the idiomatic transposition of the writer, that is one of their greatest eventualities, does not flow into internationalism but rather to another cultural province of the many in which the planet is subdivided. By this path one cannot reach the supranational category but rather the disdained national category, except that one is substituted for the other. Apart from the differences of individual flavors that they present, from their particular traditions and from their levels of development, these cultures also distinguish themselves by the power that they exercise on the rest of the planet, from there the attraction that has been exercised toward the central regions of the planet.

Here is where the debate that Julio Cortázar and José María Arguedas sustained, as clear representatives of the two poles that govern artistic behavior of the new narrative, acquires its full significance. In order to demarcate his position, Arguedas alluded to this paradoxical situation that leads to cosmopolitanism and that consists of the installation in one of the cultural provinces of the world, whether it be that of another nation, as occurred in Wilcock's case, or the province of the "supranational" that is no less closed by the fact that its values are extracted from multiple sources and are different from national values: "We are all provincials, don Julio. Provincials of nations and provincials of the supranational, that is also a closed sphere or stratus, that of 'value in itself' like you happily point out."[72]

Even though both differ in the value given to these diverse orders, they both agree in recognizing that one as much as the other are equally valid to sustain artistic production at the highest level, with which the dilemma does not refer to the attainment of beauty, which as is well-known can be fully achieved within the framework of any culture no matter its nature or level, but rather refers to the different modes in which what is beautiful is accepted according to the cultures in which it is born and the public radius in which it can enact its persuasive action. In the concrete case that concerns us, it refers to those technical mechanisms that different cultural systems accept, which ones they are and where they originate.

The transcultural pole of the avant-garde also tackles modernization, also takes charge of universal heritage, is also able to supply itself in the external technical market, but as it primarily attends to the traditional surviving culture stationed in truly defensive regions of the continent, it is through these and their individualities that it elaborates the products that are placed in the modernized lifeline through transculturating operations.[73] This work was conditioned by the zones in which it developed its action or, said another way, by the cultural elements that formed the writers born in them. While the cosmopolitans worked from the most developed cities of Latin America that have maintained for some time a permanent exchange with the external cultural centers and thus have already lived enormous transformations produced by previous modernizing impulses, transculturators emerge in the internal enclaves, sometimes of recent modernizing permeation, other times as remnants of ancient illiterate oral cultures or also zones that had splendid pasts and have been marginally displaced by progress. That is why these cosmopolitan authors are decidedly urban, not only in their subject matter but also basically in their stylistic resources that they transfer from the urbanized cultural structure, while the transculturators continue to focus on taking possession of rural zones, of abandoned towns or archaic customs, of the otherness represented by autochthonous American cultures. To the correlation between Latin American capitals and the vast Atlantic world that the cosmopolitans establish, authors like Rulfo, Arguedas, Roa Bastos, Guimarães Rosa, or García Márquez resist with equivalent operations and efforts of parallel modernization, but achieved with internal zones, call them Jalisco, Cuzco, Chaco, Mina Geraes, the Caribbean coast of Colombia. Even those who accept the urban world, like José Revueltas, Ernesto Sábato, and Juan Carlos Onetti, are reconnected to the origins, to the defenseless zones, to the marginal characters. Onetti follows Faulkner's model of recuperation of the lost order by inventing the town of Santa María that he constructs through a progressive rejection of the great city of Buenos Aires and as an idealization of the city of his birth, Montevideo, the "neighborhood that left us," as Borges would say.

Their products do not reproduce frozen folkloric nor simply regionalist models but entail a renovation that makes full use of the technical, linguistic repertoire of modernization, and in several of them the absolute presence of Faulkner has been noted; at the same time, through his placement and his transculturating project, in them the search and discovery of expressive forms, modes of narration, techniques that flow from the very heart of the internal cultures that they rework is perceptible. This is one of the innovations of the transcultural avant-garde that marks the distance in which it is situated with respect to a regional narrative whose subject matter it nevertheless extends. We also find here the novel of the land and nature and rural characters and even indigenous peoples with their invariable customs, but what is unique lies in the fact that this content is not merely incorporated as subject matter that serves as a demonstration but is perceived through the cognitive structures that correspond to the internal vision of these people. It produces a displacement from the simple fascinating thematic orbit, but seen from outside (in Gallegos, Icaza, or Rivera), to the interior vision that they have of it and that thus is secured in the mechanisms of the perception of objects and the universe and not in those objects and that universe. The reiterated affirmation of the close tie between technique and content that appears in the transcultural author is representative of this totality: from the critique of Onetti to "writers that limit themselves to using new techniques without these responding to the content"[74] to Sábato's emphatic declaration, "For me technique should emerge as the consequence of the reality that one investigates,"[75] passing through the way in which García Márquez links technical inquiry to its applicability to the discovery of a unique Latin American reality: "I believe that we have to work on investigations of language and technical forms of the story given that all this fantastic Latin American reality forms part of our books and that Latin American literature corresponds to Latin American life where the most extraordinary things happen every day."[76]

If one of the global tendencies of the avant-garde consisted in the desertion of strictly literary language, transferring it to registers of speech, simultaneously enacting the absorption of history by personal discourse, said or thought, this common denominator splits into one path that situates it at the conscious level of the writer incorporating learned discourse together with colloquialism, criticism together with description, historical information together with popular perceptions and another path that situates it at the particular level of the character, within their imaginary, their terminology, and their syntax. Oral narrative is what governs multiple short stories by Rulfo or inundates his novel *Pedro Paramo* to the point of absorbing it completely in the discourse of Juan Preciado and more urgently is what allows Guimarães Rosa to forge the narrative structure that appears as the literary articulation of the systems of oral storytelling. Faced with borderline situations, because they imply the use of characters with other (indigenous) languages, Roa Bastos and Arguedas compose syncretic languages, and in the latter, as happened previously with Asturias, poetic language appears as the appropriate approach to not only translate a worldview but organize it in literary structures. It could be, however, that it is not the character but the omniscient author who fills the totality of history, as in *One Hundred Years of Solitude*, but in this case it would appeal to a mode of storytelling that he persuasively says was learned from village women and that consists of the rigorous and equivalent leveling of realist and fantastic data within a colloquial flow, in such a way that history evolves into a discourse, attributed to the narrator or to Melquíades's cryptic text, whose technical resources come from illiterate popular narration or the wide vein of the joke and the anecdotal event. In this case, that the displacement has been achieved is obvious: the novel preserves the content that could supply a regional novel, but now this content is perceived through a narrative technique (that is simultaneously a worldview) that is supplied by the intellectual mechanisms of understanding and interpreting what is real for the people who move among this content. There is a change of level that allows writing to install itself in the field of intellectual articulations and not only in the events, even though they also remain present in discourse. These articulations are born of a concrete praxis in a real world, they are the instruments that organize a determined culture.

A similar displacement can be found in João Guimarães Rosa's narrative. Being born into powerful Brazilian regionalism, tied to the experience of a rural community that had a period of splendor and then remained enclosed, at the edge of modernization that moved to other parts of Brazil, macerating idiosyncratic cultural forms (Minas Gerais), his investigation of this culture is achieved through its central product, language, transferring him from the picturesque nature of subject matter to the mechanisms of expression and elaborating them so that language expresses what is specific to that culture, that worldview. Alfredo Bosi does well to signal that the principal that governs his mythopoetic discourse is "a radicalization of the mental and verbal processes inherent to the context that gave them the raw material of their art"[77] with which both the raw material and the technique of elaboration rise harmonically from an identical source, even though it is on the latter that the work of the writer is based, enriching it, modernizing it, thanks to its vast international cultural linguistics. This is evident in a masterful story "Bronze Face" (from *Corpo de Baile*) where the verbal structure translates the intellectual that serves to elaborate myths and offers itself as the instrument of analysis of the raw material.

In these examples we can trace the eventuality of a modernization of techniques that is based on, in the inquiry of forms that adopt an internal material, the Latin American not found in the internationalizing concept of cosmopolitanism. It is true that these transculturators receive external influence, that they are trained in the technical contributions of the great European and North American impulse of the century, and it is even possible to think that this lesson opened their eyes to a better mode of investigation within its medium. Starting with such incitements, which they owe to the avant-garde from between world wars, they are able to find equivalent autonomous systems; they obtained, like the external masters, a new reconsideration of their cultural medium that would provide them renovating techniques that are reflecting it. These, furthermore, preserved an intimate connection with the context that they produced given that both came from the same cultural framework, which meant that the techniques did not acquire an extreme visibility nor were they employed in opposition to the content. This is why the lineage of the transculturating authors is not one that offers raucous inventions, not even in the case of *One Hundred Years of Solitude*, received by Colombians as the enjoyable narrative of the familiar and to Latin Americans as the just coining of the very well-known experiences that acquired their literary expression. It is possible to say "garciamarquezco" from now on to designate them.

Within this ordering chart of literary practices, Mario Vargas Llosa holds a curious place, above all in his first works. In them the greater effort of internal recuperation of the Latin American experience coexists with the greater effort of cosmopolitan adaptation, tying them together with an extreme tension where one can see his will as writer. It would seem to be a proposal to link together the two poles, despite their abrasive collisions, in order to lose nothing of any of them. It is a project in process that has given way to a more harmonic search, but at whose foundation the extreme distance in which for this Peruvian the two cultural situations of his country, of the Andean region, have been shown. Speaking at an international meeting about the "Role of the Latin American Writer," he made this statement in defining the conflict on which his own work revolves:

> This morning we have heard very interesting statements about the problems that the electronic age sets out for the writer. Peruvian writers are far from these problems. In a certain way, the problems that we should face belong to the Stone Age.[78]

Problems of the Stone Age and narrative techniques of the Electronic Age struggle in *The Green House* without being able to find equilibrium, and this is what constitutes what is specific to Vargas Llosa's invention, the originality of his attempt, taking on this conflict that takes place at the level of writing. Given that the plan in which problems and techniques coincide is narrative language (if not language in general), namely his project implies a modernization of the optic with which it recognizes a fixed reality, which then appears as a system of unveiling. In fact writing records a protest.

An inverse of this case can be found in one who has contributed the most original narrative technique or at least the one most removed from the frequent sources of the European avant-garde. It is Macedonio Fernández,[79] who wrote *The Museum of Eterna's Novel*, which appeared posthumously in 1967, in the same center of the widening of the reading public, although it did not attract great attention from the readers of the new novel.

12

Literature within an Anthropological Framework

If we accept, following Karl Mannheim,[1] a tendency to apply successive interpretive filters on the world, derived from human effort to define oneself with respect to the absolutes that men believe govern their historical circumstances, one can also accept with him that the constitution of mass society in the nineteenth century has presaged the emergence of sociological categories that, despite their antecedents, have just recently begun constructing their systematic foundation. The pioneering work of Comte and Spencer, just like the rapid adoption of their work to literary studies by Hippolyte Taine (although Henry Thomas Buckle's *History of Civilization in England* figures as a greater influence on him), establish that new framework within which one can circumscribe historical phenomena. By 1895, a year in which the sociological inferences of Marx's thought have prevailed and in which the works of Max Weber and Vilfredo Pareto[2] are being produced, this framework already explains its autonomous methodology in the seminal book by Emile Durkheim about the rules of the sociological method.

The violent expansion of sociology from the beginning carried over to literary studies, even though literary scholars jointly claimed Romantic (and conservative) traditions set by Louis de Bonald and the verbose Madame De Staël within the French context ruled by the dominance of Hugo and Zola, but also by Frederic Le Play and Gustave Le Bon,[3] successful in their time but now forgotten. An uncommon combination, confusing and contradictory, was received in Latin America like the flag of liberation by writers who continued to fulfill all the intellectual roles in existence (lawyers, sociologists, educators, poets, politicians) and for whom the cultural conditions originating in colonial times proved especially adept for sociological categories.

Even with notorious precedents, which Salvador Giner has called the "pre-sociological phase" of Hispanic American thought in which Sarmiento's robust contribution cannot be missed, it would be the decade of the 1880s that would fully establish sociology, thanks to the work of Eugenio María de Hostos.[4] In the Dominican Republic during the decade between 1879 and 1889 de Hostos gave the lectures that constituted his posthumous *Tratado de sociología* (Treatise on Sociology, 1904) and published *Moral social* (Social Morals) in 1888. The first literary history of the continent truly informed by European sociological thought, *História da Literatura Brasileira* (*History of Brazilian Literature*) by Sílvio Romero (1851–1914), comes from this same year. As irritating as it may seem now, it continues to bear witness to the first original attempts to understand an American uniqueness and the first robust effort to autonomously structure a literary corpus, that is, *to construct a literature*. What continues to impress with Sílvio Romero, apart from his voracious understanding of literature and his discovery of popular literatures since 1879, is the reckless eloquence of his literary theorization, so informed by European criticism of his time, so syncretic and adaptable in splicing divergent trends, so true and belligerent in the wake of the famous "teuto-sergipana" school of his teacher Tobias Barreto; in short, so Latin American.[5] He reconstructed his formative years many times over with his impassioned discoveries:

> Later, a little later, Littré's *Paroles de Philosophie Positive* (Words of Positivist Philosophy) made me understand that there was something much larger to inspire the poets—philosophy. At the same time, the *History of English Literature* and *The Philosophy of Art: Art in Greece* by Taine, besides being two volumes consecrated to art in Italy and the Netherlands, showed me a long critical road based in the sciences, singularly in mesology, physiology, anthropology, ethnography, besides the indispensable psychological approaches. . . . In 1868 in Recife, my friends and I read Comte, Littré, Buckle, Taine, Max Müller, Renan, Vacherot. . . . Comte was only set aside by our love for Spencer, Darwin, Haeckel, Büchner, Vogt, Molleschott, Huxley.[6]

Although neither Araripe nor José Veríssimo,[7] both much more attentive and knowledgeable of literary phenomena, have followed him, the sociological mark forged by Romero would dominate the state of literary studies, not just in Brazil but also in critics like Alberto Zum Felde or Ricardo Rojas,[8] who very probably read him. Like in the Goethean metaphor, a "red thread" departs from here that under other lenses (nationalist, social, and Marxist) follows a large part of Latin American literary criticism. It even crosses stylistic, psychological, or structural critique, as a tenacious factory mark on the continent.

This renovation of literary styles, this splendid modernization that would become so beneficial in Latin America, should not impede us from observing its insufficiencies and, above all, the deformations that it introduced in the appreciation of literary works. This was very evident in the arrogant polemic in 1906, when Sílvio Romero hoped to annihilate Manoel Bonfim's book *A America Latina: Males de Origem* (*Latin America: Original Sins*), certainly one of the best books that has been written regarding the so-called Latin American under-development. The complete arsenal of European sociology was placed in the service of this exterminating work, without any reticence about its appropriateness or applicability to a different cultural field. If Antonello Gerbi's excellent book, *The Dispute of the New World* (1955), had already been published at the time, reasonable doubts might possibly have been raised about the usefulness of European theories, especially in relation to America. Even without it, Sílvio Romero had already been able to confront some conclusions of European sociology, above all when it put into doubt America's own existence as was the case in the determinist relationship between climate and culture that Buckle put into circulation and Taine explored in his literary investigations. It should be noted that ten years later, in honor of Sílvio Romero, this was the argument that José Enrique Rodó used to judge that Rubén Darío could not be the poet of America, since, as he states with precision: "Nor for Taine, nor Buckle, would such a personality in a similar atmosphere be a happy discovery."[9] Half a century later, Juan Marinello appealed to Rodó's testimony to reiterate a condemnation of Darío, without recognizing that at the root of such arguments not only would Darío disappear but so would Marinello himself, the complete island of Cuba, and a good part of the world, that is, all the tropical zones that according to Buckle did not produce cultures as a consequence of their destructive climates for intellectual life.

These are the stumbling blocks that servile acceptance of metropolitan thought produce and it should be remembered that we owe the pessimism of many books, like that of Mexican Francisco Bulnes or the Bolivian Alcides Arguedas, to French sociology from the second half of the nineteenth century. These theorists were crushed by the racists tendencies that came from Gobineau's work and were implemented by the Social School of Le Bon.[10]

We should also remember that the majority of intellectuals at the time felt the shadow of disgrace for belonging to mestizo peoples in which whites had mixed with blacks and indigenous peoples, or for being affiliated with the culture of corn or yuca and not that of wheat or at least rice. A more attentive exploration of the books that Latin American intellectuals read at the time of sociology's emergence, and of the errors as well as the virtues that they provide, would contribute to develop in us a cautious critical vision of contemporary material with which we furnish ourselves. As is well known, one of the mildest intellectual obsessions is a secret progressivist faith in which the latest contributions are always the best. This works like its symmetrical opposite, that is, the ineradicable faith in some truth revealed despite the modifications of subsequent history.

When I compiled all the dispersed writings that Rubén Darío had consecrated to a theme that terrified him, oneirism, in a book that he gave title to, *El mundo de los sueños* (*The World of Dreams*),[11] it surprised me that the interpretations that the author gave in a series published between 1911 and 1914 belonged to the most dissimilar literary and psychological sources. However, these interpretations never touched on the science of psychoanalysis underway that in 1900 had not yet given way to the Freudian *Traumdeutung* [interpretation of dreams]. The writings combined to give theosophist, mystical, spiritualist, and poetic explanations but never studies about sexuality. In the same way, in the reading of European books that our first literary sociologists read, I have never found a key name—that of Edward Burnett Tylor (1832–1917), who by 1871 had already published his revolutionary book *Primitive Culture*, followed in 1881 by *Anthropology*. We owe the first definition of "culture" to Tylor: "That complex whole which includes knowledge, belief, art, morals, law, custom, and any other capabilities and habits acquired by man as a member of society."[12] With him the field of "social anthropology" or "cultural anthropology" began, fields that would be influential in the twentieth century. Without losing its connection with sociology, in relation to which it appeared as the new science par excellence, it would have to deal with its own territory, curiously supported on both a material basis (geography, archaeology, cultural objects) and a speculative social horizon. This is what Lévi-Strauss's definition of anthropology signals, "It has, as it were, its feet planted on the natural sciences, its back resting against the humanistic studies, and its eyes directed towards the social sciences."[13] It offered a hybrid situation, which was, at the same time, rich with inventive consequences, above all regarding literary phenomena because this new science was formed to study illiterate societies and only later extended its scope to complex and modern societies where writing played a central role. The high attention given to language that is, obviously, the principal and most collective production of a culture, originates from the earliest studies. We owe a debt to the outstanding work of Edward Sapir, who saw languages in the Saussurean double lens, just as Lévi-Strauss could not avoid observing this, describing in anthropology that "there is the same concern to avoid separating the objective basis of language (sound) from its signifying function (meaning)."[14] Sociology has not shown the same attention to languages, and it is possible that we owe to this the visible content based tendency of the sociology of literature. This tendency has interrogated novels and their meaning with pleasure, yet shown themselves to be aloof regarding poetry and, in general, what the sound says and represents within literature. One could even venture that it costs sociology much to distance itself from its bourgeois origins and that, in particular the sociology of literature continues to be obscurely tied to its roots: the prosification of genres that accompanied the dominating emergence of the bourgeois class on the horizon of eighteenth- and nineteenth-century history and that has maintained such weight in the heirs of Marx, from Plekhanov to Lukács.[15]

The pathways, findings, polemics, and frustrations of anthropology are not our topics, but rather, its potential contribution to better understanding the literatures of Latin America. Its contribution has been less appreciated than that of sociology, despite the narrow isolation of both disciplines from Durkheim's books to the renewed proposal of a "sociology of culture" by Raymond Williams, reviving (and coloring with Marxist thought) a German path (Dilthey, Weber, Hauser).[16]

Both disciplines were born in the bosom of colonizing metropolises that founded vast universal empires through the development of powerful scientific and technical instruments that legitimized their civilizing pride with which they were able to subjugate multiple societies representative of the "otherness" of the world. They interpreted this difference—marked at one extreme as "primitive cultures"—as backwardness with respect to their presumed "progress." The unilateral evolutionist philosophy dominated European thought in the nineteenth century, from the Comtean theory of the three stages of anthropology to Morgan's theory about the three periods of social organization,[17] which underlies Darwinism as much as Marxism, and led sociological educators to propose to the world the European model of society and to justify its imperialist action through an inflexible corpus.

That is how it was understood, at least from the Latin American periphery at the turn of the century when it was introduced to the continent. Intellectuals, in large part, discredited their traditions and peculiarities, trying to exchange them for imported theories that they made sacred. The primacy that they conceded to the ethnocentric line of sociology perhaps explains the lack of interest they showed for English anthropology (with rare exceptions, like Varona's intellectual curiosity[18]). Based on the experience of otherness, which it developed in a specific way similar to the development of its own field, anthropology began to propose the opposite: the recognition of the singularity of native regions, the acceptance of their differences with the metropolis, the appreciation of the traditional norms that ruled them. This occurs within a "culturalist" tendency that would impregnate the thought of Franz Boas and that Malinowski[19] would theorize. In its early development this ideology did not attract Latin Americans who presumably would be able to see it, then, as inferior to their ambitions of transforming into European societies outright, given the hierarchy of values under which they were operating.

Curiously, they disdained one of the first basic contributions of anthropology: the affirmation of a legitimacy, independence, and self-sufficiency of any culture whatsoever, which should be measured according to its own norms and not be adjusted by those that rule other cultures. This cultural relativism would be expressed in many ways and the controversies surrounding these ideas do not matter for our purposes. Early anthropology also affirmed the constitutive organic nature that sustains and authenticates culture. These are the criteria that gained coherent systematization in Lévi-Strauss's book *Race and History*.[20] The importance of this idea in relation to racism and, in general, all ethnocentric thought has been recognized, and one could also affirm it in relation to literatures, placing them as they correspond in the active center of their respective cultures. They are cultural organic expressions, immersed in the complex web of relations that unfold as a much vaster and richer field than that of intertextuality (Kristeva) and from which they are nourished and, at the same time, to which they contribute as systems of meanings within the same cultural field. If, on the one hand, this means the indictment of a literature, starting with the assumptions that govern others, preferably those of the developed metropolises, as has been the norm, on the other, it would fully allow for an accounting of the elements that shape it and their specific functionality, accepting the presence of ancient internal forces, of original syncretic elaborations, and of tendencies that specifically permeate Latin American social life.

I believe that one can consider the culturalist tendency that characterized the first anthropological contributions that Latin America produced as significant. In the 1920s and 1930s of the twentieth century, Gilberto

Freyre's work responded explicitly to the reading of Franz Boas, to his egalitarianism that rejected racial categories. In the prologue to the first edition of *The Masters and the Slaves* (1933), Freyre says, "It is upon this criterion of the basic differentiation between race and culture that the entire plan of this essay rests."[21] Regarding the other great anthropologist of the time, the Cuban Fernando Ortiz, his affiliation with Malinowski who wrote the prologue to his *Cuban Counterpoint: Tobacco and Sugar* (1940) is well known, even though one cannot simplify his work as a version of the Polish thinker's ideas,[22] as the original concept of "transculturation," which recognizes the creative role of Latin American mestizo society in cultural invention that Ortiz developed clearly shows. More recently, the same approach would mark the Peruvian José María Argüedas, which would permit him to distance himself from the militant sociology of Mariátegui and to propose a culturalist appreciation of indigenous communities, which echoes Herskovitz's teachings,[23] and a positive valorization of mestizo transculturation.

A second basic contribution of this anthropological culturalist concept, which is already in Taylor's definition but would be refined by Radcliffe Brown and was also found in Mauss's work,[24] is what today we would call a structured vision of cultures. This vision highlights the strict correlation between its diverse forms (language, beliefs, social forms, art) in a strongly interdependent dynamic. For the purposes of the consideration of literary works, it establishes its connection with a plurality of sources (explicit or implied, but present) that constitute an unbreakable group, a way in which the modifications of any of its elements affects the others, leading to changes. This concept, which emerges in the midst of nineteenth-century organicism but with Taylor was already acquiring a clear intellectual rigor, can approach the notion of totality that sociology has developed, at the same time enriching it with a considerable and precise material base and perceiving of it as a dynamic free from its components. The literary work does not situate itself, then, between the social and the linguistic sets (Tynianov), but rather appears in turn as a global structure of signification, as a truncated model of the culture that informs it, supplied by the diverse trends that operate in society but functioning as an autonomous, not merely reflective, product.

A third basic contribution has its foundation in the notion of collective production of culture that anthropology developed, starting with the study of the arts and above all the language of primitive cultures. If this did not mean the disappearance of the individual artist, it saw artistic activity within powerful collective patterns that constituted the superior tools that a culture manipulated since before any particular invention or, after that, in the process of collective adaptation that Jakobson saw in the oral traditions dealing with folklore. Anthropology worked preferentially (and even expanded it in the diffusionist trend) with horizontal spatial distributions of cultures in which the same participative factors occur and much less, as sociology did, in vertical distributions that are more evident in complex societies than in primitive ones. At the same time, its demarcation of areas has an application for literary production, not only in the clear message but much more in the implicit. Borges already explained ingeniously that nothing proved the Pampas region was the origin of gauchesque literature better than the lack of the *ombú*, the most well-known tree of the region. The secret working of mental structures of a society in the production of its literary texts is of greatest importance because they translate into particular expressive instruments. To use the same example, the constant use of the narrative ellipsis (in contrast to the bourgeois articulation of discourse) is one of the subtle artistic devices of the rural tale.

Anthropology's attention to folklore and language comes from this attention to collective forms of literary invention as well as for craftworks. It is an attempt to span, using products filtered through the whole community, the values on which their identity lies; values that permeate the social totality even though they combine with those originating from vertical layers with being replaced by them entirely. At the margin of the debate that at the time Whorf's analysis of the Hopi language provoked, following their mental categories for the vocabulary and order of discourse, is an example of the effort to find in language the objectification of a worldview that undergirds the community that uses it, which could be subconscious, but that acts through the linguistic order that is the prime material of literary discourse. Even though advances in modern linguistics has redirected literary scholars to a greater attention for this capital component of artistic work, it has not done the same with folklore nor with the abundant production of myths that previously and now flourish in the continent and are expressed through combined languages, the majority of them urbanized. The consideration of this enormous material contributes to questioning, perhaps even dispersing, the nineteenth-century concept of literature that has continued to operate in Latin America, given above all the traditional aristocratic concept of intellectuals, based on the idea of the author who produces for an educated circle.

Paul Zumthor, after considering the voice as an instrument of prophecy, adds sinisterly: "Since the seventeenth century, Europe has spread itself

Literature within an Anthropological Framework | 323

over the world like a cancer. . . . Without a doubt, one of the symptoms of the evil was, from the very start, what we call literature, and literature has taken on consistency, prospered, become what it is—one of the vast dimensions of human beings—by challenging voice."[25] A short story by the Paraguayan author Augusto Roa Bastos,[26] whose title in the only language in which to date it has been published, Portuguese, is "O sonámbulo" (The Sleepwalker), tells the story of Coronel Silvestre Carmona, who has delivered the rebels of Cerro Corá to the Empire and thus makes a traitor of the educated man. He is condemned to have his tongue ripped out, because it is through the tongue that a people live and not in scriptural folios.[27] It is a part of Latin American myths that testify to its cultural uniqueness and it is this that has composed, more with the voice than with writing, its masterpieces.

Appendix: Publishing History of the Essays in This Volume

Mariano Azuela: Ambition and Frustration of the Middle Class (1966)

Originally titled "El perspectivismo social en la novela de Mariano Azuela," this article was published in *Revista Iberoamericana de Literatura* (Uruguay), 2nd period, no. 1 (1966): 63–94. This journal was a publication of the Department of Spanish American Literature of the Universidad de la República in Montevideo, Uruguay. It was directed by Ángel Rama and only two issues were published. The article was then modified and expanded with the title "Mariano Azuela: Ambición y frustración de las clases medias" and published in *Cuadernos de Marcha*, Segunda Época (2nd epoch or period, when it was published in Mexico, 1979–1983) in three parts. Part 1: vol. 2, no. 10 (Nov–Dec, 1980): 87–91. Part 2: vol. 2, no. 11 (Jan–Feb, 1981), 75–83. Part 3: vol. 2, no. 12 (March–April, 1981), 61–67. In 1984 it became the fourth chapter in Rama's collection of essays *Literatura y clase social* (Mexico: Folio, 1984), 144–83.

Criticism and Literature (1971)

Published as "Crítica y literatura," *Sin Nombre* 1, no. 3 (1971): 6–11.

Spanish American Literature in the Age of Machines (1972)

Published as "La literatura hispanoamericana en la era de las máquinas," *Revista de la Universidad Nacional Autónoma de México* 26, no. 6–7 (1972): 15–18.

No More Demons (1972)

Published as "El fin de los demonios. Respuesta a Vargas Llosa," *Marcha* 34, no. 1603 (July 28, 1972): 30–31. Republished as a chapter in Ángel Rama and Mario Vargas Llosa, *García Márquez y la problemática de la novela* (Montevideo: Corregidor-Marcha, 1973).

The Two Latin American Avant-Gardes (1973)

Published as "Las dos vanguardias latinoamericanas," *Maldoror* 4, no. 9 (1973): 58–64.

Literary System and Social System in Spanish America (1975)

Published as "Sistema literario y sistema social en Hispanoamérica" in *Literatura y praxis en América Latina*, ed. Fernando Alegría (Caracas: Monte Avila, 1975), 81–109. Reprinted in Ángel Rama, *Literatura, cultura, sociedad en América Latina*, ed. Pablo Rocca (Montevideo: Trilce, 2006), 94–122.

Literature and Social Class (1976)

Originally published as "Literatura y clase social," *Escritura* 1, no. 1 (1976), 57–75. It became the introduction to his book *Los gauchipolíticos rioplatenses: Literatura y sociedad* (Buenos Aires: Calicanto, 1976). Pablo Rocca changed its title to *Literatura y sociedad* when he edited Ángel Rama, *Literatura, cultura, sociedad en América Latina* (Montevideo: Trilce, 2006), 123–43.

The Literary System of Gauchesque Poetry (1977)

Originally the preface to the anthology *Poesía gauchesca*, ed. Jorge B. Rivera (Caracas: Ayacucho, 1978), ix–liii. It became chapter 7 in the second edition of *Los gauchipolíticos rioplatenses* (Buenos Aires: CEDAL, 1982) and is included as chapter 2 of Ángel Rama, *Literatura y clase social* (Mexico: Folio, 1984), 23–77.

The Boom in Perspective (1979)

Published as "El boom en perspectiva," *Escritura* 4, no. 7 (1979), 3–45. It became chapter 4 in *La novela latinoamericana: Panoramas 1920–1980* (Bogotá: Colcultura, 1982), 235–93.

A Research into Ideology in Poetry (1980)

Published as "Indagación de la ideología en la poesía (Los dípticos seriados de *Versos sencillos*)," *Revista Iberoamericana* 46, no. 112–13 (1980): 353–400.

Narrative Technification (1981)

Published as "La tecnificación narrativa," *Hispamérica* 10, no. 30 (1981): 29–82. It became chapter 7 in *La novela latinoamericana: Panoramas 1920–1980* (Bogotá: Colcultura, 1982), 294–360.

Literature within an Anthropological Framework (1984)

Published as "La literatura en su marco antropológico," *Cuadernos Hispanoamericanos* 497 (1984): 95–101. Reprinted in Ángel Rama, *Literatura, cultura, sociedad en América Latina*, ed. Pablo Rocca (Montevideo: Trilce, 2006), 158–66. This paper was presented in the "Second Conference on the Sociology of Literature," held in Madrid on November 16–18, 1983. It is the last text that Rama wrote, and the last that he presented publicly, just a few hours before the fatal accident in which he lost his life.

Notes

Introduction

1. Ángel Rama, *The Lettered City*, ed. and trans. John Charles Chasteen (Durham, NC: Duke University Press, 1996).

2. Ángel Rama, "Processes of Transculturation in Latin American Narrative," *Journal of Latin American Cultural Studies* 6 (1997): 155–71.

3. Ángel Rama, *Writing Across Cultures: Narrative Transculturation in Latin America*, trans. David Frye (Durham, NC: Duke University Press, 2012).

4. See Carina Blixen and Alvaro Barros-Lémez, *Cronología y bibliografía de Ángel Rama* (Montevideo: Fundación Ángel Rama, 1986).

5. Ángel Rama, *Diario: 1974–1983* (Montevideo: Trilce, 2001), 52.

6. Julio Ramos, *Divergent Modernities: Culture and Politics in Nineteenth-Century Latin America* (Durham, NC: Duke University Press, 2001), 60.

7. Rama, *The Lettered City*, 124–25.

8. The book was published posthumously and we do not know how Rama would have defended his approach. That Rama lived his last few years as if time was slipping away is now well known. His diary, for example, is crowded with references to his ailments and the effects of age on his body. See Rama, *Diario 1974–1983*. In a moving essay written shortly after his passing, the Argentine author and journalist Tomás Eloy Martínez suggests that it wasn't events like his 1978 bypass surgery that served as "reminders of death," but the US government's rejection of his request for a resident visa for advocating the "doctrines of world communism," leaving him unable to accept a position as distinguished scholar at the University of Maryland that changed him: "He plunged into writing like someone accepting an addiction or a fate. . . . Against all critical tradition, he started to carelessly issue warnings and predictions." "Ángel Rama o la crítica como gozo," *Revista Iberoamericana* 52, no. 135–36 (1986): 663.

9. It is surprising to see that well-established Latin Americanists confuse the few authors that Rama considered "transculturators" with all the Boom authors (and

even some pre-Boom ones) and express this in really misinformed reviews of Rama's work. Joshua Lund, in his review of the English translation of *Transculturación narrativa*, even includes writers like Borges, who Rama always used as one of the classic examples of "cosmopolitan" writers, as transculturators. See Lund, "Magic Socialism," *Cultural Critique* 92 (2016): 179–89. John Beverly, who has offered one of the most important critiques of Rama's theory, also mistakenly equates "boom writers" or "novels of the boom" with "transculturators." See Beverly, *Subalternity and Representation* (Durham, NC: Duke University Press, 1999), 10, 43, 45.

10. Rama's use of statistics—common now among contemporary digital humanities scholars—was innovative in his field at the time and it is indicative of the enormous cultural capital he possessed at the end of his career: very few other critics in the field had access to the type of information he is able to include in this article.

11. Romina Pistacchio, *La aporía descolonial releyendo la tradición crítica de la crítica literaria latinoamericana: Los casos de Antonio Cornejo Polar y Ángel Rama* (Madrid: Iberoamericana Vervuet, 2018); Javier García Liendo, *El intelectual y la cultura de masas: Argumentos latinoamericanos en torno a Ángel Rama y José María Arguedas* (West Lafayette, IN: Purdue University Press, 2017; José Eduardo González, *Appropriating Theory: Ángel Rama's Critical Work* (Pittsburgh, PA: University of Pittsburgh Press, 2017).

12. See for example Magalí Armillas-Tiseyra's use of Rama to study the figure of the dictator in world literature in *The Dictator Novel: Writers and Politics in the Global South* (Evanston, IL: Northwestern University Press, 2019); or Ignacio Sánchez Prado's work on the novel form and how contemporary literature is reframing transculturation in "The Persistence of the Transcultural: A Latin American Theory of the Novel from the National-Popular to the Global," *New Literary History* 51, no. 2 (2020): 347–74.

Chapter 1

1. Manuel Pedro González, *Trayectoria de la novela en México* (Mexico: Botas, 1951), 97–98.

2. Mariano Azuela, "El novelista y su ambiente," in *Obras completas*, vol. 3 (Mexico: Fondo de Cultura Económica, 1960), 1133.

3. Antonio Castro Leal, "Introducción" to *La novela de la revolución mexicana* (Mexico: Aguilar, 1962), 25.

4. José Luis Martínez, *Literatura mexicana siglo XX* (Mexico: Antigua Librería Robredo, 1949), 40.

5. [This is a reference to Carlos Drummond de Andrade's poem "Nosso Tempo."]

6. Azuela, "El novelista y su ambiente," 1070.

7. Martínez, *Literatura mexicana*, 40.
8. Enrique Anderson Imbert, *Historia de la literatura hispanoamericana*, vol. 2 (Mexico: Fondo de Cultura Económica, 1961), 110.
9. Georg Lukács, "Franz Kafka or Thomas Mann?" in *The Meaning of Contemporary Realism* (London: Merlin Press, 1969), 55.
10. Azuela, *Obras completas*, 1063–64.
11. James Creelman, "President Diaz, Hero of the Americas," *Pearson's Magazine* 19, no. 3 (1908): 240.
12. José Vasconcelos, "El cordonzo de San Francisco" in *Ulises criollo*, 8th ed. (Mexico: Botas, 1937), 134.
13. Vasconcelos, *Ulises criollo*, 199.
14. Azuela, *Obras completas*, 3:1181.
15. Jesús Silva Herzog, *Breve historia de la revolución mexicana*, vol. 1 (Mexico: Fondo de Cultura Económica, 1962), 41.
16. Azuela, *Obras completas*, 3:558.
17. Pablo González Casanova, "México, el ciclo de una revolución agraria," *Cuadernos Americanos* 21, no. 1 (1962): 11.
18. Nathan L. Whetten, "The Rise of the Middle Class in México," in *Materiales para el estudio de la clase media en América Latina*, vol. 2, ed. Theo R. Crevenna (Washington, DC: Union Panamericana, 1950), 17.
19. José E. Iturriaga, *La estructura social y cultural de México* (Mexico: Fondo de Cultura Económica, 1951), 31.
20. John Johnson, *Political Change in Latin America: The Emergence of the Middle Class* (Stanford, CA: Stanford University Press, 1958), 128.
21. Johnson, *Political Change*, 135–36.
22. Iturriaga, "Las clases sociales en México" in *La estructura social y cultural de México* (Mexico: Fondo de Cultura Económica, 1951).
23. Herzog, *Breve historia*, 41.
24. Vasconcelos, *Ulises criollo*, 86–87.
25. Creelman, "President Diaz," 240.
26. [Ezequiel Montes believed that positivism produced individuals without morals. As minister of public instruction in 1881 he introduced a law to bring back philosophy, ethics, and logic to elementary schools.]
27. Vasconcelos, *Ulises criollo*, 261 62.
28. Vasconcelos, 230.
29. Vera Estañol, *La revolución mexicana: Orígenes y resultados* (Mexico: Porrúa, 1957), 16.
30. Estañol, 16.
31. Estañol, 41.
32. Vasconcelos, *Ulises criollo*, 282.
33. Vasconcelos, 120.
34. Vasconcelos, 124.

35. Vasconcelos, 305.

36. José Rubén Romero, "Apuntes de un lugareño" in *La novela de la revolución Mexicana*, vol. 2, ed. Antonio Castro Leal (Mexico: Aguilar, 1962), 82.

37. [Reyismo refers to the group of people supporting general Bernardo Reyes to become Díaz's successor. About the history of this movement Héctor Aguilar Camín and Lorenzo Meyer explain: "From the Díaz-Creelman interview in June 1908, the horizon of the opposition was dominated by the figure of Gen. Bernardo Reyes, former secretary of war. Reyismo filtered into some of the most sensitive parts of Mexican political life: the Masonic lodges, the modest bureaucrats, the army. During 1908 and parts of 1909, in the North and the West of the country, Reyismo led to the creation of clubs, journals and impressive speeches. Near mid-1909, however, Reyes yielded to Díaz's pressure and quelled with silence the demands of his supporters." *In the Shadow of the Mexican Revolution* (Austin: University of Texas Press, 1993), 17.]

38. Vasconcelos, *Ulises criollo*, 400.

39. Herzog, *Breve historia*, 187–88.

40. Alfredo Maillefert, *Los libros que leí* (Mexico: Universidad Nacional de Mexico, 1942), 110.

41. Speaking frankly, Azuela says in *The Trials of a Respectable Family*: "Victoriano Huerta belonged to the same class as the *pelado* even though the eminent poet Díaz Mirón may have said when the troglodytic assassin of Madero visited the offices of *El Imparcial*: 'General Huerta yesterday visited our editorial room leaving behind an aroma of glory.'" *Two Novels of The Mexican Revolution: The Trials of a Respectable Family and the Underdogs*, trans. Frances Kellam Hendricks and Beatrice Berler (San Antonio, TX: Principia Press, 1963), 98.

42. Azuela, *Two Novels of Mexico: The Flies, The Bosses*, trans. Lesley Byrd Simpson (Berkeley: University of California Press, 1965), 72.

43. Azuela, *Two Novels of The Mexican Revolution*, 20.

44. Dante Alighieri, *Inferno*, canto iii, trans. Courtney Langdon (Cambridge, MA: Harvard University Press), 31.

45. Azuela, *Two Novels of The Mexican Revolution*, 99.

46. Karl Mannheim, *Essays on the Sociology of Culture: Collected Works Volume Seven* (Taylor and Francis e-Library, 2003).

47. Azuela, *Andrés Pérez, maderista*, in *Obras completas*, 2:786–87.

48. Azuela, 780.

49. Azuela, *Two Novels of Mexico*, 147.

50. Azuela, 159.

51. Azuela, *Obras completas*, 2:1075.

52. Azuela, 1063–64.

53. In *The Bosses* Juan Viñas says ingenuously, "Very simple. Patience and stick to it. You save a penny because with that penny you complete the stack of twenty-five. You save the quarter, because with four quarters you have a peso, and with that

peso you complete your first hundred-peso note. And you watch that note as if it were the apple of your eye until it grows to be a thousand. And so on. Patience, honesty, and stick to it. That's the secret of the rich." *Two Novels of Mexico*, 122–23.

54. Azuela, *Two Novels of The Mexican Revolution*, 157.
55. [Church of San Felipe Neri in Mexico city ("La Profesa").]
56. Azuela, *Andrés Pérez*, 765.
57. Azuela, *Two Novels of The Mexican Revolution*, 15.
58. Azuela, *Obras completas*, 3:1093.
59. Azuela, *Obras completas*, 3:1099.
60. Azuela, *Two Novels of The Mexican Revolution*, 80.
61. Mannheim, *Essays on the Sociology of Culture*, 145.

Chapter 2

1. [Arnold Hauser (1892–1978), Marxist art historian, sociologist, and author of *The Social History of Art and Literature* (1951). Heinrich Wölfflin (1864–1945), Swiss art historian. His book *Renaissance and Baroque* (1888) was influential in modern reinterpretations of the Baroque period. Leo Spitzer (1887–1960), Austrian Hispanist.]

2. [Karl Vossler (1872–1949), German Romanist.]

Chapter 3

1. [Rama employs the term "voluntarism" in many of his writings. It appears to refer mainly to the idea that gives the will supremacy over reason. It was influential on Nietzsche's work, which is where Rama came into contact with it.]

2. ["Objectivist authors" refers to writers considered precursors of the *nouveau roman*.]

Chapter 4

1. [The exchange between Rama and Vargas Llosa has been collected in the volume *García Marquez y la problemática de la novela* (Buenos Aires: Corregidor-Marcha, 1973). Two studies in which this controversy is analyzed are José Eduardo González, *Appropriating Theory: Ángel Rama's Critical Work* (Pittsburgh, PA: University of Pittsburgh Press, 2017), 88–96; and Mabel Moraña, *Arguedas/Vargas Llosa: Dilemmas and Assemblages* (London: Palgrave, 2016), 177–81.]

2. [See "Crítica y literatura," *Sin nombre* 1, no. 3 (1971): 6–11. Translated as "Criticism and Literature" in the present collection.]

3. [Instituto de las Españas at the University of Columbia was established in 1920.]

4. [Agustin Thierry (1795–1856), French historian whose approach to history was influenced by Romantic writers, like Walter Scott. Charles Augustin Sainte-Beuve (1804–1869), French literary critic who believed in the necessity of knowing an artist's biography to understand their work.]

5. [*Rameau's Nephew* (1805) by Denis Diderot is written in the form of a philosophical dialogue in defense of the Enlightenment ideas, and *Candide* (1759) by Voltaire is a novella satirizing optimistic views of the world.]

6. [Rama is referring to Jan Kott, *Shakespeare: Our Contemporary* (New York: Doubleday, 1964).]

7. [Bertrand Russell, *Proposed Roads to Freedom: Socialism, Anarchism, and Syndicalism* (London: George Allen and Unwin, 1918).]

8. [Allusion to Argentine Romantic writer Esteban Echeverría, author of *Los consuelos* (1834).]

9. [Domingo Faustino Sarmiento, *Facundo: Civilization and Barbarism* (1845) and José Marmol, *Amalia* (1851).]

10. [Rama is here poking fun at Vargas Llosa's conciliatory tone in "The Return of Satan." After Rama employs Benjamin's idea of the writer as producer when reviewing Vargas Llosa's book, the Peruvian author calls Walter Benjamin "excellent" in his response but does not seem to grasp what Rama is referring to.]

11. [Ángel Rama, *Rubén Darío y el modernismo (circunstancia socioeconómica de un arte americano)* (Caracas: Biblioteca de la Universidad Central de Venezuela, 1970).]

12. [Rama is referring to Karl Mannheim's "The Problem of the Intelligentsia," in *Essays on the Sociology of Culture* (London: Routledge and Kegan Paul, 1956), 91–170. Also mentioned in "Literature within an Anthropological Framework."]

13. [See Ángel Rama, "La dialéctica de la modernidad en José Martí," in *Estudios martianos: Memoria del Seminario José Martí*, ed. Manuel Pedro González (San Juan: Universidad de Puerto Rico, 1974), 132–46.]

14. [José Martí, "Cuaderno de apuntes, 5 (1881)," in *Obras completas*, vol. 21 (Havana: Editorial Nacional de Cuba, 1965), 163–64.]

15. [Darcy Ribeiro, "Introducción: La cultura," in *América Latina en su arquitectura*, ed. Roberto Segre (Mexico: Siglo XXI, 1975), 37.]

16. [José Medina Echavarría (1903–1977), Spanish sociologist exiled in Mexico.]

17. [Isidore Lucien Ducasse, or Comte de Lautréamont (1846–1870), author of *Les Chants de Maldoror*.]

18. [Wilhelm Reich (1897–1957), an Austrian psychoanalyst and an important figure within the Freudo-Marxist tradition. He is the author of *The Mass Psychology of Fascism* (1933).]

19. [Erich Fromm (1900–1980) and Herbert Marcuse (1898–1979) disagreed on how to combine the theories of Marx and Freud. While Fromm believed that Freud's views needed to be revised (e.g., abandoning the libido theory), Marcuse believed that Freud's theory already contained an implicit critique of the established order.]

Chapter 5

1. *Sincerismo* refers to a literary style that comes after modernismo and is characterized by a rejection modernismo's cosmopolitanism and its evasion of Latin American reality. It began in 1911 with the publication of the poem "Tuércele el cuello al cisne de engañoso plumaje" ("Wring the neck of the swan with the deceiving plumage") by Mexican poet Enrique González Martínez.

2. [Translations of both books by Tablada can be found in Tablada, *The Experimental Poetry of José Juan Tablada*, trans. A. Scott Britton (Jefferson, NC: McFarland, 2016).]

3. [Vicente Huidobro, *The Poet is a Little God*, trans. Jorge García-Gómez (Las Cruces, NM: Xenos Books, 1990), 5.]

4. [Mario de Andrade, *Hallucinated City: Pauliceia Desvairada*, trans. Jack E. Tomlins (Nashville, TN: Vanderbilt University Press, 1968), 37.]

5. [César Vallejo, *The Complete Poetry*, ed. and trans. Clayton Eshelman (Berkeley: University of California Press, 2007), 167.]

6. [Gabriel García Márquez, *One Hundred Years of Solitude*, trans. Gregory Rabassa (New York: Penguin Books, 1973), 372.]

7. [Vicente Huidobro, *Selected Poetry of Vicente Huidobro*, ed. David M. Guss (New York: New Directions, 1981), 25.]

8. [Rama's text says "Amauta," but judging from the rest of the paragraph, he means Avance or *Revista de Avance*, a Cuban avant-garde magazine.]

9. [Hans Magnus Enzensberger, *Consciousness Industry: On Literature, Politics and the Media* (New York: Seabury Press, 1974), 17.]

10. [Famous public square in Paris.]

11. [Bateau-Lavoir was the name given to a building in Paris where several famous artists and writers took up residence at the turn of the twentieth century. *Le Surréalisme au service de la révolution* was a periodical published by members of the Surrealist movement from 1930 to 1933.]

12. [Georges Raynaud (1865–194[?]) was a professor of ancient American religions at the Sorbonne. He is known for his French translations of ancient pre-Columbian documents.]

13. [Closerie de Lilas is a famous café in Paris frequented by artists and writers.]

14. [Pablo de Rokha was the pen name of Carlos Díaz Loyola (1894–1968), a Chilean avant-garde poet.]

15. [César Vallejo, "XXVI" in *The Complete Poetry*, 217.]

Chapter 6

1. Within the nationalist climate that surrounded the centenary celebration of Independence, Ricardo Rojas finalized the process of aesthetic vindication for gauchesque poetry, devoting one of the volumes of his *History of Argentine Literature*

(1916) to it. Since 1960, writers have undertaken a similar task to dignify the lyricists of *mezzomúsica* in all of America: Gabriel Zaid in his *Omnibus of Mexican Poetry* (Mexico: Siglo XXI, 1971) has attempted to reconstruct the "poetic totality" of the country; Idea Vilariño dedicated a book of stylistic analysis to *Las letras del tango* (Buenos Aires: Schapire, 1966), giving them the same hierarchy as the learned poets. Other similar revisions in the field of theater are also in progress. In general, the theory of genres as well as the recuperation of trivial literatures has undergone intense modifications.

2. [Calixto Oyuela (1857–1935), was an Argentine writer and critic.]

3. This can be connected to Michel Foucault's views in "On the Archeology of the Sciences: Response to the Epistemology Circle" where he states, "In fact, the systematic effacement of merely given units makes it possible, first, to restore to the statement its singularity as an event. It is no longer regarded merely as the intervention of a linguistic structure, nor as the episodic manifestation of a deeper significance than itself; it is dealt with at the level of its historical irruption; an attempt is made to direct attention at the incision it constitutes, this irreducible—and often minute—emergence." *The Essential Foucault*, eds. Paul Rabinow and Nikolas Rose (New York: New Press, 1994), 401.

4. Darcy Ribeiro's book *El dilema de América Latina* (Mexico: Siglo XXI, 1971) has made a significant contribution to this point. A revision of the ideas presented there about social stratification and an updating of the structures of power in Latin America can be found in Dary Ribeiro's article "América Latina. Clases y poder" in *Participación* (Lima), no. 2 (February 1973). For the historical revision of the process, see Tulio Halperin Donghi's books, in particular *Historia contemporánea de América Latina* (Madrid: Alianza Editorial, 1969), and Sergio Bagú's *Estructura social de la Colonia* (Buenos Aires: El Ateneo, 1952) and *Evolución histórica de la estratificación social* (Caracas: Instituto de Investigaciones Económicas y Sociales, 1969).

5. Both Octavio Paz and Carlos Fuentes have referred to the problem of the appropriation of a foreign language. See Carlos Fuentes, *La nueva novela hispanoamericana* (Mexico: Joaquín Mortiz, 1969).

6. ["Los Podestá" was a circus family that travelled between Argentina and Uruguay responsible for staging theatrical performances of popular plays.]

7. [Rama is probably alluding to Manuel González Prada's book *Ortometría: Apuntes para una rítimica* (Lima: Universidad Nacional Mayor de San Marcos, 1977).]

8. See "On Literary Evolution" in Yuri Tynianov, *Permanent Evolution: Selected Essays on Literature, Theory and Film* (Boston: Academic Studies Press, 2019), 267–82.

9. See Eliseo Verón, ed., *El proceso ideológico* (Buenos Aires: Tiempo Contemporáneo, 1971); Colloque de Cluny, *Litterature et ideologies* (Paris: Nouvelle Critique, 1971); and Lucio Collettti, *Ideología e societá* (Bari: Laterza, 1969).

10. Cintio Vitier, "Los *Versos sencillos*," in *Temas martianos* (Havana: Biblioteca Nacional José Martí, 1969).

11. In particular with his main work, *The Philosophy of Symbolic Forms*, trans. Ralph Mannheim (New Haven, CT: Yale University Press, 1955), but also in his partial studies, like *Antropología filosófica* (Mexico: Fondo de Cultura Económica, 1970) or *Mito y lenguaje* (Buenos Aires: Galatea-Nueva Visión, 1959). We should also consider the contributions of Claude Lévi-Strauss regarding the transposition of psychic patterns like those studied in "The Effectiveness of Symbols" in *Structural Anthropology*, trans. Monique Layton (Chicago: University of Chicago Press, 1983).

12. Octavio Paz, "Prólogo," in *Poesía en movimiento* (Mexico: Siglo XX, 1966).

13. [Esteban Echeverría (1805–1851), Argentine Romantic writer, author of *The Captive*.]

14. [Pedro Henríquez Ureña (1884–1946), Dominican literary critic, author of *Literary currents in Hispanic America* (Cambridge, MA: Harvard University Press, 1945).]

15. Luis Alberto Sánchez, *Balance y liquidación del Novecientos*, 3rd ed. (Lima: Universidad Nacional Mayor de San Marcos, 1968).

16. Multiple studies exist about Spanish American cultural dependency and the function of the writer, consistent with the sociology of the writer, but there are no contributions about the problem of "writing" in situations of dependency. In the journal *Casa de las Américas*, La Habana, nos. 45 and 47 [1967–1968], one can find abundant material. A good debate about different theses is found in Alfredo Chacón's book *Contra la dependencia* (Caracas: Síntesis Dosmil, 1973).

Chapter 7

1. See my essay, "Un proceso autonómico: de las literaturas nacionales a la literatura latinoamericana" in *Estudios filológicosy linguisticos: Homenaje a Rosenblat en sus 70 años* (Caracas: Instituto Pedagógico, 1974).

2. [Ricardo Rojas (1882–1957) was an Argentine intellectual, historian, literary scholar, and politician. As the first professor of Argentine literature at the University of Buenos Aires, Rojas is known for his studies on the history of Argentine literature. Pedro Henríquez Ureña (1884–1946) was a Dominican journalist and literary critic who lived and worked in Cuba, Mexico, Spain, the United States, and Argentina. Ureña's work centers on Latin American culture and history as well as grammar and linguistics. Alberto Zum Felde (1888–1976) was a Uruguayan poet and literary critic recognized for his work on the history of intellectual and literary trends in Uruguay. Mexican diplomat, intellectual, and essayist Alfonso Reyes (1889–1959) focused on Mexican identity and culture. He was the director of the Mexican Academy of the Spanish Language. Chilean novelist and literary critic Hernán Díaz Arrieta (1891–1984), who wrote under the pseudonym Alone, is known for his support of Chilean authors and his intellectual work on the history

of Chilean literature. Federico de Onís (1885–1966) was a Spanish intellectual and literary critic celebrated for his work on Latin American language and literature.]

3. [Juan Marinello (1898–1977) was a Cuban poet and essayist. Politically active with the Communist Party, Marinello's works focus on Cuban literature, in particular José Martí. Luis Alberto Sánchez (1900–1994) was a Peruvian intellectual and politician known for his political activism and his work on the indigenous communities in Peruvian literature. The Chilean Ricardo Latcham (1903–1965) also combined left-wing political activism with his interest in Chilean literary history.]

4. [Mariano Lorenzo Melgar Valdivieso (1790–1815) was a Peruvian poet who fought during the Peruvian War of Independence. Mariátegui studies him in his *Seven Interpretive Essays on Peruvian Reality*.]

5. See my essay, "Literary System and Social System" [chapter 6 in the present collection.]

6. Robert Escarpit, *Le littéraire et le social* (Paris: Flammarion, 1970), 10.

7. In his groundbreaking essay, Arnold Hauser had noted this situation, suggesting "it would have to portray the development of art by the use of cross-sections, and that would make people realize that in art, there are always several different traditions running parallel, and would dispose of the dogma that everything contemporary must be organically connected." "Educational Strata in the History of Art: Folk Art and Popular Art," in *The Philosophy of Art History* (Evanston, IL: Northwestern University Press, 1985), 280. This study speaks of the multiple difficulties of this project, recognizing the scarcity of information available, as much in establishing the distinction that he ensures (art of the people and popular art) as in reconstructing continuously a history of the first.

8. [All of these scholars compiled works focusing on folklore in Latin America: Juan Alfonso Carrizo (1895–1957) with Argentine oral poetry, Vicente T. Mendoza (1894–1964) with the Mexican corrido, Augusto Raúl Cortázar (1910–1974) with Argentine folk music, Luis da Camara Cascudo (1898–1986) with Brazilian folklore. Carlos H. Magis (1926–1988) was a Mexican literary critic known for his study of contemporary poets, most notably Octavio Paz.]

9. Roman Jakobson and Petr Bogatyrev, "Folklore as a Special Form of Creation," trans. John M. O'Hara, *Folklore Forum* 13, no. 1 (1980): 1–21.

10. Hauser, 279.

11. Abraham Moles, *Sociodynamique de la culture* (Paris: Mouton, 1967).

12. Amado Alonso, "Americanismo en la forma interior del lenguaje," in *Estudios lingüísticos: Temas hispanoamericanos* (Madrid: Gredos, 1953).

13. Alexander Lipschutz, *El indoamericanismo y el problema racial en las Américas* (Santiago de Chile: Nascimento, 1944).

14. [Eduardo Mallea (1903–1982) was an Argentine novelist, essayist, and cultural critic. His novels include *La bahía de silencio* (*The Bay of Silence*, 1940), *Las Águilas* (*The Eagles*, 1943), and *Todo verdor perecerá* (*All Green Shall Perish*, 1941). Eduardo Caballero Calderon (1910–1993) was a Colombian novelist and cultural

critic. His works include *El Cristo de espaldas* (*Christ on His Back*, 1952), *Siervo sin tierra* (1954), and *El buen salvaje* (*The Good Savage*, 1966).]

15. [Rudolf Grossmann, *Historia y problemas de la literatura latinoamericana* (Madrid: Revista de Occidente, 1972), 293.

16. See Antonio Candido's essay, "Manuel Antonio de Almeida: o romance en moto-continuo," in *Formaçao da literatura brasileira* (São Paulo: Livraria Martins, 1952).

17. Georg Lukács, *The Historical Novel*, trans. Hannah Mitchell and Stanley Mitchell (Lincoln: University of Nebraska Press, 1983).

18. Soares states:
"If here and there some sought after and well found vocabulary effects are suggested and from phraseological jousts, intention and excellent caricaturesque expressivity, as, among many cases, the Sermon of *Sé*, the two voices and languages, the mistranslation of some proverbs, paroxysms of judiciary and tabloid language, intentional popularisms and neologisms: if such searches and findings are frequent in the language of the Romantic, they also worked with a reasonable legacy of currency of the highest quality of classicism and respectable antiquity, which does not thus stop being abundant, nor stop being the same language, crude syntactic structures, with a popular origin and large popular circulation: confused forms of treatment, ambiguous relations. (Antonio Soares Amora, *O Romanticismo* [São Paulo: Editora Cultrix, 1973], 137.)

19. Alfredo Bosi, *Historia concisa da literatura brasileira* (São Paulo: Editora Cultrix, 1972).

20. Amado Alonso, "Gramática y estilos folclóricos en la poesía guachesca," in *Estudios lingüisticos: Temas hispanoamericanos* (Madrid: Gredos, 1953).

21. Lauro Ayestarán, *La primitiva poesía guachesca en el Uruguay* (Montevideo: El Siglo Ilustrado, 1950).

22. [In his edition of this text, Pablo Rocca adds the following: "This refers to José Artiga's decree, during his brief government after Argentina's independence, that instigated agrarian reform in the region known as the Banda Oriental at the time." See footnote in Rama, *Literatura, cultura, sociedad en América Latina* (Montevideo: Trilce, 2006), 140.]

23. [Francisco Acuña de Figueroa, *Diario histórico del sitio de Montevideo en los años 1812–1814*. Montevideo: Ministerio de educación y cultura, 1978.]

24. Ángel Rama, "El area cultural andina (hispanismo, mesticismo, indigenismo)," *Cuadernos Americanos* 23, no. 6 (1974). [It became chapter 3 in Rama's *Writing Across Cultures: Narrative Transculturation in Latin America*, ed. and trans. David Frye (Durham, NC: Duke University Press, 2012).]

25. [All of these painters and writers are known for promoting indigenous communities and themes in their works. José Sabogal (1888–1956) was a Peruvian painter and muralist. Oswaldo Guayasamín (1919–1999) was an Ecuadorian painter and sculptor. Enrique López Albújar (1872–1966) was a Peruvian writer

and poet. Jorge Icaza (1906–1978) was an Ecuadorian novelist and playwright. His novel *Huasipungo* (1934) is one of the most important documents within the indigenista canon.]

26. [*Colónida* was the name of a literary magazine in Peru at the beginning of the twentieth century, around which a literary movement emerged. It was a reaction against traditional literary norms and forms. Its founder was Abraham Valdelomar (1888–1919).]

Chapter 8

1. The title of Ezequiel Martínez Estrada's book, *Muerte y transfiguración de Martín Fierro* [*Martín Fierro's Death and Transfiguration*] (Mexico: Fondo de Cultura, 1948) is followed by a subtitle that announces its main purpose: "The essay of interpretation of Argentine life." Then, legitimately one sees it as the crowning achievement of an interpretative project whose previous steps were *Radiografía de la pampa* (1933) and *La cabeza de Goliat* (1940). It is between these two that one must place his essay-prologue to *Martín Fierro* (1938), which is the point of departure of his great posterior work.

2. Roman Jakobson, "La nouvelle poésie russe," in *Question de poétique* (Paris: Du Seuil, 1973), 15.

3. Of the abundant literature on the topic, I would recommend Ricardo Rodríguez Molas's *Historia social del gaucho* (Buenos Aires: Maru, 1968), which even though it contains ideas previously presented by the author, presents a more modern view than the one in Emilio Coni's *El gaucho: Argentina-Brasil-Uruguay* (Buenos Aires: Sudamericana, 1945) or that of Fernando Assuçao, *El gaucho* (Montevideo: Imprenta Nacional, 1963), focused on the eighteenth century.

4. Jorge Luis Borges, *Aspectos de la literatura gauchesca* (Montevideo: Número, 1950), reprinted in the second edition of *Discusión* (Buenos Aires: Emecé, 1955) with the title "La poesía gauchesca." Borges has repeated this idea in several texts that deal directly or indirectly with guachesque poetry, of which, a good example, in the same work and edition, is "The Argentine Writer and Tradition" [in Jorge Luis Borges, *Selected Non-Fictions* (New York: Viking, 1999), 420–27.]

5. Carlos Alberto Leumann, *La literatura gauchesca y la poesía gauchesca* (Buenos Aires: Raigal, 1953).

6. In *La primitiva poesía gauchesca en el Uruguay (1812–1838)* (Montevideo: El Siglo Ilustrado, 1950), Lauro Ayestarán reviewed this and other gauchesque topics that had become commonplace. For his part, Jorge Luis Borges, in *Aspectos de la literatura gauchesca*, establishes a distinction to which he returned in later texts. In *The "Martín Fierro,"* Buenos Aires, 1953, he says: "It is not, unlike its name suggests, a poetry made by gauchos; educated persons, gentlemen for Buenos Aires and Montevideo composed it." In "The Argentine Writer and Tradition" (incorporated

into *Discusión*, 1955), he says: "[gauchesque] poetry, which has produced—I hasten to repeat—admirable works, is as artificial as any other literary genre." Borges, *Selected Non-Fictions*, 421.

7. We suspect that some anonymous texts, like the famous "Cielito del blandengue retirado" from the Cisplatine period or the *décimas* of those who took part in the Great Siege of Montevideo collected by Francisco Acuña de Figueroa in *Diario histórico* [Montevideo: Biblioteca Artigas, 1978], were created by country people, or strictly by gauchos. Any of those examples shows an expressive quality that the learned Juan Baltazar Maziel in his "Canta un guaso" recognized as the first sample of "gauchesque literature." See Horacio Jorge Becco, *Antología de la poesía gauchesca* (Madrid: Aguilar, 1972). Among the few compilations of spontaneous songs to come out of the gauchos army that participated in the civil wars, it is worth mentioning the ones copied in Abdón Arózteguy, *La revolución oriental de 1870* (Buenos Aires: Félix Lajoune, 1889). They are persistently of lower expressive quality.

8. [In 1837, Marcos Sastre started a "Salón literario" where writers would meet to discuss the latest literary fashions and present their own works. They also debated cultural and political topics, as well as social and philosophical theories.]

9. Ángel Battistesa belligerently criticized this literary history commonplace in his essay "José Hernández" in *Historia de la literatura Argentina*, by Rafael Alberto Arrieta (Buenos Aires: Peuser, 1949), 123–259. The documentation he presents, however, corroborates the marginalized position in which contemporary cultured writers placed even authors like José Hernández, a journalist, politician, and, in addition, member of parliament.

10. Juan Carlos Ghiano, who also insists on identifying the gauchesque poets as writers coming from cities, adds: "Hidalgo resembles more the pseudo-classical poets of *La Lyra* than to payadores mentioned in his similes." Ghiano, "Bartolomé Hidalgo entre los poetas de mayo" in *Algunos aspectos de la cultura literaria de mayo* (Buenos Aires: Universidad Nacional de la Plata, 1961).

11. José Hernández, *El Gaucho Martín Fierro: A Bilingual Edition*, trans. C. E. Ward (Albany: State University of New York Press, 1967), 20.

12. I have studied the workings of literary sequences and levels, with their peculiar structure of producers, public, and internal communications in "Sistema literario y sistema social en Hispanoamérica" in *Literatura y praxis en América Latina* (Caracas: Monte Ávila, 1975). [Included in the present volume as "Literary System and Social System in Spanish America."]

13. Among the modern studies about the cultural problematic of the period of River Plate independence, interesting information can be found in Raúl J. Catagnino, *Milicia literaria de mayo* (Buenos Aires: Nova, 1960); and *Algunos aspectos de la cultura literaria de mayo* (Buenos Aires: Universidad Nacional de La Plata, 1961). On the relationship between writer and public at the beginning of the Romantic period, one can consult the chapter "El público de nuestros mejores libros" in *Sociología del público*, by Adolfo Prieto (Buenos Aires: Leviatán, 1956);

and Félix Weinberg's excellent introduction to *El Salón Literario* (Buenos Aires: Librería Hachette, 1958). With respect to the concrete situation of the poet and the gauchesque genre, Jorge B. Rivera, *La primitiva literatura gauchesca* (Buenos Aires: Jorge Álvarez Editor, 1968) is indispensable.

14. Roman Jakobson, "Linguistics and Poetics" in *Twentieth-Century Literary Theory*, ed. K. M. Newton (London: Palgrave, 1997), 71–77.

15. [Rama is translating from the French edition of Julia Kristeva's *Semeiotike*. The English version says, "Literary scholarship is one branch of the study of ideologies [which] . . . embraces all areas of man's ideological creativity." Quoted by Julia Kristeva, in *Desire in Language: A Semiotic Approach to Literature and Art*, ed. Leon S. Ruidiez, trans. Thomas Gora, Alice Jardine, and Leon S. Roudiez (New York: Columbia University Press, 1980), 73.]

16. Ricardo Rojas, *Historia de la literatura argentina: Los gauchescos*, vol. 2 (Buenos Aires: Guillermo Kraft, 1960), 403.

17. Jorge Luis Borges and Bioy Casares say that "toward mid-nineteenth century, gauchos in these republics were not exotic characters; it was difficult, almost impossible, not to know who they were," preface to *Poesía gauchesca*, vol. 1 (México: Fondo de Cultura Económica, 1955), viii. The gauchesque poets had a different view since the middle of the century. They never stopped repeating that the gaucho was about to disappear, being almost unknown for their countrymen, more exactly, for the upper urban class that was leading the country. The latter replaced real knowledge with stereotypes (debased or beautified, depending on the case) like those Juan Manuel Blanes employed in his genre painting.

18. Quoted in J. Caillet Bois, "Hilario Ascasubi," in *Historia de la literatura argentina*, by Rafael Alberto Arrieta (Buenos Aires: Peuser, 1949), 79.

19. Juan María Gutiérrez, "La literatura de mayo" in *Los poetas de la revolución* (Buenos Aires: Academia Argentina de Letras, 1941), 11. The cultured class never had doubts about the *usefulness* of gauchesque poetry to transmit information to the illiterate population and to guide them ideologically during the civil war period. Leaders and politicians and even caudillos did not have any doubts either, as is exemplified by the professional link between Hilario Ascasubi and Urquiza. I suspect that something similar must have happened in the case of Luis Pérez and many of the verse-makers of the conflict between unitarios and federales. Hence the importance of José Hernández's *Martín Fierro*, in which the poet occupies again, like genre founder Hidalgo once did, the function of interpreter of the helpless masses' demands to the authorities at the time.

20. Lauro Ayestarán, *La primitiva poesía gauchesca en el Uruguay* (Montevideo: El Siglo Ilustrado, 1950).

21. Rama, "Condicionamientos sociales de las formas literarias en la literatura de la emancipación," presented at the Fifteenth Congreso Iberoamericano de Literatura (which took place in Lima, August 1971) in *Literatura de la emancipación hispanoamericana y otros ensayos* (Lima: Universidad Mayor de San Marcos, 1972)

and republished in the volume *Los gauchipolíticos rioplatenses: Literatura y sociedad* (Buenos Aires: Calicanto, 1976).

22. Bernardo Prudencio Berro, *Escritos selectos* (Montevideo: Biblioteca Artigas, 1966).

23. "La sexta lectura de Lugones, 'El linaje de Hércules' " in *El payador*, by Leopoldo Lugones (Buenos Aires: Ediciones Centurión, 1961), with preliminary comments by Leopoldo Lugones's son.

24. Darcy Ribeiro, *Las Américas y la civilización*, 2nd ed. (Buenos Aires: Centro Editor de América Latina, 1972).

25. On the argument about the genre, see Jaime Alazraki's essay "El género literario del *Martín Fierro*," *Revista Iberoamericana* 40, no. 87–88 (April–Sept 1974): 433–58.

26. Pedro Henríquez Ureña, *Las corrientes literarias en la América Hispánica* (Mexico: Fondo de Cultura Económica, 1949).

27. Ángel Rosenblat, *Lengua literaria y lengua popular en América* (Caracas: Cuaderno del Instituto de Filología Andrés Bello, 1969), 23. Later, he points out that "America after independence has been more purist than Spain on matters of language, and academic authority had more weight there than in the metropolis." Rosenblat, *Lengua literaria*, 47–48.

28. This is the classification Horacio Jorge Becco employs for his *Antología de la poesía gauchesca* (Madrid: Aguilar, 1972) distributing the poems he selected into two sections, titled "Gauchesque poetry in rural language" and "Gauchesque poetry in general language."

29. Estrada, *Muerte y transfiguración*, 2:427.

30. "Cuatro palabras de conversación con los lectores," preface to Hernández, *La vuelta de Martín Fierro*.

31. In Félix Weinberg, ed., *El Salón Literario* (Buenos Aires: Hachette, 1958), 186. Florencio Valencia establishes a rigid distinction between ideas and language: "I do not agree that because we are reading in Castilian our spirit will be influenced by ideas from Spanish authors. I believe that only those who lack judgement and *discernment run that risk, but not those who read, reflect and choose distinguishing between the good and the bad.*"

32. Rosenblat, *Lengua literaria*, 24.

33. In Weinberg, ed., *El Salón Literario*, 145. Gutiérrez's discourse bears the title "Fisonomía del saber español: Cuál debe ser entre nosotros."

34. In Weinberg, ed., *El Salón Literario*, 196.

35. Amado Alonso, *Estudios lingüísticos: Temas hispanoamericanos* (Madrid: Gredos, 1953), 439.

36. On the distance between a gaucho language and gauchesque poetry language, see chapter "El habla del paisano" in Estrada, *Muerte y transfiguración*, vol. 2, "Las perspectivas," fifth part; José Pedro Rona, "La reproducción del lenguaje hablado en la literatura gauchesca," *Revista Iberoamericana de Literatura* (Montevideo)

4, no. 5 (1962); chapters 7 ("La gauchesca y el 'Martín Fierro'") and 8 ("La lengua poética") in Emilio Carilla, *La creación del 'Martín Fierro'* (Madrid: Gredos, 1973).

37. Quoted in Coni, *El gaucho*, 177. [We have used Stephen Paullada's translation of this passage in "Some Observations on the Word Gaucho," *New Mexico Quarterly* 31.2 (1961): 152.]

38. Alonso, "Gramática y estilo folklóricos en la poesía gauchesca" in *Estudios lingüísticos*.

39. Estrada, *Muerte y transfiguración*, 425.

40. Alonso, "Americanismo en la forma interior del lenguaje" in *Estudios lingüísticos*, 61–83.

41. Louis Hjelmslev, *Prolegómenos a una teoría del lenguaje* (Madrid: Gredos, 1971), chap. 13.

42. Alonso, "Americanismo en la forma interior del lenguaje," 154. [Alonso argues that gauchos divide the vegetable world they see above ground into these four groups. In the 1971 edition that we consulted the quote appears on page 69. See note 40.]

43. Edward Sapir, "The Status of Linguistics as Science," in *Culture, Language and Personality: Selected Essays*, ed. David G. Mandelbaum (Berkeley: University of California Press, 1949), 69. The empirical application of this idea can be followed in B. L. Whorf's *Language, Thought, and Reality* (Cambridge, MA: MIT Press, 1957). There is a discussion about this point in Adam Schaff, *Langage et connaissance* (Paris: Anthropos, 1969).

44. Basil Bernstein, "Social Class, Language and Socialization," in *Class, Codes and Control: Theoretical Studies towards a Sociology of Language*, vol. 1 (New York: Routledge, 2003), 133.

45. See the entire third section, "Language in Social Strata and Sectors" in *Readings in the Sociology of Language*, ed. Joshua A. Fishman (The Hague: Mouton, 1972), especially the contributions by W. Labov ("The Reflection of Social Processes in Linguistic Structures") and by Roger Brown and Albert Gilman ("The Pronouns of Power and Solidarity").

46. Bernstein, "Social Class," 136.

47. Pier Paolo Pasolini made the same observations with respect to the Gospel According to Matthew and tried to apply them systematically to the syntax of his latest films.

48. She says: "In reality *Versos sencillos* are truncated décimas; décimas with the link between the two central verses suppressed to leave them converted into cuartetas revealing not a visible link but a transcendental one." *Temas martianos* (Havana: Biblioteca Nacional José Martí, 1969).

49. Antonio Machado, "From My Notebook," in *Border of a Dream: Selected Poems of Antonio Machado*, trans. Willis Barnstone (Port Townsend, WA: Copper Canyon Press, 2003).

50. Greimas, "To reconcile the two types of approaches, to read a poetic text both as taxon and as story (as a group of symmetries that appear on several levels and whose value resides essentially in being places of transformation) seems to characterize at this moment a type of strategy for deciphering poetic objects." *Essais de sémiotique poétique* (Paris: Larousse, 1972), 18. In the same preface, Greimas comments: "In large part, the options for the organization of a poetic text are determined, in equal measure, by two parallel discourses, in which expression restricts content, or the other way around."

51. In Manuel Mújica Láinez, *Vidas del gallo y el pollo* (Buenos Aires: Centro Editor de América Latina, 1966), 80–81. It was not always like that: the definition does not apply to the works of Lussich, for example, where there are various characters of equal importance, who are recounting alternatively their lives and enter a debate where they defend diverse political positions, whose importance is equivalent.

52. In Ayestarán, *La primitiva poesía*.

53. Jorge Luis Borges and Adolfo Bioy Casares, *Poesía gauchesca* (Mexico: Fondo de Cultura Económica, 1955), xx.

54. Jorge Luis Borges, *Discusión* (Buenos Aires: Emecé, 1955).

55. In "Linguistics and Poetics" Jakobson mentions Sol Saporta's thesis about the emotional differences of the text that are not linguistic elements "attributable to the delivery of the message and not to the message." See Saporta, "The Application of Linguistics to the Study of Poetic Language" in *Style in Language*, ed. Thomas Sebeok (Cambridge, MA: MIT Press, 1960), 88.

56. In "Literature and Signification," in *Critical Essays*, trans. Richard Howard (Evanston, IL: Northwestern University Press, 1972).

57. Arnold Hauser, *The Philosophy of Art History* (London: Routledge, 1959), 88.

58. See Fermín Chávez, *Poesía rioplatense en estilo gaucho* (Buenos Aires: Ediciones Culturales Argentina, 1962); Domingo A. Caillava, *Historia de la literatura gauchesca en el Uruguay* (Montevideo: Claudia García, 1945).

59. A vision of this homogeneous horizon of the "school" in contrast to the regime of selection in the anthologies of fundamental works is present in Eneida Sansone de Martínez's study, *La imagen en la poesía gauchesca* (Montevideo: Facultad de Humanidades y Ciencias, 1962), which employs indistinctively examples from different artistic sources, although all of them from the same gauchesque genre. Another observation to take into account about the dimensions of the production, in comparison to the more reduced field studied by critics, can be seen in Juan María Gutiérrez. In "La literatura de mayo," he points out that there is another source of cielitos, which are widely diffused among the people who are less appreciated by educated people because they are too explicit. Gutiérrez comments: "They are not licentious nor cynical; but they call mundane things by their name and stay away from the artifice of metaphors and this gives their expression a very *graphic* accent." The well-known prudish Spanish American character has rejected

the pornographic aspect of the gauchesque, which has been transmitted orally and never been registered in books.

60. Jakobson [and Bogatyrev] in "Folklore as a Special Form of Creation," trans. John M. O'Hara, *Folklore Forum* 13, no. 1 (1980): 1–21: "The existence of a work of folklore requires a group to accept and sanction it for its continuation" (7). "In folklore the relationship between the work of art on the one hand, and its objectivization—i.e., the so-called variants of this work as performed by different individuals—on the other, is completely analogous to the relationship between langue and parole" (9). "Oral poetic creation remains collective even in the cases of separation between producer and consumer, except that then the collective aspect takes on specific qualities" (19).

61. Indeed, Bally says: "If one is asked to explain how the language of a specific social group usually reflects thought, which is a modest request, this is like asking for the psychological portrait of this social group, something we have barely begun to work on." *Traité de stylistique* (Paris: Klincksiek, 1951), 20. The psychological character of Bally's proposition and the long polemic about the fundamentals of stylistics can be followed in Pierre Guiraud and Pierre Kuentz's *La stylistique* (Paris: Klincksieck, 1970) and the excellent summary by Alicia Yllera, *Estilística, poética y semiótica literaria* (Madrid: Alianza Universitaria, 1974). At the margin of any purely linguistic approach (Bruneau) stylistics (be it intuitive or scientific, idealist or positivist) has been developing as it is applied to literary texts. Like Louis Hjelmslev recognizes in his *Prolegomena to a Theory of Language* (Madison: University of Wisconsin Press, 1969) connotative semiotics ("whose content plane is a semiotic," 114) incorporate different concepts of style, language, tone, and physiognomies: "Stylistic form, style, value-style, medium, tone, vernacular, national language, regional language, and physiognomy are solidary categories, so that any function of denotative language must be defined in respect to them all at the same time" (116). However, the modern trends in stylistics, part of a generalized abandonment of historical criteria and of diachronic views of literature, has been replaced with analysis of the workings of the synchronic system and, even more restrictively, of the individual text, abandoning the idea of style as a school, movement, and epoch and instead has focused on author's individual styles, or more specifically, on a work's style. The bibliography on this topic is immense. The most effective contribution might be Michael Riffaterre's *Essais de stylistique structurale* (Paris: Flammarion, 1971), especially because he replaces the criteria of "deviation" from linguistic norm with a study of "context," which is not only linguistic but also literary—the work thus emerges from a rich and codified literary context. See, especially, his chapter "L'étude stylistique des formes littéraires conventionelles" where he detects the possibility of creatively employing the highly conventional style of a period: "Literary conventions are no more reproachable or arbitrary than the laws that govern a language. In fact, these rules, this rhetoric are not artificial; they are a grammar and it depends only on the poet to use conventional things naturally or conventionally." Riffaterre, *Essais*, 202.

62. Henri Meschonnic, *Pour la Poétique* (Paris: Gallimard, 1970), 42. "The system of language is based on an established code, handed down. The system of literary works too. But in contrast to language, which is characterized by stability, a relative community of different values, the value of the literary work depends only on the *conflict* between the inner necessity of the individual *message* (which is creativity) and the *code* (genre, language, style of an era) common to a company or to a group, a code which is the ensemble of old, existing values, "commonplaces." We cannot study the message without the system, nor the system without its message (this is the error of those who today define . . . poetry only on a syntactic level). All this places the problem of the existence of value in the code (of the work, in, for example, the "genre") and its approach.

63. Hauser, *The Philosophy of Art History*, 97.

Chapter 9

1. In José María Castellet's "La actual literatura latinoamericana vista desde España," a paper presented in Havana in 1968 and published in *Panorama de la actual literatura latinoamericana* (Madrid: Fundamentos, 1971), the author talks about the "chaotic knowledge about Latin American literature" in Spain. An attempt at re-organization is visible in Rafael Conte's book, *Lenguaje y violencia: Introducción a la nueva novela hispanoamericana* (Madrid: Al–Borak, 1972), and in José María Valverde's *Historia de la literatura latinoamericana* (Barcelona: Planeta 1974).

2. [Emilio Díaz Valcarcel (1929–2015), Puerto Rican novelist and playwright known for his novel *Schemes in the Month of March* (1972).]

3. [Salvador Garmendia (1928–2001), Venezuelan author.]

4. [*Adan Buenosayres* (1948) is a novel by Leopoldo Marchal that parodies the Argentine avant-garde of the 1920s, following the protagonist—an avant-garde writer—through three days of a metaphysical journey.]

5. Tomás Eloy Martínez, "América: la gran novela," *Primera Plana* 5, no. 234, Buenos Aires, 20–26 June 1967.

6. Information about the presentations can be found in the art pages of *El Nacional* newspaper, Caracas, July and August 1972, especially July 29, and in the issues 14 (August 1972) and 16 (December 1972) of *Zona Franca*.

7. The first diary entry of *El zorro de arriba y el zorro de abajo* appeared in *Amaru* 6, April/June 1968, Lima. Cortázar answered in *Life en español* (New York, April 7, 1969) and José María Arguedas replied in his article "Inevitable comentario a unas ideas de Julio Cortázar" in *El Comercio* (Lima, June 1, 1969).

8. The documents related to this polemic have now been collected in Oscar Collazos, Julio Cortazar, and Mario Vargas Llosa, *Literatura en la revolución y revolución en la literatura* (México: Siglo XXI, 1970).

9. The polemic was published as *Gabriel García Márquez y la problemática de la novela* (Buenos Aires: Corregidor–Marcha, 1974).

10. Mario Vargas Llosa, *Zona Franca* 3, no. 14, August 1972.

11. In José Miguel Oviedo, "Cortázar a cinco rounds" *Marcha* (Montevideo) 34, no. 1634, March 2, 1973). Also in Ernesto González Bermejo, *Conversaciones con Cortázar* (Barcelona: Edhasa, 1978).

12. [David Viñas (1927–2011), Argentine cultural critic, playwright, and novelist.]

13. [Jules Regis Debray (1940–), French philosopher who taught at the University of Havana (Cuba) in the late 1960s and was later an associate of Che Guevara when Guevara was killed in Bolivia. Debray was also linked with Salvador Allende's government in Chile after he sought refuge there upon his release from prison in Bolivia.]

14. José María Castellet in "La actual literatura" includes the search for identity as one of the four characteristics of the new Latin American novel.

15. José Donoso, *The Boom in Spanish American Letters: A Personal History*, trans. Gregory Kolovakos (New York: Columbia University Press, 1977).

16. Donoso, *The Boom in Spanish America Letters*, 2–3.

17. [Ciro Alegría (1909–1967), Peruvian novelist and politician most known for his novel *Broad and Alien is the World* (1941). Marco Denevi (1922–1998), Argentine journalist and author known for his works *Rosaura a las diez* (1955) and *Secret Ceremony* (1960), the latter of which was turned into a 1968 film starring Elizabeth Taylor, Mia Farrow, and Robert Mitchum.]

18. Carlos Barral, *Años de penitencia* (Barcelona: Seix Barral, 1975).

19. Barral, 139.

20. *Zona Franca*, issues previously quoted.

21. Manuel Pedro González, "Crisis de la novela en América" in *Revista Nacional de Cultura* (Caracas, 1962) 150.

22. Luis Alberto Sánchez, "La novela de Hispanoamérica en el contexto de la internacional" in *Coloquio de la novela hispanoamericana* (Mexico: Tezontle, 1967). The volume is a collection of presentations for a conference that took place at Washington University in 1966. Ivan Schulman, Juan Loveluck, and Fernando Alegría participated and their positions were very different from Manuel Pedro González's.

23. Sánchez, "La novela de Hispanoamérica," 63.

24. Carlos Fuentes, *La nueva novela hispanoamericana* (Mexico: Joaquín Mortiz, 1969); Mario Vargas Llosa, "Novela primitiva y novela de creación en América Latina" in *Revista de la Universidad de México* 23, no. 10, 1969. More legitimate is Alejo Carpentier's opposition to the regionalist novel in several texts (see his *Tientos y diferencias* [Mexico: Universidad Nacional Autónoma, 1964]), because being older he grew up during the period where it was the dominant mode and constructed his original narrative as a rejection of it.

25. [These are all novels from the late 1920s and early 1930s: Mario de Andrade (Brazil) *Macunaíma* (1928), Macedonio Fernández (Argentina) *Papeles de recienvenido* (1929), Miguel Ángel Asturias (Guatemala) *Leyendas de Guatemala*

(1930), Vicente Huidobro (Chile) and Hans Arp (France/Germany) *Tres inmensas novellas* (1931), Gilberto Owen (Mexico) *Novela como nube* (1928).]

26. Luis Harss, *Los nuestros*, 3rd ed. (Buenos Aires: Sudamericana, 1969); and Luis Harss and Barbara Dohmann, *Into the Mainstream: Conversations with Latin American Writers* (New York: Harper and Row, 1967).

27. Harss, *Los nuestros*, 463.

28. Donoso, *The Boom in Spanish American Letters*, 108.

29. Alejo Carpentier, *Afirmación literaria americanista* (*Encuentro con Alejo Carpentier*) (Caracas: Ediciones de la Facultad de Humanidades y Educación, 1978).

30. One can read negative critiques in José Blanco Amor, *El final del boom literario* (Buenos Aires: Cervantes, 1976), a collection of articles previously published in *La Nación* newspaper from Buenos Aires. A positive evaluation is found in Emir Rodríguez Monegal, *El boom de la novela latinoamericana* (Caracas: Tiempo Nuevo, 1972). A political–social evaluation is found in Jaime Mejía Duque's chapter, "El boom de la narrativa latinoamericana," in *Narrativa y neocoloniaje en América Latina* (Buenos Aires: Crisis, 1974).

31. [Luis Spota (1925–1985), Mexican writer, boxing official, and film director. Mario Benedetti (1920–2009), Uruguayan novelist and poet. Silvana Bullrich (1915–1990), Argentine novelist, translator, screenwriter, and academic. Manuel Scorza (1928–1983), Peruvian novelist, poet, and political activist known for the Silent War series of novels that begins with *Drums for Rancas* (1970). Miguel Otero Silva (1908–1985), Venezuelan writer, journalist, and politician. Corín Tellado (1927–2009), prolific Spanish author of romance books. Tellado published more than four thousand titles. Henri Charrière (also known as Papillon) (1906–1973), French writer whose autobiography *Papillon* (1970) was an international bestseller.]

32. "La violencia: miradas opuestas," *La Nación* (Buenos Aires), August 6, 1972, sec. 3, 2.

33. [José María Vargas Vila (1860–1933), Colombian modernista writer.]

34. [Hugo Wast (1883–1962), Argentine novelist and scriptwriter. Roberto Arlt (1900–1942), Argentine journalist, novelist, and playwright. Arlt is known for his novels *Mad Toy* (1926) and *The Seven Madmen* (1929).]

35. Donoso, *The Boom in Spanish American Letters*, 109.

36. Fernando Tola de Habich and Patricia Grieve, *Los españoles y el boom* (Caracas: Tiempo Nuevo, 1972).

37. John S. Brushwood, *The Spanish American Novel: A Twentieth Century Survey* (Austin: University of Texas Press, 1975).

38. Brushwood, *The Spanish American Novel*, 211.

39. Martínez, "El boom: esplendor y después," *El Nacional* (Caracas), September 3, 1978.

40. [Osvaldo Soriano (1943–1997), Argentine author. Griselda Gambaro (1928), Argentine novelist and playwright Antonio Skármeta (1940), Chilean novelist and playwright best known for his novel *Burning Patience* (1985). Sergio Ramírez (1942–),

Nicaraguan writer and politician, serving as vice president of Nicaragua under Daniel Ortega from 1985–1990. Luis Britto García (1940–), Venezuelan novelist and playwright known for his works *Rajatabla* (1970) and *Aprapalabra* (1979). Héctor Manjarrez (1945), Mexican novelist who was part of the *Onda* movement known for his works *Lapsus: algunos actos fallidos* (1971) and *No todos los hombres son románticos* (1983). Luis Rafael Sánchez (1936), Puerto Rican novelist and playwright known for his play *Macho Camacho's Beat* (1976). Jorge Aguilar Mora (1946–), Mexican academic and novelist. Norberto Fuentes (1943–), Cuban writer. Plinio Apuleyo Mendoza (1932–), Colombian novelist. Lisandro Chávez Alfaro (1929–2006), Nicaraguan novelist and poet. Hector Libertella (1945–), Argentine novelist.]

41. Information was provided by Francisco Porrúa in a personal letter to the author of this article, dated Sept 6, 1972. Porrúa was the architect of the transformation of Sudamericana from an international publisher to a national and Latin American one in the 1960s.

42. Same letter previously mentioned.

43. A longer and at times more diverse list is given by John Brushwood, *Spanish American Novel*, 337–51.

44. Carpentier, "Problemática del tiempo y del idioma en la moderna novela latinoamericana," *Escritura* 1, no. 2 (July–December 1976).

45. [H. A. Murena (1923–1975), Argentine intellectual, poet, and translator.]

46. [All of these figures were instrumental in the intellectual life of their country in their lifetimes: Dominto Faustino Sarmiento (1811–1888) as an intellectual and eventual president of Argentina, Manuel González Prada (1844–1918) as a social critic and director of the National Library in Peru, and José Vasconcelos (1882–1959) as Secretary of Education in Mexico.]

47. [Fernando Solanas (1936–2020) was instrumental in the Third Cinema movement in Spanish America. With Octavio Getino, he directed *The Hour of the Furnaces* (1968), a lengthy experimental political documentary that focuses on neocolonialism and violence in Latin America.]

48. [Arturo Uslar Pietri (1907–2001), Venezuelan intellectual, novelist, and television producer.]

Chapter 10

1. José Martí, "Cartas de verano: En las montañas" in *Obras completas*, vol. 12 (Havana: Editorial Nacional de Cuba, 1964), 441. For the place of Martí's articles in different editions of his complete works, see Carlos Ripoll, *Índice universal de la obra de José Martí* (New York: Eliseo Torres and Sons, 1971).

2. Martí, prologue to *Versos Sencillos: Simple Verses*, trans. Manuel A. Tellechea (Houston, TX: Arte Público Press, 1997), 13. [The poems by Martí analyzed in this chapter, with the exception of "Dos milagros," come from this translation of *Simple Verses*.]

3. [Martí, *Versos Sencillos*, 15.]
4. [Martí, 13.]
5. [Frederic Nietzsche, *The Nietzsche Reader*, eds. Keith Ansell Pearson and Duncan Large (Malden, MA: Wiley Blackwell, 2006), 337.]
6. Cintio Vitier and Fina García Marruz, *Temas martianos* (Havana: Biblioteca Nacional José Martí, 1969), 167. It is helpful to note that this is an exceptional book within the abundant (and many times tedious) bibliography about Martí.
7. See K. Kosik, *Dialéctica de lo concreto* (México: Grijalbo, 1967); and Terry Eagleton's insightful book, *Criticism and Ideology* (Norfolk, CT: Verso Editions, 1978), chapters 2 and 3.
8. A summary of critical positions can be found in Mostafa Rejai's article "Ideology" in *Dictionary of the History of Ideas*, vol. 2, ed. Philip Wiener (New York: Charles Scribner's Sons, 1973).
9. This text by Martí serves as a description of the function of ideology at the time of poetic production: "Regarding poetics, understanding is not the principal thing, nor is memory, but rather a certain state of confused and tempestuous spirit in which the mind functions as a mere aid, placing and taking away what comes from outside it until it remains in music." "Francisco Sellén," in *Obras completas*, vol. 5 (Havana: Editorial de Ciencias Sociales, 1964), 190.
10. See Clifford Geertz's article, "Ideology as Cultural System" in *Ideology and Discontents*, ed. David E. Apter (New York: Free Press, 1964); and his book *The Interpretation of Cultures* (New York: Basic Books, 1973). In the application of the sociology of knowledge, see the classic essays by Karl Mannheim, *Ideology and Utopia*, trans. Louis Wirth and Edward Shils (New York: Harcourt Brace Jovanovich, 1985); and Arnold Hauser, *The Philosophy of Art History* (Evanston, IL: Northwestern University Press, 1985). Also note the excellent contributions of Eliseo Veron, *Conducta, estructura y comunicación*, 2nd ed. (Buenos Aires: Tiempo Contemporáneo, 1972); and *El proceso ideológico* (Buenos Aires: Tiempo Contemporáneo, 1971); Joseph Gabel, *La fausse conscience: essai sur la reification* (Paris: E. de Minuit, 1963); Nicos Poulantzas, *Pouvoir politique et clases sociales* (Paris: Maspero, 1968); and "Semiotica delle ideologie" in *Le forme del contenuto*, by Umberto Eco (Milan: Bompiani, 1972).
11. Robert Weimann is among the most recent to explore this problem. See Weimann, "French Structuralism and Literary History: Some Critiques and Reconsiderations," *New Literary History* 4 (1973): 437–69; Marc Zimmerman, "Exchange and Production: Structuralist and Marxist Approaches to Literary Theory," *Praxis* 4 (1978): 151–68. Within a wider framework, see the scientific research of Ilya Prigogine and Isabelle Stengers, *La Nouvelle Alliance* (Paris: Bibliothéque des Sciences Humaines, 1979).
12. [See Roland Barthes, "Literature and Signification," in *Critical Essays*, trans. Richard Howard (Evanston, IL: Northwestern University Press, 1972). Also mentioned in "The Literary System of Gauchesque Poetry."]

13. Martí, "Clubs y Libros. El Club de los trece . . ." in *Obras completas*, vol. 13 (Havana: Editorial de Ciencias Sociales, 1992), 458.

14. Cintio Vitier and Fina García Marruz, *Temas martianos* (Havana: Biblioteca Nacional José Martí, 1969), 163.

15. See Dorothy C. Clarke, "Redondilla and copla de arte menor," *Hispanic Review* 9, no. 4 (1941): 489–93.

16. Fina García Marruz, "Los versos de Martí" in *Revista de la Biblioteca Naiconal José Martí* 3, no. 10 (1968): 35–38, now in the volume *Temas Martianos*, 240–67.

17. See Noé Jitrik, *Las contradicciones del modernismo: Producción poética y situación social* (Mexico: El Colegio de México, 1978).

18. See D. C. Clarke, "Redondilla and copla de arte menor" and "Miscellaneous Strophe Forms in the Fifteenth Century Court Lyric," *Hispanic Review* 16, no. 2 (1948): 142–56.

19. The behavior signaled by the metric matrix has its canonical form in poems XX, XXIX, and XXXIX and shows irregularities in XII and XXV, through combinations of consonant with assonant rhymes. Poem XX, which is the first diptych written by Martí, if we accept that the book as we know it responds in chronological order to its composition, would seem to reveal a difficulty in accepting a uniform rhyme scheme; poem XXXV includes in the second stanza an assonant rhyme of the consonant rhyme in the first: ABBA/C(b)DDC(b).

20. See his essays about the reading of myths and the shamanic healing in *Structural Anthropology*, trans. Claire Jacobson and Brooke Grundfest Schoepf (New York: Basic Books, 2008).

21. Martí, "Dos milagros," in *Obras completas*, vol. 15 (Havana: Centro de Estudios Martianos, 2007), 168. www.josemarti.cu/obras-completas/tomo-15/.

22. See Claude Lévi-Strauss, *Introduction to the Work of Marcel Mauss*, trans. Felicity Baker (London: Routledge and Kegan Paul, 1987).

23. Gilles Deleuze, *The Logic of Sense*, ed. Constantin Bondas, trans. Mark Lester and Charles Stivale (New York: Columbia University Press, 1990); and *Difference and Repetition*, trans. Paul Patton (New York: Columbia University Press, 1994).

24. Michel Foucault, *Archeology of Knowledge*, trans. A. M. Sheridan Smith (New York: Routlegde, 1972), 15.

25. Martí, "Monumento a los peregrinos," in *Obras completas*, vol. 12 (Havana: Editorial Nacional de Cuba, 1964), 290.

26. Martí, *Obras completas*, vol. 21 (Havana: Editorial Nacional de Cuba), 387.

27. Federico de Onís, *España en América* (Río Piedras: Ediciones de la Universidad de Puerto Rico, 1955).

28. [See Rubén Darío, *Songs of Life and Hope* (Lewisburg, PA: Bucknell University Press, 2004), 54–60.]

29. [Rama is interpreting Martí's question, "¿Quién piensa en mí," as meaning both "Who thinks of me?" and "Who thinks inside of me?"]

30. [Deleuze, *The Logic of Sense*, 50–51.]

31. Martí, "Muerte de Emerson," in *Obras completas* vol. 9 (Havana: Centro de Estudios Martianos, 2004), 337. www.josemarti.cu/obras-completas/tomo-12/.

32. Claude Lévi-Strauss, *Introduction to the Works of Marcel Mauss*, trans. Felicity Baker (London: Routledge, 1987), 65. Regarding symbols in Martí's works, see Iván Schulman, *Símbolo y color en la obra de José Martí* (Madrid: Gredos, 1960).

33. See Giovanni Meo Zilio's excellent analysis in *De José Martí a Sabat Ercasty* (Montevideo: El Siglo Ilustrado, 1967), reproduced in *Anuario martiano* 2 (1970): 9–94.

34. Martí, "Clubs y Libros," 460.

35. "He does not force the comparison, and in truth does not compare, but says what he sees or remembers with a graphic and incisive complement, and confident of the general impression he is about to give, employs his skills, which he hides completely, in reproducing the elements of his painting with the same disorder that he observed in Nature." Martí, "El poeta Walt Whitman," in *Obras completas*, vol. 25 (Havana: Centro de Estudios Martianos, 2013), 260. www.josemarti.cu/obras-completas/tomo-25/.

36. Martí, "La exhibición de pintura del ruso Vereschagin . . ." in *Obras completas*, vol. 15 (Havana: Editorial Nacional de Cuba), 431.

37. [Words with *aguda* accents have the stress on the last syllable. Words with *grave* accents have the stress on the penultimate syllable.]

38. Martí, "Francisco Sellén," 191.

39. Martí, "La Revolución del trabajo. Grandes huelgas . . ." in *Obras completas*, vol. 23 (Havana: Centro de Estudios Martianos, 2011), 95. www.josemarti.cu/obras-completas/tomo-23/. In his article "Nueva York y el arte. Nueva exhibición de los pintores impresionistas," he points out that these artists pretend to "put on the canvas things with the same splendor and grandeur with which they appear in life," highlighting their tendency to "paint with fraternal tenderness and with brutal and sovereign anger the misery in which the poor live. These are the hungry ballerinas! There are the alcoholic workers! These are the dry mothers of the peasants! These are the perverted children of the wretched! There are the women of pleasure! This is how they are: shameless, pompous, hateful and brutal!" Martí, "Nueva York y el arte," in *Obras completas*, vol. 24 (Havana: Centro de Estudios Martianos, 2012), 94–95. www.josemarti.cu/obras-completas/tomo-24/. [Jean-François Millet (1814 1875) was a French realist painter known for his paintings of peasant farmers.]

40. Martí, "Coney Island" in *Obras completas*, vol. 9 (Havana: Centro de Estudios Martianos, 2004), 133–38. www.josemarti.cu/obras-completas/tomo-9/.

41. The summer in New York is evoked in "Por la bahía de Nueva York": "From one chimney to another, looking for less scorching bricks, the exhausted workers pass half undressed, like imps, hair tangled, mouth fallen, swearing and staggering, ridding themselves of the trickles of sweat with their hands as if they were unweaving their entrails." Children do not generate any less startling images:

"The little ears of girls do not have a drop of blood. There are mouths that are open wounds. Many are blind in one eye and many are mangy." Marti, "Por la bahía de Nueva York," in *Obras completas*, vol. 29 (Havana: Centro de Estudios Martianos, 2019), 135, 137. www.josemarti.cu/obras-completas/tomo-29/.

42. [Augusto Ferrán (1835–1880), Spanish Romantic poet and translator. Gustavo Adolfo Bécquer (1836–1870), influential Spanish Romantic poet.]

43. [The Spanish word *gozque* refers to a small dog and has the connotations of a dog that barks a lot. It can also be used similarly to the English word mongrel when referring to a dog.]

44. [*Les Chants de Maldoror* by Lucien Isidore Ducasse is about a figure who renounces morality.]

45. [Juan Antonio Pérez Bonalde (1846–1892), Venezuelan poet and translator.]

46. Martí, "La exhibición de pinturas del ruso Vereschagin . . ." 431.

47. Ernst Cassirer, *The Philosophy of Symbolic Forms*, vol. 2 (New Haven, CT: Yale University Press, 1955), 31.

48. [Rubén Darío, *Selected Poems of Rubén Darío*, ed. and trans. Alberto Acereda and Will Derusha (Lewisburg, PA: Bucknell University Press), 165.]

49. Martí, "Muerte de Emerson," 330–32.

50. Karl Marx, *Grundrisse: Introduction to the Critique of Political Economy* (New York: Vintage, 1973). 85.

51. Marx, *The German Ideology* in *The Marx-Engels Reader*, 2nd ed., ed. Robert Tucker (New York: W. W. Norton), 154.

52. Marx, *Grundrisse*, 83.

53. Martí, "Tipos y costumbres bonaerenses," in *Obras completas*, vol. 20 (Havana: Editorial Trópico, 1939), 199.

54. Martí, "El arte en los Estados Unidos," in *Obras completas*, vol. 28 (Havana: Centro de Estudios Martianos, 2018), 27. www.josemarti.cu/obras-completas/tomo-28/.

55. I analyzed this in "La dialéctica de la modernidad en José Martí," in *Estudios martianos* (San Juan: Editorial Universitaria, 1974), 129–97.

56. [Poem XLII—"Mucho señora daría / por tender sobre tu espalda / tu cabellera bravía / tu cabellera de gualda."]

57. Martí, "Impressions of America (by a Very Fresh Spaniard) II," in *Obras completas*, vol. 7 (Havana: Centro de Estudios Martianos, 2003), 140. www.josemarti.cu/obras-completas/tomo-7/.

58. Martí, "Impressions of America," 140–41.

59. Martí, "Suma de sucesos," in *Obras completas*, vol. 17 (Havana: Centro de Estudios Martianos, 2010), 60–75. www.josemarti.cu/obras-completas/tomo-17/.

60. Martí, *Selected Writings*, ed. and trans. Esther Allen (New York: Penguin Books, 2002), 62.

61. Martí, "Tipos y costumbres bonaerenses," 192.

62. [José Enrique Rodó (1871–1917), Uruguayan intellectual most noted for his essay "Ariel" (1900).]

63. [Dioscuri refers to the twin brothers Castor and Pollux from Greek mythology. They were reunited in the sky after Castor's death and are considered patrons of athletes and sailors.]

64. José Enrique Rodó, *The Motives of Proteus*, trans. Angel Flores (New York: Bretano's, 1928), 1–2.

65. Martí, "Muerte de Emerson," 330.

66. ["esa nube que se va" to "esa nube que's Eva."]

67. The enshrinement of Martí as hero can explain the scarcity of psychoanalytical readings of his works. Very recently José A. Portuondo censured the sickly sweet biography *Martí el Apóstol* by Jorge Mañach for dedicating so much space to the love life of the writer (*Martí y el diversionismo ideológico* [Havana, 1974].)

68. Gilles Deleuze and Félix Guattari, *Anti-Oedipus: Capitalism and Schizophrenia*, trans. Robert Hurley, Mark Seem, and Helen Lane (Minneapolis: University of Minnesota Press, 1983).

69. [Friedrich Nietzsche, "Fragment 75," in *Beyond Good and Evil*, eds. Rolf-Peter Horstmann and Judith Norman, trans. Judith Norman (Cambridge: Cambridge University Press, 2002), 60.]

70. Marx, *A Contribution to the Critique of Political Economy*, trans. S. W. Ryazanskaya (New York: International Publishers, 1970), 125.

71. Martí, "Informe a la Conferencia Monetaria de Washington," in *Obras completas*, vol. 22 (Havana: Editorial Trópico, 1940), 16.

72. The same year in which Martí wrote *Simple Verses* saw the scandalous sale of a bank ("La política internacional de los Estados Unidos," in *Obras completas* vol. 12 [Havana: Editorial Nacional de Cuba, 1964], 383–90. Also, motivated by the Panic of 1884, "Un domingo de junio," in *Obras completas*, vol. 17 (Havana: Centro de Estudios Martianos, 2010), 224–35. www.josemarti.cu/obras-completas/tomo-17/; and "La procession moderna. Una columna de veinte mil trabajadores . . ." in *Obras completas*, vol. 17 (Havana: Centro de Estudios Martianos, 2010), 236–49. www.josemarti.cu/obras-completas/tomo-17/.

73. Martí, "Un Congreso antropológico en los Estados Unidos," in *Obras completas*, vol. 29 (Havana: Centro de Estudios Martianos, 2019), 81. www.josemarti.cu/obras-completas/tomo-29/.

74. Martí, "Cartas de verano, La universidad de los pobres," in *Obras completas*, vol. 12 (Havana: Editorial Nacional de Cuba, 1964), 438.

75. Martí, "Política internacional y religión. Haití y los Estados Unidos . . ." in *Obras completas*, vol. 12 (Havana: Editorial Nacional de Cuba, 1964), 413–22. On the same topic: "Crímenes y problemas," in *Obras completas*, vol. 22 (Havana: Centro de Estudios Martianos, 2011), 27–37. www.josemarti.cu/obras-completas/tomo-22/; "Cisma católica en Nueva York," in *Obras completas*, vol. 25 (Havana:

Centro de Estudios Martianos, 2013), 120–33. www.josemarti.cu/obras-completas/tomo-25/; "El confilcto religioso en los Estados Unidos," in *Obras completas*, vol. 26 (Havana: Centro de Estudios Martianos, 2015), 88–100. www.josemarti.cu/obras-completas/tomo-26/; "La religion en los Estados Unidos," in *Obras completas*, vol. 28 (Havana: Centro de Estudios Martianos, 2018), 175–82. www.josemarti.cu/obras-completas/tomo-28/.

76. [Manuel Gutiérrez Nájera (1859–1895), Mexican modernista poet and intellectual.]

77. Martí, "Monumento a los peregrinos," 288.

78. Norman Friedman argues that in Max Muller's "Lectures of the Science of Languages" at the Royal Institution in 1861–1864, "the nature of metaphor—hitherto almost categorized out of existence by the traditional rhetoricians—became once again an opener question." "Imagery," in *Princeton Encyclopedia of Poetry and Poetics*, ed. Alex Preminger (Princeton, NJ: Princeton University Press, 1974), 364.

79. At the level of post-surrealist aesthetic, the poet Octavio Paz can no longer conceive of poetry without the image, which he defines as the consubstantial and atemporal element of poetry. See the chapter "La imagen," in *El arco y la lira* (Mexico: Fondo de Cultura Económica, 1967).

80. I studied the topic in the prologue and edition of Rubén Darío's *Poesías* (Caracas: Biblioteca Ayacucho, 1977), xxiii–xxx.

81. Martí, "Joaquín Tejada," in *Obras completas*, vol. 5 (Havana: Editorial de Ciencias Sociales, 1992), 287.

82. Martí puts into place diverse grammatical procedures to obtain poetic objectivity; above all, he abandons the deictic coordinates frequent in his earlier work and still perceptible in *Simple Verses* (personal pronouns, adverbs, and demonstrative pronouns), which he avoids the egocentric situation of the statement, replacing it with another more impersonal one, reinforcing it through the remission of all actions to third person (whose unique volatilization of the statement Benveniste has signaled) elected in the *definite* category. Then he uses for the two terms of Series A an unmarked class of sentences, declarative in nature, and furthermore with a neutral, not modal, characterization that in Spanish we attribute to the present indicative, making them revolve around the copulative verb *llevar* (take), with which he reduces the temporal category to a constative present. These verb tenses correspond, according to Harald Weinrich's classification (*Estructura y función de los tiempos en el lenguaje* [Madrid: Gredos, 1974]) to those of the commented world, whose non-narrative quality opposes those of the told world, but furthermore "the verb tenses of the commented world show that the statement in question immediately affects the listener-reader as well as the acting person." "Les temps et les personnes," *Poétique* 39 (September 1979), 340.

83. [Gabriela Mistral (1914–1957), Chilean poet and diplomat. Mistral was the first Spanish American writer to be awarded the Nobel Prize in literature.]

84. Roman Jakobson, "Structures linguistiques subliminales en poésie," in *Questions de poétique* (Paris: E. du Seuil, 1973). The musical component is analyzed in Susanne Langer's book *Feeling and Form* (New York: Scribner, 1953).

85. Juan Marinello talks of "a delight in the internal torture that comes at the blessing of pain" in "La españolidad literaria de José Martí," *Archivo Martí* 4 (Dececmber 1941): 42–66; and now in *Ensayos Martíanos* (Santa Clara: Universidad Central de la Villas, 1961).

86. See Paul Ricoeur, *Freud and Philosophy: An Essay on Interpretation*, trans. Denis Savage (New Have, CT: Yale University Press, 1970).

87. "In the social struggle, Martí does not come to admit the inevitability of violence on the part of the exploited to rid themselves of the yoke of the exploiters." José Cantón Navarro, "Influencia del medio social norteamericano en el pensamiento de José Martí," *Anuario Martíano* 6 (Havana, 1976), 31. Martí's resistance to violence remains consigned to his annotations at the death of Marx "Suma de sucesos," in *Obras completas*, vol. 17 (Havana: Centro de Estudios Martianos, 2010), 60–75. www.josemarti.cu/obras-completas/tomo-17/; and abundantly in the series of articles in which he narrates the social agitation of 1886, which culminates in the trial of the anarchists: "Los trabajadores se apaciguan," in *Obras completas*, vol. 23 (Havana: Centro de Estudios Martianos, 2011), 136–40. www.josemarti.cu/obras-completas/tomo-23/; and "El proceso de los anarquistas," in *Obras completas*, vol. 24 (Havana: Centro de Estudios Martianos, 2012), 206–13. www.josemarti.cu/obras-completas/tomo-24/.

Chapter 11

1. [Rubén Darío, *Songs of Life and Hope: Cantos de vida y esperanza*, ed. and trans. Will Derusha and Alberto Acereda (Lewisburg, PA: Bucknell University Press, 2004).]

2. [Oswald de Andrade (1890–1954), Brazilian novelist and cultural critic most known for his *Anthropophagist Manifesto* (1928). Vicente Huidobro (1893–1943), Chilean avant-garde poet. Huidobro founded the literary movement Creationism and is known for his work *Altazor* (1931).]

3. [While Rama does not mention which book by Toynbee he is referring to, Toynbee's interest in the consequences of the Jesuits separating technology and religion as part of their strategy to establish themselves in China and Japan appears in texts such as *The World and the West* (London: Oxford University Press, 1952), 51–62.]

4. *Marcha*, 2nd section (Aug. 7, 1964): 2–32.

5. Ángel Rama, "La generación hispanoamericana de medio siglo: una generación creadora," in *La crítica de la novela iberoamericana contemporánea*, ed.

Aurora Ocampo (Mexico: Universidad Nacional Autónoma de México, 1973), 17–23. Originally published in *Marcha*, 2nd section (Aug. 7, 1964): 2.

6. [Rosario Castellanos (1925–1974), influential Mexican intellectual, novelist, and poet. Castellanos is noted for both her critical work (*Mujer que sabe latín*, 1973) and her creative output (*Oficio de tinieblas*, 1962) and *Poesía eres tú* (1972). Álvaro Cepeda Samudio (1926–1972), Colombian journalist, novelist, and filmmaker. Cepeda Samudio collaborated with the Barranquilla Group, of which Gabriel García Márquez was also a member. Salvador Garmendia (1928–2001), Venezuelan author. Martínez Moreno (1917–1986), Uruguayan novelist. José Donoso (1924–1996), Chilean novelist. He is most known for *The Obscene Bird of Night* (1970). Adriano González León (1931–2008), Venezuelan novelist known for his work *País portátil* (1968). Mario Benedetti (1920–2009), Uruguayan journalist, poet, and novelist. Augusto Roa Bastos (1917–2005), Paraguayan novelist most known for his fictionalization of the José Gaspar Rodríguez de Francia dictatorship in his novel *I, the Supreme* (1974). David Viñas (1927–2011), Argentine cultural critic, playwright, and novelist.]

7. Rama, "La generación hispanoamericana," 21.

8. These were included in Joaquín Neyra's book, *Ernesto Sábato* (Buenos Aires: Ministerio de Cultura y Educación, 1973).

9. Opinions recorded by Jorge Rufinelli, in Juan Carlos Onetti, *Requiem para Faulkner y otros artículos* (Montevideo: Arca-Calicanto, 1975), 199.

10. [Rómulo Gallegos (1884–1969), Venezuelan politician and writer. Gallegos was elected president of Venezuela in 1948 and governed for nine months. He is most known for his novel *Doña Bárbara* (1928). Mariano Azuela (1873–1952), Mexican writer best known for *The Underdogs* (1929).]

11. Rama, "Diez problemas para el novelista latinoamericano," in *Casa de las Américas* 26 (Oct.–Nov. 1964): 3–43. It has been reproduced as a book (with the same title), *Diez problemas para el novelista latinoamericano* (Caracas: Editorial Síntesis 2000, 1972).

12. [Lino Novás Calvo (1903–1983), Cuban novelist. José Revueltas (1914–1976), Mexican writer and political activist. Juan Rulfo (1917–1986), Mexican author best known for his novel *Pedro Páramo* (1955).]

13. James Irby, *La influencia de William Faulkner en cuatro narradores hispanoamericanos* (Mexico: UNAM, 1956).

14. Rama, "La generación hispanoamericana," 28.

15. [Mario de Andrade (1893–1945), Brazilian novelist and intellectual best known for his work in ethnomusicology and his novel *Macunaíma* (1928).]

16. [Roberto Arlt (1900–1942), Argentine journalist, novelist, and playwright. Arlt is known for his novels *Mad Toy* (1926) and *The Seven Madmen* (1929).]

17. Alejo Carpentier, "Problemática de la actual novela latinoamericana," *Tientos y diferencias y otros ensayos* (Barcelona: Plaza y Janés, 1987), 26.

18. Carpentier, "Problemática," 24.

19. Carpentier, 25–26.

20. [José Hernández (1834–1886), Argentine journalist and poet best known for his epic poem *Martín Fierro* (1872) and *The Return of Martín Fierro* (1879).]

21. "Cultura uruguaya," in *Marcha* (Montevideo: Aug. 4, 1939). Later compiled in *Requiem para Faulklner y otros artículos* (Montevideo: Arca, 1975).

22. Onetti, "Cultura uruguaya," 24.

23. Collected in Onetti, *Requiem para Faulkner y otros artículos.*

24. Stanley Stein and Barbara Stein, *The Colonial Heritage of Latin America* (New York: Oxford University Press, 1970), 192–93.

25. United Nations Economic Commission for Latin America, *Report of the Executive Secretary to the Eighteenth Session of the Commission*, April 18–26, 1979, 81.

26. Report by Elena Poniatowska, "Al fin un escritor que le apasiona escribir, no lo que se diga de sus libros," in *Antología mínima de Mario Vargas Llosa* (Buenos Aires: Tiempo Contemporáneo, 1969), 7–81.

27. In Óscar Collazos et al., *Literatura en la revolución y revolución en la literatura* (Mexico: Siglo XXI, 1970). The debate is recounted between Óscar Collazos, Julio Cortázar, and Mario Vargas Llosa.

28. Immanuel Wallerstein, *The Modern World-System: Capitalist Agriculture and the Origins of the European World Economy in the Sixteenth Century* (New York: Academic Press, 1976).

29. The relation of this "autonomy" with political eviction has been studied by Jean Franco in a brilliant essay, "Modernización, resistencia y revolución: La producción literaria de los años sesenta," in *Escritura* 2, no. 3 (Jan.–June 1977), 3–19.

30. *Guerra del tiempo: Tres relatos y una novela* ("El camino de Santiago," "Viaje a la semilla," "Semejante a la noche," "El acoso") (Mexico: Compañía General de Ediciones, 1958).

31. *Afirmación literaria americanista* (Caracas: Ediciones de la Facultad de Humanidades y Educación, 1978), 29.

32. [Mariano Brull (1891–1956), Cuban poet associated with the Symbolist movement.]

33. [Bernardo Ortiz de Montellano (1899–1949), Mexican poet and literary critic.]

34. [Rama is probably referring to the following article, Wolfgang A. Luchting, "El lector como protagonista de la novela: Onetti y *Los adioses*," *Nueva Narrativa Hispanoamericana* 1, no. 2 (Sept. 1971), 175–84.]

35. Günter Lorez, *Dialog mit Lateinamerkia* (Tübingen: Horst Erdman Verlag, 1970).

36. From the Spanish translation, Lorenz, *Diálogo con América Latina* (Valparaiso: Ediciones Universitarias, 1972).

37. In *El escritor y sus fantasmas* (Buenos Aires: Aguilar, 1963); and in *Tres aproximaciones a la literatura de nuestro tiempo: Robbe-Grillet, Borges, Sartre* (Santiago: Editorial Univesitaria, 1968); Ana María de Rodríguez's *La creación corregida: estudio*

comparativo de la obra de Ernesto Sábato y Alain Robbe-Grillet (Caracas: Universidad Católica Andrés Bello, 1976) deals with the topic as well.

38. Onetti, "Reflexiones literarias," *Acción* (Montevideo: Nov. 13, 1966). Reproduced in *Requiem para Faulkner y otros artículos*.

39. Onetti, "Reflexiones literarias," 200.

40. [José Lezama Lima (1910–1976), influential Cuban writer and poet. Guillermo Cabrera Infante (1929–2005), Cuban novelist and essayist best known for his novel *Three Trapped Tigers* (1965). Pablo Armando Fernández (1929–), Cuban poet and novelist. Reinaldo Arenas (1943–1990), Cuban poet, novelist, and playwright. Severo Sarduy (1937–1993), Cuban poet, novelist, and playwright.]

41. [Pablo de Rokha (1894–1968), Chilean poet. Carlos Droguett (1912–1996), Chilean novelist. Alfonso Alcalde (1921–1992), Chilean novelist and poet. Enrique Lafourcade (1926–2019), Chilean novelist.]

42. [The Mexican "new wave" was a group of young writers who began publishing fiction written by youth about youth in Mexico in the 1960s. Gustavo Sáinz (1940–2015), Mexican novelist. José Agustín (1944–), Mexican novelist. Agustín wrote his first novel, *The Tomb* (1964), when he was sixteen.]

43. [Leopoldo Marechal (1900–1970), Argentine writer and cultural critic best known for his novel *Adam Buenosayres* (1948).]

44. [Ezequiel Martínez Estrada (1895–1964), Argentine novelist, poet, and literary critic. José Bianco (1908–1986), Argentine novelist and editor of the important periodical *Sur*. J. Rodolfo Wilcock (1919–1978), Argentine novelist, poet, cultural critic, and translator.]

45. [Luis Cardoza and Aragon (1901–1992), Guatemalan novelist, poet, and diplomat. Jorge Zalamea (1905–1969), Colombian journalist, novelist, and poet. Jacques Stephen Alexis (1922–1961), Haitian novelist, poet, and political activist.]

46. [Luis Britto García (1940), Venezuelan novelist and playwright. Germán Espinosa (1938–2007), Colombian novelist and poet.]

47. José María Castellet, *Panorama de la actual literatura latinoamericana* (Madrid: Fundamentos, 1971).

48. [Rubén Darío, *Selected Poems of Rubén Darío*, eds. and trans. Will Derusha and Alberto Acereda (Lewisburg, PA: Bucknell University Press, 2001).]

49. Mario Vargas Llosa's comments are compiled in *Día domingo* (Buenos Aires: Amadis, 1971). Those of García Márquez appear in the conversation with Vargas Llosa in Gabriel García Márquez and Mario Vargas Llosa, *La novela en América Latina: Diálogo* (Lima: C. Milla Batres, 1968). Curiously, Julio Cortázar, in his response to Óscar Collazos (*Literatura en la revolución*) does not seems to believe that anyone has forwarded such a position.

50. Emir Rodríguez Monegal, "Novedad y anacronismo en *Cien años de soledad*," *Revista Nacional de Cultura* (Caracas) 29 (July–Dec. 1968): 2–20.

51. Stein and Stein, *The Colonial Heritage*, 195.

52. Albert O. Hirschman, "The Political Economy of Import-Substituting Industrialization in Latin America," in *A Bias for Hope: Essays on Development and Latin America* (New Haven, CT: Yale University Press, 1971).

53. Onetti, *Requiem para Faulkner*, 185.

54. [Néstor Sánchez (1935–2003), Argentine novelist and translator. Guillermo Cabrera Infante (1929–2005), Cuban novelist and translator best known for *Three Trapped Tigers* (1967). Salvador Elizondo (1932–2006), Mexican writer known for his experimental novel *Farabeuf* (1965). Alberto Duque López (1936–2010), Colombian journalist and novelist. Héctor Libertella (1945–2006), Argentine novelist. José Balza (1939–), Venezuelan novelist.]

55. [Carlos Martínez Moreno (1917–1986), Uruguayan novelist. Vicente Leñero (1933–2014), Mexican novelist and playwright. German García (1944–2018), Argentine novelist. Manuel Puig (1932–1990), Argentine writer most known for his novel *Kiss of the Spider Woman* (1976).]

56. [Antonio Skármeta (1940), Chilean novelist and playwright best known for his novel *Burning Patience* (1985). Luis Rafael Sánchez (1936), Puerto Rican novelist and playwright known for his play *Macho Camacho's Beat* (1976). Griselda Gambaro (1928), Argentine novelist and playwright. Plinio Apuleyo Mendoza (1932), Colombian novelist.]

57. Rama, "Mezzo secolo di narrative latinoamericana," in *Latinoamericana: 75 Narratori*, vol. 1, ed. Franco Mogni (Florence: Vallecchi, 1973), 3–72. [A Spanish translation of this essay appears as "Medio siglo de narrativa latinoamericana (1922–1972)" in Rama, *La novela en América Latina: panoramas 1920–1980* (Bogota: Colcultura, 1980), 99–202.]

58. I have explored this theme in a prologue to Rubén Darío's *El mundo de los sueños* (San Juan: Editorial Universitaria, 1971).

59. Article published in *El Economista Americano*, New York, July 1888, and compiled in José Martí, *Nuestra América* (Caracas: Biblioteca Ayacucho, 1977), 205.

60. Published in *Temps Modernes*, no. 83, September 1952, compiled in *Hygiéne des lettres: Littérature dégagée* (Paris: Gallimard, 1955).

61. Using this statement as epigraph, Michel Berveiller conducted a systematic investigation on Borges that led to his book *Le cosmopolitisme de Jorge Luis Borges* (Paris: Didier, 1973).

62. Jorge Luis Borges, "The Argentine Writer and Tradition," in *Selected Non-Fictions*, ed. Eliot Weinberger, trans. Esther Allen, Suzanne Jill Levine, and Eliot Weinberger (New York: Viking, 1999), 420–27. Borges concludes his explanation thus, "Precisely because I had abandoned myself to the dream, I was able to achieve, after so many years, what I once sought in vain."

63. Silvia Molloy, *La diffusion de la littérature hispano-américaine en France au XXe siècle* (Paris: Presses Universitaires de France, 1972).

64. Molloy, 236.

65. Cortázar, "Para una poética," in *La Torre* 2 (July–Sept. 1954).

66. Gustavo Luis Carrera, *Nuevas Viejas preguntas a Julio Cortázar* (Caracas: Ediciones de la Facultad de Humanidades y Educación, 1978). José Donoso has also considered his move, as he has said his "unpacking," as the key to his new creation outside the country as he explains in his *Historia personal del boom* (Barcelona: Anagrama, 1972).

67. Carlos Fuentes, "Situación del escritor en América Latina," dialogue with Emir Rodríguez Monegal in *Mundo Nuevo*, July 1966.

68. [José Asunción (1865–1896), Colombian modernista poet and author. Carlos Reyles (1868–1838), Uruguayan novelist.]

69. [Manuel Mujica Láinez (1910–1984), Argentine novelist and cultural critic.]

70. [Enrique Larreta (1875–1961), Argentine intellectual and writer.]

71. [This expression is from Darío, "Mi esposa es de mi tierra; mi querida de Paris," who says it in his "Palabras liminares" to *Prosas profanas*.]

72. "Inevitable comentario a unas ideas de Julio Cortázar," in *El Comercio*, Lima, June 1, 1969.

73. See my essay, "Processes of Transculturation in Latin American Narrative," in *Revista de Literatura Hispanoamericana* (Maracaibo) 5 (April 1974). [A translation of this article can be found in *Journal of Latin American Cultural Studies* 6, no. 2 (1997): 155–71.]

74. Onetti, *Requiem para Faulkner*, 201.

75. Quoted by Loveluck in *Coloquio sobre la novela hispanoamericana* (Mexico: Tezontle, 1967).

76. García Márquez and Vargas Llosa in *La novela en América Latina: Diálogo* (Lima: Ediciones Copé, 2013), 54.

77. Alfredo Bosi, *História concisa da literatura brasileira* (São Paulo: Cultrix, 1972), 488.

78. "Papel del escritor en América Latina," *Mundo Nuevo* 5, Nov. 1966, 27.

79. [Macedonio Fernández (1874–1952), Argentine novelist and poet.]

Chapter 12

1. Karl Mannheim, "The Problem of the Intelligentsia," in *Essays on the Sociology of Culture* (London: Routledge and Kegan Paul, 1956), 91–170.

2. [Vilfredo Pareto (1848–1923) was an Italian thinker famous for his contributions to the fields of mathematics, economics, and sociology.]

3. [Louis de Bonald (1754–1840) was a French philosopher and politician. His works were later used as a theoretical framework for French sociology. Germaine de Staël (1766–1817), French Romantic author of novels, travel literature, and literary criticism. Frédéric Le Play (1806–1882), French mining engineer and later

sociologist. Gustave Le Bon (1841–1931), French academic known for his work in anthropology, psychology, sociology, medicine, and physics. His best-known work is *The Crowd: A Study of the Popular Mind* (1895).]

4. "El pensamiento sociológico de Eugenio María de Hostos," *Revista de Ciencias Sociales de la Universidad de Puerto Rico* 7, no. 3 (Sept. 1963): 218.

5. [Tobias Barreto de Meneses (1839–1889) was a Brazilian Romantic strongly influenced by German culture.]

6. Quoted in Antonio Candido, *O método crítico de Silvio Romero* (São Paulo: Boletim, 266, 1963).

7. [Tristão de Alencar Araripe Junior (1848–1911), Brazilian lawyer, literary critic, and author. José Veríssimo (1857–1916), Brazilian journalist and literary critic who was a founding member of the Brazilian Academy of Letters.]

8. [Alberto Zum Felde (1888–1976) was a Uruguayan poet and literary critic recognized for his work on the history of intellectual and literary trends in Uruguay. Ricardo Rojas (1882–1957) was an Argentine intellectual, historian, literary scholar, and politician. As the first professor of Argentine literature at the University of Buenos Aires, Rojas is known for his studies on the history of Argentine literature.]

9. José Enrique Rodó, "Rubén Darío. Su personalidad literaria, su última obra" [1899], in *Obras Completas*, ed. Emir Rodríguez Monegal (Madrid: Aguilar, 1967), 169.

10. [Arthur de Gobineau (1816–1882), a French writer who helped develop racist theories later adopted by others. He wrote the pseudoscientific work *An Essay on the Inequality of Human Races* in 1853.]

11. Rubén Darío, *El mundo de los sueños*, ed. Ángel Rama (San Juan: Editorial Universitaria, 1973).

12. Edward Burnett Tylor, *Primitive Culture*, vol. 1 (London: J Murray, 1871), 1.

13. Claude Lévi-Strauss, *Structural Anthropology*, trans. Claire Jacobson and Brooke Grundfest Schoepf (New York: Basic Books, 2008), 359.

14. Lévi-Strauss, 365.

15. [Georgi Plekhanov (1856–1918), a Russian revolutionary and Marxist theoretician. He is the author of *Art and Social Life* (1912), where he declares that the main function of art was to improve the social system.]

16. Raymond Williams, *The Sociology of Culture* (New York: Schocken Books, 1982); and Raymond Williams, *Problems in Materialism and Culture* (London: Verso Edition, 1980).

17. [Lewis Henry Morgan (1818–1881), North American sociologist known for his text *Ancient Society* (1877). The three periods were savagery, barbarism, and civilization.]

18. [Enrique José Varona (1848–1933), Cuban thinker.]

19. [Bronisław Malinowski (1884–1942), Polish anthropologist.]

20. Claude Lévi-Strauss, *Race and History* (Paris: UNESCO, 1952). [This later became chapter 18 in *Structural Anthropology*, 324–63.]

21. Gilberto Freyre, *The Masters and the Slaves*, trans. Samuel Putnam (New York: Knopf, 1946), 3.

22. See Julio Le Riverend's prologue to Fernando Ortiz's *Cuban Counterpoint, Tobacco and Sugar* (Caracas: Biblioteca Ayacucho, 1978).

23. [Melville Jean Herskovits (1895–1963), North American anthropologist.]

24. [Marcel Mauss (1872–1950), French sociologist.]

25. Paul Zumthor and Walter Ong, *Oral Poetry: An Introduction* (Minnesota: University of Minnesota Press, 1990), 225.

26. [Augusto Roa Bastos (1917–2005), Paraguayan novelist most known for his fictionalization of the José Gaspar Rodríguez de Francia's dictatorship in his novel *I, the Supreme* (1974).]

27. Augusto Roa Bastos, "O sonàmbulo," in *Cándido López* (Parma: Francesco Ricci, 1982).

Bibliography

Acuña de Figueroa, Francisco. *Diario histórico de Montevideo de los años 1812–1814.* Montevideo: Biblioteca Artigas, 1978.
Alazraki, Jaime. "El género literario del *Martín Fierro*." *Revista Iberoamericana* 40, no. 87–88 (1974): 433–58.
Alighieri, Dante. *Inferno.* Translated by Courtney Langdon. Cambridge, MA: Harvard University Press, 1918.
Alonso, Amado. *Estudios Lingüísticos: Temas Hispanoamericanos.* Madrid: Editorial Gredos, 1953. Reprinted in 1971.
Amor, José Blanco. *El final del boom literario.* Buenos Aires: Cervantes, 1976.
Anderson Imbert, Enrique. *Historia de la literatura hispanoamericana.* Mexico: Fondo de Cultura Económica, 1961.
Andrade, Mario de. *Hallucinated City: Pauliceia Desvairada.* Translated by Jack E. Tomlins. Nashville, TN: Vanderbilt University Press, 1968.
Arguedas, José María. "Inevitable comentario a unas ideas de Julio Cortázar." *El Comercio* (Lima), June 1, 1969.
Armillas-Tiseyra, Magalí. *The Dictator Novel: Writers and Politics in the Global South.* Evanston, IL: Northwestern University Press, 2019.
Arózteguy, Abdón. *La revolución oriental de 1870.* Buenos Aires: Félix Lajoune, 1889.
Assuçao, Fernando. *El gaucho.* Montevideo: Imprenta Nacional, 1963.
Ayestarán, Lauro. *La primitiva poesía guachesca en el Uruguay (1812–1838).* Montevideo: El Siglo Ilustrado, 1950.
Azuela, Mariano. *Obras completas.* 3 vols. Mexico: Fondo de Cultura Económica, 1960.
———. *Two Novels of the Mexican Revolution: The Trials of a Respectable Family and the Underdogs.* Translated by Frances Kellam Hendricks and Beatrice Berler. San Antonio, TX: Principia Press, 1963.
———. *Two Novels of Mexico: The Flies, The Bosses.* Translated by Lesley Byrd Simpson. Berkeley: University of California Press, 1965.
Bagú, Sergio. *Estructura social de la Colonia.* Buenos Aires: El Ateneo, 1952.
———. *Evolución histórica de la estratificación social.* Caracas: Instituto de Investigaciones Económicas y Sociales, 1969.

Bally, Charles. *Traité de stylistique*. Paris: Klincksiek, 1951.
Barral, Carlos. *Años de penitencia*. Barcelona: Seix Barral, 1975.
Barthes, Roland. "Literature and Signification." In *Critical Essays*. Translated by Richard Howard. Evanston, IL: Northwestern University Press, 1972.
Battistessa, Ángel. "José Hernández." Vol. 3 of *Historia de la literatura Argentina*, edited by Rafael Alberto Arrieta. Buenos Aires: Peuser, 1949.
Becco, Horacio Jorge. *Antología de la poesía gauchesca*. Madrid: Aguilar, 1972.
Bernstein, Basil. "Social class, language and socialization." Vol. 1 of *Class, Codes and Control: Theoretical Studies towards a Sociology of Language*. New York: Routledge, 2003.
Berro, Bernardo Prudencio. *Escritos selectos*. Montevideo: Biblioteca Artigas, 1966.
Berveiller, Michel. *Le cosmopolitisme de Jorge Luis Borges*. Paris: Didier, 1973.
Beverly, John. *Subalternity and Representation*. Durham, NC: Duke University Press, 1999.
Blixen, Carina, and Alvaro Barros-Lémez. *Cronología y bibliografía de Ángel Rama*. Montevideo: Fundación Ángel Rama, 1986.
Borges, Jorge Luis. *Aspectos de la literatura gauchesca*. Montevideo: Número, 1950.
———. *Discusión*. Buenos Aires: Emecé, 1955.
———. *Selected Non-Fictions*. Edited by Eliot Weinberger. Translated by Esther Allen, Suzanne Jill Levine, and Eliot Weinberger. New York: Viking, 1999.
Borges, Jorge Luis, and Aldofo Bioy Casares. *Poesía gauchesca*. Mexico: Fondo de Cultura Económica, 1955.
Bosi, Alfredo. *História concisa da literatura braileira*. Sao Paulo: Editora Cultrix, 1972.
Brushwood, John S. *The Spanish American Novel: A Twentieth Century Survey*. Austin: University of Texas Press, 1975.
Caillava, Domingo A. *Historia de la literatura gauchesca en el Uruguay*. Montevideo: Claudia García, 1945.
Caillet Bois, J. "Hilario Ascasubi." In *Historia de la literatura Argentina*. Edited by Rafael Alberto Arrieta. Buenos Aires: Peuser, 1949.
Camín, Héctor Aguilar, and Lorenzo Meyer. *In the Shadow of the Mexican Revolution*. Austin: University of Texas Press, 1993.
Candido, Antonio. *Formaçao da literatura brasileira*. São Paulo: Livraria Martins, 1952.
———. *O método critico de Silvio Romero*. São Paulo: Boletim 266, 1963.
Cantón Navarro, José. "Influencia del medio social norteamericano en el pensamiento de José Martí." *Anuario Martiano* 6, Havana (1976).
Carilla, Emilio. *La creación del "Martín Fierro."* Madrid: Gredos, 1973.
Carpentier, Alejo. *Afirmación literaria americanista (Encuentro con Alejo Carpentier)*. Caracas: Ediciones de la Facultad de Humanidades y Educación, 1978.
———. *Guerra del tiempo: Tres relatos y una novela*. Mexico: Compañía General de Ediciones, 1958.
———. "Problemática del tiempo y del idioma en la moderna novela latinoamericana." *Escritura* 1, no. 2 (July–December 1976): 191–206.

———. *Tientos y diferencias*. Mexico: Universidad Nacional Autónoma, 1964.
Carrera, Gustavo Luis. *Nuevas Viejas preguntas a Julio Cortázar*. Caracas: Ediciones de la Facultad de Humanidades y Educación, 1978.
Casanova, Pablo González. "México: el ciclo de una revolución agraria." *Cuadernos Americanos* 21, no. 1 (1962): 7–29.
Cassirer, Ernst. *Antropología filosófica*. Mexico: Fondo de Cultura Económica, 1970.
———. *Mito y lenguaje*. Buenos Aires: Galatea-Nueva Visión, 1959.
———. *The Philosophy of Symbolic Forms*. Translated by Ralph Mannheim. New Haven, CT: Yale University Press, 1955.
Castellet, José María. "La actual literatura latinoamericana vista desde España." In *Panorama de la actual literatura latinoamericana*. Edited by Jorge Enrique Adoum, et al. Madrid: Fundamentos, 1971.
Castro Leal, Antonio. *La novela de la revolución mexicana*. Mexico: Aguilar, 1962.
Catagnino, Raúl J. *Milicia literaria de mayo*. Buenos Aires: Nova, 1960.
———, ed. *Algunos aspectos de la cultura literaria de mayo*. Buenos Aires: Universidad Nacional de La Plata, 1961.
Chacón, Alfredo. *Contra la dependencia*. Caracas: Síntesis Dosmil, 1973.
Chávez, Fermín. *Poesía rioplatense en estilo gaucho*. Buenos Aires: Ediciones Culturales Argentina, 1962.
Clarke, Dorothy C. "Miscellaneous Strophe Forms in the Fifteenth Century Court Lyric." *Hispanic Review* 16, no. 2 (1948): 142–56.
———. "Redondilla and copla de arte menor." *Hispanic Review* 9, no. 4 (1941): 489–93.
Collazos, Óscar, Julio Cortazar, and Mario Vargas Llosa. *Literatura en la revolución y revolución en la literatura*. Mexico: Siglo XXI, 1970.
Collettti, Lucio. *Ideología e societá*. Bari: Laterza, 1969.
Colloque de Cluny. *Literature et ideologies*. Paris: Nouvelle Critique, 1971.
Coni, Emilio. *El gaucho: Argentina-Brasil-Uruguay*. Buenos Aires: Sudamericana, 1945.
Conte, Rafael. *Lenguaje y violencia: Introducción a la nueva novela hispanoamericana*. Madrid: Al-Borak, 1972.
Cortázar, Julio. "Para una poética." *La Torre* 2 (July–September 1954).
Creelman, James. "President Diaz, Hero of the Americas." *Pearson's Magazine* 19, no. 3 (1908): 231–77.
Darío, Rubén. *El mundo de los sueños*. Edited by Ángel Rama. San Juan: Editorial Universitaria, 1973.
———. *Selected Poems of Rubén Darío*. Translated and edited by Alberto Acereda and Will Derusha. Lewisburg, PA: Bucknell University Press, 2001.
———. *Songs of Life and Hope: Cantos de vida y Esperanza*. Translated and edited by Will Derusha and Alberto Acereda. Lewisburg, PA: Bucknell University Press, 2004.
Deleuze, Gilles. *Difference and Repetition*. Translated by Paul Patton. New York: Columbia University Press, 1994.

———. *The Logic of Sense*. Edited by Constantin Bondas. Translated by Mark Lester and Charles Stivale. New York: Columbia University Press, 1990.

Deleuze, Gilles, and Félix Guattari. *Anti-Oedipus: Capitalism and Schizophrenia*. Translated by Robert Hurley, Mark Seem, and Helen Lane. Minneapolis: University of Minnesota Press, 1983.

Donghi, Tulio Halperin. *Historia contemporánea de América Latina*. Madrid: Alianza Editorial, 1969.

Donoso, José. *The Boom in Spanish American Letters: A Personal History*. Translated by Gregory Kolovakos. New York: Columbia University Press, 1977.

Duque, Jaime Mejía. *Narrativa y neocoloniaje en América Latina*. Buenos Aires: Crisis, 1974.

Eagleton, Terry. *Criticism and Ideology*. Norfolk, CT: Verso Editions, 1978.

Eco, Umberto. *Le forme del contenuto*. Milano: Bompiani, 1972.

Enzensberger, Hans Magnus. *Consciousness Industry: On Literature, Politics and the Media*. New York: Seabury Press, 1974.

Escarpit, Robert. *Le litteraire et le social*. Paris, Flammarion, 1970.

Estañol, Vera. *La revolución mexicana: Orígenes y resultados*. Mexico: Porrúa, 1957.

Etiemble, Rene. *Hygiène des lettres: Littérature dégagée*. Paris: Gallimard, 1955.

Fishman, Joshua A., ed., *Readings in the Sociology of Language*. The Hague: Mouton, 1972.

Foucault, Michel. *Archeology of Knowledge*. Translated by A. M. Sheridan Smith. New York: Routledge, 1972.

———. "On the Archeology of the Sciences: Response to the Epistemology Circle." In *The Essential Foucault*. Edited by Paul Rabinow and Nikolas Rose, 392–422. New York: The New Press, 1994.

Franco, Jean. "Modernización, resistencia y revolución: La producción literaria de los años sesenta." *Escritura* 2, no. 3 (January–June 1977): 3–19.

Freyre, Gilberto. *The Masters and the Slaves*. Translated by Samuel Putnam. New York: Knopf, 1946.

Fuentes, Carlos. *La nueva novela hispanoamericana*. Mexico: Joaquín Mortiz, 1969.

———. "Situación del escritor en América Latina." Dialogue with Emir Rodríguez Monegal in *Mundo Nuevo* (July 1966): 5–21.

Gabel, Joseph. *La fausse conscience: Essai sur la reification*. Paris: Minuit, 1963.

García Liendo, Javier. *El intelectual y la cultura de masas: Argumentos latinoamericanos en torno a Ángel Rama y José María Arguedas*. West Lafayette, IN: Purdue University Press, 2017.

García Marruz, Fina. *Temas martianos*. Havana: Biblioteca Nacional José Martí, 1969.

———. "Los versos de Martí." *Revista de la Biblioteca Naicional José Martí*. Havana (January–April 1968): 35–38.

García Márquez, Gabriel. *One Hundred Years of Solitude*. Translated by Gregory Rabassa. New York: Penguin Books, 1973.

García Márquez, Gabriel, and Mario Vargas Llosa. *La novela en América Latina: Diálogo*. Lima: C. Milla Batres, 1968.
Geertz, Clifford. "Ideology as Cultural System." In *Ideology and Discontents*. Edited by David E. Apter. New York: Free Press, 1964.
———. *The Interpretation of Cultures*. New York: Basic Books, 1973.
Ghiano, Juan Carlos. "Bartolomé Hidalgo entre los poetas de mayo." In *Algunos aspectos de la cultura literaria de mayo*, edited by Raúl J. Catagnino. Buenos Aires: Universidad Nacional de La Plata, 1961.
Giner, Salvador. "El pensamiento sociológico de Eugenio María de Hostos." *Revista de Ciencias Sociales de la Universidad de Puerto Rico* 7, no. 3 (September 1963): 215–29.
González Bermejo, Ernesto. *Conversaciones con Cortázar*. Barcelona: Edhasa, 1978.
González, José Eduardo. *Appropriating Theory: Ángel Rama's Critical Work*. Pittsburgh, PA: University of Pittsburgh Press, 2017.
González, Manuel Pedro. "Crisis de la novela en América." *Revista Nacional de Cultura* (Caracas) 150, 1962.
———. *Trayectoria de la novela en México*. Mexico: Botas, 1951.
Greimas, Julien. *Essais de sémiotique poétique*. Paris: Larousse, 1972.
Grossmann, Rudolf. *Historia y problemas de la literatura latinoamericana*. Madrid: Revista de Occidente, 1972.
Guiraud, Pierre, and Pierre Kuentz. *La stylistique*. Paris: Klincksieck, 1970.
Gutiérrez, Juan María. "La literatura de mayo." In *Los poetas de la revolución*. Buenos Aires: Academia Argentina de Letras, 1941.
Habich, Fernando Tola de, and Patricia Grieve. *Los españoles y el boom*. Caracas: Tiempo Nuevo, 1972.
Hauser, Arnold. *The Philosophy of Art History*. Evanston, IL: Northwestern University Press, 1985.
Harss, Luis. *Los nuestros*. Buenos Aires: Sudamericana, 1966.
Harss, Luis, and Barbara Dohmann. *Into the Mainstream: Conversations with Latin American Writers*. New York: Harper and Row, 1967.
Henríquez Ureña, Pedro. *Las corrientes literarias en la América Hispánica*. Mexico: Fondo de Cultura Económica, 1949.
———. *Literary currents in Hispanic America*. Cambridge, MA: Harvard University Press, 1945.
Hernández, José. *El Gaucho Martín Fierro: A Bilingual Edition*. Translated by C. E. Ward. Albany: State University of New York Press, 1967.
Hjelmslev, Louis. *Prolegomena to a Theory of Language*. Translated by Francis Whitfield. Madison: University of Wisconsin Press, 1963.
Huidobro, Vicente. *The Poet is a Little God*. Translated by Jorge García-Gómez. Las Cruces, NM: Xenos Books, 1990.
———. *Selected Poetry of Vicente Huidobro*. Edited by David M. Guss. New York: New Directions, 1981.

Hirschman, Albert O. *A Bias for Hope: Essays on Development and Latin America.* New Haven, CT: Yale University Press, 1971.
Irby, James. *La influencia de William Faulkner en cuatro narradores hispanoamericanos.* Mexico: UNAM, 1956.
Iturriaga, José E. *La estructura social y cultural de México.* Mexico: Fondo de Cultura Económica, 1951.
Jakobson, Roman. "Linguistics and Poetics." In *Twentieth-Century Literary Theory*, edited by K. M. Newton, 71–77. London: Palgrave, 1997.
———. *Question de poétique.* Paris: Seuil, 1973.
Jakobson, Roman, and Petr Bogatyrev. "Folklore as a Special Form of Creation." Translated by John M. O'Hara. *Folklore Forum* 13, no. 1 (1980): 1–21.
Jitrik, Noé. *Las contradicciones del modernismo: Producción poética y situación social.* Mexico: El Colegio de México, 1978.
Johnson, John. *Political Change in Latin America: The Emergence of the Middle Class.* Stanford, CA: Stanford University Press, 1958.
Kieffer, E. Gudiño. "La violencia: Miradas opuestas." *La Nación* (Buenos Aires), August 6, 1972.
Kosik, Karel. *Dialéctica de lo concreto.* Mexico: Grijalbo, 1967.
Kott, Jan. *Shakespeare, Our Contemporary.* New York: Doubleday, 1964.
Kristeva, Julia. *Desire in Language: A Semiotic Approach to Literature and Art.* Edited by Leon S. Ruidiez. Translated by Thomas Gora, Alice Jardine, and Leon S. Roudiez. New York: Columbia University Press, 1980.
Langer, Susanne. *Feeling and Form.* New York: Scribner, 1953.
Lorenz, Günter. *Diálogo con América Latina.* Valparaiso: Ediciones Universitarias, 1972.
———. *Dialog mit Lateinamerkia.* Tübingen: Horst Erdman Verlag, 1970.
Leumann, Carlos Alberto. *La literatura gauchesca y la poesía gauchesca.* Buenos Aires: Raigal, 1953.
Lévi-Strauss, Claude. *Introduction to the Work of Marcel Mauss.* Translated by Felicity Baker. London: Routledge and Kegan Paul, 1987.
———. *Race and History.* Paris: UNESCO, 1952.
———. *Structural Anthropology.* Translated by Claire Jacobson and Brooke Grundfest Schoepf. New York: Basic Books, 2008.
Le Riverend, Julio. Prologue to *Contrapunteo cubano del tabaco y el azúcar*, by Fernando Ortiz. Caracas: Biblioteca Ayacucho, 1978.
Lipschutz, Alexander. *El indoamericanismo y el problema racial en las Américas.* Santiago de Chile: Nascimento, 1944.
Luchting, Wolfgang A. "El lector como protagonista de la novela: Onetti y *Los adioses*." *Nueva Narrativa Hispanoamericana* 1, no. 2 (September 1971): 175–84.
Lugones, Leopoldo. *El payador.* Buenos Aires: Ediciones Centurión, 1961.
Lukács, Georg. *The Historical Novel.* Translated by Hannah Mitchell and Stanley Mitchell. Lincoln: University of Nebraska Press, 1983.

———. *The Meaning of Contemporary Realism*. Translated by John and Necke Mandar. London: Merlin Press, 1969.
Lund, Joshua. "Magic Socialism." *Cultural Critique* 92 (2016): 179–89.
Machado, Antonio. *Border of a Dream: Selected Poems of Antonio Machado*. Translated by Willis Barnstone. Port Townsend, WA: Copper Canyon Press, 2003.
Maillefert, Alfredo. *Los libros que leí*. Mexico: Universidad Nacional de Mexico, 1942.
Mannheim, Karl. *Essays on the Sociology of Culture: Collected Works*. Vol. 7. Taylor and Francis e-Library, 2003.
———. *Ideology and Utopia*. Translated by Louis Wirth and Edward Shils. New York: Harcourt, 1955.
Marinello, Juan. *Ensayos Martianos*. Santa Clara: Universidad Central de la Villas, 1961.
———. "La españolidad literaria de José Martí." *Archivo Martí* 4, Havana (December 1941): 42–66.
Martí, José. *Nuestra América*. Caracas: Biblioteca Ayacucho, 1977.
———. *Obras completas*. 27 vols. Havana: Editorial de Ciencias Sociales, 1992–1994.
———. *Obras completas*. 28 vols. Havana: Editorial Nacional de Cuba, 1963–1973.
———. *Obras completas*. 29 vols. Edited by Cintio Vitier and Fina García Marruz. Havana: Centro de Estudios Martianos, 1983–2019.
———. *Obras completas*. 74 vols. Edited by Gonzalo de Quesada y Miranda. Havana: Editorial Trópico, 1936–1953.
———. *Selected Writings*. Edited and Translated by Esther Allen. New York: Penguin Books, 2002.
———. *Versos Sencillos: Simple Verses*. Translated by Manuel A. Tellechea. Houston, TX: Arte Público Press, 1997.
Martínez Estrada, Ezequiel. *Muerte y transfiguración de Martín Fierro*. Mexico: Fondo de Cultura, 1948.
Martínez, José Luis. *Literatura mexicana siglo XX*. Mexico: Antigua Librería Robredo, 1949.
Martínez, Tomás Eloy. "América: La gran novela." *Primera Plana* (Buenos Aires) 5, no. 234, June 20–26, 1967.
———. "Ángel Rama o la crítica como gozo." *Revista Iberoamericana* 52, no. 135–36 (1986): 663.
———. "El boom: Esplendor y después." *El Nacional* (Caracas). September 3, 1978.
Marx, Karl. *A Contribution to the Critique of Political Economy*. Translated by S. W. Ryazanskaya. New York: International Publishers, 1970.
———. *The German Ideology* in *The Marx-Engels Reader*. Edited by Robert Tucker. New York: Norton. 1978.
———. *Grundrisse: Introduction to the Critique of Political Economy*. New York: Vintage, 1973.
Meschonnic, Henri. *Pour la Poétique*. Paris: Gallimard, 1970.
Moles, Abraham. *Sociodynamique de la culture*. Paris: Mouton, 1967.

Molloy, Silvia. *La diffusion de la littérature hispano-américaine en France au XXe siècle*. Paris: Presses Universitaires de France, 1972.
Moraña, Mabel. *Arguedas/Vargas Llosa: Dilemmas and Assemblages*. London: Palgrave, 2016.
Mújica Láinez, Manuel. *Vidas del gallo y el pollo*. Buenos Aires: Centro Editor de América Latina, 1966.
Neyra, Joaquín. *Ernesto Sábato*. Buenos Aires: Ministerio de Cultura y Educación, 1973.
Nietzsche, Frederic. *Beyond Good and Evil*. Edited by Rolf-Peter Horstmann and Judith Norman. Translated by Judith Norman. Cambridge: Cambridge University Press, 2002.
———. *The Nietzsche Reader*. Edited by Keith Ansell Pearson and Duncan Large. Malden, MA: Wiley Blackwell, 2006.
Onetti, Juan Carlos. *Requiem para Faulkner y otros artículos*. Montevideo: Arca-Calicanto, 1975.
Onís, Federico de. *España en América*. Río Piedras: Ediciones de la Universidad de Puerto Rico, 1955.
Ortiz, Fernando. *Contrapunteo cubano del tabaco y el azúcar*. Caracas: Biblioteca Ayacucho, 1978.
Oviedo, José Miguel. "Cortázar a cinco rounds." *Marcha* (Montevideo) 34, no. 1634, March 2, 1973.
"Papel del escritor en América Latina." *Mundo Nuevo* 5 (November 1966).
Paullada, Stephen. "Some Observations on the Word Gaucho." *New Mexico Quarterly* 31, no. 2 (1961): 151–62.
Paz, Octavio. *El arco y la lira*. Mexico: Fondo de Cultura Económica, 1967.
———. *Poesía en movimiento*. Mexico: Siglo XX, 1966.
Pistacchio, Romina. *La aporía descolonial releyendo la tradición crítica de la crítica literaria latinoamericana: Los casos de Antonio Cornejo Polar y Ángel Rama*. Madrid: Iberoamericana Vervuet, 2018.
Poniatowska, Elena. "Al fin un escritor que le apasiona escribir, no lo que se diga de sus libros." In *Antología mínima de Mario Vargas Llosa*, 7–81. Buenos Aires: Tiempo Contemporáneo, 1969.
Portuondo, José Antonio. *Martí y el diversionismo ideológico*. Havana: Biblioteca Nacional José Marti, 1974.
Poulantzas, Nicos. *Pouvoir politique et clases sociales*. Paris: Maspero, 1968.
Preminger, Alex, ed. *Princeton Encyclopedia of Poetry and Poetics*. Princeton, NJ: Princeton University Press, 1974.
Prieto, Adolfo. *Sociología del público*. Buenos Aires: Leviatán, 1956.
Prigogine, Ilya, and Isabelle Stengers. *La Nouvelle Alliance*. Paris: Bibliothéque des Sciences Humaines, 1979.
Rama, Ángel. "El area cultural andina (hispanismo, mesticismo, indigenismo)." *Cuadernos Americanos* 23, no. 6 (1974): 136–73.

———. "La dialéctica de la modernidad en José Martí." In *Estudios martianos: Memoria del Seminario José Martí.* Edited by Manuel Pedro González, 132–46. San Juan: Universidad de Puerto Rico, 1974.

———. *Diario: 1974–1983.* Montevideo: Trilce, 2001.

———. "Diez problemas para el novelista latinoamericano." *Casa de las Américas* 26 (October–November 1964): 3–43.

———. *Diez problemas para el novelista latinoamericano.* Caracas: Editorial Síntesis 2000, 1972.

———. *García Marquez y la problemática de la novela.* Buenos Aires: Corregidor-Marcha, 1973.

———. *Los gauchipolíticos rioplatenses: Literatura y sociedad.* Buenos Aires: Calicanto, 1976.

———. "La generación hispanoamericana de medio siglo: Una generación creadora." In *La crítica de la novela iberoamericana contemporánea*, edited by Aurora Ocampo, 17–23. Mexico: Universidad Nacional Autónoma de México, 1973.

———. *The Lettered City.* Edited and translated by John Charles Chasteen. Durham, NC: Duke University Press, 1996.

———. *Literatura, cultura, sociedad en América Latina.* Montevideo: Trilce, 2006.

———. *Literatura y praxis en América Latina.* Caracas: Monte Ávila, 1975.

———. "Mezzo secolo di narrative latinoamericana." In *Latinoamericana: 75 Narratori*, edited by Franco Mogni, 3–72. Firenze: Vallecchi, 1973.

———. *La novela en América Latina: Panoramas 1920–1980.* Bogotá: Colcultura, 1980.

———. "Un proceso autonómico: De las literaturas nacionales a la literatura latinoamericana." In *Estudios filológicos y linguisticos: Homenaje a Rosenblat en sus 70 años*, 125–39. Caracas: Instituto Pedagógico, 1974.

———. "Los *procesos de transculturación* en la narrativa latinoamericana." *Revista de Literatura Hispanoamericana* (Maracaibo), April 5, 1974.

———. "Processes of Transculturation in Latin American Narrative." *Journal of Latin American Cultural Studies* 6, no. 2 (1997): 155–71.

———. Prologue to *El mundo de los sueños*, by Ruben Darío, 5–54. San Juan: Editorial Universitaria, 1971.

———. Prologue to *Poesía*, by Ruben Darío. Caracas: Biblioteca Ayacucho, 1977.

———. *Rubén Darío y el modernismo (circunstancia socioeconómica de un arte americano).* Caracas: Biblioteca de la Universidad Central de Venezuela, 1970.

———. *Writing Across Cultures: Narrative Transculturation in Latin America.* Edited and translated by David Frye. Durham, NC: Duke University Press, 2012.

Rama, Ángel, and Mario Vargas Llosa. *García Marquez y la problemática de la novela.* Buenos Aires: Corregidor-Marcha, 1973.

Ramos, Julio. *Divergent Modernities: Culture and Politics in Nineteenth-Century Latin America.* Durham, NC: Duke University Press, 2001.

Rejai, Mostafa. "Ideology." Vol. 2 of *Dictionary of the History of Ideas*. Edited by Philip Wiener. New York: Charles Scribner's Sons, 1973.
Ribeiro, Darcy. "América Latina: Clases y poder." *Participación* (Lima), February 2, 1973.
———. *Las Américas y la civilización*. Buenos Aires: Centro Editor de América Latina, 1972.
———. *El dilema de América Latina*. Mexico: Siglo XXI, 1971.
———. "Introducción: La cultura." In *América Latina en su arquitectura*, edited by Roberto Segre. Mexico: Siglo XXI, 1975.
Ricoeur, Paul. *Freud and Philosophy: An Essay on Interpretation*. Translated by Denis Savage. New Have, CT: Yale University Press, 1970.
Riffaterre, Michael. *Essais de stylistique structurale*. Paris: Flammarion, 1971.
Ripoll, Carlos. *Índice universal de la obra de José Martí*. New York: Eliseo Torres and Sons, 1971.
Rivera, Jorge B. *La primitiva literatura gauchesca*. Buenos Aires: Jorge Álvarez Editor, 1968.
Roa Bastos, Augusto. "O sonàmbulo." In *Cándido López*. Parma: Francesco Ricci, 1982.
Rodó, José E. *The Motives of Proteus*. Translated by Angel Flores. New York: Brentano's, 1928.
———. "Rubén Darío: Su personalidad literaria, su última obra" [1899]. In *Obras Completas*, edited by Emir Rodríguez Monegal. Madrid: Aguilar, 1967.
Rodríguez, Ana María de. *La creación corregida: Estudio comparativo de la obra de Ernesto Sábato y Alain Robbe-Grillet*. Caracas: Universidad Católica Andrés Bello, 1976.
Rodríguez Molas, Ricardo. *Historia social del gaucho*. Buenos Aires: Maru, 1968.
Rodríguez Monegal, Emir. *El boom de la novela latinoamericana*. Caracas: Tiempo Nuevo, 1972.
———. "Novedad y anacronismo en *Cien años de soledad*." *Revista Nacional de Cultura* (Caracas) 29 (July–December 1968): 2–20.
Rojas, Ricardo. *Historia de la literatura argentina: Los gauchescos*. Buenos Aires: Guillermo Kraft, 1960.
Romero, José Rubén. "Apuntes de un lugareño." In *La novela de la revolución mexicana* 2. Edited by Antonio Castro Leal. Mexico: Aguilar, 1962.
Rona, José Pedro. "La reproducción del lenguaje hablado en la literatura gauchesca." *Revista Iberoamericana de Literatura* (Montevideo), 1962.
Rosenblat, Ángel. *Lengua literaria y lengua popular en América*. Caracas: Cuaderno del Instituto de Filología Andrés Bello, 1969.
Russell, Bertrand. *Proposed Roads to Freedom: Socialism, Anarchism, and Syndicalism*. London: George Allen and Unwin, 1918.
Sábato, Ernesto. *El escritor y sus fantasmas*. Buenos Aires: Aguilar, 1963.
———. *Tres aproximaciones a la literatura de nuestro tiempo: Robbe-Grillet, Borges, Sartre*. Santiago: Editorial Universitaria, 1968.

Sánchez, Luis Alberto. *Balance y liquidación del Novecientos*. Lima: Universidad Nacional Mayor de San Marcos, 1968.
Sánchez Prado, Ignacio. "The Persistence of the Transcultural: A Latin American Theory of the Novel from the National-Popular to the Global." *New Literary History* 51, no. 2 (2020): 347–74.
Sansone de Martínez, Eneida. *La imagen en la poesía gauchesca*. Montevideo: Facultad de Humanidades y Ciencias, 1962.
Sapir, Edward. "The Status of Linguistics as Science." In *Culture, Language and Personality: Selected Essays*, edited by David G. Mandelbaum, 65–77. Berkeley: University of California Press, 1949.
Saporta, Sol. "The Application of Linguistics to the Study of Poetic Language." In *Style in Language*, edited by Thomas Sebeok, 82–93. Cambridge, MA: MIT Press, 1960.
Schaff, Adam. *Langage et connaissance*. Paris: Anthropos, 1969.
Schulman, Ivan. *Símbolo y color en la obra de José Martí*. Madrid: Gredos, 1960.
Schulman, Ivan, Manuel Pedro González, Juan Loveluck, and Fernando Alegría. *Coloquio sobre la novela hispanoamericana*. Mexico: Tezontle, 1967.
Silva Herzog, Jesús. *Breve historia de la revolución mexicana*. Mexico: Fondo de Cultura Económica, 1962.
Soares Amora, Antonio. *O Romanticismo*. São Paulo: Editora Cultrix, 1973.
Stein, Stanley, and Barbara Stein. *The Colonial Heritage of Latin America*. New York: Oxford University Press, 1970.
Tablada, José Juan. *The Experimental Poetry of José Juan Tablada*. Translated by A. Scott Britton. Jefferson, NC: McFarland, 2016.
Tylor, Edward Burnett. *Primitive Culture*. London: J. Murray, 1871.
Tynianov, Yuri. *Permanent Evolution: Selected Essays on Literature, Theory and Film*, 267–82. Boston: Academic Studies Press, 2019.
United Nations Economic Commission for Latin America. *Report of the Executive Secretary to the Eighteenth Session of the Commission*, April 18–26, 1979.
Vallejo, César. *The Complete Poetry*. Edited and translated by Clayton Eshelman. Berkeley: University of California Press, 2007.
Valverde, José María. *Historia de la literatura latinoamericana*. Barcelona: Planeta, 1974.
Vargas Llosa, Mario. *Día domingo*. Buenos Aires: Ediciones Amadis, 1971.
———. *Historia de un deicidio*. Barcelona: Barral Editores, 1971.
———. "Novela primitiva y novela de creación en América Latina." *Revista de la Universidad de México* 23, no. 10, 1969.
Vasconcelos, José. *Ulises criollo*. Mexico: Botas, 1937.
Verón, Eliseo. *Conducta, estructura y comunicación*. Buenos Aires: Tiempo Contemporáneo, 1972.
———, ed. *El proceso ideológico*. Buenos Aires: Tiempo Contemporáneo, 1971.
Vilariño, Idea. *Las letras de tango: La forma, temas y motivos*. Buenos Aires: Schapire, 1966.

Vitier, Cintio. *Temas martianos.* Havana: Biblioteca Nacional José Martí, 1969.
Vitier, Cintio, and Fina García Marruz. *Temas martianos.* Havana: Biblioteca Nacional José Martí, 1969.
Wallerstein, Immanuel. *The Modern World-System: Capitalist Agriculture and the Origins of the European World Economy in the Sixteenth Century.* New York: Academic Press, 1976.
Weimann, Robert. "French Structuralism and Literary History: Some Critiques and Reconsiderations." *New Literary History* 4 (1973): 437–69.
Weinberg, Félix, ed. *El Salón Literario.* Buenos Aires: Hachette, 1958.
Weinrich, Harald. *Estructura y función de los tiempos en el lenguaje.* Madrid: Gredos, 1974.
———. "Les temps et les personnes." *Poétique* 39 (September 1979): 340.
Whetten, Nathan L. "The Rise of the Middle Class in México." Vol. 2 of *Materiales para el estudio de la clase media en América Latina*, edited by Theo R. Crevenna. Washington, DC: Union Panamericana, 1950.
Whorf, Benjamin L. *Language, Thought, and Reality.* Cambridge, MA: MIT Press, 1957.
Williams, Raymond. *Problems in Materialism and Culture.* London: Verso Edition, 1980.
———. *The Sociology of Culture.* New York: Schocken Books, 1982.
Yllera, Alicia. *Estilística, poética y semiótica literaria.* Madrid: Alianza Universitaria, 1974.
Zaid, Gabriel. *Omnibus of Mexican Poetry.* Mexico: Siglo XXI, 1971.
Zilio, Giovanni Meo. *De José Martí a Sabat Ercasty.* Montevideo: El Siglo Ilustrado, 1967.
Zimmerman, Marc. "Exchange and Production: Structuralist and Marxist Approaches to Literary Theory." *Praxis* 4 (1978): 151–68.
Zumthor, Paul, and Walter Ong. *Oral Poetry: An Introduction.* Minneapolis: University of Minnesota Press, 1990.

Index

Anthropology, 7, 47, 71, 103, 113, 212, 274, 316, 318–22
Arenas, Reinaldo, 59, 290–92
Arguedas, José María, 113, 173, 177, 201, 205, 212, 297, 301, 309, 310–11, 317, 321
Arlt, Roberto, 85, 90–91, 176, 194, 203, 271, 290
Ascasubi, Hilario, 126, 131–32, 137–38, 140, 146, 151–52, 155, 158–62, 165–67
autonomy, 55, 56, 77, 95–96, 100–102, 106, 114, 124, 144–45, 154–55, 185, 187, 203, 212, 215, 223–25, 244, 275–79, 283–84
Avant-Garde, 8, 10, 56–57, 77–91, 112, 172–73, 180, 189–89, 204, 211, 214, 258, 263, 265, 267–69, 271, 278, 280, 284–85, 297–301, 304–305, 309–13
Azuela, Mariano, 5, 6, 13–46, 84, 176, 189, 269

Balzac, Honoré de, 70, 72, 74
Baroque, 48, 89, 271–73, 286
Barral, Carlos, 186–87, 195–96
Barthes, Roland 47, 61, 69, 164, 222
Baudelaire, Charles, 174, 236, 244
Bello, Andrés, 99, 145, 147, 211

Benjamin, Walter, 1, 9, 65, 70, 174, 238
Blanchot, Maurice, 47
Boom, the, 11, 171–218, 265, 275, 288, 298, 303
Borges, Jorge Luis, 80, 83, 85, 88, 130–31, 143, 162, 165, 172–73, 176, 179, 182, 184, 191, 194–97, 200, 205–206, 210, 212, 214, 216, 242, 266–69, 274, 290, 292, 294, 301, 304–305, 307–308, 310, 322

Cabrera Infante, Guillermo, 60, 183, 198, 298
Candido, Antônio, 10
Cárdenas, Lázaro, 18
Carpentier, Alejo, 1, 69, 82–83, 88–89, 176, 182, 191, 195–96, 198, 201, 205, 210, 212, 266–67, 269–73, 284–87, 290, 292, 305, 307–308
Calvino, Italo, 62, 69, 291
Cassirer, Ernst, 101, 114, 237
Cortázar, Julio, 62–63, 83, 117, 172–73, 176–79, 181–82, 189, 191, 195–96, 199–201, 205–206, 210, 212, 274, 278–80, 288, 290–92, 295, 297–98, 301, 305–309
Cuban Revolution, 1, 172, 179, 180, 219

378 | Index

cosmopolitanism, 10, 85, 110, 189, 264, 301–10, 312–13
cronyism, 49, 52

Darío, Rubén, 15, 51, 70, 84, 90, 99, 102, 104, 106, 149, 168, 194, 203, 214, 222, 230, 237, 242–46, 248, 258, 265, 271–72, 274, 279, 295, 300, 302, 306–307, 317–18
decadence, 56, 66, 289, 294, 297
density of literature, 5–6, 94–96, 102–103, 107–27, 164, 272
Del Campo, Estanislao, 124, 126, 132, 134–38, 140, 146, 155, 166–67
dependency, 55–56, 87, 88, 102, 106, 180
de Onís, Federico, 66, 106, 111
Díaz, Porfirio, 17, 20–21, 22, 25, 29, 30, 32, 38

Echeverría, Esteban, 69, 83, 102, 136, 142, 146, 148–49
escapism, 6, 39
estridentista movement, 81
EUDEBA (Editorial Universitaria de Buenos Aires), 185–86

Faulkner, William, 266, 270, 291, 310
Freud, Sigmund, 72–73, 248, 260–61, 318
folklore, 110, 166, 322
foreign influence, 8–10, 22, 25, 28, 30, 33, 55–56, 61–62, 69, 88, 90, 94–95, 106–107, 117, 143, 147–51, 172, 180, 183, 187, 269, 270, 272–73, 276–81, 297, 300, 304–307
Freud, Sigmund, 72–73, 248, 260–61, 318
Fuentes, Carlos, 59, 63, 69, 173, 177, 181–83, 189–91, 195–96, 198, 201, 205–206, 210, 212, 267, 270, 274, 289–91, 295, 297–99, 301, 303, 306–307
Futurists, 58, 78

Gallegos, Rómulo, 60, 84, 152, 176, 189, 269, 293, 310
García Márquez, Gabriel, 1, 61, 65–66, 69, 80, 176, 183, 191, 195–96, 198, 200–201, 206, 213–14, 267, 270, 291–93, 295, 298, 301, 303, 310–11
gauchesque genre, 1, 5, 8, 10–11, 94, 105, 124–12, 129–70, 322
globalization, 10
Guzmán, Martín Luis, 40

Harss, Luis, 61, 190–91, 197
Hauser, Arnold, 48, 118, 137, 165, 170, 319
Hernández, José, 107, 124, 126, 132, 134, 136, 138, 141–46, 151–52, 157, 159–60, 162, 165–67
Henríquez Ureña, Pedro, 102, 111, 113
Hidalgo, Bartolomé, 125–26, 131–32, 134–37, 139–40, 144, 146, 152, 159, 161–63, 166–67
Hippolyte Taine, 112, 315–17
Huidobro, Vicente, 78, 81, 83, 88, 102, 257–58, 266, 300–301

ideology, 5, 10, 19, 24–25, 30, 46, 57, 72, 100–101, 106, 109, 132–33, 136–37, 139–41, 216, 219–62, 268, 320
indigenismo, 112, 128
intellectuals, 1, 4–6, 34, 36–42, 45, 50, 52, 82, 132, 136, 179, 184, 190, 205, 211, 213, 318–19, 322
imperialism, 56, 61, 78, 84, 87, 101, 277, 319
import substitution industrialization (ISI), 9, 275, 296–97

Jakobson, Roman, 129, 133, 157, 169, 259, 322

Lautréamont, Comte de (Isidore Lucien Ducasse), 72, 82, 86
letrado, 2–5, 11
Lévi-Strauss, Claude, 58, 113, 225, 227, 229, 233, 274, 318–19
Lewis, Oscar, 59
Literary Salon, 10, 116, 131–32, 148–49
literary system, 3, 4, 6, 8, 10–11, 48, 86–91, 93–108, 129–70, 221, 307
Lugones, Leopoldo, 80, 98, 102, 129, 141–43
Lukács, Georg, 19, 71, 249, 319

Madero, Francisco I., 16, 17, 20–21, 24–25, 29–30, 32, 37–38, 40, 42–43, 109, 226
Mannheim, Karl, 40, 70, 315
Marcha, 1, 65, 177, 267
Martí, José, 51, 70, 80–81, 90, 101–102, 107, 144, 149, 157, 194, 203, 219–62, 300, 302
Mariátegui, José Carlos, 71, 90, 112, 180, 321
Marx, Karl, 70, 97, 122–23, 237–38, 253, 261, 315
Marxist criticism, 56, 69–70, 73, 94–95, 111–13, 317–19
mass media, 11, 133, 173, 178, 198, 214–16, 272
mediocrity, 49–50
Mexican Revolution, 1–2, 5–6, 13–29, 36–46, 109, 188
metropolis, 56, 103, 120, 199, 264, 266, 271, 273, 275–76, 283, 319–20
modernismo, 1, 6, 8, 10–11, 38–39, 50–51, 79–80, 99, 102–105, 109–10, 212, 127, 144, 149, 167–68, 172, 194–95, 202–204, 211, 223, 230–31, 235, 245, 268–71, 274, 276, 283, 295, 300, 307
modernization, 3–4, 10, 51, 94, 106, 109, 175, 180, 230, 295, 298–304, 309–13, 317
nature, 78, 86, 101, 149, 153, 219, 229–60

Neoclassicism, 147–48, 159, 168
Neruda, Pablo, 88, 193, 206, 267
Nietzsche, Friedrich, 220, 248, 304
New Criticism, 94, 296
North American literature, 51, 57–58, 61, 82, 189, 197, 209, 213, 235–37, 266–67, 284, 293, 306, 312
Nouveau roman, 186, 288–91, 296

Ocampo, Victoria, 213
Onetti, Juan Carlos, 176, 181–83, 191, 195–96, 198, 200–201, 210, 212, 214, 267–68, 270, 274–78, 285, 288–89, 297, 299, 305, 310–11
orality, 99, 115, 117–18, 120, 124, 126, 157–59, 161, 163–64, 168–69, 310–11, 322
Orfila Reynal, Arnaldo, 185–86
Ortiz, Fernando, 113, 321

Padilla, Heriberto, 179
Paz, Octavio, 51–52, 62–63, 87, 101, 181, 193, 212, 296
periphery, 9, 55–56, 82, 86–87, 90–91, 277, 286, 319
professionalization, 10–11, 131, 202–204
provincialism, 49, 211
publishing houses, 11, 172, 175, 179, 183–88, 199–202, 203, 209, 215, 280
Puerto Rico, 49, 50, 52, 172

Ramos, Julio, 4
raw materials, 150, 276, 282, 296–97
realism, 13–15, 84, 86, 122, 249, 278, 289, 299
regionalism, 57, 85, 105, 168, 184, 312
Reyes, Alfonso, 52, 111, 120, 212, 308
Ribeiro, Darcy, 71, 113, 143
Rimbaud, Arthur, 51, 86, 153, 236
Rivera, José Eustasio, 84, 176, 189–90, 293
Rodó, José Enrique, 4, 194, 211, 245–46, 248–49, 317
Romanticism, 5, 10, 39, 66, 68–72, 74, 78, 94, 102, 104, 112, 117–19, 121–23, 132, 139–40, 146–50, 163, 168, 170, 231, 235, 260, 271, 273
Romero, Sílvio, 110, 316–17
Rulfo, Juan, 8, 182, 189, 191, 195–96, 201, 202, 205, 212, 267, 270, 297, 301, 305, 310–11

Sapir, Edward, 113, 154, 319
Sarmiento, Domingo Faustino, 4, 70, 142, 145, 149, 212, 316
Saussure, Ferdinand de, 86, 319
Seix Barral, 183–84, 186–87, 196, 201, 206
social change, 94, 104–105, 271
social class: lower class, 23, 142, 262; middle class, 19–46, 62, 97, 104, 109, 110, 112, 121, 289; upper class, 24, 29–30, 32, 36, 156
Social Imaginary, 98, 100, 102–104
Sociology, 1, 20–21, 25, 31, 40, 50, 58, 60, 70, 73, 94, 98, 100–105, 112–14, 130, 176, 182, 210, 220, 239, 315–22
Spivacow, Boris, 185–86
Structuralism, 3, 48, 69, 94, 111, 268, 296
Surrealism, 58, 83, 118, 260, 287, 306
Symbolism, 48, 78, 79, 94, 109, 168, 271

techniques, 7–10, 39, 62, 85, 135–36, 167, 173, 189, 215, 232, 263–314
technology, 8–9, 56–63, 71, 209, 214, 264, 266, 275–76, 280, 282–83
television, 11, 203, 215
theater, 61, 112, 133, 141, 164, 214, 216, 222
transculturation, 2–3, 7–11, 297, 301–304, 309–13, 321
Tynianov, Yuri, 86, 99, 281, 321

Ultraísmo, 80, 194
university, 3, 23, 51, 180, 185, 186, 203, 212

Valéry, Paul, 83, 204
Vallejo, César, 79, 83, 90, 267, 300–301
Vargas Llosa, Mario, 1, 56, 63, 65–75, 172–73, 176–77, 181, 183, 189–92, 195–96, 198, 201, 205–206, 210, 212, 267, 278, 285, 289–91, 295, 299, 313
Vasconcelos, José, 15, 17, 23, 28, 31, 34, 37, 40, 46, 212
Vitier, Cintio, 51, 90, 101, 220, 223

Weber, Max, 70, 315, 319

www.ingramcontent.com/pod-product-compliance
Lightning Source LLC
Chambersburg PA
CBHW031703230426
43668CB00006B/86